IMPULSE to ACT

IMPULSE TO ACT

A New Anthropology of Resistance and Social Justice

Edited by Othon Alexandrakis

Indiana University Press

Bloomington and Indianapolis

This book is a publication of

Indiana University Press
Office of Scholarly Publishing
Herman B Wells Library 350
1320 East 10th Street
Bloomington, Indiana 47405 USA

iupress.indiana.edu

The paper used in this publication meets the minimum
requirements of the American National Standard for Information
Sciences—Permanence of Paper for Printed Library Materials,
ANSI Z39.48-1992.

Manufactured in the United States of America

Cataloging information is available from the Library of Congress.

ISBN 978-0-253-02278-3 (cloth)
ISBN 978-0-253-02311-7 (paperback)
ISBN 978-0-253-02326-1 (ebook)

1 2 3 4 5   21 20 19 18 17 16

For my colleagues and friends who have helped to make this volume possible.

Let those who heavy feel
The cupreous hand of fear
Under slavery's yoke live;
Mettle and virtue is what
Freedom wants.

She (and myth belies the mind of truth)
Gave wings to Icarus.
But he,
Still winged,
Even though he fell
And drowned
In the sea,

Fell from high heights
And thus died free.

And if you become
The slaughter of a tyrant
With no honor,
Do think the grave as a horror.

—"Fourth Ode, To Samos" Andreas Kalvos
    (translated by Neni Panourgiá)

Contents

Acknowledgments

THE IDEA FOR this book emerged from field research I conducted on citizenship and civic engagement in Athens, Greece, during the turbulent years of 2007 to 2010. I was a doctoral student at the time and, as I make clear in the introduction to this volume, found myself in the position of rethinking what I thought I knew about resistance and what I thought I knew about fieldwork. This rethinking of resistance and fieldwork stayed with me.

I wish to thank the Social Sciences and Humanities Research Council of Canada for their support of my research in Athens. I am also grateful to the Seeger Center for Hellenic Studies at Princeton University, where I was Hannah Seeger Davis Post-Doctoral Research Fellow between 2010 and 2011. This time at Princeton afforded me the opportunity to reflect with colleagues from various disciplines on the challenges of studying resistance action playing out on highly dynamic terrain. These conversations led to a workshop in 2013 at the International Center for Hellenic and Mediterranean Studies (CYA), "Athens in 'Crisis': Reimagining Ethnographic Writing," and a roundtable later that year at the Modern Greek Studies Association Symposium, "Greece in Transition: Reconsidering Anthropological Approaches to 'Crisis.'" I'd like to thank Aimee Placas for co-organizing the workshop with me, and the participants in both the workshop and the roundtable for their insights and questions. I began work on this volume soon after these events.

Early drafts of this work inspired a plenary session at the 2014 annual meeting of the Canadian Anthropological Society, "Unsettled Politics and Radical Potential: Figuring the Impulse to Act." A number of presenters in those sessions contributed chapters to this volume. I wish to thank Daphne Winland, Antonio Sorge, and Maya Shapiro for co-organizing the plenary with me, my colleagues Albert Schrauwers and Zulfikar Hirji for their work on the conference, and the paper presenters, discussants—especially John Borneman and David Nugent— and audience for their helpful comments and questions.

I am also very grateful to Gary Dunham, Rebecca Jane Tolen, Janice Frisch, and the anonymous reviewers at Indiana University Press. One anonymous reviewer in particular provided comments that inspired a comprehensive reorganization of this volume—to this individual I am truly grateful. I would also like to thank Christopher Kelty, Hannah Landecker, James Faubion, Nia Georges, and Stephen Tyler for inspiring and encouraging me to think critically and creatively about fieldwork and ethnography, and my friends and colleagues with whom I've had numerous conversations about studying resistance over the years, especially Tina Palivos, Heath Cabot, and Neni Panourgiá. A special thanks also to the participants in my PhD seminar in methodology at York University, and to Kathe Gray, Parinaz Adib, Janita Van Dyk, and Nadine Ryan for their help in preparing the manuscript for this volume and for their support and enthusiasm.

Finally, my deepest thanks go to my partner, Jordana, and to our little ones, Sofia and Theo, who—each in their own way—taught me to always follow my heart when on uncertain ground.

IMPULSE TO ACT

Introduction

Resistance Reconsidered

Othon Alexandrakis

IN RECENT YEARS the spread of conflict and war zones, the creep of neoliberalism and its economies of abandonment, the uncertainty of environmental change, and other ruinous trends and unsettling conditions have sparked responses of all description around the world. These responses regularly capture both headlines and the attention of academics, in part because they are often unexpected and intense, but also because they have—in recent years especially—varied considerably in form, content, and direction: whereas some scenes of unrest have appeared to be familiar (at least at first blush), many new formations of resistance have caused observers to question whether they were witnessing politics at all. These actions continue to push against engrained mythologies and orthodoxies of politics, to challenge us to question what we know about the political, and—critically—to challenge us to revisit *how* we know it.

This volume begins a conversation about rethinking resistance politics from the perspective of innovation in methodology. We will reconsider the political in terms of the challenge of new resistance actions, and related political forms, to ethnographic method. Affect and agency will be our two central concerns, as these recombine fieldwork and theory work in new ways and, together, highlight new analytical possibilities of political ethnography and engagement, and political ethnography as engagement.

What Is Really Happening, on the Ground?

The question of what is really happening, on the ground, marks an interdisciplinary contact zone. For one, this question locates as "witness" anthropologists, political scientists, sociologists, and other researchers who conduct ethnographic fieldwork—and especially long-term participant observation—in places where resistance actions defy expectations. This witnessing, Taussig (2011) explains, sees inside and outside, translates, but also has the power to *up* the provisional connection behind the question of what is really happening to a mode of participation itself. As Neni Panourgiá and Alex Khasnabish so clearly argue in this volume, the capacity to connect diverse publics, and to build these connections to another order of more consequential engagement, is certainly one of the challenges and promises of the ethnography of resistance.

Of course, "what is really happening?" is also a question most researchers ask themselves at various junctures as we conduct research and write. Fieldwork-based ethnography, with its openness to various approaches and tools, also provides space to play, to figure things out (see Fortun 2009) in tune with fluctuations in our connections with and within field sites. In the context of unexpected, dynamic ground, in the midst of the kinds of resistance actions we consider here, recognizing new challenges and retooling in response to them is not only a matter of critical importance but also, as Marianne Maeckelbergh reminds us in this volume, a matter of ethical integrity. Taken together, the following chapters sketch an approach to understanding "what is really happening" based on attentiveness to affect and agency—arguably, the two human fundamentals at the heart of the political. To illustrate this approach, and the challenges of figuring things out in the field, let us consider an example from my research in Athens, Greece.

* * *

Between 2006, when I began field research for my dissertation, and 2008, when—as I describe later—Athens was rocked by intense and in many ways unusual resistance action, I became very interested in political tipping points, or *activations*. In that period, critical commentators and scores of protest actions in Athens had cataloged what was a growing list of devastating economic, political, and social problems, including an already-obvious impending national economic catastrophe, growing disenfranchisement among youth and young adults, mismanagement of public infrastructures, widespread corruption, and government policy that actively discriminated against the most vulnerable members of society while benefiting the elite. Greece seemed to be on the verge of a transformative political moment, for better or worse.

I would eventually come to understand the broad intensive questioning I was seeing in Athens as part of a larger global trend of questioning the parameters, modes, and ethics of neoliberal governmentality and as casting doubt on the legitimacy of this mode of governance (Povinelli 2011). This questioning appeared to feed the explosive public reaction to the murder of a fifteen-year-old boy, Alexis Grigoropoulos, by a Special Forces police officer on December 6, 2008 (Dalakoglou 2011; Goodale and Postero 2013). In the days and weeks following the murder, crowds seemed to agglomerate spontaneously, over and over, across Greece and beyond, and participants acted boldly but did not communicate a clear demand or message beyond a general expression of outrage. I was conducting research, at the time, with anti-establishment youth, members of the local Roma (Gypsy) community, and undocumented migrants living in and around the city's core. Nearly all my interlocutors took to the streets along with an unexpected—for Greece—mix of other political actors, primarily anarchists, unionists, pensioners, university students, soccer (and other kinds of) hooligans, mainstream political party supporters, and documented migrants. However, it seemed to me that I was witnessing something more than spontaneously coalescent if distinct responses to a murder by individuals and groups were jointly motivated by broader concerns with the social, political, and economic state of affairs.

As the protests continued and spread, most commenters noted what they considered the unusual form and temporality of the street action. Common frames of analysis failed to explain the politics we were witnessing. On the one hand, familiar categories like "solidarity" and "civil action" appeared to function better as descriptive tools than as analytical prisms. On the other, and as per my discussion with Athena Athanasiou later in this volume, the December events (as they came to be known locally) also appeared to trouble even broader political categories. Indeed, they didn't resemble proceduralist politics, that is, politics grounded in the actions of autonomous individuals pursuing their own self-interests. The actions also exceeded the terms of communitarian politics, that is, politics grounded in the actions of self-identified groups engaged in resistance and advocacy in order to acquire public recognition and empowerment. Some observers began to ask whether Greece was perhaps turning to a kind of direct global street politics (Economides and Monastiriotis 2009). Other observers wondered whether Greece was undergoing some kind of fundamental "political realignment" (Kalyvas 2010, 351).

I had a different perspective on the December events. In the days that followed each night of action, my interlocutors would talk to me about standing with others in the cold, the risk of being caught in running street battles between various groups of agitators and the police, and the experience of being active "at this time." While standing on the streets, my interlocutors couldn't make sense of the action (much like other participants and observers)—they didn't feel solidarity with others, they didn't speak with others, they weren't all sympathetic to the murdered boy, and so on—but at home, they understood the action as a meaningful, important, powerful intervention. Standing on the streets, then looking back, then returning to the streets, then looking back again—this mirrored the recursive ontology of the acting mass and informed what became my approach, and eventually my methodology. I began to understand the December events as a mode of resistance that became intelligible, at least to participants and in terms of form and direction, when repeated remembering combined, recombined, and brought to the present residues of affect and praxis.

What I would eventually refer to as my "looking-back" research methodology came together as I began to understand that the December events differed from the established modes and patterns of protest and political disruption in Athens. This realization led me to question my presuppositions about politics, and it inspired me to reflect on my research tools. What was I not asking? What do we make of participant observation if presence isn't enough to "know" resistance action? Of course, as this volume demonstrates, the challenge the December events posed to my thinking about the political and to my fieldwork was not unique, nor was my approach to figuring things out on the basis of attention to affect and agency.

Toward a Reconsideration of Resistance

In selecting essays for this volume, my motivation was not to represent the diversity of new resistance action; to collect essays dealing with "major" social movements, hot spots, or forms of resistance; or to examine resistance in one geographic location or another. Doing so would have oversimplified and/or obscured economic and political interconnectedness across the globe. Social phenomena not immediately legible as resistance action would also have been left out. The "ground" shared by the following chapters—the site they engage—is resistance action and related forms that challenge ethnographic research methods. The chapters do not describe straightforward "bodies in the streets" scenes; rather, they approach politics from the granularity of human experience, often focusing on unexpected locations and configurations of contest and contestation. Pushing against habituated ways of looking for and perceiving resistance challenges our normative understandings of politics.

The December 2008 events in Athens are an example of the resistance action we consider in this volume not only because of its unusual form, content, and uncertain direction, but because of the methodological challenge it posed. I wish to stress that the December events are merely an example. It is tempting to recall Balibar's (2004, 2) suggestion: "If Europe is for us first of all the name of an unresolved political problem, Greece is one of its centers, not because of the mythical origins of our civilization . . . but because of the current problems concentrated here." In this sense, the December events in Athens might be taken as symptomatic of and/or for Europe, "a local projection of forms of confrontation and conflict characteristic of all of Europe" (Balibar 2004, 5) and, perhaps, beyond. We should resist the temptation to locate Athens at the forefront of some kind of global political moment, and by extension to locate the conditions, histories, and struggles in Greece as somehow common to or situated centrally within the global system. The December events in Athens did not set off some kind of global resistance action. Nor should we take neoliberalism—along with insecurity, capitalism, debt, and other disappointments of citizenship—as some universal, or general condition, driving or inspiring resistance actions around the world today.

Rather, the December events simply happened to precede and in some cases coincide with an explosion of unexpected action around the world: the rise of the Occupy movement, antiausterity protests across Europe, the Arab Spring revolts, new environmental activism across the Global South, experimental forms of representation in postsocialist states, the June Journeys in Brazil, movements against experiences of collective confinement across Europe and South Asia, and more. These actions varied tremendously. Some were episodic, others were part of ongoing and recurrent social and political movements, some were revolutionary, and others appeared to be responsive but diffused and uncertain. These actions shared little beyond the fact that they all occurred recently, qualifying them as "third wave" action following the struggles of the nineteenth century and the action of the 1960s (Juris 2012) while, like Athens, also providing new sites for reflection and expanding our understanding of the political.

Context and Approach

This volume comes at a critical moment for the study of resistance and politics more generally. A steady succession of innovative work since the mid-1990s has pushed research in this area to consider new analytical approaches to the political, including culture and identity (Rosaldo and Flores 1997), social process (Delanty 2002), transnational flow and neoliberalism (Greenhouse 2010; Ong 2006; Goodale and Postero 2013), and the subjective experience of political life (Povinelli 2011; Das et al. 2000; Stewart 2007). The latest research on resistance, and political action more generally, draws on diverse theory to engage with the political at various sites of innovation and experimentation with forms of resistance (Maeckelbergh 2009; Razsa and Kurnik 2012; Razsa 2015; Greenberg 2014; Juris 2012; Mitchell, Harcourt, and Taussig 2013). Since 2008, there has also been an increase in commentary calling for the crafting of engaged, affirmative ethnographic texts (Borneman 2011; Razsa 2012) and in works reconsidering the political quality of ethnography (Biehl and McKay 2012; Panourgiá 2012; Juris and Khasnabish 2013). These later contributions—the commentary and the work on ethnography—mark a refreshing stocktaking sparked by new resistance actions.

Indeed, with the shift to late liberalism many social scientists—and certainly anthropologists—began to ask (once again) what the coming period would demand of our disciplines, how fieldwork would change, and what forms ethnography might take (see, for example, Faubion and Marcus 2009; Rabinow and Stavrianakis 2013; Fassin 2014; Taussig 2011). Resistance actions intensified that asking. Researchers were pressed to reconsider the politics they thought they understood in the places they studied, and to reconnect their audiences to what many considered unexpected and certainly astonishing acts of resistance playing out over diverse and often highly dynamic ground. To this end, many researchers committed to returning to the field and became involved or otherwise invested in various actions, and ultimately most researchers found themselves rethinking the questions they had been asking or intending to examine. This interest in new forms of resistance combined with introspection and a commitment to a grounded reengagement with politics is the context for this volume.

The following chapters explore analytical possibilities that address fluctuations in our understanding of core political concepts brought about by new resistance action. The approach we take, in terms of affect and agency, emerged from the collection itself. In broad terms, the first part of the volume reengages with our understandings of collectivities from the perspective of affect and in terms of belonging. We will show that affects are intensities that can disrupt or even rupture discourse-based, "formal" or "traditional" political communities while—to borrow from Félix Guattari (1995)—territorializing new collectives around sometimes unexpected, microsocial, or *little* affective connections. The first part challenges us to think about the impulse to act in terms of the connections between individuals, and between individuals and worlds. In the second part of this volume we will examine representation from the perspective of agency and in terms of action and critique. We will show that collective practice can produce intense potentialities, or sites of reflection and evaluation, that—borrowing from Foucault (1980, 1997)—may root critique that disrupts established political projects founded on high-scale moral narratives. The second part challenges us to think about the formation of political horizons in terms of practice and agonism.

The Political, Revisited

Carl Schmitt's classic work *The Concept of the Political* (1976 [1927]) and Talcott Parsons's *The Structure of Social Action* (1968 [1937]) offer early parameters of the project we take up here. In *The Concept of the Political*, Schmitt casts politics as a sphere of value that is not based on substantive distinction. According to this work, there is no absolute that determines the limits of the political. Instead, political community is founded on individuals sharing a sense of belonging to a collective of individuals who self-identify with some common characteristic, whereas political action refers to the (collective) work of protecting or preserving the community from external threat. The sovereign state persists, Schmitt argues, as long as this sense of belonging is strong and as long as members of the community are willing to protect it. Some ten years later, in *The Structure of Social Action*, Parsons would offer a more nuanced examination of collective action, focusing on the motivations of individual subjects. This text laid the foundation for thinking about resistance in terms of microscale or subjective decisions, and in terms of complicated webs of actors.

In these early works, belonging informed by difference and voluntary action inspired by differential belonging constitute the heart of politics. Yet these works also establish a number of assumptions and orthodoxies that, moving into the latest period of political action, become problematic. Beyond setting out a structuralist approach to politics, which continued to influence scholarship in the social sciences for the better part of the twentieth century (Habermas 1991; Touraine 1977; Escobar 1995), these works also bound belonging and identity together in a way that, first, limited considerations of politics to communitarian and proceduralist formations and actions and, second, fixed the locations and temporalities of resistance politics to particular historical complexes and serial trajectories.

This meant, for example, that assemblages of actors and collectives advancing diverse, if compatible, ideals were illegible as political forms. Such political assemblages were cast as manifestations of an abnormal civil body, or were simply regarded as dominant parts and problematic fringes. This also meant that direct interventions into one or another state of affairs effecting informal or nongovernmental realms, variously construed, often fell outside the political altogether. In the present volume we keep belonging and action, the political substance defined by Schmitt and Parsons, the political substance that continues to inform thinking on collectives and representation; however, as anthropologists and other social scientists have done in the past and in response to the demands of their day, we offer a ground-up critique (Barth 1969; Benhabib 1996; Holston 2008; Brettell and Reed-Danahay 2012; Castles and Davidson 2000; Cohen 1982). How else might we think of and with belonging and action, the relationship between them, and the actions they produce and inform?

* * *

Let me return once again to the December events in Athens. As mentioned already, I observed multiple collectives and individuals who did not identify with any collective; I observed multiple and diverse belongings, all on the street at once, again and again and again. No single group or individual organized the action. Instead, protesters simply came together, chanted, sang, yelled, fought, and occupied, following no overall protest strategy and producing no single discernable message. Indeed, it was possible to trace multiple conversations within the action—conversations that did not merge or harmonize over time on the street, but rather revealed multiple simultaneous motivations and interests. Considering all this, we might regard the action as some kind of anomaly, or explain it away by accounting for the individuals and groups on the street separately. These approaches, like others that preserve and privilege established approaches to politics, simultaneously reproduce a "politics as usual" narrative while foreclosing the possibility of seeing the December events as differing from the local political status quo. An alternative approach is to think of the protest as an assemblage: an arrangement of heterogeneous elements that fit together in such a way as to give rise to something novel, some activating process that expresses through collective practice. This kind of assemblage is not reducible to a sum of its parts; rather, the meaning of the collective form emerges from the relations among its constituent elements, relations that influence their becoming as they produce a unique mass effect.

While my interlocutors may have joined the resistance action for different reasons—reasons they expressed clearly—their understanding of the street action and their own roles in it changed over time. This change marks, by my estimation, the emergence of something novel. Participants in the protest experienced themselves in the social space of the action not in terms of relations of opposition, but in terms of a "polyphonic interlacing" with the collective (Guattari and Genosko 1996, 267). They all stood together and shouted against "authority," for something better: the individual, on her or his own or in a group, began to resonate with the broader collective; the forms internal to the assemblage came together as they exceeded their codes. The dynamics and effects of this interlacing became visible when my interlocutors thought back to their participation in the action. Again, when remembering the action they noted the heterogeneity of the mass; however, they also noted the production of a collective expression of anger that transcended the specific sentiments and demands of the constituent elements of the mass. This collective feeling indexed the interlacing, the interstitial relations, that produced the assemblage as such.

As the street action persisted and various individuals and groups moved in and out of the protest space, thought back to it, talked about it, and otherwise engaged and reengaged with the broader assemblage, the collective feeling became increasingly legible and increasingly intense. The repeated work of connecting and reconnecting to the resonant assemblage—the angry mass on the streets—produced a refrain that structured the affective into an existential territory (Guattari 1995, 28): the assemblage itself took on the qualities of a common ground. This territorialization opened the individual to new becomings (Biehl and Locke 2010). This is not to say that my interlocutors abandoned their individual and collective projects. I am also not suggesting that disparate political actors somehow merged toward some kind of ideological point of gravity. Instead, the assemblage emerged conditions for a kaleidoscopic multiple political becoming. In this, difference was preserved, but individual immanent possibilities of what a life can do began to harmonize with the mass effect of the assemblage. The result was twofold: first, my interlocutors began to describe wanting to act with others, not motivated by common identity; second, as the action persisted week to week, my interlocutors began to describe a common political horizon.

Talking to me about the action, my interlocutors continued to refer to the work of bringing about changes consistent with their political commitments.

However, they also evoked what Agamben (1993) has referred to as an inessential commonality. They did not see themselves as sharing some quality with other protesters; rather, my interlocutors described acting with diverse others for change. This commonality cannot be explained in terms of community or solidarity; it did not compel my interlocutors to support their political rivals in other spheres or to reconsider their own commitments. Rather, these individuals saw a range of political positions and issues—issues broadly defined before 2008—as elemental to the unconventional political form of the assembled collective and, moreover, as its source of authority. They described feeling empowered by simply being part of the action and, critically, empowered in a way not accessible to them through traditional forms of political action. This feeling of empowerment expanded my interlocutors' sense of what was possible while also rooting an ethic of caring and acting with others (see Massumi 2002, 255) that opposed fragmentation and abandonment.

This has not inspired some kind of mass social project, nor have protest participants described caring about preserving a vibrant political ecology. However, I would see another political assemblage, hear about belonging to a collective based on inessential commonality, and observe an ethic of caring and acting with others again during the 2010 Athens antiausterity protests. At this time neoliberal governmentality became a more clear and present concern. My interlocutors described the mass action as familiar and encouraging. They knew what to expect of the assemblage and how to act in the space of the protest. This was another cycling back, in this case to the December events of 2008. It produced a refrain that made the ontology and ethics of this mode of resistance more legible as antithetical to a state that dominates and dispossesses (Povinelli 2011, 25).

Thinking back to the December events and later actions like the 2010 antiausterity protests brought to my interlocutors' minds affective states that made commonality visible, albeit a commonality not based on some shared identity, political ideology, history, or even experience of precarity. Also, when thinking back, my interlocutors shared stories of "having been there"; and while the details of these stories differed considerably, they all made reference to a common set of values that ethically marked particular actions and dispositions. Affect and agency were at the heart of a politics and ethics of resistance that effervesced as individuals invested in unconventional action, and as dynamics and conditions on the ground consolidated. My interlocutors were motivated by diverse politics and commitments when they took to the streets, and the action certainly didn't erase these differences. However, the December events rooted something radical, something unlike Greek politics as usual. They achieved a manifestation of "the people," reclaimed democracy and the unconditionality of public space.

New Analytics: Drawing Lines of Flight

This volume can be read in different ways. Readers may wish to follow my grouping of essays, taking the affect and agency chapters as complementary sections. This grouping will allow the reader to concentrate on rethinking the political in terms of the impulse to act and political horizons, as it were, more systematically. Alternatively, readers wishing to focus more directly on the challenge of new action to methodology may find the following groupings interesting: rethinking intersubjectivities and collectives (Greenberg, Avramopoulou, Peano, Ahmad), spatiotemporalities (Postill, Rethmann, Howe, Faubion), and reimagining political ethnography (Maeckelbergh, Panourgiá, Khasnabish). As it is, the chapters talk to one another on various levels, forming rich cross-conversations.

In the first chapter, Jessica Greenberg explores the politics of disappointment in postrevolutionary Serbia. She takes up disappointment as an affectively complex and analytically revealing category. While developing a rich ethnographic description of the postsocialist and post-Yugoslav terrain in Serbia, Greenberg delves into the tensions between older and younger generations of disappointed activists. She explains that, in planning future actions, older generations of activists adhere to a moralistic "being" versus the pragmatic engagement of the younger generation's "doing." We'll rejoin the issue of being versus doing in Eirini Avramopoulou's chapter on queer struggles in Istanbul, and in Tania Ahmad's innovative chapter exploring resistance informed by the moral register of respectability.

In chapter 2, Eirini Avramopoulou continues our reconsideration of activist communities and desire as political affect through an examination of LGBT activism in Istanbul, Turkey. She explores the tension between desire and the demand for legal recognition, subject formation and subjectivation, to remap action from the perspective of the "unfulfilled human." Specifically, the chapter addresses the relation between the demand for legal recognition and the desire for visibility as this mediates the political activism of LGBT people in Istanbul while they are trying to resist legal prohibitions, social exclusions, and psychic displacement. Deriving insights from performativity theory and psychoanalysis in order to unpack the complicated relation between subject formation and subjectivation, Avramopoulou situates the analysis of desire within the "political economy" of visibility, defined both in terms of the effects of neoliberal processes of commodification affecting identity claims and gender performances and as a psychic process affected by the cultural and legal regulations working to discipline bodies and legitimize civic and social policing of genders, sexualities, pleasures, and satisfactions.

Irene Peano focuses more directly on political activations and emergent political formations in chapter 3, investigating militant practices that revolve around the control of immigration and the exploitation of migrant labor in contemporary Italy. Her chapter is based on sustained engagement and participant observation in a number of militant contexts, and particularly with an activist network that concentrates predominantly on the exploitation of agricultural labor, through activities that aim to understand forms of exploitation and repression, to bring solidarity to migrants, and to break the isolation into which they are forced by a regime of *exception*, in Giorgio Agamben's formulation. If the migrants in question are formally deprived of their political subjectivity, in a system that confines them in ghettos or camps and denies them any opportunity to obtain regular work (regardless of their legal status and right to work), Peano asks how this militant political practice might begin to build alternative subjectivities out of the encounter between citizens and noncitizens across different locations. She does so by reflecting on the notion of subjectivity as it has been deployed in critical thought, putting it in dialogue with analytical models that stress the trans-subjective, affective dimensions of such thought, and with the militant notion of composition as it has been reworked outside the orthodox "class" paradigm.

In chapter 4, James Faubion challenges our approach to political collectives by staking out a systematic critique of the exclusion of religion from politics. He argues that allowing what Foucault characterized as the "figures of spirituality" into the normative political imagination affords a different understanding of the political grounds we implicitly separate as Other, including, for example, the current versions of Islamist activism. He achieves this by drawing portraits of the Seventh-Day Adventists (specifically, Branch Davidians) and Earth First, movements that demand social changes that transcend the limits of politics, social changes that are vitalist in their expansiveness, their cosmologicopolitics. Taken together with Peano's consideration of bare life and Avramopoulou's thinking on subjectivation and the unfulfilled human, Faubion's chapter rounds out a fascinating conversation about refiguring the human within the political.

Neni Panourgiá's chapter ends this section with a summative question: how does one give an account of one's own precarity? Panourgiá looks at different ways in which young people in Greece are attempting to own and disown precarity. She considers discourses of mourning and loss as they are erected in Athens among the young who participate in new formulations of being, as they are attempting to carve out a sense and an articulation of self out of what she calls "cinders of global capital," as the wake and the refuse of phatic accountabilities performed from the vacated spaces of real responsibilities. The chapter offers a fractured text that mirrors the disruption of the distant and objectifying analytic voice Panourgiá problematizes, and it echoes the subjective Greek experiences of disorder and social unraveling. Throughout this poetic work, the author revisits political affect and community while challenging the ethnographer to write for a broader political responsiveness. In this, the final chapter in the first part directly engages with the first chapter in the second part.

Chapter 6, by Tania Ahmad, opens the second part of this book, exploring agency, ethics, and political horizons. In this chapter Ahmad offers an account of a movement in Karachi based on a politics of the ordinary. She details the emergence of the *intolerants*, or ordinary people who reject violence in favor of a banal everyday, a rejection articulated in terms of respectability—a primarily moral register. Ahmad suggests that the broad taking up of a pious morality generates a normative imaginary that rejects the current state of political affairs, effectively rooting something radical. Considering the formation of political horizons, Ahmad's chapter can be read with Peano's reworking of composition in mind. The authors provide reflections on very different modes of collectivization, from active aggregation to the (almost) incidental, and dynamics of collectivity, from the directly interventionist to the critically passive and diffused—yet they both describe self-organization and the emergence of resistance actions.

In chapter 7, Cymene Howe offers a reading of activist engagements—for gay rights in Managua and against a wind farm in Oaxaca, Mexico—that refuse to be called movements. She uses these refusals as a way to explore social movement scholars' preoccupation with dramatic and spectacular faces of activism and to redirect us toward other more quotidian forms of quiet engagement, even moments when nothing seems to be happening. Howe suggests that times when seemingly nothing is happening or, to use her term, the "negative space" between one and another activist episode, are the periods that bring out the finer contours of the political ecologies of activism and transformative social action. Along with John Postill's chapter, this work engages with resistance temporalities, the unfolding of critical agonism, and political horizons.

Petra Rethmann begins chapter 8 by asking how art can (and does) function as a technique for the emergence of political possibilities. She offers an examination of how the Russian political-artistic collective *chto delat'*—what should be done—uses in its protests pamphlets that reconnect the present and the past, the living and the dead, in communicating a sense of capitalist disenchantment. She argues that art, and art objects specifically, can maintain a space outside hegemonic historical constructions of the past, which can inspire a disruptive imagining in the present. This chapter engages directly with questions of ethics and critique, and the emergence of new action. What's more, Rethmann, together with Postill, begins a conversation about the rise of new forms of discourse and innovative practice that extend across different periods. In this, they challenge the reader to consider a (multiply) dislocated rooting of resistance, evoking Howe's discussion of negative spaces.

In chapter 9, John Postill provides a reading of the multilinearity of the Spanish Indignados, or 15-M movement, assessing its multiple timelines with Sewell's

(2005) concepts of events, trends, and routines. This chapter lays out the very different temporalities, as well as the striking continuities and discontinuities, of the movement, especially during the dramatic year of 2011. It offers a model of how scholars can track the rise of new forms of discourse, innovative practices with regard to public space, trends on social media, and routinized practices that extended across different periods, even as they take on new significance in their new settings.

In chapter 10, Marianne Maeckelbergh continues our consideration of ethics and critique by engaging directly with the question of the ethical researcher: academics in the field feeling their way through situations they often don't know how to negotiate. This chapter returns us to the question of the researcher as ethical subject and prompts a reconsideration of the challenge resistance actions pose to the imaginative logic of discovery at the heart of field-based ethnography. Through an exploration of the complementary and contradictory ethical frameworks that the ethnographer negotiates as part of participant observation during long-term fieldwork, this chapter argues that to gain access to the lifeworld of activists, the researcher needs to privilege the (multiple) ethical codes of activists themselves over other possible ethical frameworks. Maeckelbergh questions the agency of the researcher, the challenges of access to different fields of activity, the sometimes-uncertain building of an understanding of how actions unfold, and the promises of ethnography based on participant observation. This chapter can be read in relation to Panourgiá and Khasnabish's discussion of ethnography's contributions to political horizons.

The final chapter of this part, chapter 11, addresses the limits of dominant frameworks for cataloging and assessing radical movements, and what insights this might provide for researchers hoping to contribute to those actions. Alex Khasnabish draws on his experience with radical social justice activists and his work with the Radical Imagination Project in Halifax, Nova Scotia, and argues for the taking up of engaged research practiced in an ethic of solidarity. He combines the question of representation with a consideration of "radical imagination" to show how the academy can help produce critical and collective moments of deep reflection that may inform established social projects and/ or produce new resistance initiatives. Building on Maeckelbergh's consideration of negotiating fieldwork practice, this chapter brings the key themes of this part of the book—ethics and agency—to a consideration of ethnography as engagement.

The conclusion to this volume is in the form of a conversation with Athena Athanasiou—a format that represents the ongoing work of "figuring things out." The chapter tacks back to the December 2008 events in Athens to discuss agonism, desubjugation, and political assemblages. This chapter reconnects with the major themes in the book and explores some of the analytical and political possibilities we might look for in new resistance actions.

References

Agamben, Giorgio. 1993. *The Coming Community, Theory out of Bounds*. Minneapolis: University of Minnesota Press.

Balibar, Étienne. 2004. *We, the People of Europe? Reflections on Transnational Citizenship*. Princeton, NJ: Princeton University Press.

Barth, Fredrik. 1969. *Ethnic Groups and Boundaries: The Social Organization of Culture Difference*. Boston: Little, Brown.

Benhabib, Seyla. 1996. *Democracy and Difference: Contesting Boundaries of the Political*. Princeton, NJ: Princeton University Press.

Biehl, João, and Peter Locke. 2010. "Deleuze and the Anthropology of Becoming." *Current Anthropology* 51 (3): 317–337.

Biehl, João, and Ramah McKay. 2012. "Ethnography as Political Critique." *Anthropological Quarterly* 85 (4): 1209–1228.

Borneman, John. 2011. "Oedipal Roots of Revolt in the Middle East." *Anthropology News* 52 (5): 17.

Brettell, Caroline, and Deborah Reed-Danahay. 2012. *Civic Engagements: The Citizenship Practices of Indian and Vietnamese Immigrants*. Stanford, CA: Stanford University Press.

Castles, Stephen, and Alastair Davidson. 2000. *Citizenship and Migration: Globalization and the Politics of Belonging*. Basingstoke, UK: Macmillan.

Cohen, Anthony P. 1982. *Belonging: Identity and Social Organization in British Rural Cultures, Social and Economic Papers*. St. John's, NL: Institute of Social and Economic Research.

Dalakoglou, Dimitris. 2011. "Crisis and Revolt in Europe." *Anthropology News* 52 (9): 11–14.

Das, Veena, Arthur Kleinman, Mamphela Ramphele, and Pamela Reynolds. 2000. *Violence and Subjectivity*. Berkeley: University of California Press.

Delanty, Gerard. 2002. "Two Conceptions of Cultural Citizenship: A Review of Recent Literature on Cultural Citizenship." *Global Review of Ethnopolitics* 1: 60–66.

Economides, Spyros, and Vassilis Monastiriotis, eds. 2009. *The Return of Street Politics? Essays on the December Riots in Greece*. London: Hellenic Observatory, London School of Economics.

Escobar, Arturo. 1995. *Encountering Development: The Making and Unmaking of the Third World*. Princeton Studies in Culture/Power/History. Princeton, NJ: Princeton University Press.

Fassin, Didier. 2014. "True Life, Real Lives: Revisiting the Boundaries between Ethnography and Fiction." *American Ethnologist* 41 (1): 40–55.

Faubion, James D., and George E. Marcus. 2009. *Fieldwork Is Not What It Used to Be: Learning Anthropology's Method in a Time of Transition*. Ithaca, NY: Cornell University Press.

Fortun, Kim. 2009. "Figuring Out Ethnography." In *Fieldwork Is Not What It Used to Be: Learning Anthropology's Method in a Time of Transition*, edited by James D. Faubion and George E. Marcus, 167–183. Ithaca, NY: Cornell University Press.

Foucault, Michel. 1980. *The History of Sexuality*. New York: Random House.

———. 1997. "What Is Critique?" In *The Politics of Truth*, edited by Sylvère Lotringer, 41–82. New York: Semiotext(e).

Goodale, Mark, and Nancy Postero. 2013. *Neoliberalism, Interrupted: Social Change and Contested Governance in Contemporary Latin America*. Stanford, CA: Stanford University Press.

Greenberg, Jessica. 2014. *After the Revolution: Youth, Democracy, and the Politics of Disappointment in Serbia*. Stanford, CA: Stanford University Press.

Greenhouse, Carol J. 2010. *Ethnographies of Neoliberalism*. Philadelphia: University of Pennsylvania Press.

Guattari, Félix. 1995. *Chaosmosis: An Ethico-Aesthetic Paradigm*. Bloomington: Indiana University Press.

Guattari, Félix, and Gary Genosko. 1996. *The Guattari Reader*. Blackwell Readers. Oxford, UK: Blackwell Publishers.

Habermas, Jürgen. 1991. *The Structural Transformation of the Public Sphere: An Inquiry into a Category of Bourgeois Society*. Cambridge, MA: MIT Press.

Holston, James. 2008. *Insurgent Citizenship: Disjunctions of Democracy and Modernity in Brazil*. Princeton, NJ: Princeton University Press.

Juris, Jeffrey S. 2012. "Reflections on #Occupy Everywhere: Social Media, Public Space and Emerging Logics of Aggregation." *American Ethnologist* 39 (2): 259–279.

Juris, Jeffrey S., and Alex Khasnabish. 2013. *Insurgent Encounters: Transnational Activism, Ethnography, and the Political*. Durham, NC: Duke University Press.

Kalyvas, Andreas. 2010. "An Anomaly? Some Reflections on the Greek December 2008." *Constellations* 17 (2): 351–365.

Maeckelbergh, Marianne. 2009. *The Will of the Many: How the Alterglobalisation Movement Is Changing the Face of Democracy, Anthropology, Culture and Society*. London: Pluto Press.

Massumi, Brian. 2002. *Parables for the Virtual: Movement, Affect, Sensation*. Durham, NC: Duke University Press.

Mitchell, W. J. T., Bernard E. Harcourt, and Michael T. Taussig. 2013. *Occupy: Three Inquiries in Disobedience*. Chicago: University of Chicago Press.

Ong, Aihwa. 2006. *Neoliberalism as Exception: Mutations in Citizenship and Sovereignty*. Durham, NC: Duke University Press.

Panourgiá, Neni. 2012. "Anthropology's Europe." *Anthropology News* 53 (4): 32–33.

Parsons, Talcott. 1968 [1937]. *The Structure of Social Action: A Study in Social Theory with Special Reference to a Group of Recent European Writers*. 2 vols. New York: Free Press.

Povinelli, Elizabeth A. 2011. *Economies of Abandonment: Social Belonging and Endurance in Late Liberalism*. Durham, NC: Duke University Press.

Rabinow, Paul, and Anthony Stavrianakis. 2013. *Demands of the Day: On The Logic of Anthropological Inquiry*. Chicago: University of Chicago Press.

Razsa, Maple. 2012. "Toward an Affirmative Ethnography." *Anthropology News* 53 (9): 35.

——. 2015. *Bastards of Utopia: Living Radical Politics after Socialism*. Bloomington: Indiana University Press.

Razsa, Maple, and Andrej Kurnik. 2012. "The Occupy Movement in Žižek's Hometown: Direct Democracy and a Politics of Becoming." *American Ethnologist* 39 (2): 238–258. doi: 10.1111/j.1548-1425.2012.01361.x.

Rosaldo, Renato, and William Flores. 1997. "Identity, Conflict, and Evolving Latino Communities: Cultural Citizenship in San Jose, California." In *Latino Cultural Citizenship: Claiming Identity, Space and Politics*, edited by William Flores and Rina Benmayor, 57–96. Boston: Beacon Press.

Schmitt, Carl. 1976 [1927]. *The Concept of the Political*. New Brunswick, NJ: Rutgers University Press.

Stewart, Kathleen. 2007. *Ordinary Affects*. Durham, NC: Duke University Press.

Sewell, W. H., Jr. 2005. *Logics of History: Social Theory and Social Transformation*. Chicago: University of Chicago Press.

Taussig, Michael. 2011. *I Swear I Saw This: Drawings in Fieldwork Notebooks, Namely My Own*. Chicago: University of Chicago Press.

Touraine, Alain. 1977. *The Self-Production of Society*. Chicago: University of Chicago Press.

PART I

AFFECT AS POLITICAL CONDITION

1 Being and Doing Politics

Moral Ontologies and Ethical Ways of Knowing at the End of the Cold War

Jessica Greenberg

At a debate in Southern California in 2007, the French philosopher Alain Badiou informed the French philosopher Étienne Balibar that he, Balibar, was a reformist. "And you, monsieur," Balibar replied, "are a theologian."
—Bruce Robbins, "Balibarism!," *N+1* (2013)

IN THIS CHAPTER, I want to address three questions with methodological import for the analysis of political practice in contemporary Europe. First, how is it that we are still at a point in political thought where it makes sense to pose a choice between political theology and reform? Second, how are our categories of analysis denatured and flattened when we map the world of political possibility around these two opposing poles? And third, what has been the toll on activists who live and work in the shadow of such binaries? At issue is whether it is possible to imagine a progressive politics outside the terms that have dominated the European left for much of the twentieth (and apparently the early twenty-first) century. Is reform antithetical to an affectively rich and hopeful vision of a just world? Does pragmatism, and its ugly stepchild disappointment, truly spell the death of a utopian politics?

In approaching these questions, I hope to move beyond the binaries of revolution and reform, utopia and apologia, moral purity and compromise, as fixed starting points in defining political possibility. The remainder of Robbins's (2013) article cited in the epigraph to this chapter is a spirited defense of Étienne Balibar's reformism and a refusal that it is less politically pure than utopianism. In this spirit, I examine the ideological and affective structure of what I call elsewhere "a politics of disappointment" (Greenberg 2014). I argue that pragmatism, so often negatively understood as the absence of sentiment, is in fact a form of aspirational political desire, best understood through the lens of disappointment.

Such disappointment engenders a particular relationship to human agency in the face of (im)possible change. Disappointment is thus the beginning, rather than the end, of a practical political engagement. Pragmatism (and relatedly, reformism) is thus not merely an effect of seeing the world "as it really is." Neither is it a cynical response motivated by the absence of hope. It is a space of desire that emerges in dialogic relation with totalizing visions of political and moral transformation. In the attempt to rethink the experience of pragmatism as itself a form of affective intensity, I hope to show that the categories of "reformist" and "theologian," "pragmatist" and "idealist," are not opposites. Rather they are co-constituting and historically emergent categories that entail very different theories of human agency and thus call forth different approaches to activism.

On Hope and Disappointment

In part, this chapter is a response to recent scholarship on what might be called the post-hope generations of late liberalism. For young people, caught between their parents' modernist ideals and the stark economic and social realities of the contemporary world, boredom (Mains 2007), shame (Jeffrey 2010), and disconnectedness (Allison 2009) emerge as effects of stalled expectations and deferred dreams. For many young people, such states are mapped along the progressive space of a life cycle (Durham 2008; Johnson-Hanks 2002) that intersects with broader geopolitical configurations of development and modernity (Koselleck 2004; Ferguson 1999). This contemporary scholarship is important in highlighting new features of coming of age in an insecure world. Yet at times, it runs the risk of reinscribing a binary of hope and disappointment that defines the "negative" affective experience as a form of loss.

At the same time that we are lamenting the absence of hope, we are also increasingly invested in the project of finding it in new places. We look to globalizing forms of protest, what Hardt and Negri (2011) have termed a "cycle of struggles," or the reconfiguration of old domains of capital into sites of concentrated political possibility (Harvey 2000). Hope has become an aspirational horizon in which scholars are increasingly invested: if the world gives us disappointment, we might anecdotally (or ethnographically) locate hope in unlikely places. In such an intellectual and political context, disappointment is a starting point for inquiry. But it is rarely an enduring focus of analysis. In the attempt to take new democratic spaces seriously—both politically and analytically—we lose sight of disappointment as a social form in its own right.

Yet disappointment is neither loss—of hope or possibility—nor the aftereffect of "real" politics having taken place at another time or in another place. Indeed, it appears that disappointment is the dominant experiential frame of many contemporary political movements. We apprehend such disappointment in the narratives of frustrated activists and citizens. We experience it in the painful compromises and gripes of former revolutionaries turned technocrats, politicians, or nongovernmental organization workers. Scholars and activists alike often frame disappointment in the same terms as those that opened this article—those of the theologian versus the reformist, the revolutionary versus the pragmatist. Yet such binaries do not capture the complexities of practice. Increasingly, disappointment is the ruling ethos of many new (and not-so-new) democracies. It is a condition of democratic practice, not its failure.

In my 2014 book, I develop the frame of a politics of disappointment by tracking how student activists in Serbia after the democratic revolution of 2000 manage the contradictions of democratic practice as they play out in real time (Greenberg 2014). Here disappointment emerged not only as people compared the expectations of revolution to the realities of democracy in an impoverished country marked by war, state violence, and corruption. It also emerged as people contended with the murkiness and contingency of political agency under such conditions. Student activists were often at the center of these processes. They were charged objects of disappointment given long-standing ideological investment in youth revolutionary politics. And they were well poised to confront the contingencies of activism as they moved between street protest and institutionally based democratic reform.

I elaborate on student activists' negotiation of changing meanings of youth politics in the postrevolutionary, postsocialist democratic period. I argue that they engaged in a "politics of disappointment" defined by a subtle awareness and negotiation of the contingency of action. They were, to put it plainly, well aware that their democratic practices would inevitably be contradictory and disappointing to others. In showing how such action unfolded and was made meaningful, I sought to show "the conditions under which the coherence of practice is impossible, and yet action takes place nonetheless" (Greenberg 2014, 8). To this extent, student activists were both shadowed by and able to move beyond the burden of the defining whether or not they were truly (and still are) revolutionary subjects.

Was There, or Was There Not?

For many activists in newly emerging democracies, the absolutisms of twentieth-century politics are no longer convincing ways of authorizing political engagement. Indeed, the investment in twentieth-century notions of revolutionary transformation has come under fire not only from scholars but also from many activist circles (see Graeber 2009). Certainly, in formerly socialist Eastern Europe, the collapse of state socialism has called into question the totalizing nature of revolutionary politics. On the one hand, the actually lived experience of "permanent revolution," with its ongoing ideological and social contradictions, disabused socialist citizens of the idea that revolution could ever be a coherent or fully finished project. On the other hand, the disappointments of Western leftists in actually-existing socialism, from 1956 to 1968 and finally 1989, slowly eroded the belief that socialist utopia was at hand.

This terrain of post–Cold War politics is perfectly captured in the popular 2006 Romanian movie *12:08 East of Bucharest*. I begin with an analysis of this film because it captures the affective experience and ethical stakes of living in the shadow of a revolution. In working between the space of "was there, or was there not?" the film points to how our assumptions about human political agency emerge in relationship to the knowability (and unknowability) of historical truth.

The farcical film—its Romanian title is *A fost sau n-a fost?* (Was There or Was There Not)—takes place over the course of a day in a small town east of the Romanian capital of Bucharest on the sixteenth anniversary of the Romanian Revolution. The film's English title refers to the precise moment when Romanian dictator Nicolae Ceaușescu and his wife, Elena, fled the Presidential Palace in Bucharest by helicopter. They were later arrested and executed by firing squad. In the movie, a local television host, well connected and shadowed by corruption, hosts an anniversary program to determine whether there was or was not a revolution in their town. At stake is whether the small town participated in Romania's democratic transformation. The integrity of those who claimed authority based on their resistance to the communist regime is also in question.

The host invites two citizens: an elderly man best known for dressing up as Santa Claus for the local children and a schoolteacher and intellectual whose moral authority is compromised by his heavy drinking. What follows is an hour of bickering, accusation, and counteraccusation. The spirit of revolution is reduced to a "he said, she said" tale of whether the schoolteacher was really in the square protesting *before* the 12:08 flight of Ceaușescu. In the process, the revolution becomes terrain for petty grievances and minor cruelties. The film itself deserves more elaboration than I have room for here. What is important is the way the film focuses on the importance of establishing historical timelines in order to pinpoint moral and political integrity. Establishing whether it did or did not happen is inseparable from establishing whether the town was complicit or courageous. Revolutionaries were present in the square. Petty liars and drunks were not. At stake is not just what happened but people's essential moral being.

The film is funny and tragic because it reduces world-historical transformations to small-town disputes over meaningless details. The meaning of revolution and the status of the revolutionary are contingent on a mundane sequencing of events. This sequence forms the architecture of moral possibility through a process of post hoc reckoning. At the beginning of the film, the host and guests are certain they can get to the bottom of things. By the end, the beleaguered participants confront the limits of knowledge, and thus the limits of their own moral authority and political integrity. Not only does the film throw into question the possibility that revolution might be a knowable historical event. It also questions the very relevance of revolution as a metric of human value and political agency.

What, then, is left for a disappointed, backward-looking town, mired in the irrelevance of its own postsocialist disappointment? And to what extent is it the burden of revolution itself that stymies new imaginaries for the future? One particular moment in the film throws these questions into stark relief. It also suggests alternatives to fighting over control of historical memory and political significance. Toward the end of the film, the host turns to outside callers with questions for the panelists. Up to this point, the callers have engaged in accusations and counteraccusations to attempt to fix the exact timeline of events in the town's main square. One caller has a different memory to share. Just before the show within the movie ends, the host asks if there is another call. There is a pause, and a woman's voice fills the void. The following exchange occurs:

CALLER: My name is Tina. My son died on December 23 in Otopeni, Bucharest.

HOST: I'm very sorry, ma'am, but we want to know what happened in our town.

CALLER: I'm not about to reproach you, Mr. Jdersecu. I'm just calling to let you know that it's snowing outside.

HOST: It's snowing?

CALLER: Yes, it's snowing big white flakes. Enjoy it now. Tomorrow it will be mud . . . Merry Christmas, everybody.

The panelists are momentarily stunned into awkward silence, and they are only able to wish her a Merry Christmas in the moments after she has hung up.

We know nothing about Tina, or her motivations for calling: only that she lost her son (likely one of the many killed in the protests in 1989). What is significant in this moment is that the entire enterprise of "was there, or was there not" that defines postsocialist political accountability is made utterly irrelevant. Instead, the woman's recollection takes places along a different timeline, that of a human connectedness that eschews the temporal logic of political change. When the *definitional* becomes the terrain of politics, then everyday lived experience is lost. For the woman caller, what is significant about that day was not the inexorable march of historical change, but the interweaving of revolutionary time with affective intensities of memory and loss. For Tina, life's meaning unfolded unexpectedly, not according to a fixed timeline based on rupture and hindsight. Her revolution was a different kind of transformation. Its significance could never be apprehended through a perfect and knowable sequencing of events. Time and distance (the bird's-eye view of history), makes the revolution no less knowable. Yes, snow indeed turns to mud. But in the moment, one must experience and enjoy it—to do so is to be present in, rather than haunted by, time.

In this moment, *12:08 East of Bucharest* proposes another way of understanding historicity. One's essential relationship to political possibility in the future need not be determined by one's position within the official histories of the past. Moving beyond "did it or did it not" happen is a key condition of possibility for post–Cold War politics. The very logic that structures our ability to distinguish revolution from reform—a temporal sequencing of events in which a moment of pure transformation might be apprehended, let alone made meaningful—is upended. For Tina the ability to define historical truth takes a backseat to a present-focused affective intensity that resists definition. It is in this space—and not the project of definitive knowledge—that ethics is grounded.

And yet the stakes of simply walking away from modernist frameworks for defining and apprehending change are high. Indeed, the problem is that "did it" or "did it not happen" is not merely the animating question of modernist ideologies of political transformation. The question of defining, naming, and knowing historical events has its roots in other political crises of twentieth-century Europe. To this extent, one cannot decenter the binary of revolution and reform without understanding the particular significance of "knowing" (did it happen or didn't it?) in European political imaginaries. In turn, defining history becomes the basis for producing ethical subjectivity (whether one was or was not *really* a revolutionary).

The act of defining history is central to twentieth-century revolutionary politics and to modern European moral commitments. The stakes of "knowing historical truth" have been shaped by two intersecting failures. The first was the failure of the European left to anticipate or counter the totalizing crimes of fascism. The second was the failure of 1968 to reshape the conditions of political and social possibility in the name of humanist socialism: to effect a true revolution not only of state but also of society. In both cases, a totalizing vision gave way to a moral reckoning that forced a shattered left to try to pick up the pieces of history. There was an urgency to making sense of what really happened and why. The ability to set the record straight requires that one have temporal and spatial perspective: the moral capacities enabled by the twentieth-century bird's-eye view of a complex, secular world. Bearing witness is at its heart an ethics of producing historical truth. The project of leftist politics in modern Europe was inextricably bound to such a project of history. The proper sequencing of events might encompass memory without reproducing the violence of rupture.

In such a context, politics of continuity (reform) became necessarily suspect. How could there be a moral basis for the pragmatic? Didn't practical engagement imply at best acquiescence and at worst complicity? These moral and political stakes are necessary to understanding the weight of the distinction between revolution and reform. These are not merely different approaches to political change.

They are different orientations to the past that dictate one's ethical position in the present and the future.

Human Rights and Postutopian (Un)certainties

These dilemmas—the ethics of bearing witness and the confrontation with the contingency of historical knowledge and truth—come together in the modern history of human rights. Speaking of the international human rights movement, Samuel Moyn (2010, 213) notes:

> The international human rights movement became so significant, then, neither because it offered a rights-based doctrine alone nor because it forged a truly global vision for the first time. Rather, it was the crisis of other utopias that allowed the very neutrality that had made "human rights" wholly peripheral to the aftermath of World War II . . . to become the condition of their success. Human rights could break through in that era because the ideological climate was ripe for claims to make a difference not through political vision but by transcending politics.

Moyn argues that the antipolitics of the human rights era opened up space for new, moralizing utopian horizons in the wake of revolutionary, anticolonial, and communist disappointments (see also Fassin 2011; Ticktin 2011). What links these dilemmas to those that open this chapter is a broader context in which twentieth-century certainties, anchored by powerful and competing utopian frameworks, are no longer available to stabilize social and ethical forms of praxis.

These two strains of politics—the moral commitment of bearing witness and the limits of twentieth-century revolutionary consciousness—came into sharp relief in the wake of the Yugoslav Wars of Succession. Indeed, Moyn has suggested that these modern human rights regimes are deeply tied to those wars. He notes that, in the wake of Cambodian genocide, and "certainly by the mid-1990s resurgence of 'ethnic cleansing' on the European continent—genocide prevention is now among the first items on the human rights agenda" (Moyn 2010, 220). It is noteworthy that the Balkans, while operating as a causal factor in Moyn's analysis, is only obliquely named. "Ethnic cleansing" on the European continent stands metonymically for the complex histories of violence of the Yugoslav Wars of Succession. Here Moyn gets only half the significance of the Yugoslav scene—it has become inextricably linked to contemporary ideas of rights, justice (transitional and otherwise), and definitions of humanity (and its limits). But what makes the Yugoslav case significant in the story of rights is that it is also a terrain across which the other central feature of rights discourse has played out—the actually existing and lived experience of the death of utopia.

Thus, to ask how rights have been configured in the shadow of twentieth-century utopias and genocidal violence, one can turn to no better source than activists in the region who are struggling with precisely how to live and enact a postconflict, post–Cold War ethical politics. Human rights activism in the former Yugoslavia thus sheds light not only on the lived terms of rights work but on the lived conditions of postrevolutionary politics as well. It is at this point that the ontological and epistemological struggles over being versus doing politics intersects with the struggle over whether it is any longer possible to *be* a revolutionary or *do* revolution?

I now turn to look at two approaches to human rights in contemporary Serbia. I hope to demonstrate the epistemological and ontological commitments that underlie particular approaches to the practices of postutopian, post–Cold War politics in contemporary Europe. This terrain is both bound to and far more complicated than the terms of debate that opened this chapter: reform versus revolution, moral and political purity versus contingency and compromise.

Being versus Doing: Human Rights Activism in Serbia

I conducted my initial field research with student activists in the years immediately following the October 5 revolution that toppled Serbian dictator Slobodan Milošević. Even in the heady early days of postrevolutionary student activism, one of the common refrains I encountered among student activists was that they needed to be practical and strategic. In the face of accusations of being "political," or of betraying more altruistic revolutionary ideals, student activists then, and now, foregrounded the importance of a pragmatic politics within new democratizing contexts. I examined the conditions under which young activists were no longer compelled by totalizing visions of rupture. How and why are practicality, strategy, and compromise the new terrain of democratic activists? And what does this commitment to reform (within compromised state and juridical institutions marred by violent legacies of the past) say about the new shape of activism in contemporary Europe? In other words, how and why are democratic activists compelled by a pragmatism that was anathema to an older generation of European progressives?

Like the farcical rejection of a revolutionary historicity (whether it did or did not happen), activists that I encountered embraced the nonsovereign nature of political agency. Their activism was pragmatic because it questioned the terms under which one could anticipate, or even assess, the moral and political authenticity of action. This did not mean that they abandoned certainty altogether. Rather, certainty was based on doing (engaging in) rather than knowing the complex world around them. It was based on a praxis that operated in terms of epistemological contingency rather than on the ontological certainty of bearing witness. It is to this dynamic that I now turn in more detail.

Doing and Being Human Rights Politics in Serbia

It was a warm summer night in Belgrade. Milena (a pseudonym) and I met in a crowded, outdoor pub strung with Christmas lights and cluttered with tables. We had to lean our heads together and raise our voices to be heard above the din, but we were both thrilled to be out. It was a rare treat for both of us, mothers of young children, working full-time, with partners who were stretched equally thin between family and work. It was hard not to think back to earlier evenings together, staying up late to watch bad action movies or Eurovision song contests. A decade earlier, in 2003, Milena was still a university student. She was not yet widely known in the larger Serbian human rights community. But the unflinching nature of her convictions was already evident. Also present was her general sense that the rank and file could rarely be trusted to make the right decision when it came to progressive issues—a trait that had earned her the joking name "Lenin" during one meeting at her student organization. At the same time, like many other student activists and young people her age, Milena had a finely tuned cynicism and distrust of anything "political." By this she meant the kind of backroom, underhanded, and self-serving negotiations that characterized formal politics in Serbia. From the earliest days that I had known her, Milena had combined a kind of hopeful naïveté and frustrated cynicism and disappointment in the ethical capacities of others.

Now in 2013 Milena was poised to become head of a well-respected civil society organization in Belgrade. The transition was far from easy, however. We spoke at length about Milena's frustration with the organization as it was currently run. The then-current leaders were well-respected, longtime progressive activists in Serbia, and Milena held them in extremely high regard. Yet she was also at times frustrated with their approach to running the organization, including their egalitarian managerial style (particularly related to the hiring and firing of staff). Milena drew a link between her boss's leftist politics and egalitarian ethos. It was simply not practical for running an organization. This is not to say that Milena saw herself as a technocrat. She spoke of the need for passion and inspiration in one's activist work. But for Milena, this passion was integrally tied to a kind of practicality necessary to realizing activist work in the most efficient way possible.

In part the need for practicality was a lesson Milena had learned from watching older generations of activists burn out or become consumed by their work. She recounted an argument that she had with an older activist, a human rights advocate in the country. Milena had incredible respect for this woman, and yet she also saw how her all-consuming passion was a personal and "strategic" problem. Milena detailed for me a fight she had with this older activist over the issue of a Serbian truth and reconciliation commission, which activists in the region had been trying to get up and running for some time. The latest efforts to establish the commission included getting one million signatures across the former Yugoslavia. Milena was ever attentive to issues of strategic framing—a skill that she had finely honed within her student organization a decade before. She suggested to this same older, respected colleague involved in the effort that that they would have to be particularly careful in presenting the commission when trying to get signatures in Serbia and among Serbs in other parts of the region.

Milena was trying to work within, as well as against, the widespread denial of and silence on Serbia's role in ethnic cleansing in the Yugoslav Wars of Succession during the 1990s. She was also attuned to the competitive victim narratives that characterize Serbian official discourse about this period. Milena felt that emphasizing the commission's role in justice for Serbian victims would be more widely acceptable. For her, the larger goal was to attain the one million signatures, even though she understood the ethical and political implications of the framing she was proposing. The truth commission is too important to not be strategic, she told me. "We get one chance at this, and if not now, then it will be another twenty years." Milena recounted how when she made this point to her older colleague, her colleague became enraged and accused Milena of being a nationalist—an accusation targeted to hurt. She told Milena that she, Milena, was trying to make this woman "not into a traitor" and she wanted to be a traitor. For this older and highly respected activist, being a traitor signaled a particular moral stance in which anything that smacked of compromise was necessarily complicit with the violence committed in the name of Serbia and Serbian nationalism. For her, Milena's "strategic thinking" was at worst a justification of that violence and at best naïve within a culture of denial. The desire not only to betray the nation but also to be branded a traitor was all-consuming and necessitated utterly uncompromising activism, to the point of alienating large swaths of a potential public.

At the heart of this argument were two very different understandings of the relationship among moral ambiguity, passionate commitment, and political action. For the older activist, it was necessary to create certainty in the face of moral ambiguity by modeling a moral absolutism: one must and can only ever be a traitor. The state of betrayal was thus necessary to ensuring ethical political engagement. The older activist needed to *be* a traitor at heart, and to act like one. For Milena, it was also necessary to create some kind of certainty in the face of moral ambiguity. But here, certainty emerged through "practical" action. Milena did not express the need to *be* in any particular way. For her, being, as an essential political act, was not the starting point for activist engagement. This does not mean that she felt the practical less urgently, or that its animating spirit was less emotionally charged for Milena. Indeed, her sentiment that "we get one chance at this" was entirely about urgency and passion for her work, for which she had made personal sacrifices. For Milena the stance of being uncompromising was not tenable. Inflexibility was precisely part of the problem.

This rough schematization is not meant to map absolutely onto particular styles of political engagement or approaches to activism. Rather, it points to moral absolutism and institutional compromise as a defining tension in post–Cold War politics in Europe. The debate over political compromise (like the one that opened this chapter) signal different possible relationships to agency, knowledge, and ethics. I call these different bundles of relationships among action, agency and ethics "being" and "doing" politics.

Both being and doing politics designate different repertoires of action and modes of framing activism. That these often map onto different generational affiliations does not mean that they necessarily must. Rather, these are embodied genres of activist practice that entail becoming new kinds of selves in the act of articulating in and with the world. Being and doing politics thus work as meta-ethical frameworks for making sense of activist practice and inhabiting activist subjectivity. What I am pointing to are differences in the ethical and ontological ground that mediates the dynamic relationship of subject and world. The emphasis on "doing" involves a skepticism toward certainty or knowability as the ground of political action. An emphasis on "being" entails material and social forms of praxis that ground activism in a moral certitude. People may move back and forth between ways of knowing and assessing self and world and acting in the dialogic space between the two.

Being Politics: Ontologies as Ethics

Framing one's politics in terms of being entails drawing lines in the sand by which moral certainties can be known, defined, and enacted. Such a politics assumes that praxis emerges from and is productive of an ontological state—being (a traitor) requires the subject him- or herself to be the terrain and enactment of a politics of refusal. Here, being as action anchors ethics and politics to an essential (if not essentialized) subject through the practices of documentation and bearing witness. Such anchoring makes sense in response to a context that can be described only as a constant battle over the meaning of the past—"perspective" is itself a form of power often used by the former regime, current apologist politicians, and broader mass-media representations of Serbian victimhood. In Serbia, narratives about the meaning of the past are a constantly shifting battleground in which facticity and evidence are not anchoring points capable of grounding the relationship between experience and reality, self and other (Gordy 2013; Živković 2011). As I have written elsewhere, this constant sense that meaning is up for grabs, that reality can be unlinked from narrative, has produced a particular desire for agency in postwar Serbia in which people might fix intentionality to efficacy in the world (Greenberg 2011). In such a context, activists may ground themselves by situating a self in relationship to absolute moral truth.

For the older activist discussed earlier, betrayal is an irrepressibly uncompromised ethical stance. It is rooted in the ability to truly define the relationship between action and counteraction, cause and effect. Like the debates on whether "there was or was not" a revolution, bearing witness entails a definitional politics that is rooted in both temporal and scalar logics of knowability. It stands to reason, then, that if one knows, one can act *only* in the mode of betrayal, of moral absolutism and certainty. For a certain kind of human rights work, particularly in response to the denial of war crimes, this moral absolutism emerged as an absolutely necessary strategy and ethics in response to Serbian state-led and supported violence. From this perspective compromise is not only unacceptable; it is simply nonsensical. To engage with institutions that were structurally complicit was itself a form of violent complicity. For a particular generation of human rights activists, revelation and documentation formed the backbone of resistance to widespread denial and silence. Exhaustive documentation was also a response to the morass of relative and competitive victim narratives, which downplayed the structural systematicity of mass crimes committed in the name of Greater Serbia.

The political terrain of Serbia in the past twenty years has been defined by a complicated and uncomfortable relationship between moral absolutism and institutional compromise. Early feminist and antiwar activism in Serbia was premised on a commitment to speaking out against violence and war atrocities. Organizations like Women in Black and human rights practitioners and documenters like those involved in the Humanitarian Law Center and the Helsinki Committee for Human Rights put a great deal on the line in documenting human rights violations across the region. For this work, these (largely) woman activists were declared traitors to the nation and often (and continue to be) excoriated in the mainstream press and threatened verbally and physically. For many of these activists, engagement with corrupt and morally compromised institutions was antithetical to activist work—a stance of betrayal was an essential moral and political stance.

Such an ontological politics is all the more urgent given the complexities of identity in the context of postsocialist upheaval. Ethnographers of the region have documented people's sense that the social and semiotic conditions for anchoring a stable sense of identity were upended (Schäuble 2014; Helms 2013; Green 2005; see also Dunn 2008; Manning 2007). The sense of a self unmoored from continuities between past, present, and future has produced a profound sense of crisis (Shevchenko 2009). At the same time, the experience of continuity is forged through the ideological and social architecture that essentializes and grounds identity in forms of gendered difference (Helms 2013; Žarkov 2007; Gal and Kligman 2000). Thus, on the one hand, there is a widespread sense that it is impossible to moor a sense of self to a set of consistent ethical commitments and norms. On the other hand, feminist and antinationalist activists and scholars have pointed to the ways that gendered and ethnicized identities have become even more entrenched and naturalized. As Elissa Helms has argued in the case of Bosnia, the work of postconflict peace building and critical feminist activist engagement has thus taken place on a highly contradictory terrain. Activists must ground ethical action in the face of shifting social norms. And they must challenge new ethnicized essentialisms forged in the context of gendered violence.

The impact of this shifting moral and political terrain was a central theme for feminist activists during the Yugoslav Wars of Succession. These women came face-to-face with the challenge of grounding either action or ethics in identities outside ethnicized essentialisms. Lepa Mladjenović, Vera Litricin, and Tanya Renne captured the emerging dilemmas vividly in a 1993 piece titled "Belgrade Feminists 1992: Separation, Guilt and Identity Crisis." Despite a rich history of feminist action and solidarity across the former Yugoslav space, the violence of the wars produced a new set of uncertainties for activists that centered on the interplay of action, structural and war violence, complicity, and subjectivity. In this context, women faced "completely new questions . . . : Can a feminist be a nationalist chauvinist? Can a pacifist be a nationalist?" (Mladjenović, Litricin, and Renne 1993, 117). Activists confronted some of the most central questions of the nature of human subjectivity. Here the performative nature of gender and the materiality of gendered violence revealed themselves through complex positionalities that left women feeling "split within themselves" (Mladjenović, Litricin, and Renne 1993, 117). From the perspective of woman activists in Serbia, their unwilling but inevitable alignment with perpetrators funded and armed by the Serbian state, in the name of Serbian nationhood, forced difficult questions about the relationship between guilt and responsibility.

The fact of social reification has become the major battleground for articulating an activist versus a gendered nationalist politics (Helms 2013). In this context, grounding oneself in alternative ontologies offered a particular kind of agency. Here I take a (perhaps unexpected) page from Jane Bennett (2010), who, among others, is interested in the vital lives and actions of things and their enmeshment with human subjects. Bennett and other theorists of objects, assemblages, and ontologies seek to displace the primacy of human agency and action in favor of the action and effects of things in and on the world. What if, however, humans also fashion themselves in and through the ontological image of the thing itself? What if people also operate ontologically like objects? Can we also understand rights politics as the production of a kind of thingified state of being, a way to ground and hold form as if the human were a recalcitrant yet vital object? Indeed, Bennett (2010, 10), quoting John Frow, argues that the differences between human and object need to be "'flattened, read horizontally as a juxtaposition rather than vertically as a hierarchy of being. It's a feature of our world that we can and do distinguish . . . things from persons. But the sort of world we live in makes it constantly possible for these two sets of kinds to exchange properties.'"

Take, for example, the case of Women in Black, one of the oldest and most active feminist, antiwar groups in Serbia. Bojan Bilić (2012) has argued (following the analysis of Women in Black activists themselves) that collective identity has been central to Women in Black's incredible survival and persistence as an organization. I would argue that part of this collective identity is constituted through the practices of occupying space through a recalcitrant ontological presence—a politics of being. Like the politics of being (a traitor) as the basis for bearing witness, the power of Women in Black is the power of presence. Women in Black is best known for its powerful, silent vigils during which its members stand, utterly silent, unmoving and recalcitrant as objects that humans must contend with in public space. In positioning themselves in public space as immovable, bystanders must at least contend with *something* beyond their own control. Women in Black thus effects a transformative relationship to how people must position themselves as bodies in material space (see Fridman 2011; Dević 1997). It is a politics of reification and vital, unmovable "thingness" that throws into relief the stubborn interconnectedness of human and no longer human (if we can consider the dead the most vital objects of all). This connectedness underlies the project of social responsibility. Here, peace and feminist activists are themselves enmeshed in networks and cultures of materiality—material evidence, documentation, exhumed remains, black clothing. Bearing witness as an ethical project is inseparable from the moral and epistemological architecture made possible by webs and networks of these material objects.

A politics of being (or being politics) as the site of moral possibility is a logical consequence of a human rights politics. The epistemological struggles of the late twentieth-century post-utopia have produced a need for a politics that grounds the human in an "essential" truth. But more important, one cannot understand the kinds of agency implied in human rights activism without understanding that human rights activism is a struggle over the conditions of human ontology in the wake of violent processes of human reification. This is by no means to say that humans are (only) objects. But rather, people may choose to "exchange properties" with objects—persistence, recalcitrance, immutability—as a political and ethical strategy. Thus, I take Bennett (2010, 10) seriously when she proposes that we need to consider "human power [as] itself a kind of thing power." More to the point, one might harness the qualities of the thing to better the human soul, rather than the other way around.

When women stand, quietly but stubbornly, they stand as objects, facts, data, and not only as symbols. It is a bearing witness that relies on a fundamentally ontological logic. Such activisms are embedded in social and legal cultures that necessitate particular material architectures in and through which to materialize concepts as elusive as guilt and responsibility (see Gordy 2013). As Orli Fridman has documented, the politics of knowing was (and remains) essential to anti-war, feminist, and human rights activism in Serbia. Recognizing and publically speaking about the crimes of the 1990s and their continued denial and silencing in Serbia is central feature of the work of many human rights activists, particularly those of a generation that feels responsible for the wars (Fridman 2011). Here knowledge is central, but it is also not enough. Indeed, Fridman (2011, 518) quotes one activist who notes, "'The first time I stood [in a silent vigil] was in 1997 in memory of Srebrenica. This was the first time I exposed myself in the street, which was a great difference from only knowing and recognizing that something happened." As Fridman argues, public, alternative voices are crucial to combatting the way that "socially constructed silence is part of the framing of public understanding of events" (509). In the face of the relativism that underpins the project of maintaining collective silence, one must also remain firm and immovable—bodies become facts in themselves. The praxis of publically knowing entails political practices that link knowledge to place through the ontology of bodies in public space.

From Ontological to Epistemological Activism

"To be" a traitor, then, is to take on the qualities of a very particular kind of object—the reified human, the vital ethical thing. Yet this is not the only approach to grounding ethical action. Other feminist activists in the region have navigated political ethics not in terms of, but against, the urgency of moral absolutism. The activist and scholar Ana Bitoljanu perfectly captures the challenge of a political ethics in her 2007 piece "Ethics and Peace Work—The Unbearable Lightness of Acting." Bitoljanu's starting point is also that of the crisis of self and meaning in the chaos of postsocialist and post-Yugoslav transformations. She notes, "In societies where everything is relative, it is good to have a constant, even if the constant is this very thing: everything is relative and everything can be relativized" (Bitoljanu 2007, 241). In examining how to ground a political ethics, Bitoljanu both diagnoses the complex dialectic of "building" and "deconstructing." She offers a path of ethics in action that takes into account the positionality of activists within "groups and environments that, whether we want it or not, determine us in various ways" (242). In pushing for ethical judgment that is valid in practice, Bitoljanu holds the theoretical and the practical in constant tension, arguing for an ethics that emerges from dialogic relation. For her, then, the role of peace work is "re-introducing ethics into everyday vocabulary," to effect a new vocabulary for "the concept of social responsibility" (245). Ultimately,

Bitoljanu's practical ethics mean "that we respond to the main alibi statements of today about there being no tried and safe ethical patterns and therefore no pattern should be respected, by establishing some sort of patterns even if they are not tried, even if we change them" (250). Action is guided by a framework for establishing lasting ethical principles—even if one of these central principles is the flexible mutability of the framework in response to changing conditions.

This approach is exemplary of what I call epistemological activism. It is an approach that is founded on the contingency of knowledge. It is both born of a need to ground action ethically, and it emerges in the context of social uncertainty. It is thus neither wholly "building" nor "deconstructing." This is a position different from a human rights "minimalism" in which all we can hope for is limiting violence (see Ignatieff 2001; Brown 2004). A dialectic of building and deconstructing is both generative and contingent, foundational and antifoundational in turn.

I later return to the case of Milena, the young activist leader who saw herself at odds with her older counterpart, but no less committed to the project of human rights. Milena's emphasis on strategy and practicality is a kind of epistemological, as opposed to an ontological, praxis. For Milena, as for Bitoljanu, the politics of being could not trump the importance of doing. If knowledge and meaning were contingent, certainty could emerge only through action. This doing approach to activism did not require knowing the world (and anchoring that knowledge through one's most essential self) so much as strategically shaping and directing the actions of others.

The idea of practicality and strategic thinking was part of a larger sense of self that Milena had long cultivated. Milena understood herself as a logical person, but logic and reason were not external to activist passion; they were necessary to its realization. When it comes to human rights and activism, she notes in one interview: "At every step I encounter misunderstanding. But this doesn't drain my strength. On the contrary, it motivates me to do something more. If others won't [do it] then you must [*Ako neće drugi, onda moraš ti*]."[1]

Yet her uncompromising approach to activism is structured by the kind of moral ambiguity that she showed in the encounter described previously. In talking about being an independent person and thinker later in the interview, Milena further elaborates a politics of disappointment. She notes:

> I distanced myself from all types of political manipulation. I have sister who was only four years old in 1999 during the [NATO] bombing [of Serbia]. I couldn't bring myself to explain to her that those who were bombing us weren't all bad and that in fact we were bad, but that we weren't so bad, but that rather among us there were some who were bad, which is why these others who we saw as bad were bombing us. It was then that I decided that I would never be part of a political party, because I wouldn't be able to see things with a broad enough perspective.

Milena's rejection of formal politics is framed here as both a need to comfort her sister and the necessity of doing justice to the complexity of the world around her. It is typical of political coming-of-age narratives among the revolutionary generation of student activists in Serbia, in which an awareness of the complexities of the world is tied to both a rejection of formal politics and an embrace of action over moral certainty. As I detail elsewhere (Greenberg 2014), the pragmatic nature of this engagement was grounded in both a disappointment (in others, in older generations) and a confusion and frustration with the complexity of the political and social world in which they found themselves—an inability to "cognitively map" a world of topsy-turvy social relations and changing political values (Živković 2011).

If the affective structure of democracy is disappointment, then its activist-oriented manifestation is pragmatism. We often understand pragmatism as a response to the overwhelming saturation of new political spaces with optimism—and hope. Here pragmatism is a withdrawal into a practical stance, a kind of shutting down of the utopian impulse. Yet as the case of Milena demonstrates, pragmatism itself is often an intensely felt set of commitments. These are commitments that differently configure the relationship between ontological states (the being of being a traitor) and political action. Rather than being, the practical and strategic is focused on doing. The subjective state of doing emerges in relationship to contingency, it emerges from recognition of the ambiguity of action and intention that conditions action. In some ways Milena, like other student activists of her generation, knows that she will be disappointed—in others, in the results of her actions. And yet this spurs her to action—action that she sees as practical precisely because it anticipates the conditions of disappointment that necessitate it in the first place.

These tensions between Milena and her older colleagues were political and ethical. They were also contingent on the women's different social locations among generations of activists in Serbia (for an important comparative perspective on generational waves of activism in Croatia, see Stubbs 2012). The widespread "NGOization" of politics in the region (Stubbs 2012) necessitated a host of new practices rooted in institutional engagement, compromise, and—in the perspective of some—complicity with international donor goals and forms of power.

But in addition to the different institutional terrain of new NGO and donor-driven activism, younger generations of Serbian activists were also differently positioned in relation to the moral projects of their older counterparts. In many ways this is the debt Milena owes to the ontological activism of an older generation: the ability to take human rights violations not as the terrain of activist battle, but as a fact in the world. Although it is a fact that is contested or denied by many, Milena has inherited a vocabulary for articulating such violations. Milena is deeply invested in projects of documentation and widespread education about human rights to counteract denial and promote accountability. Yet she sees herself less as bearing witness (in other words, being the embodied and living anchor of truth to reality) than as a force for raising awareness and beginning a process of institutional redress.

Milena does not fear that her essential self is compromised by complicity for having allowed and participated in a society in which such crimes could be committed. Thus, in in the interview cited earlier, Milena states:

> When they ask me why I am so persistent in [my involvement] in the story of human rights, I don't have an answer, because for me, this story of rights is taken-for-granted. Also, since I started to work on human rights, each step of the way I have encountered incomprehension. That hasn't drained my strength, on the contrary, it motivated me to do something more.

Milena's understanding of human rights as implied (*podrazumeva*) or taken-for-granted is key. The conditions of possibility for human rights to be implied included a long-term struggle to articulate the terms of debate at all. Milena benefits from a moral confidence that an older generation of activists and intellectuals could never have. Here Milena does not have to configure her own sense of her essential self, her political subjectivity, as a mechanism for anchoring moral truth to reality. Her knowledge of the truth (and others' incomprehension and denial) drives her activism forward. Her sense of the contingency of action and meaning does not necessarily extend to her own moral certainty. Rather, she sees such contingency as a terrain to be engaged, the resistance she meets as a source of strength and motivation. Nowhere in the interview is her sense of self in question. It is this that makes the moral complexity and ambiguity of practicing rights not a threat but a feature of her social engagement. Practicality is not the opposite of moral truth; it is a different register for configuring the possible in the face of uncertainty.

Practicing with Politics

The examples I give here are not universal models for responding to the disappointments of politics in the shadow of revolution and violent conflict. As a reviewer of this piece rightly pointed out, not all activism that emerged in the shadow of twentieth-century utopian politics embraced engagement with dominant forms of governance. There are politics of doing that are infused with creative visions of world making: prefigurative political activism and radical direct action, for example (Juris 2008; Graeber 2009) Indeed, Maple Razsa (2015) has shown that among radical leftist youth activists in Croatia, disappointment in the project of socialist revolution produced new and hopeful political practices. Such activists would likely reject outright binaries such as utopian or pragmatic, reformist or revolutionary, in describing their own praxis (Ringel 2014; Maeck-elbergh 2009).

At the same time, I've hoped to make clear that the pragmatic is not at heart about accession to and compromise with dominant forms of power. The practical is a specific ethical and epistemological stance toward the contingency of knowledge. And it is a skepticism of political purity that emerged when activists become students not only of their own disappointment but also of the nonfinal-izability of action and subjectivity. Like many of the authors in this volume, I am interested in the conditions of possibility for promiscuous and experimental politics in the face of seemingly impossible challenges (see the chapters here by Avramopoulou and Peano). Recent scholarly and popular writing has often focused on the creativity and hopefulness of new youth activism. Without dismissing the power and significance of such world-making practices, the "new" youth activism is not the only site of experimentation. In part because our terms of analysis are also marked by the binaries that opened this chapter (pragmatism and utopia, revolution and reform), we miss the creativity that informs the mundane, the technical, the organizational, and the disappointing. As Tania Ahmad shows elsewhere in this volume, claims to ordinariness or even normalcy can be important ways to ground moral and political subjectivity, particularly in contexts of violence (see also Kolind 2007; Greenberg 2011; Jansen 2015). And it is worth noting that the celebration of political transformation and revolutionary activism itself often has gendered dimensions (see Winegar 2012). There is, as Sara Ahmed has pointed out, much that is politically critical and efficacious in the work of the killjoy (a figure that appears here not coincidentally as feminist; see Ahmed's research blog *feministkilljoys*, at http://www.feministkilljoys.com).

The social work of compromise is not inherently less creative than a politics that enunciates its own imaginative force. Nor is it *necessarily* an accession to dominant forms of power and governance—although it may at times be that. The creativity of the pragmatic is difficult to apprehend because the affective work the ordinary does necessitates erasures of ordinariness's world-making possibilities. And at the same time, as the recent participatory democratic plenums in Bosnia have shown, the day-to-day work of the ordinary over time can also ground community in ways that foster moments of radical political possibility and novelty (see Hromadžić and Kurtović, forthcoming). Indeed, we likely cannot have one without the other: not reform *or* revolution, pragmatism *or* utopia, but the cease-less movement between them that propels us to a better world.

At stake between whether it did or did not happen, at the heart of the conflict between revolution and reform, theological absolutism and pragmatism are profoundly different ways of constituting human agency. Might we ground moral truths and commitments through the ontologization of our very souls? Might we eschew the terrain of absolute definitions in favor of a negotiated and meandering ethics of practice? What does it mean to know what is right in the grand arc of history? To return to the debate that opened this piece, I wonder what costs and possibilities the legacy of political absolutism offer. Indeed, Robbins (2013, 2) noted: "There is never any shortage of bad stuff. And yet it doesn't follow that the job of the left is always and everywhere to harp on it." At question here is not only the best or most pragmatic approach to progressive social change. As long as the terrain of debate is one of either-or, we miss the complex forms of personhood (and objecthood) that constitute different ways of doing or being politics.

Note

1. This interview appeared in a curated collection by a local nongovernmental organization. To maintain the integrity of the pseudonym, I do not include the link or full citation in this chapter.

References

Allison, Anne. 2009. "The Cool Brand, Affective Activism and Japanese Youth." *Theory, Culture & Society* 26 (2–3): 89–111.

Bennett, Jane. 2010. *Vibrant Matter: A Political Ecology of Things.* Durham, NC: Duke University Press.

Bilić, Bojan. 2012. "Not in Our Name: Collective Identity of the Serbian Women in Black." *Nationalities Papers* (40) 4: 607–623.

Bitoljanu, Ana. 2007. "Ethics and Peace Work: The Unbearable Lightness of Action." In *20 Pieces of Encouragement for Awakening and Change: Peacebuilding in the Region of the Former Yugoslavia,* edited by Helena Rill, Tamara Smidling, and Ana Bitoljanu, 241–250. Belgrade: Center for Non-Violent Action.

Brown, Wendy. 2004. "The Most We Can Hope For . . .": Human Rights and the Politics of Fatalism. *South Atlantic Quarterly* 103 (2–3): 451–463.

Dević, Ana. 1997. "Anti-War Initiatives and the Un-Making of Civic Identities in the Former Yugoslav Republics." *Journal of Historical Sociology* 10: 127–156.

Dunn, Elizabeth. 2008. "Postsocialist Spores: Disease, Bodies, and the State in the Republic of Georgia." *American Ethnologist* 35 (2): 243–258.

Durham, Deborah. 2008. "Apathy and Agency: The Romance of Agency and Youth in Botswana." In *Figuring the Future,* edited by Deborah Durham and Jennifer Cole, 151–178. Santa Fe, NM: SAR Press.

Fassin, Didier. 2011. *Humanitarian Reason: A Moral History of the Present.* Berkeley: University of California Press.

Ferguson, James. 1999. *Expectations of Modernity: Myths and Meanings of Urban Life on the Zambia Copperbelt.* Berkeley: University of California Press.

Fridman, Orli. 2011. "It Was Like Fighting a War with Our Own People": Anti-War Activism in Serbia during the 1990s. *Nationalities Papers* (39) 4: 507–522.

Gal, Susan, and Gail Kligman. 2000. *The Politics of Gender after Socialism*. Princeton, NJ: Princeton University Press.

Gordy, Eric. 2013. *Guilt, Responsibility, and Denial: The Past at Stake in Post-Miloševic Serbia*. Philadelphia: University of Pennsylvania Press.

Graeber, D. 2009. *Direct Action*. Edinburgh: AK Press.

Green, Sarah. 2005. *Notes from the Balkans*. Princeton, NJ: Princeton University Press.

Greenberg, Jessica. 2011. "On the Road to Normal: Negotiating Agency and State Sovereignty in Postsocialist Serbia." *American Anthropologist* 113 (1): 88–100.

———. 2014. *After the Revolution: Youth, Democracy and the Politics of Disappointment in Serbia*. Stanford, CA: Stanford University Press.

Hardt, Michael, and Antonio Negri. 2011. "The Fight for 'Real Democracy' at the Heart of Occupy Wall Street: The Encampment in Lower Manhattan Speaks to a Failure of Representation." *Foreign Affairs*, October 11. https://www.foreignaffairs.com/articles/north-america/2011-10 -11/fight-real-democracy-heart-occupy-wall-street.

Harvey, David. 2000. *Spaces of Hope*. Berkeley: University of California Press.

Helms, Elissa. 2013. *Innocence and Victimhood: Gender, Nation, and Women's Activism in Postwar Bosnia-Herzegovina*. Madison: University of Wisconsin Press.

Hromadzić, A., and L. Kurtović (forthcoming). "Cannibal States, Empty Bellies: Protest, History and Political Imagination in Post-Dayton Bosnia." *Critique of Anthropology*.

Ignatieff, Michael. 2001. *Human Rights as Politics and Idolatry*. Princeton, NJ: Princeton University Press.

Jansen, Stef. 2015. *Yearnings in the Meantime: Normal Lives and the State in a Sarajevo Apartment Complex*. New York: Berghahn Books.

Jeffrey, Craig. 2010. "Timepass: Youth, Class, and Time among Unemployed Young Men in India." *American Ethnologist* 37 (3): 465–481.

Johnson-Hanks, Jennifer. 2002. "On the Limits of Life Stages in Ethnography: Toward a Theory of Vital Conjunctures." *American Anthropologist* 104 (3): 865–880.

Juris, Jeffrey. 2008. *Networking Futures. The Movements Against Corporate Globalization*. Durham, NC: Duke University Press.

Kolind, Torsten. 2007. "In Search of 'Decent People': Resistance to the Ethnicization of Everyday Life among the Muslims of Stolac." In *The New Bosnian Mosaic*, edited by Xavier Bougarel, Elissa Helms, and Ger Duijzings, 123–140. London: Ashgate.

Koselleck, Reinhart. 2004. *Futures Past*. New York: Columbia University Press.

Maeckelbergh, M. E. 2009. *The Will of the Many: How the Alterglobalization Movement Is Changing the Face of Democracy*. London: Pluto Press.

Mains, Daniel. 2007. "Neoliberal Times: Progress, Boredom, and Shame among Young Men in Urban Ethiopia." *American Ethnologist* 34 (4): 659–673.

Manning, Paul. 2007. "Rose Colored Glasses? Color Revolutions and Cartoon Chaos in Post-Socialist Georgia." *Cultural Anthropology* 22 (2): 171–213.

Markell, Patchen. 2003. *Bound by Recognition*. Princeton, NJ: Princeton University Press.

Mladjenović, Lepa, Vera Litricin, and Tanya Renne. 1993. "1992: Separation, Guilt and Identity Crisis." *Feminist Review* 45: 113–119.

Moyn, Samuel. 2010. *The Last Utopia: Human Rights in History*. Cambridge, MA: Harvard University Press.

Razsa, Maple. 2015. *Bastards of Utopia*. Bloomington: Indiana University Press.

Ringel, Felix. 2014. "Post-Industrial Times and the Unexpected: Endurance and Sustainability in Germany's Fastest-Shrinking City." *Journal of the Royal Anthropological Institute* 20: 52–70.

Robbins, Bruce. 2013. "Balibarism!" *N+1*. http://nplusonemag.com/balibarism.

Schäuble, Michaela. 2014. *Narrating Victimhood. Gender, Religion, and the Making of Place in Post-War Croatia*. Oxford, UK: Berghahn Books.

Shevchenko, Olga. 2009. *Crisis and the Everyday in Postsocialist Moscow*. Bloomington: Indiana University Press.

Stubbs, Paul. 2012. "Networks, Organizations, Movements: Narratives and Shapes of Three Waves of Activism in Croatia." *Polemos* 15 (2): 11–32.

Ticktin, Miriam. 2011. *Casualties of Care: Immigration and the Politics of Humanitarianism in France*. Berkeley: University of California Press.

Winegar, Jessica. 2012. "The Privilege of Revolution: Gender, Class, Space, and Affect in Cairo." *American Ethnologist* 39 (1): 67–70.

Žarkov, Dubravka. 2007. *The Body of War*. Durham, NC: Duke University Press.

Živković, Marko. 2011. *Serbian Dreambook: National Imaginary in the Time of Milošević*. Bloomington: Indiana University Press.

2 The Affective Echoes of an Overwhelming Life

The Demand for Legal Recognition and the Vicious Circle of Desire in the Case of Queer Activism in Istanbul

Eirini Avramopoulou

"A Right to Life"

"Our understanding of human rights is basic. It means a right to life"—these were the words used by a volunteer of the LGBT organization Lambda Istanbul, a few days after an unexpected police raid in their office.

On April 7, 2008, two months before Pride Week, twelve police officers unexpectedly raided the office of Lambda. The excuse they provided was having vague suspicions against "wrongful activities," and it was only the following day that the activists were informed that an accusation had been filed against the organization for participating in illegal prostitution and encouraging transsexual sex work. Lambda had secretly been under police surveillance for days before the knock on the door. On that day, the police turned the place upside down, looking in every drawer, reading all of Lambda's documents, looking at all of the organization's CDs. In the end, the police did not find the "evidence" that they were looking for, but they took Lambda's financial documents and membership list, ultimately raising fears and concerns because of the confidentiality at stake, as well as the danger involved when all these names were in the hands of the police, including possible archival for use in the future.

The activists' reaction to this unexpected "visit" was instant. They immediately demanded to see the warrant and called their lawyer, asking for his intervention to ensure that legal procedures would be followed according to their rights. Later, the activists investigated the situation and notified all of their national and international networks through press releases and signature campaigns denouncing the act.

The police invasion once again marked Lambda as a target, accentuating a recent history of accusations. In June 2006, the Provincial Associations Directorate of the governor's office of Istanbul (responsible for nongovernmental organizations) had initiated a legal process to close Lambda on the following basis: article 41 of the Turkish Constitution declares that "the family is the foundation of Turkish society" and that "the state shall take the necessary measures and establish the necessary organisation to ensure the peace and welfare of the family." Article 54 of Turkish law on associations permits the suspension of organizations on "public morality" grounds, among others. Article 56 of Turkish civil law, which declares that "no association can be established against law," was used to open the case, and the use of the non-Turkish-language name Lambda was also cited as an unlawful act. In February 2007, the prosecutor's office reached a decision to allow the group to continue to operate, but after the governor's office's appeal, the case was again taken to the higher court. In July 2007 a second hearing was ordered and a trial followed. Although other LGBT organizations, in Ankara (KAOS GL) and Bursa (Pembe Hayat–Pink Life), had received threats of being banned, the local courts and prosecutor's office had declined appeals to close them down. For this reason, Lambda's trial was the first to reach the higher court, and in the series of hearings that followed, experts were called to give their opinion.

On May 29, 2008, a month after the police invasion of Lambda, the sixth hearing of the legal case opened at the Third Civil Court of Beyoğlu. While reaching the court in the company of a group of activists from Lambda, I was assured by their initial reactions that they were not expecting a negative verdict. Considering that in recent years the LGBT activists' lobbying had been very effective in attempting to "mainstream" LGBT visibility in the public sphere—however hard it might be to reach such a goal—Lambda was operating with the support of national and international networks and was receiving financial help from COC Netherlands (one of the oldest LGBT organizations in the world), the International Lesbian and Gay Association, and George Soros's Open Society Foundations. This support was raising constant debate among members of Lambda because some perceived the affiliation with Soros's foundation and the constraints attached to finding funding by other European countries as impeding their political ideologies and visions of being part of a social movement or a collective. However, in the legal jargon of rights negotiations at the moment of the trial, this support was expected to have a good exchange value. Also, the positive report submitted by experts prior to the trial eased the fears of receiving a negative verdict and so brought a serene, cheerful mood to those heading to the trial.

This calm, relaxed, and positive atmosphere, however, was immediately replaced by the surprise, shock, fear, and anger that materialized in people's faces and movements. "What happened?" we all asked while waiting and seeing those coming out of the court rushing, calling out in haste, discussing feverishly, and organizing a reading of a press release. "The decision was negative," someone answered. "We will find justice in the Supreme Court and if not in the European Court of Human Rights," they stated in front of the few reporters and representatives of Human Rights Watch and Amnesty International. A few days later, Lambda organized the "Hands off My Association" rally in Istiklal Street, announcing their press release, which read:

> The verdict is the result of an obsolete understanding of "morality." This verdict is the result of our absence from the equality clause. This verdict is the result of an impairment of the justice system. We are aware that it takes a lot of time and effort to legitimise a struggle for rights. Therefore, we will continue our efforts to increase the basis of our legitimacy through legal recognition.

These words also emphasized the need for the vast mobilization of international and national support that followed and that was reflected in the participation of a few thousand people—including feminist, leftist, anarchist, and independent groups—marching in Istiklal Street to express solidarity with LGBT people and their right to visibility, against the court's decision to close down the organization. This positive atmosphere worked to replace the injurious affects of loneliness, precariousness, and injustice that they were experiencing, especially when murders of trans and gay people were frequently reported in the news and when violent assaults against trans people, either by the police or by individuals in cases of hate crimes, were also hovering in the air, clouding the possibility of reclaiming the public sphere.

"Our understanding of human rights is basic. It means a right to life," said a Lambda volunteer, a few days after the unexpected police raid in the organization's office and before the court decision. Indeed, in this chapter, I ask, what does that mean, asking for the right to life? How differently can one live life and ask, demand, or desire to be recognized under this right, the right to life? But also how does life exceeds its limits, how does it turn into an overwhelming life?

Reflecting on what it means to seek political presence and queer visibility in the affective economy of a public sphere where life appears to feel overwhelming, in what follows I focus on a moment when a person who refuses to be named, or else to self-identify as a certain gender (man, woman, or other) goes to a police station to report a street assault, exercising the right to be perceived by the law as a human possessing rights, like the right to life. This incident occurred in 2009, a few days after the Seventeenth Annual Pride Week, a time when accusations of harming the morality of Turkish society and family structure were aimed at the closure of the Lambda organization, and a time when the Pride March had been marked by the police's sovereign presence and the then-recent deaths of several trans people. The elaboration in this chapter is the result of ethnographic research conducted from 2007 until 2010, in Istanbul, Turkey, and it aims to address how questions of agency, affect, and subjectivity mediate the rights struggle of LGBT people.

Similarly to Jessica Greenberg's elaborations elsewhere in this volume, my concern is with unpacking the dilemmas that activists face when confronted the language of rights, which entails certain compromises or, rather, sacrifices. Greenberg poignantly argues that one should consider what political subjectivity, agency, and resistance mean without getting caught in a binary presupposition between revolution and reform. Deriving insights from performativity theory and psychoanalysis that assist in unpacking the complicated relation between subject formation and subjectivation, my intention is also to expose through ethnography quandaries of resistance that relate to the conflicting subject positions that an individual acquires, such as when positioned as a radical activist challenging the state but at the same time seeking police protection. In order to understand how these conflicts work and how they come to form subjects, a focus on desire is necessary. For this reason, this chapter addresses the relation between the *demand* for legal recognition and the *desire* for visibility as it mediates the political activism of LGBT people in Istanbul, Turkey, as they try to resist legal prohibitions, social exclusions, and psychic displacement. I thus attempt to situate the analysis of desire within the "political economy" of visibility that is defined both in terms of the effects of neoliberal processes of commodification as they affect identity claims and gender performances and in terms of psychic processes affected by the cultural and legal regulations that discipline bodies and legitimize the civic and social policing of genders, sexualities, pleasures, and satisfactions.

By offering a gendered criticism of human rights claims and by analyzing the conflicting subject positions emerging in activism, I argue that human rights should be perceived as a mechanism that sustains a melancholic attachment to the vicious circle of a person's unfulfilled desire both for resisting normative inscriptions of humanness and for seeking recognition and justice along with attention, affection, and love. In other words, the right to claim that one is the "human" in possession of rights should be perceived as a mechanism that sustains this melancholic attachment, echoing a failed resistance or a loss (of a different vision of life) that cannot be (publicly) mourned.

At the fringes of a nation-state that has inscribed its own historical path into the exercise of gender and ethnic violence; at the threshold of a city built upon neoliberal structures of governance, severe policing, and cosmopolitan aesthetics; at the crossroads where the meaning of "human life" flirts with death, violence, precarity, mourning, and melancholia, but also with subversion, affection, pleasure, thrill, and desire—*there*, in that space, one needs to situate the story that follows. *There*, in that place, one might also want to keep repeating the following question: "What does it mean, asking for the right to life?"

A Year Later: At Home

The notes from my ethnographic diary during the summer of 2009 read as follows:

> It was late at night when we returned home to Cema's apartment, where I was living during the last months of my ethnographic fieldwork, during the summer of 2009. Pride Week was over but the lingering effect of the constant movement of excitement and exhaustion, the ongoing discussions, and the new actions that needed to be organized were still defining everyday life and were interwoven with that day's tired mood. Erkan Oğur's melody was the soundtrack for the shared silence between Cema, Barış, and myself before going to sleep. Words were avoided. Then Barış started to cry. It was unexpected. S/he started crying in silence. But then, her silent tears started aching inside our ears as her face started to moan, as the veins of her neck stretched out. S/he was staring at us with her poignant, frightened eyes and in throaty spasms ... a scream was coming out unuttered. A vocal paralysis stuck as a tight knot in her throat, marking each teardrop as sonorous. Her body started crouching down, curling up, shrinking in on itself ... all of which was leading to the escalation of our confusion. "What is wrong?" we tried to ask, but there was no space for reason, for explanations. A delirium of fears, fantasies, dreams, realities, blended together. But we could only guess at them.
>
> S/he calmed down only for a moment. It was the moment when both Cema and I were lying next to her, side by side, in an effort to cuddle a part of this mourning. S/he gave us a smile back in recognition. The tears drained after a while. In that moment Cema fell asleep while still being rolled over on her arm. With the sudden sound of a bottle falling under the table, she woke up. "Thank you, *canim* [dear]," Barış said to her. "Go to sleep. I will be OK." At that moment, I thought it would be over. But then it only became more severe. "It is OK, it is over, it will be over soon" was the only thing I could whisper and at times shout, especially when s/he started running out of breath, almost ready to faint. This went on for three hours. Two of Erkan Oğur's CDs. That's how I could keep track of time. The calm tunes of spiritual music against the horrifying affect of excessive pain, fear, and mourning. Before the last CD was over, I decided to stop the music. I walked out of the room. I was not thinking anymore. When I came back, I found her sitting down on the floor watching her masculine hairy feet, caressing the beard on her face, playing with her toes. I stayed on the floor with her, watching her movements, watching her watching herself. In silence. S/he lay down. I put a blanket over her. S/he fell asleep. I also went to sleep. Next morning I got up and s/he had already left.

* * *

The moment "when existence hangs on a push of the lungs" is an echo, Adriana Cavarero (2005, 169) writes.[1] In Ovid's myth, Echo is a nymph, a vocal discussant who possesses the art of rhetoric. After Juno's intervention and Echo's encounter with Narcissus in the forest, she is condemned to exist only as a pure or mere voice. She no longer speaks but repeats the words of others. She follows the repetition of words outside their context; that is, she is turned into a being who speaks only after, or as a result of, what has already been uttered. Echo, then, is a sound that speaks only after something has happened.

Indeed, if one thinks of an emotional breakdown as an echo, rather than as a mere psychic pathology, one might want to be attentive to the nonrepresentational and subversive potentialities that this could carry. At the same time, it might be unavoidable to wonder where pain comes from, what it indicates, what it tries to communicate, and how one can make sense of it. These were also my initial questions, as I elaborate later. The story that follows starts from here in order to place and displace such questions by offering critical meditations on the subjective crossroads that might lead to such a break, and by asking what this might tell us more broadly about the gendered nature of human rights claims and about the affective responses connected to such claims. I return to the affective echoes of this pain at the end of this chapter.

A Walk on a Street

"Too many small things gathered inside and found their way out"—that's what Barış told Cema and me the next afternoon, when our paths crossed somewhere on Istiklal Street. S/he was coming from a meeting at Lambda and was running to another one, as always, in haste. "There are things that one can talk about and other things that you cannot," s/he said when I approached her in anticipation of a more detailed explanation regarding the previous night. A minute of silence followed and then s/he repeated in a lighter manner: "Eh, we laugh, we cry, it is all the same, isn't it?" "Is it?" I wondered, and s/he continued: "Life is *overwhelming* sometimes. That's all."

We arranged to meet later in the evening to have ice cream and to take a walk. Even though I was not expecting a more detailed explanation of "what happened" or "what was wrong," those questions still were remaining suspended.

Istiklal Street was very crowded that evening, something not unusual during the summer. We got an ice cream from an Italian place near Tünel, and started to walk toward Taksim Square. For Barış, having an ice cream from this place was one of those ordinary rituals that provide a kind of coziness that accompanies homely desires. At the age of twenty-one, Barış had already traveled to many places around the world, mainly funded by international networks of LGBT activism, but as s/he once told me: "When I am saying that I am coming back home, I mean I am going back to Istanbul, actually I refer to Taksim. No, actually, I mean Istiklal. Istiklal for me is home." Indeed, s/he was claiming Istiklal as "home" while being fully aware that "home" is not only a space of comfort and familiarity but also a place haunted by discomfort, uneasiness, inequality, and violence.

Walking down Istiklal in an androgynous body, with dreadlocks, a beard, fully haired legs, at times wearing skirts and feminine makeup, Barış can be rendered multiply ambiguous or violently "unsexed" through a "Huh?" or a "What . . . is . . . this?" (Weston 2002), reactions that attempt to immediately resexualize her body's presence by declaring *it* a freak, a weirdo, a woman-man-woman, a queer, a dyke, a trans, an intersexed, a-whatever-*this*-might-be. But at the same time, s/he knows very well how to command respect in this area, being already familiar with the streets' topography and the people who inhabit it. In other words, s/he knows very well how to be "visible" in queer looks and how to demand presence in the street, how to feel "at home" in this body, in this street.

After all, it was just few days ago, on the day of the Pride March, when s/he was holding a microphone in her hands, raising the spirits of a big crowd of people facing the protracted police line. That day, a forty-meter-long rainbow flag was slowly unraveled in Taksim Square as it waited to be carried down Istiklal Street, signaling in a celebratory manner the beginning of the Pride March.[2] In 2009, more than three thousand people gathered in Taksim Square in anticipation of the march, marking a significant increase from 2003, when only thirty people had come to support the first Pride March in Istanbul. But more than an hour had passed and the crowds were thwarted in their desire to march down the street. An extensive line of police was blocking the path from Taksim Square to Istiklal Street. No official permission for the march had been granted beforehand, as had become customary since Workers' Day, May 1, 1977, a performance of mass violence when police freely opened fire against demonstrators. But small gatherings, press conferences, and marches occur almost every day unless the police are given different orders, as was feared by the demonstrators on that day.

That day, one had to be standing near this line to understand the severity and intensity of the negotiations taking place between the police and the activists who were mobilizing the presence of famous politicians and human rights representatives, both from Turkey and abroad, to make this event happen.[3] This power struggle could not easily be grasped from a position behind that line while mingling with the crowd. Here, one could easily gain the impression that the event had already begun. People were already dancing to the rhythm of drums, adding to the cheerful mood that was spreading and creating a euphoric atmosphere that was transmitting itself across and against the limits set by the severe policing. But holding on to this euphoria was not easy; "Istiklal is no paradise." These were the words used by Batur on that day while standing next to his sister, who had come to support his struggle.

"During the march I felt like Istiklal Street was endless, the distance from Taksim Square to Galatasaray Lyceum felt like walking from Istanbul to Ankara . . . endless," Batur's sister, Ferya, mentioned to me a little later, when the police had decided to let the march begin. Ferya was a young Kurdish, religious woman wearing a headscarf. She had come that day to support her gay brother. The painful and long path Ferya had to traverse before understanding, accepting, and supporting her brother was reflected in that street on the day of the Pride March, especially when family matters were exposed to the voyeuristic curiosity of the media cameras. The media could not miss the moment when a modestly dressed trans woman, holding a banner that read "Educational rights for trans-vestites and for headscarved women," walked next to Ferya, herself wearing a light-purple silk scarf in the "new veiling" chic style and holding a banner that read "I am his sister and I support him." Both were shouting the slogan "hands off my association" declaring the shared intimacy of a political struggle for rights and recognition. That moment was as "catchy" as the drag performance of Seda. As Seda was posing for the media cameras and the other gazes, she could not expose the suture of her wounds through the thin purple ribbon embroidered on a strapless glossy green top that stretched over her postoperational breasts. Her extravagant tufted wig, the multicolored makeup, the way she was waving the feather fan in her hand and proudly enjoying her ability to ignite desire while balancing charmingly on top of a pair of high-heeled, shiny silver platform boots was indeed attracting all attention. However, when her photos featured in the next day's press coverage, there would be no Barthesian "punctum" (Barthes 1981) to remind the readers of either the "cleansing operation" in the 1990s— when gentrification projects aimed to attack trans people as well as stray dogs— or the recent deaths of gay and trans people around the periphery of the city. This performance will be delegated to feature in the next day's media coverage in the absence of citations underlying the fear of facing harassment, abuse, violence, and ultimately death, each time a drag crosses the ordinary life of this street.

It is at this point that one should be reminded that in between the precarious-ness of life designated for a trans woman and the voyeuristic curiosity that escorts most of the gazes cast upon her, there is an uneasiness connected to the texture of the "subterranean texts" on which these people tread (Kandiyoti 2002). And it is at this point that one might also need to ask: How can one disentangle the shared intimacy between a religious and a trans woman against its possible registration as simple decoration in the city's architectural multiculturalism? How can one's "political presence" become vocal in between the competing sovereignties of the secular and Islamic projects of regional appropriation of Beyoğlu and Pera, both shaping Istanbul's path in tandem with global economy, transforming cities into "aestheticised commodities" and injecting certain political struggles with a sort of identity-politics anesthesia (see Bartu Candan and Kolluoğlu 2008, 13)?

So, as we were walking on Istiklal Street with Barış, enjoying our ice cream, I could not help but remember what had happened few days earlier, on the day of the Pride March. When we reached the outside of the Galatasaray Lyceum with Barış, we reached the same point at which days earlier three thousand people were standing still in order to read a press release in which they were asking for the right to a life without hate, without anger. After the press release, a list of names followed, a list of names in memory of those absent that day:

> On 10 March, 2009, trans woman Ebru Soykal was stabbed to death at her home in Cihangir, Istanbul. On 20 March, 2009, transvestite L.D. (29) was stabbed in the stomach and wounded by three people in Eskişehir. In March 2009, the body of a transvestite, whose head and sexual organ had been cut off, was found in a rubbish container in Bursa. On 27 March, 2009, Yaşar Sert (35) killed Şükrü Gençer (57) for suggesting a sexual relation (Edirne).

And the list continued. A moment of silence was kept, in commemoration, in mourning, in fear and hope. Difficult as it was to create a moment of piercing silence among a crowd of three thousand people, it was almost impossible to stop their wild clapping when Barış and Alida started kissing by the window of a nearby restaurant. Everybody's head turned and people vigorously started clapping. The melancholia of the silent mourning and the joyful clapping over this kiss—the transmission from one emotion to another—echoed the fact that what dies in certain deaths is the inability to publicly celebrate certain (unacknowledged) desires. This was made even more audible in the wave of booing and hissing that followed to denounce a waiter's attempt to interfere, separate, and throw the two queers out of the restaurant—a reminder that policing is not only the job of the police; a reminder of the historicity of persecution haunting the limits cast upon certain desires; a reminder also that Istiklal Street can serve as an illuminating conjunction for reflecting on what it means for LGBT activists to seek visibility in the affective economy of a public sphere while facing the effects of legal prohibitions, social exclusions, and psychic displacements, even if (or especially when) they might be given the space and, at times, the "choice" to demand and desire the right to (another) life. Because when some bodies, some desires, or some lives "carry" upon them, carry in them, the intensity or agony reflected in the aporia of what constitutes as "human" the right to a differently livable life, this question, then, sometimes, also hovers in the air, loiters among us in the street.

~~Names~~

As the experiences of the previous week were lingering in the memory of the body, and as we were passing by the same corner, there, in front of Galatasaray

Lyceum on Istiklal Street, I tried to start a conversation regarding the previous night. However, Barış was protecting her silence by claiming tiredness. It was already late, and s/he was feeling exhausted at the end of another long day that was full of meetings and discussions. But in any case, s/he had already explained everything: "Sometimes life becomes overwhelming. That's all."

Similarly overwhelming was what followed when s/he turned around to answer insults uttered by some people walking behind us. Then everything happened very fast.

Three tall and muscular men quickly isolated Barış in the corner, leaving me a step behind. "What? What did you say?" one of them yelled at her and slapped her aggressively. S/he did not react. In a provocative expression of apathy, s/he continued to eat her ice cream while staring at him with a tough, indifferent, cold gaze. Without thinking much, I tried to interfere, but her silence and gaze were denoting that this was something s/he had to deal with on her own. One of the men, though, got more irritated, as it was clear that he expected to start a fistfight. He punched Barış in the face and s/he started bleeding, remaining still and inactive, but not numbed.

In that moment, two male friends of Barış who were passing by ran toward us. One of them shouted "How dare you?!" to imply, "What kind of 'man' would hit a woman?" The codes of honor invoked lingered ambivalently, especially when one was first attacked as man-to-man and then was defended or "protected" as a woman (by other men). It was either that or the fear of police intervention that made Barış's attackers step back and walk away. But as they were heading off, one of them shouted in repugnance "Is . . . *this* . . . a girl?"—words that underlined both the fascist machismo attack against a "weirdo" (a boy in dreadlocks) and the homophobic chauvinist assault against a "freak" (a boy that appears to be a girl). "Is . . . *this* . . . a girl?" he repeated while laughing in a violent hate-speech act.

Reactions like "Huh?" or a "What . . . is . . . this?" define a moment of ambivalence that Kath Weston (2002) has coined as "unsexed" or a "zero moment," a moment of suspension and confusion when one's gender cannot be immediately decoded, when one's sex is not transparent, and when one could be later denounced as a freak, a weirdo, a woman-man-woman, a queer, a dyke, a trans, an intersexed, a-whatever-*this*-might-be. For Weston, then, when gender zeros out and bodies become unsexed, the zero moment holds the ambiguity and suspension before the actual disciplinary moment acts to rename. But this moment is not a stage of liminality, as one does not remain in limbo for long. It is a moment of a lack of meaning that neither is emancipatory nor leading to political irruption; it is neither a presexual nor an asexual moment; it is neither an androgyny nor a lack of identity. Rather, it is a "placeholder" of the material history and temporality of social classification that reveals the impossibility of holding on to the anxiety created by ever-shifting social categories and genders (see Weston

2006, 104–113). In particular, Weston argues that the proliferation of accounts of "who is who" and "how one will be seen" (e.g., queer, dyke, femme, butch, FTM, MTF, trans, intersexed) ascribe to a historical period, in the aftermath of Fordism and flexible specialization, when the political economy of global capitalism designates a process by which every relation is being transformed into an identity commodity.

Indeed, during that period, by refusing to be named, Barış seemed to be enjoying the moment of suspension through which the process of identification could remain ambiguous. S/he was refusing not only to be named as either a man or a woman but also to be identified as a (female to male) trans person or intersexed. Through this stance, s/he would also answer back to the exercised pressure to tick a box and define who s/he "is." "I can be whatever you want me to be," s/he would answer to children's teasing reactions. S/he would "act" as a man when being "read" as one and "play out" her feminine side when this was considered more suitable. "I don't ascribe to names" was her stance whenever someone from Lambda would challenge her to declare her sexual identification. Some activists from Lambda would question Barış's attitude as arrogant and elitist; they argued that they had paid a lot of money to go through breast implants and other operations to become "real" women, conforming to society's norms. Hence, they were claiming that one's position in refusing to be named as man or woman was the same as announcing that one is beyond these gendered categories or that one is privileged enough to consider oneself as not conforming to society's norms.

At the same time, Barış had to answer to family pressure. Having accepted her relationships with other women, her family was expecting her to "appear" as one, and hence either shave her beard and legs or go through biological examinations in order to be "diagnosed" as something else, letting science "prove" who she "really" is. Therefore, s/he was constantly asked to answer as to whom s/he was claiming visibility as and to comply with recognizable modes of address while also denouncing any name that would define her felt experience of her "self."

By claiming to be "unnamed," it was as if Barış were answering to the feeling of pressure exercised through the repetitiveness of the question of classification, even if s/he was in a position to know very well that asking not to be named does not mean that names will not be projected upon someone, at times even violently. Hence, her stance in remaining unnamed was not untroubled. Her own feelings of ambivalence, uncertainty, fear, and confusion would become more concrete at times, when this pressure would loom large. Like when Barış had called me in anger, sadness, and frustration one day, as s/he was traveling by bus to Izmir to visit her family. Although in the Turkish language one might escape being interpellated by the use of grammar—since there is only one personal pronoun (*o*) to define all three genders (she, he, and it/neuter)—entering the grammar of the public space is nevertheless a deeply gendered and sexualized experience. Traveling by bus is only one such aspect of this, as the passenger is asked to tick the box "male" or "female" to be seated accordingly. Apparently, the woman who was next to Barış read her as a man and created a scene implicating the bus driver and the other travelers. And that was only one of a series of similar occasions, defining the confusion of the "unsexed moment" and the personal violation and humiliation one might experience in retrospect.

In this sense, claiming to be unnamed can relate to the critical moment that denounces the economy of gazes haunting the visibility and divisibility of the endless processes of gendering. At the same time, claiming to be unnamed is a speech act that denotes much more than just the intention to be beyond identities and categories. It might expose, I suggest, the condensed historicity of social exclusions, psychic displacements, and abjections that emerge as echoes when the pressure to be classified overwhelms, or in the violent encounter with forced reclassification. In other words, then, to understand the "political eco-nomy of visibility"—that is, the politics of the laws (*nomos*) of the home (*oikos*) regulating visibility—we need to take into account, on the one hand, the effects of global economy and the neoliberal processes of commodification that affect and define identity claims and gender performances, as Weston (2002) has poignantly argued. On the other hand, one might also need to re-view one's alertness to social, cultural, and legal codes and norms, which act in such a way so as to interpellate bodies by enforcing and legitimizing the social policing of different sexualities, desires, and pleasures. Put differently, one might need to be equally alert to another eco-nomy (*oiko-nomy*): the laws of *oikos*, or home, that regulate the (im)possibilities of uttering a re-action. This is especially so when claiming to be "unnamed" echoes how difficult it might feel at times to bear the performative act of responding.

It is for this reason that I understand, in this case, the position to claim to be "unnamed" as carrying the critical effect of undecidability as theorized by Jacques Derrida (1988, 148–149). To rephrase, undecidability is not an inability to decide (or to "choose" a gender identification); rather, it is a moment that exposes the very act of decision (to take a side) as aporetic. It is because all names come at a cost (even the unnamed) that keeping the decision in suspense, and hence inhabiting the suspension of the decision (a state that of course does not last for long, like the unsexed), against the enumeration of possible decisions, is destabilizing. Therefore, while the "unsexed" critically refers to the economy of perceptions revealing their ascribed deadlock and the impossibilities attached to referentiality,[4] the unnamed echoes such (im)possibilities in the responsibility of a response attached to a differing economy of visions. It then exposes that this kind of speech act can be a performative one.

This is how I see Weston's (2002) "Gender in Real Time" and Butler's (1990) "Gender Trouble" as meeting, if one reads performativity theory against its possible translation as a speech act that celebrates agency but that also exposes agency's impossibilities. It is because of the fact that names and naming expose the ambivalent relation between the emplacement and displacement of the moment of decision (on one's sex or gender) that claiming agency (to choose, or decide one's sex or gender) is not free of misfires. This becomes evident if one reviews the difference between performance and performativity as suggested by Butler (1993). The performative act is not a "free" game in which one can choose a gender performance and enact it (see also Athanasiou 2007, 212). Indeed, a performance can be performative, but performativity is not about performance. A nonnormative act is performative because if in every act, or in the repetition of an act (e.g., speech act, citation, performance) there is a possibility of identification, then the act of repetition carries the potential to deinstitute the classifications through which identities are institutionalized and naturalized. However, at the heart of the potential undoing of norms there is no celebration of agency; rather, this process reveals that an act of noncomplicity with the norms comes at the price of discipline, punishment, and violence.

For Barış, then, the disavowal of names might be read as a way to denounce identity politics and the constant shifting of genders; it might be a way to ask to prolong the suspension and ambiguity before naming occurs (in violent or other forms), but at the same time this claim cannot but expose that ultimately one is implicated in what one attempts to transgress. For this reason, in this case, it would also be crucial to think about how power works to define the cultural, social, and psychic political economy of the subject's formation in order to understand processes of subjectivation and desubjectivation. It is important to investigate how one becomes formed in names, codes, and norms, especially because when one asks to be unnamed this does not mean that a speech act can set the subject free of names. An act does not undo the norms but carries the potential of exposing what is suspended in them. As Butler (1997, 149) explains, "A radical refusal to identify suggests that on some level an identification has already taken place, an identification has been made and disavowed, whose symptomatic appearance is the insistence, the overdetermination of the identification that is, as it were, worn on the body that shows."

Human Rights: The Vicious Circle

Barış uttered her own "that's enough" to the scene of assault differently than her male friends who ran to her defense. "No need for this," s/he said. "What's the need for this?" That's what she replied to her friends who expressed an eagerness to chase the other men and "give them a 'proper' lesson." "What's the need for more violence? Why should we all get beaten up?" s/he told me later when we went to calm down in a bar. But our feelings were on edge because of the reverberating anger and frustration that could not find a place to calm down. S/he stayed calm while refusing to talk or find consolation in words. Her bruised and swollen lips were hurting, and her mouth was still bleeding. Still, there was no evident mark of pain in her facial expressions. The only moment when her eyes shone was when an idea emerged. "There was a CCTV camera there. Yes, I know. We were standing at the exact point where the camera is. Everything must have been recorded. We have proof. Should we go and report it to the police?" s/he asked me in anticipation of a positive response, even if s/he retained her doubts. "Let's go and make the police do their job—why not?" S/he immediately called Lambda's lawyer and asked for advice. S/he was familiar with such procedures through her activist experience in human rights training.

We ended up at the Beyoğlu police station, which is located next to Lambda's office, a few minutes' walk from the point of the assault. We were at a police station that is infamous for the "cleansing operation" days, when it targeted stray dogs and trans people, back in the 1990s when the president and former prime minister Recep Tayyip Erdoğan was the mayor of Beyoğlu. We were at a police station that even more recently had raided the office of Lambda under the pending court decision to close down the organization. Barış "forgot" to refer to the aforementioned operation and raid but made a similar comment: "It's a bit ironic," s/he said. "The only time that I have been beaten up in my life was by the police during the May 1 demonstration and now I have to go to them to report this."

However, that day we were both treated in a very polite manner with a seriousness that also hinted at indifference. While we were asked to wait in a room inside the police station, our mood began to lighten, probably as a result of taking some sort of action—an action that felt *as if* we could take the situation in our hands, *as if* we were not "victims" of violence, *as if* violence might not be disarming. After s/he gave an official testimony, we had to go to a hospital and receive another report. The whole procedure lasted several hours. We were promised that a letter of evidence would be found. This letter never arrived. However, this action felt at that moment *as if* it were "righting" the wrong. Put differently, it felt *as if* we were doing something "right" when we were exercising our right to have rights. It felt *just*. But is this so? What can be considered here right or wrong (just or unjust) when someone is exercising her right to ask the law to be protected as a "human of rights"? Do rights bring justice? More than that, what does "righting" wrongs imply?

Many authors have criticized human rights as a discursive utterance, as a verbal performance appearing through a social Darwinist assumption "about what it means to help and about those who are represented as forever 'in need' of our help" (Cornell 2010, 106; see also Spivak 1988).[5] For this reason, many ethnographies emphasize that any discourse on rights will always be inclined to fall into the rhetorical reductionism of trying to find "someone to save someone else," as if this "someone" could not be heard otherwise, such that the possibility of people voicing demands in their own terms is foreclosed (see Abu-Lughod 2002; Strathern 2004; Englund 2006). Therefore, human rights activism is rendered suspect and for good reasons.

At the same time, though, the discourse of human rights is also criticized by the activists who use it, even if it might also form the rough ground for the creation of coalitions. These coalitions might be based on disagreement and a politics of dissensus (Avramopoulou 2013), or they might be formed through processes of composition, as Irene Peano indicates in her ethnographic research on southeastern Italy elsewhere in this volume. More precisely, the LGBT activists whom I worked with are positioned very critically with regard to universal ideas, and for that matter, human rights discourse and practices, but this does not mean that they do not employ the discourse of human rights to ask for such legitimization. This is especially so when Lambda is defined as a human rights organization, or when it holds panels to discuss and debate LGBT human rights, or when it uses this language to form coalitions with other activist groups, or in the case here, as when one thinks that he or she has the "choice" to go to the police to report the violation of rights. But how does this incommensurability between what one says and what one does become reconciled? Or what kind of "choice" might that be?

In her research in a small town in Hawaii on victims of violence against women, Sally Engle Merry (2003) argues that rights are chosen by subjects from other possibilities so as to engage in dialogue with their own traumas. In this process, a new identification emerges in negotiation with "interactions with police officers, prosecutors, probation officers, judges, shelter workers, feminist advocates and even bailiffs [who] affect the extent to which an individual victim is willing to take on this new identity" (Merry 2003, 347). Merry continues: "In going to the law, a woman takes on a new subject position, defined in the discourses and social practices of the law. She tries it on, not abandoning her other subject positions as partner or wife, member of a kinship network. . . . She is, in a sense, seeing how it goes" (349–350). But these moments entail a risk, as Merry thoroughly explains, because they bring changes to the social, cultural, and gendered status of subjects.

From this perspective, the "shift in subjectivity" occurs as a result of perceiving the "self" as occupying multiple and contradictory subject positions, a theoretical analysis Merry uses through reference to Henrietta Moore. Indeed, Moore (2007, 17) draws attention to the necessity of distinguishing between a self, an individual, and a subject:

Individuals are multiply constituted subjects who take up multiple subject positions within a range of discourses and social practices. Some of these subject positions will be contradictory and conflicting, and individuals constitute their sense of self through several, often mutually contradictory, positions rather than through one singular position.

For this reason, to understand the subject position in relation to the workings of power, ideology, and subjectivation, it is important to review the question of desire. As Moore (2007, 41–42) emphasizes, "Fantasy, desire and unconscious motivation are at work, alongside strategy, rationalization and emotional intelligence in the process of making and sustaining a self through identification with multiple subject positions." However, this is exactly what Merry's analysis does not foreground, that the relation between the formation of the subject and the constitution of subjectivity is a complex process, as psychoanalysis reminds us—a point emphasized by Moore's suggestion to provide such analytical lenses for reviewing "the subject of anthropology."

In other words, if the question of desire is not taken into consideration, then to cause a "shift in subjectivity" presupposes a degree of agency worked through an analytical perspective that renders subjectivity as either occasional or operational, either "it happens to me" or "I make it happen." This is exactly the problem with the liberal perception of rights as providing a choice, which nevertheless comes at a cost. But the problem of "choice" is deeper than that. Merry's assertion as to how women choose to use human rights language seems to restore a figure of a choosing humanist subject potentially seeking emancipation while enacting the will expressed by the demand of decision. But what kind of decision is this? Let me explain further the critical questions I am raising.

Renata Salecl (1995, 1132), for example, argues that "the invention of democracy brought with it the notion of a forced choice and a sacrifice the subject had to make in order to become a member of the community." Hence, "if the subject does not 'choose' community, it excludes itself from the society and falls into psychosis" (1133)—a cost incurred by exposure to symbolic castration. In other words, the demand to have rights and to be able to seek those rights as a human member of a community raises the question of acquiring a new status and attaining a degree of agency. But of course the creation of the emancipatory fantasy fails, the illusion of choice dissolves, and hence there is the cost, or the loss.

This loss occurs because the demand for rights reveals the economy of needs, wishes, and fears translated in a legal language that exposes not only demands but also desires (Douzinas 2000, 312). In the Lacanian meaning of desire, however, what one demands from the other is the fulfillment of a need, as an expression of attention, affection, and love. This is why Salecl (1995, 1133) argues that rights can appear to serve the function of the "object a," the object cause of desire that operates as the substitute of castration and renders all other substitutes insufficient, hence always suspending the moment of desire as a desire for something else. The object a represents the excess of demand over need, and hence the demand to meet one's needs comes at a cost, which is the realization of the loss incurred while confronting a lack that cannot be fulfilled or realized (Douzinas 2000, 313). For this reason, when the desire for rights confronts the social domain, Salecl argues that there is a "symbolic castration," that the forced choice is not a real choice, that it does not relate to intentionality or to conscious decision (as it appears to in Merry's ethnographic analysis); instead, it is the result of entering language and the symbolic order.

The universality of human rights, the right to have rights, in this sense does not express the filling of a void but the displacement and emplacement of a lack that makes the subject exist as a desiring subject. That is why rights as universal ideas do not exist but insist (or "ex-sist"). This is why they belong to the Real and cannot be articulated in language, like the object a of desire (Salecl 1995, 1134). But even if Salecl introduces an important perspective for understanding the workings of desire in the demand for the right to have rights, one might need to question her final position that the universality of human rights is a "good enough" concept because it at least reveals social antagonisms.

The desire to be in language so as to exist in law brings the subject close to the object, but most often in painful ways, and for this reason, one needs to ponder more the effect of the vicious circle of desire opened through the path of demanding the right to have rights as claimed by Douzinas (2000, 317–318). Let me now return to my ethnographic example.

Barış's claim not to be named and identified with a socially recognizable gender code would seem not to contradict her right to ask to be protected by the police as a *human* with rights. Still, this would mean that s/he has to suspend and/or forget the fact that the *human* of rights is not a genderless universal category (also see Asad 2003, 2006; Das 2006),[6] as well as the fact that in the history of violence exercised against queer people, the police have played a constitutive role. At the same time, even if it is not through gender that Barış addressed the police (indeed, gender is not the only one of the identifications working to constitute the subject) her antimilitarist, antinationalist, and antiauthoritarian politics, which s/he perceives as constitutive aspects of the ways that heteronormativity has been legitimized in society, made her immediately confront the paradox inscribed in the moment of asking the police to "protect" her as a human of rights (as if *human* could be devoid of political identifications). Can we then say that s/he is "choosing" to "shift" subject positions? If so, what is the cost of this "choice" if it is implied that s/he has to suspend (to forget) the history or the memory of violence s/he has been exposed to in order to be and/or to act as the human of rights? One needs to ask what kind of estrangement can be staged, there, in this police station.

As psychoanalysis foregrounds, law enters the subject and forms subjectivity even before the actual individual is given a set of choices through which it can invent and possibly invert its subject position. Therefore, we should also ponder the impossibilities opened by a demand to have the right to have human rights, as a "human." It is true that the experiences of a body have to be translated into a language intelligible for the self and for the other (including for the law and its bureaucracy), and human rights serve this purpose. But at the same time a person cannot but confront the history and the memory of trauma, failure, violence, and persecution, which is also inscribed in the act of seeking the right to exercise rights. That is why for every liberating act there is another one that may appear to be oppressive, mournful, and dark. And this is also how the unfulfilled desire gets trapped in a vicious circle, instead of only exposing an enlightening paradox, as Salecl finally argues. For this reason, I argue that the universality of human rights appears to be a mechanism that sustains a melancholic attachment to the vicious circle of the unfulfilled desire for recognition and justice, as it deprives a person from the possibility of confronting this loss differently. Hence, instead of enlightening paradoxes, the process reveals how violently unfulfilled the need to face desire as a whole might remain.

In rereading Freud's essay "On Narcissism," Butler (1997, 142) argues that "melancholy is both the refusal of grief and the incorporation of loss, a miming of the death it cannot mourn." If mourning ends the relationship to the loss of the object, melancholia sustains this interrelation but in displaced forms.

To claim the right to have rights is crucial and critical, but for this reason doing so sustains and prolongs the unresolved relation to the paradox of desiring more in the act of asking for recognition, a recognition that does not come. It is not that recognition does not come because the letter did not arrive: that is expected. It is more the satisfaction of seeking recognition by the act of reporting the assault, which *felt* as if it "righted" the wrong. But did it? What can be defined as "wrong" here? What kind of wrongs do rights aim to make right in this case?

If the wrong here is to be limited to the street assault, then having the right to report an attack can be seen as righting the wrong. But if going to the police as a person who has already experienced violence by the police, and therefore suspending one subject position at the expense of another (to be recognized as a subject with rights rather than as a person who denounces policing), then it is not that a "shift in subjectivity" occurs; rather, the incommensurability of these positions exposes that certain deaths in the "I" cannot be mourned, or that the law gives the subject the right not to mourn Other deaths—deaths that matter in the political constitution of the human life, or in losing the right to claim a differently livable political life.

* * *

With life's tragic irony, it was only earlier that day that I had asked Barış about what was wrong after witnessing the affect of a pain that exceeds the limits of the body, that mourns something that cannot find correspondence in words. It was only one day later that the assault took place.

I initially implied that the voice of such penetrating pain was an echo. Spivak (1996, 184) wonders whether Echo (the nymph she then analyzes as an echoing voice) should be perceived as "the impossible experience of identity as wound? The *a-venir* of history not written?" Could one similarly claim that the echo of Barış's suffering was the "*a-venir* of history not written"? Spivak's response answers both these questions: "But this can only be the radical interruption of ethical hope, which must be cut down to logical size so a calculus can be proposed" (184). It is for this reason that Spivak then argues, "Echo comes to echo farewell, to echo the rites of mourning," and she "provides a cure against the grain of her intention" (184, 186).

In other words, the political echo of a mourning that does not pathologize trauma, and does not correspond to the logic of understanding pain as passive pathology, might carry within it the rhythm of a passion that "provides a cure against the grain of [its] intention" when escorting the desire of asking for a right to a different vision of life. Then, being overwhelmed—rather than the echo of an ineffable excess, an idle chatter, a passive voice, or the experience of trauma as pathology—emerges as an *affect* that is present and demands attention in its intense, albeit painful, political suggestiveness: being overwhelmed is an affective state that is neither ex-static (i.e., finding "exits," or turning into "becomings") nor static (i.e., overshadowed by structural violence). Instead, it echoes the passion escorting the question posed in repetition: "What does it mean, asking for the right to life?"

Notes

1. For Cavarero (2005, 207), Echo destabilizes the economy of the patriarchal symbolic system in which the privileging of semantics of language renders any other "sign" (e.g., the "woman") and "sound" (e.g., "feminine" voice) as "idle chatter," a mere voice not yet having acquired the vocality of speech. Writing against the rationality attached to logos (i.e., to the signifying and significant utterance), Cavarero argues: "Through the fate of Echo, logos is stripped of language as a system of signification and is reduced to a pure vocalic. And yet this is not just any vocalic, but rather a vocalic that erases the semantic through repetition" (168). The insistence of feminist writers in returning to this myth and closely listening to the sounds Echo utters has to do with the fact that this myth forces us to reconsider what is at stake in re-posing the central question regarding the ethical responsibility of responsiveness. In a similar manner, for Spivak (1996), Echo's voice has the potential to undo Narcissus's self-absorption. Her voice becomes an antiphone (not an aphonia) sending back to Narcissus the words he utters.

2. Since 2007, this ritual aimed to occupy the street's geometry in width and length, while people held the flag on each side, making it move in tremulous waves, transmitting the vibrant effect of finding presence "out of the closet" and in the street's topography, thereby declaring visibility in the public sphere. *Rainbow* was the name, after all, that had been intended for a group of LGBT people who had wanted to create a cultural space of interaction but who remained clandestine until 1996, as their activities were banned by the police under the orders of the governor of Istanbul in the name of protecting public morality. However, such accusations have not been put to rest even though the organization Lambda Istanbul launched its presence through legal channels of official recognition in 1996.

3. The names and presences of famous artists and politicians were used as the activists' protective shield against those restrained at the hands of the police, like the singer Hande Yener, the writer Esmahan Aykol, the feminist psychiatrist and rights activist Şahika Yüksel, the doctor and rights activist Mustafa Sütlaş, Stuart Milk (the nephew of the first openly gay US politician Harvey Milk), as well as representatives of the German Green Party, European MP Ska Keller, and Mechthild Rawert of the German Social Democratic Party. Additionally, the economic and moral support coming from international organizations such as COC, the International Lesbian and Gay Association, and Human Rights Watch, were also used in negotiations with the police to allow the Pride March that day.

4. Thinking through the temporality given in an "interval" in which a metasign—the zero moment—would encompass all divisions, Weston (2002, 39) is critical in her engagement with the multiple repetitions and citations of genders as analyzed in the theory of performativity introduced by Judith Butler (1990). Weston questions the promise of agency inscribed in acts of repetition, citation, and iteration, and the potentiality of an agency that could undo the ascribed norms. Indeed, the important analytical contribution of thinking through the "unsexed moment" is that it provides us with a strategy of resignification against other perspectives that focus on the liberating agency of bisexuality or on the freedom attained by the enumeration of sexual identifications. However, according to Butler, performativity is not reduced to a "free" game of meaning that takes place on a representational level, or on the level of visual iconoclasm, as I explain.

5. Also, human rights have been criticized for offering a "good enough" base of negotiations against state violence because they never appear, in the end, to do the "good" they might initially proclaim. See, for example, the debate between Ignatieff (2001) and Brown (2004), as well as Greenberg's chapter in this volume.

6. Talal Asad (2003, 137) has argued that, ironically, when the Universal Declaration of Human Rights, signed in 1948, proclaims that *inalienable* rights should be guaranteed for all members of the *human family*, it does not equate "humans" to citizens of a nation-state; instead, it refers to a state of nature out of which every human, irrespective of his or her political and cultural background, should hold the same rights qualities. The irony lies in the fact that, as Hannah Arendt (2004) long ago made explicit, the protection of human rights points to national sovereignty. At the same time, in reading Asad's suggestion that in modernity the human rights that are proclaimed to be protected are legitimated by the person's pure humanness, Veena Das (2006) is compelled to take a further stance. She denotes that the way "nature" has been actually conceptualized in the modern secular world seems to presuppose the emergence of a subject that cannot in any way be free of all its other significations but, instead, is a sociolegal subject who also performs gendered roles. In critically analyzing the way that the figure of the father or citizen has dominated our imaginations of humanness and our fantasies of the political community, Das questions any indications of personhood emerging from a "natural" condition.

References

Abu-Lughod, Lila. 2002. "Do Muslim Women Really Need Saving? Anthropological Reflections on the Cultural Relativism and Its Others." *American Anthropologist* 104 (3): 783–790.

Arendt, Hannah. 2004. *The Origins of Totalitarianism*. 1951. New York: Schocken Books.

Asad, Talal. 2003. *Formations of the Secular: Christianity, Islam, Modernity*. Stanford, CA: Stanford University Press.

———. 2006. "Responses." In *Powers of the Secular Modern*, edited by David Scott and Charles Hirschkind, 206–241. Stanford, CA: Stanford University Press.

Athanasiou, Athena. 2007. *Ζωή στο Όριο: Δοκίμια για το Σώμα, το Φύλο και τη Βιοπολιτική*. Athens: Εκκρεμές.

Avramopoulou, Eirini. 2013. "Signing Dissent in the Name of 'Woman': Reflections on Female Activist Coalitions in Istanbul, Turkey." In "Migration, Gender, and Precarious Subjectivities in Times of Crisis," edited by Athena Athanasiou and Giorgos Tsimouris. Special issue, *Review of Social Sciences: The Greek Review of Social Research* 140–141, Β'-Γ': 233–246.

Barthes, Roland. 1981. *Camera Lucida: Reflections on Photography*. New York: Hill and Wang/Noonday Press.

Bartu Candan, Ayfer, and Biray Kolluoğlu. 2008. "Emerging Spaces of Neoliberalism: A Gated Town and a Public Housing Project in Istanbul." *New Perspectives on Turkey* 39: 5–46.

Brown, Wendy. 2004. "'The Most We Can Hope For . . .'": Human Rights and the Politics of Fatalism." *South Atlantic Quarterly* 103 (2–3): 451–463.

Butler, Judith. 1990. *Gender Trouble: Feminism and the Subversion of Identity*. New York: Routledge.

———. 1993. *Bodies That Matter: On the Discursive Limits of "Sex."* New York: Routledge.

———. 1997. *The Psychic Life of Power: Theories in Subjection*. Stanford, CA: Stanford University Press.

Cavarero, Adriana. 2005. *For More Than One Voice: Toward a Philosophy of Vocal Expression*. Stanford, CA: Stanford University Press.

Cornell, Drucilla. 2010. "The Ethical Affirmation of Human Rights: Gayatri Spivak's Intervention." In *Can the Subaltern Speak? Reflections on the History of an Idea*, edited by R. C. Morris, 100–114. New York: Columbia University Press.

Das, Veena. 2006. "Secularism and the Argument from Nature." In *Powers of the Secular Modern*, edited by David Scott and Charles Hirschkind, 93–112. Stanford, CA: Stanford University Press.

Derrida, Jacques. 1988. "Afterword: Toward an Ethic of Discussion." In *Limited Inc.*, 111–154. Evanston, IL: Northwestern University Press,.

Douzinas, Costas. 2000. *The End of Human Rights: Critical Legal Thought at the Turn of the Century*. Oxford, UK: Hart.

Englund, Harri. 2006. *Prisoners of Freedom: Human Rights and the African Poor*. Berkeley: University of California Press.

Ignatieff, Michael. 2001. *Human Rights as Politics and Idolatry*. Princeton, NJ: Princeton University Press.

Kandiyoti, Deniz. 2002. "Pink Card Blues: Trouble and Strife at the Crossroads of Gender." In *Fragments of Culture: The Everyday of Modern Turkey*, edited by D. Kandiyoti and A. Saktanber, 277–293. London: I. B. Tauris.

Merry, Sally Engle. 2003. "Rights Talk and the Experience of Law: Implementing Women's Human Rights to Protection from Violence." *Human Rights Quarterly* 25 (3): 343–381.

Moore, Henrietta L. 2007. *The Subject of Anthropology: Gender, Symbolism and Psychoanalysis.* Cambridge, UK: Polity.

Salecl, Renata. 1995. "Rights in Psychoanalytic and Feminist Perspective." *Cardozo Law Review* 16: 1121–1137.

Spivak, Gayatri Chakravorty. 1988. "Can the Subaltern Speak?" In *Marxism and the Interpretation of Culture*, edited by C. Nelson and L. Grossberg, 271–313. Urbana: University of Illinois Press.

———. 1996. "Echo." *The Spivak Reader: Selected Works of Gayatri Chakravorty Spivak*, edited by D. Landry and G. M. MacLean, 175–202. New York: Routledge.

Strathern, Marilyn. 2004. "Losing (Out on) Intellectual Resources." In *Law, Anthropology, and the Constitution of the Social: Making Persons and Things*, edited by A. Pottage and M. Mundy, 201–233. Cambridge: Cambridge University Press.

Weston, Kath. 2002. *Gender in Real Time: Power and Transience in a Visual Age*. New York: Routledge.

———. 2006. "Kath Weston's 'Gender in Real Time': Power and Transience in a Visual Age—An Interview by Stefan Helmreich." *Body & Society* 12 (3): 103–121.

3 Emergenc(i)es in the Fields

Affective Composition and Countercamps against the Exploitation of Migrant Farm Labor in Italy

Irene Peano

THE PRACTICES I DESCRIBE in this chapter belong to a heterogeneous and morphing militant network that currently goes by the name Campagne in Lotta, which might be translated as "fields of struggle," referring to the agro-industrial context within which its actions unfold. I have been an active part of this project since the summer of 2012, when the recently established network first organized what was defined, in militant jargon, as an "intervention" (*intervento*) in the province of Foggia, southeastern Italy. Yet deeper, multiple genealogies can be conjured that link the network's formation to previous experiences of collective organization and mobilization, as well as of spontaneous rebellion—some of which I trace here in order better to explore the rationale behind the network's evolving practice and political significance.

However, although some such mobilizations were staged largely or exclusively by migrants, and more specifically by seasonal farm laborers, what I seek to describe here are not, strictly speaking, migrants' struggles.[1] Indeed, I propose to analyze these self-conscious militant practices in terms of *composition*, a process that the network itself actively seeks as one of its aims, alongside and through self-organization and the breaching of the isolation into which seasonal migrant laborers in the agricultural sector are plunged—perhaps more than any other socioeconomic subject—in present-day Italy and beyond.

A classic Marxist category, political composition (or recomposition) has been analyzed from a number of perspectives, most particularly within that strand of Marxist thought known as "workerism," for which it designated the behavior of the working class "as a subject autonomous from the dictates of both the labor movement and capital" (Wright 2002, 3). For autonomous Marxists, whose legacy persists into the present and informs a large part of social movement politics in contemporary Italy and elsewhere, political composition made for an antidote against representative (and reformist) party and union politics. However, while certainly this notion of composition has a significant influence on the militant practices I describe and I am part of, here I approach it from a different, if related, perspective. More specifically, I employ the characterization that Colectivo Situaciones (2007, 77) gave of this notion: for them, composition defines a militant practice that seeks to make "the elements of a noncapitalist sociability more potent," developing particular types of *relations* among members of a collective or movement. Following Spinoza, they think of composition as "relations between bodies." Composition, Colectivo Situaciones argues, "does not refer to agreements established at a discursive level but to the multidimensional flows of affect and desire the relationship puts in motion" (77). Thus, it refers to the creation of encounters that can, in turn, produce subjects, where the stress is more on the process than on the product.

What composition points to, therefore, is an overcoming of divisions (but not necessarily of differences)—such as those between migrants and citizens, workers and activists, intellectual and manual laborers, but also those between women and men, or between migrants of different origins—with which Campagne in Lotta as a network is confronted over and again in its militant activities. In this sense, composition might be thought of as a form of (ever-shifting) territorialization, in the sense in which several contributions to the present volume employ this notion: the formation of an assemblage or a collectivity, however ephemeral, through the catalyst of different affective intensities, where belonging does not imply monolithic identification. At the same time, in the collective experience I describe, the compositional aim has also implied reinforcing or establishing divisions and boundaries, which points to the fact that composition is never entirely rid of conflict. Indeed, conflict is integral to compositional processes. To understand how the network's practices might begin to overcome certain disconnections (while at times reinforcing others) with a compositional aim, it is first of all necessary to point to, and analyze, the specific lines of fracture that traverse its field of action. In particular, reflecting on the experience of the past years, I ask what kinds of spaces or places constitute such fields, what kinds of power flow cross them, and then how Campagne in Lotta seeks to contrast such emplaced dispositifs of containment, inserting itself in their cracks and creating novel spaces for sociality and action. What I am describing here is not only much more than, and different from, migrant farmworkers' struggles, but in many ways it also exceeds the national dimension and its sovereign boundaries. These struggles are situated at the juncture of overlapping geographies and multiple borders. This reflects current dynamics of global dispossession and exploitation (Mezzadra and Neilson 2013), but also, and for this very reason, it points to a potentially effective and in many ways innovative set of practices to resist them.

The reflections presented in this chapter, from the more matter-of-fact to the theoretically elaborate, were actively developed in dialogue with several members of the network, as well as with others, during the course of our activities and in ad hoc interviews. The collective's own practices, in fact, include protracted, continuous, and critical reflection and self-reflection as a constituent component of action, which in some ways makes my contribution, if not redundant, one of enhancement, and indeed of composition. If it may also contain traces of diminishment, these are unintended if not in a truly constructive spirit. In any case, it is a voice among many, driven by a specific personal, intellectual, and existential trajectory, but certainly it is not reducible to a single-handed work of individual authorship. I want to express my deep gratitude to all those who shared their reflections and knowledge (and much more), and I hope to be able to render justice to them, at least partially, in what follows.[2]

Precarity, Exception, and the Camp

The continuously evolving history and self-narration of Campagne in Lotta has been developing since the summer of 2011, emerging from meetings, collectively authored articles, radio programs, and numerous public presentations of its activities. The "Who We Are" section of its website (www.campagneinlotta.org) succinctly summarizes the network's composition and aims as follows:

> The Campagne in Lotta network was born with the aim of connecting workers in the agro-industrial sector—mostly foreigners living and working in Italy—with single individuals and militant collectives. The goal is to set up a network in order to get to know and coordinate each other, endorsing and actively supporting self-determination and self-organization processes that can lead to the composition of the struggle in different contexts and sectors.

The stated aims of the network are arguably, and in some ways necessarily, exceeded by its actual practices.

Yet to begin with, I wish to highlight two of the main events that its members identify as foundational for the network itself: the so-called Rosarno riots of 2010 and the Nardò strike of 2011, contextualizing them in the "globalized" Italian countryside (Corrado and Colloca 2013). In both instances, outbursts of rage and rebellion were sparked by seasonal farmworkers, mainly from sub-Saharan Africa, against conditions of extreme exploitation, and of general precarity, in which they find themselves as a result of intersecting histories, flows, and *dispositifs* of power and control. Here, I employ the notion of precarity as developed by a number of critical thinkers, to designate

> all possible shapes of unsure, not guaranteed, flexible exploitation: from illegalised, seasonal and temporary employment to homework, flex- and

temp-work to subcontractors, freelancers or so-called self-employed persons. But its reference also extends beyond the world of work to encompass other aspects of intersubjective life, including housing, debt, and the ability to build affective social relations. (Neilson and Rossiter 2005)

The relationship between these different aspects of precarity is particularly important in connection with the network's methodology of action, as will become apparent. But first it is necessary to specify how precarity sketches the contours within which Campagne in Lotta works.

As far as migrant farm labor in many parts of Italy (as elsewhere) is concerned, from north to south, extreme precarity is epitomized first and foremost by the absence of any labor guarantees, often regardless of immigrant workers' legal status. Especially in the southern regions, characterized by a wider spread of "informal" and "illicit" economic activities and by more pronounced and generalized work precarity, in the majority of cases no contracts are granted for farm labor, or they are mere formalities that only serve to protect the employer in case of inspections. For migrants, and in many cases for Italians too, in this as in other sectors, cash-in-hand salaries are, on average, less than half the minimum wage, and working hours far exceed those established by the sector employment agreements of each province, which also prescribe systematically violated overtime pay increases and other guarantees.[3] It is customary for agricultural producers to pay workers on a piece rate, once again against labor regulations, or to demand free labor, for example in loading trucks with orange crates, as workers testify in relation to the case of Rosarno, or as compensation for workers' "right" to inhabit farmers' abandoned houses, as in parts of Capitanata (Foggia Province).

The absence (or ineffectiveness) of any contractual form, as well as the nature of agricultural labor itself and the way it is regulated, also imply no certainty as to the number of workdays one can scrape together during the harvest seasons across most agribusiness areas. Such structural precarity is made worse by the presence of a large, seasonal, and mobile "reserve army" of potential workers in each agro-industrial district, a consequence of several waves of immigration from North Africa since 2011 (the result of a cycle of wars) and from Eastern Europe (especially after the enlargement of the European Union in 2007). The situation has been further exacerbated by the economic crisis and the closure of factories in the northern regions, which had employed large numbers of migrant workers, who then were the first to lose their jobs.

Sub-Saharan African workers often move between the olive groves during the autumn, the orange and clementine fields during the winter months, and the tomato and watermelon farms during the summer, across different regions in the south. Alternatively, if they can find employment, seasonal migrant workers settle in the northern, richer area around the town of Saluzzo, Cuneo Province

(Piedmont), for the harvest of different types of fruit, from June to November, or in other similar settings.

Especially as far as the sub-Saharan African labor force is concerned, it is often the same workers who migrate seasonally between different harvesting areas, although one can also find more occasional laborers, particularly among newcomers. In general, though, once in this circuit it is difficult to escape it, on account of the low pay and the absence of contracts, which—together with other legal and institutional hurdles—make the renewal of residence and work permits increasingly arduous.[4] As for the European workers, who face fewer restrictions on their mobility, they tend to work in one specific area and, when work is over, spend the rest of the year back in their country of origin.

Further adding to workers' exploitation, many agricultural producers rely on gangmasters, or *caporali* (*capi neri*, or "black bosses," in African workers' parlance), to recruit and control their labor force. Another illicit practice in the Italian agricultural sector, gangmastership entails the curtailment of parts of workers' already-miserly wages for "services" such as recruitment, supervision, transport, food and water provision (which according to legally binding collective agreements should all be provided free of charge by employers). Cases of physical violence and threats are often reported—especially by European workers, whose entire journey is organized by gangmasters. In many instances workers complain that they do not receive any form of payment for their labor, and they are often left with no legal or other recourse. Moreover, in the south documented migrants' benefit rights are often usurped by bogus Italian laborers, who may pay for employers to seal contracts in their name so they can have access to unemployment, pension, and maternity subsidies in the place of those who actually work in the fields. Across the national territory, when valid contracts are in fact granted, pay slips grossly underestimate the number of actual days worked, for employers to avoid tax and insurance payments. This also results in seasonal laborers' inability to claim unemployment benefits, which in agriculture are calculated according to the number of workdays recorded in any given year.

Predictably, precarity in these conditions extends also to the living and social spheres, as workers with such bleak prospects adapt to sleeping in abandoned and derelict houses, often with no running or drinking water or electricity; in self-constructed shacks or tents; or even in the open air, if the climate allows it. They may be subjected to roundups and raids by police, which force them to relocate—and may consign those without valid documents to detention and perhaps deportation—or to arbitrary attacks and robberies by local gangs. Indeed, it was one such episode, the latest in a long series, that in January 2010 sparked the well-known riots in Rosarno—followed by heavy repression against the migrants and by their mass deportation. The following year, after the criminalizing logic subtending to the government of poverty, and of the poor's migration (see

Wacquant 2009) had exercised its full force, a governance apparatus made up not only of state institutions (and more specifically of Protezione Civile, the agency in charge of managing emergencies) but also of local administrations and charities organized a further response to the (largely unchanged) situation of migrant workers, mostly from sub-Saharan Africa. This materialized in the form of a tent camp, built on the outskirts of Rosarno, in the industrial area adjacent to the Port of Gioia Tauro—one of the largest container ports in Europe, as well as one of the main hubs for the import of different sorts of illegal commodities (from drugs to arms and pirated goods) managed by the 'Ndrangheta cartels. In several politicians' intentions, the harbor should also be declared Italy's first special economic zone.

The tent camp, of the sort employed to host displaced populations after natural disasters, paradoxically appeared to respond to the endemic precarity of migrant laborers by means of emergency measures that, through time, became themselves more and more permanent, institutionalizing precarity and thus making manifest its structural nature, and indeed blurring the distinction between exception and norm (see Agamben 1998, 2005—though, as we shall see, this conflation exceeds the domain of sovereignty and the law). In late winter of 2012, a second camp replaced the first, which in the meantime had become overcrowded and had consequently spilled into another ghetto, built with scrap materials by those who could not be accommodated in the "official" tent structures. I return to this transition later in the chapter, for at this point in time the network had already established a presence in the informal side of the camp and supported its inhabitants' claims vis-à-vis police, state, and local administrations.

Here, I want to point to the way the tent camp, and the government-by-emergency that gave birth to it (beginning from an institutionalization of precarity in its wider, existential sense), also had the effect of fostering abjection, epitomized by the piles of garbage accumulating at every corner (a common sight on the streets and country roads of the wider area too). The tale of one of the camp's inhabitants is emblematic in this sense: describing life conditions in such space, and particularly the food provided by the Evangelical organization in charge of managing it, he vividly remembered the image of the cook, a man who, he kept repeating, was "dirty, but really, really . . . dirty." And food, it goes without saying, was disgusting, to the point that camp dwellers started making their own. A month after the beginning of the 2012 harvest season, the large, communal tent that served as a canteen and praying space (and that sported the bleakly ironic motto *Gesù ti ama*—"Jesus loves you"—on its side) was finally occupied by those who could not find accommodation in the regular tents.

Stories circulated among inhabitants regarding the camp's management, who were accused of demanding payments for "favors" such as the filing of applications for the renewal of documents or allowing access to other housing structures (which, however, never materialized). Once again, exception ruled. In addition, the presence in the Gioia Tauro Plain of "illicit" traffics, controlled by the organized mafialike cartels known as 'Ndrangheta (whose involvement in the management of migration and of migrant farm labor has been partly documented by judicial inquiries, journalistic reports, gray literature, and academic accounts), further reveals how a normal exceptionality (and the precarity it engenders) here governs not only the lives of migrant workers but life in general. And this goes, to different degrees, for other areas where Campagne in Lotta has been establishing its presence, and especially for the Capitanata Plain, where other powerful cartels exercise their influence without attracting much attention from the media.

Here, I employ the notion of exception in relation to those of precarity and emergency to denote symbolic and/as material apparatuses of governance. Although one of the most sophisticated, influential, and cited analyses of exception, that of Giorgio Agamben, views exception exclusively in terms of the sovereign (political-legal) power to suspend, and thereby establish, the norm, it is evident how in this case the "exception" refers to a much more complex topography of power. As a first point to note, we are clearly witnessing a "government through illegality" (see Foucault 1979; De Genova 2002) by which the state and the mafia (together with local administrations, third-sector organizations, and capital) blur not so much in legal as in governmental, and hence also economic and administrative, terms. It is also, or rather, a matter of capitalist governmentality, a form of nonsovereign rule that brutally controls and exploits flows of (often illegalized) commodities, including labor.

Critics of Agamben have pointed out precisely how states of destitution, dispossession, and displacement might be produced and maintained by a variegated set of powers other than the sovereign one (e.g., Butler and Spivak 2007, 10–11), and therefore how sovereignty no longer operates to support or vitalize the state, but rather represents a "reanimated anachronism" (Butler 2004, 53), a lawless and prerogatory "rogue" power, in which governmentality (whose object is the management of populations) represents the condition for its new exercise. Governmentality establishes the law as a "tactic" with an instrumental rather than a binding value (Butler 2004, 62). A focus on the political-legal domain alone, and on "bare life" as the central figure of this conceptual architecture, overlooks one of the core issues pertaining to the spaces I am concerned with here: that of labor, its control and exploitation in spaces that are, at one and the same time, larger and smaller than those delimited by the sovereign boundaries of the nation-state (Mezzadra and Neilson 2013; Ong 2006). Furthermore, it also writes off the productive side of the exception (see Bojadžijev, Karakayali, and Tsianos 2004; Hardt and Negri 2000).

A proliferation of different camp forms (see Rahola 2006) shapes these power-ridden sociogeographical spaces. Yet, once again, these are not, or not only, places where certain kinds of subjects are deprived of their political prerogatives, included through their exclusion at the level of the symbolic, in Agambenian terms. In all the localities mentioned, several ghettolike settlements have been developing since the early 1990s alongside more institutionalized spaces for the segregation, containment and discipline of migrant labor and mobility—such as tent camps, container camps, lodges reserved for migrant workers, but also refugee and asylum-seeker reception centers and even immigrant detention centers. Should migrants have the "privilege" of a contract (and hence of a valid permit), they can access labor camps or lodges with strict regulations concerning time of occupancy (no staying during the day), payment (which, as in the case of the container camp installed in Saluzzo in 2012, can be demanded "also in the form of community service work," as stated by the municipality deliverance disciplining it), and rights of access (strictly reserved for *migrant* laborers, who cannot invite guests, unless properly authorized, and who in some cases may bring their families and partners, but only if they are able to provide valid marriage certificates).

What appears significant is the contiguity between ghettos and the labor, tent, refugee, and detention camp, where the latter often spill and morph into the former, or vice versa, in Rosarno as in Palazzo San Gervasio (Potenza), Saluzzo, Borgo Mezzanone (Foggia), but also across distant areas. In 2011, the NATO bombing of Libya and the reaction of Gaddafi's regime forced tens of thousands of sub-Saharan Africans out of the country where they had lived and worked, often for years. Most of them landed on Italian shores after hazardous sea journeys, and the Italian government declared a "Northern Africa Humanitarian Emergency." Refugee status was denied to most of those displaced migrants, who for two years were left in a suspended state of near abandonment, in which public money allocated for their maintenance in many cases was dissipated without providing proper accommodation, food, training or guidance of any kind. Only after much protesting was a form of short-term humanitarian protection granted that would give these migrants the right to stay and work. Since 2012, a large number of them ended up in ghettos and camps in Foggia, Rosarno, and Saluzzo, hoping to make ends meet and find some work as farm laborers or prostitutes. The same situation is repeating itself since 2015, with the recent influx of hundreds of thousands of new asylum seekers again mostly from sub-Saharan Africa.

Here, the legal and the illegal are increasingly indistinguishable, in the name and through the logic not so much, or not only, of a sovereign exception as of a (governmental) control of the pace of subjects' mobility, for their quality as potential labor power that needs to be disciplined and controlled. Camps as ghettos thus act as "decompression chambers" (Papadopoulos, Stephenson, and Tsianos 2008; Mezzadra and Neilson 2013), functioning to contain a reserve army of labor that might become potentially destabilizing for the system, as the revolt in

Rosarno, the strike in Nardò, and the numerous protests staged by those expelled from Libya testify. Segregation and containment thus characterize this form of labor, located at sociospatial junctures where structural and street-level racism converge to create vulnerable, deeply fragmented, ethnicized workforces.[5]

In a sense, the camp form, whether in its institutional dress or in more "informal" guises, seems to blur the boundaries between detention and work, where both are concerned with the pacing of mobility and the containment of potentially productive (but also subversive) bodies. Significantly, the shantytown and adjacent container camp, built next to the cattle market in Saluzzo, were named "Guantánamo" by their inhabitants, brilliantly crystallizing the prisonlike nature of these spaces (but also suggesting how detention can function as a form of labor control). From human and social refuse to workforce and back again, according to the "just-in-time" model of labor recruitment and migration regulation (Düvell 2004), migrant laborers' precarity follows specific temporalities and modes of living in abjection, which shape subjectivities and relations.

Within this analytical and experiential framework, it is on the attempted subsumption of the intersubjective, affective dimension of life by a form of capitalist accumulation that can be characterized as "biopolitical" that I want to focus my attention. The ghetto, like the camp and the prison in their different manifestations, delineates a space where intersubjective relations become especially difficult, where affective attachments are rare, where suspicion and mutual exploitation are often the key to interpersonal exchanges (see Wacquant 2001). Perhaps the most evident instantiation of this tendency toward intersubjective anomie (or decomposition) is represented by the so-called Grand Ghetto near Foggia, formerly known as "New York" by virtue of its "attractions"—namely, several shops, bars, and restaurants that also offer music, drugs, and the sexual services of several dozen prostitutes, mostly from Nigeria. Apart from sex and other reproductive services (e.g., food and board), living in the ever-expanding Grand Ghetto often means having to pay also for hot water or to charge one's mobile phone. The shacks are often owned and managed by those same people who operate as gangmasters (or by their partners) and who recruit workmanship according to "fidelity" to other services they sell, and of course to docility. The Grand Ghetto is thus a controlled space where it is difficult to know who to trust and where many things (commodities, services, affects, and relations—and especially open forms of resistance) have a price. Yet, of course, countertendencies are also identifiable, on which the militant practices of Campagne in Lotta attempt to graft themselves.

Against this background, the revolt in Rosarno and the strike in Nardò appear as two instances of rebellion against extreme forms of precarity that invest subjects in their totality, even and especially in their most intimate spheres. While the riots of Rosarno might be interpreted as pre- or apolitical outbursts of rage, by virtue of the absence of any clear agenda or demand, they can be read also as a demand for recognition of common humanity through the exercise of violence, which forced the acknowledgment of vulnerability as structuring each and every subject, regardless of citizenship, skin color, origin, and/or background. By threatening the inhabitants of Rosarno and attacking their property, African migrants reminded them of their common humanity (understood here in terms of vulnerability) and obtained at least the cessation of physical attacks against them. Judith Butler (2004) has defined the unrecognized vulnerability of certain categories of humans in terms of "precariousness," which, unlike its cognate term *precarity*, designates that fundamental characteristic of bodies as socially constituted, exposed, and attached to others. For Butler (2004, 33), recognizing such vulnerability and mourning the injury that may result from it is precisely a step toward "an insurrection at the level of ontology" that would return "the Other" to the sign of the human from which it is excluded. Yet in this case it was not through a "peaceful" act of mourning performed by public opinion or by civil society, as Butler implies, but through acts of rebellion enacted by those Others in response to repeated attacks that a demand for recognition was articulated. However, beyond violence and the immediate public recognition it allowed, the riots gave rise to longer-term political projects. In particular, the revolt spurred the creation of the Africalabria association in Rosarno, which gathered African and Italian members with the aim of overcoming racism, exclusion, and exploitation, as well as of the Assembly of Rosarno's African Workers in Rome (Assemblea dei Lavoratori Africani di Rosarno a Roma, ALAR). Following the deportation of hundreds of those more or less directly involved in the revolt, some of them were hosted by an occupied social center, CSOA ExSNIA, where their meetings took place for several months, before individual life trajectories parted their ways. Through such meetings, demonstrations were organized that ultimately led to the regularization of migrants' juridical status through the granting of permits on the ground of the heavy exploitation they had to endure in Rosarno, thus giving some clearer "political" recognition to the struggle.

On the contrary, in Nardò it was because of an explicit labor issue—the demand for a fairer wage—that around five hundred migrant workers revolted against gangmasters and landowners (something more immediately recognizable as "political" action) and started a two-week-long strike, one of the first of its kind in Italy. They obtained a pay increase and significant media visibility, while the legislative and judiciary branches of government were spurred to react and close in on gangmastership. Parliament upgraded it to a penal offense, and several people were arrested; their trial is ongoing. If both the drafting of the bill and the police investigation long preceded the strike, this arguably precipitated their epilogue. While in Rosarno migrants revolted spontaneously and unsupported, in Nardò the strike took shape within the protected space of Masseria Boncuri, a camp set up by two associations, a local and a national one, for workers to find "dignified" living conditions, health care, legal support, language training regardless of their legal status, and information on their basic labor rights.[6] Once the strike started, activists also gathered monetary support for workers. In the words of one of the activists involved in this experience:

> It was an attempt to create free spaces where self-organisation is possible . . . an open camp, a countercamp [*un contro-campo*] . . . where there were [proper] sleeping places but anyone could come and pitch their tent and access services, even if they didn't live there . . . whilst nobody ever dreamed of saying that we [activists] initiated the strike—[]I believe it would have happened anyways—the difference was that [in Boncuri] people found a place where they could carry on and build up [the labor protest] . . . the conditions were created for people to be able to organize.[7]

During the strike, activists from across the country and beyond flocked to Nardò, and from some such encounters and meetings the Campagne in Lotta as a project took shape. The countercamp model had initially been experimented with by one of the associations, Brigate di Solidarietà Attiva (Active Solidarity Brigades) as an alternative to the heavily militarized, rights-suspending, exceptional camp spaces set up in the aftermath of the earthquake that shook the area around the city of L'Aquila in 2009. It was then transposed to a context that, though different in many respects, shared some of the characteristics of a postearthquake state of emergency—at least as far as its institutionalization goes, as I have already argued. It is this model that would become the main experimental ground for the network's activities, whereby precarity is exploited for its creative potentials in terms of organization, seeking

> to accept and exploit the flexibility inherent in networked modes of sociality and production. . . . In the exception, the rule becomes indistinguishable from its application, or, to put it another way, each event or action rewrites the grammar of the system. The innovative action is thus not simply a transgression that breaks the rules—a kind of avant-garde contestation of existing institutional arrangements. Rather, it is an action that involves an abrogation of rules, a fundamental recasting of grammatical propositions, and a consequent redefining of future generative possibilities. For all this, it is not a sovereign action (a kind of *creatio ex nihilo* that finds its apotheosis in the romantic ideal of the artist as god). Innovative action is necessarily intersubjective action, forged in the complex and unstable relations between brains and bodies. Its model is not the sovereign who decides on the exception but the language or form-of-life that changes through what might be called a non-sovereign decision, at once distributed and diffuse, or, if you like, an exception-from-below. (Neilson and Rossiter 2005)

Contro-Campi: Anthropological Experiments

A bike workshop, a radio, and an Italian-language school were the first activities set up by Campagne in Lotta in the Grand Ghetto in summer 2012.
After a year of meetings, contact building, and field research, an open call for
volunteers was circulated through social networks, mailing lists, and blogs to
start a project that would build on the experience of Nardò. The strike had
by no means brought positive changes alone: as many African migrants complained, it was impossible for them to find work there the following year, when
employers preferred to hire Eastern Europeans to avoid trouble and circum-
vent inspections and checks. The strike also created divisions among workers,
which resulted in episodes of physical violence, while those activists who had
been most exposed suffered threats and aggressions from those whose interests
they were jeopardizing. The confederate trade union (Confederazione Generale
Italiana del Lavoro, CGIL) that had somehow appropriated the mobilization
and its spokespersons (against the logic of self-organization that animated the
countercamp) had also ratified an employment agreement in the province of
Lecce that introduced legitimate piecework payment in agriculture, which of
course meant legitimizing a more intensive work pace. Fear of dangerous over-
exposure on the part of militants and workers led to the decision to keep a "low
profile" in the Grand Ghetto, which was understood to be a heavily controlled
space because of the presence of gangmasters, some of whom were the same as
in Nardò and who were believed to be tied to powerful cartels. Hence, rather
than directly addressing the issue of exploitation, this was tackled laterally by
means of activities that could breach isolation as well as provide instruments
for mutual encounters and understanding, and for self-organization and emancipation.

Furthermore, according to some of its protagonists, the experience of Masseria Boncuri had also evidenced some limitations concerning the relationships between militants/volunteers and migrant workers, who were then clearly
distinguished subjects—with militants in charge of managing the space while
at the same time seeking to minimize their intrusiveness. This, in a sense, re-
inforced their distance from workers, who were identified as the sole legitimate
subjects of organization, as it clearly emerged from several conversations I had
with some of those who took part in the events, and particularly with Tania,[8]
who would later become one of the core figures in the network project:

> If self-organisation is to be such, you cannot intervene and say, "You don't do it
> this way." In that occasion [during the strike] we were perhaps too silent from
> that point of view, for fear of guiding, of directing, of . . . putting too much of
> our own in it, we stepped back too much. So we simply acted as buffers, with
> the guarantee that nothing would happen to us, because in a fight we would

not be attacked—but we risked nonetheless. . . . So then you ask yourself, "Why am I doing this? What does this lead to if not to the destruction of the group of people that initially came together?" One must question one's goals. If the goal is that of bringing forward a certain kind of conflict, with precise political claims against labor exploitation, which then lead, for example, to the revision of the law against gangmastership as criminal offence, then the Nardò strike can certainly be considered a success, if you want . . . a first-timer for sure. . . . But without detracting from the experience, from the point of view of a different kind of militancy (from that of parliamentary debate or the relationship with institutions, which has a progressivist and legalistic outlook), what was the result? The result was awful, if you wish, because apart from perhaps a few remaining contacts . . . no group was created. . . .

Me: Though the network was born . . .

Tania: Surely . . . and from the point of view of relationships, this shifted the attention to the issue of labor . . . and put other groups in touch, with other experiences, perhaps as powerful—if different, like the Rosarno riots. . . . They are reactions to the same system . . . and must enter in connection, and [this] created a different path. . . . There is first of all no direct management of anything, of any structure [like it was with the Masseria] . . . which for us was . . . double-sided—on the one hand you lived in things all day every day, for three months, but on the other hand, as much as you place yourself in a dimension of egalitarian management, of co-management of spaces, they [workers] will always perceive you as someone who is managing them, or responsible for something. . . . The difference is that the following experiences [with Campagne in Lotta] were designed in a different way . . . a process was set in motion.

Thus, the network represented the evolution of practices first tested out elsewhere, toward a more horizontal and inclusive, compositional structure.

Rather unusually for a radical militant project, the activities in the Grand Ghetto were organized within an already-existing volunteer camp, run by Catholic missionaries, whose outlook seemed to be far enough from the mere provision of charity relief to be at least partly compatible with the aims of the network, and whose many years of experience on the ground proved crucial as a first introduction into such difficult terrain.[9] Yet the aims of their volunteer camp were partly at odds with those of the network, and certainly their languages were different: as stated on the missionary project's website (http://www.iocisto.eu), the goal of the camp is "to offer seasonal migrants the chance of an encounter with young volunteers and Italian institutions for a more positive and constructive vision" through language training and information on services; sensitization to rights and duties; and active commitment against "discrimination, abuse, prejudice, exploitation, injustice, enslavement," and "to allow youth to discover human beings' natural diversity in its essence, in an increasingly multicultural society, for an intercultural relationship that respects alterity for mutual growth."

Indeed, composition within the network has acquired unexpected shapes, being focused not only on establishing horizontal relations with migrant workers, but also with and between local organizations that often have rather different goals and methods. Thus, its first collective project saw volunteers, who often had radical political backgrounds and views, living and working side by side with missionaries, would-be priests, nuns, and scouts. Before being confronted with migrant workers, militants were faced with another kind of alterity, perhaps equally, if not more, distant in terms of experiences and outlooks. While differences were never completely bridged (as they never are within any collective, even where members come from similar political and existential backgrounds), and would determine progressive, even conflictual distancing from both sides after initial enthusiasms subsided, many activists were positively impressed by the Catholics' curiosity and openness, which brought some of them to join the network and participate in general meetings and subsequent projects for some time. Jokes and banter were the main vehicle for the establishment of relationships, together with the exchange of knowledge. Yet political criticism by militants against Catholics (rather than vice versa) was often fierce and scathing, leaving little to the imagination.

Here as elsewhere, a process of attempted composition, which is about the creation of subjectivities out of encounters, clashed with preconstituted subject positions. Yet while radical militant experience and religious subjectivities may diverge on a number of counts, they nonetheless share an "internalization of ideals" (Milanesi 2010, 28, my translation), whereby both militant politics and religion are processes of active subjectivation. Indeed, it was precisely on this account that coexistence and collaboration had become possible in the first place. Both militants and Catholics were engaging in a practice of active, creative, willful commitment, for personal as well as social change. Political battle is fought not only against opposing ideas and different views within one's own side, but also "*in interiore homine*, submitting the subject to a theoretical tension that finds a counterpart only in the shades of religious experience" (Milanesi 2010, 28). In this view, militancy as religion represents a constant, totalizing type of commitment that involves life in its entirety and in all its expressions, comprising the public and the private dimensions (32). However, it is important to stress the processual, ever-incomplete character of such processes of subjectivation (and of composition itself). As mentioned, such composition did not last. While some of the network's members had a years- or decades-long history of political commitment, many of the volunteers who joined in the network's first and subsequent projects had little or no previous militant experience. But despite this caveat, it is fair to call those experiences (however brief and idiosyncratic) of full immersion into the reality of ghettos and camps, with a transformative purpose, "militant"—precisely on account of their totalizing character, of the fact that they absorbed the energies, desires, affects, time, and work of their participants, leaving little or no space for anything else, and that they engaged volunteers in creative practices aimed at transforming reality. Here is how Tania explains the rationale behind such a project:

> Already in 2010, the first year in Nardò, we talked about a "farmworkers' league," which . . . in our imagination was to be the answer to that kind of phenomenon [the exploitation and marginalization of farm laborers], a farmworkers' organisation, foreigners and nonforeigners, precisely because there is a total lack of interest from confederate and grassroots trade unions in this phenomenon—because of forces, concern, political will. Hence, [we sought] bottom-up self-organization, but the real thing . . . After three years, now I see that this thing is beginning to be there, after a very long and thorough work, of a construction that if not day-by-day at least has been of total dedication.

These experiences of course evolved over time. The network's first project was only partly different from the experiment of Masseria Boncuri: it did not directly manage a living space *for* (and to some extent *with*) migrant workers—which in some sense may be seen as a necessary step forward against the risks of establishing hierarchies and barriers, but in another represented an act of withdrawal—and it could create only limited spaces for mutual, horizontal encounters. Among these, the "pirate" radio was perhaps paramount, together with film nights, a farewell party, and the myriad informal discussions and moments of sociality that were established in the Grand Ghetto on the side of scheduled activities.

Above all, the volunteer camp model confined militants and Catholics in an enclosed and isolated space: a former rehabilitation center for people with drug addiction issues, turned into a shelter and open workshop space for health-related prevention and the promotion of "social inclusion." Some among the militant volunteers jokingly compared it to an asylum-seeker shelter or even a migrant detention center. Of course the differences are many and clearly evident, but a sense of entrapment, total institutionalization, and discipline did characterize the experience of living in the space, where life rhythms were paced rather strictly according to bans against smoking and drinking, gender-segregated sleeping spaces, cleaning and cooking shifts, scheduled training and discussion moments, and the time spent in the Grand Ghetto. Rather than a countercamp, at times it felt like a redoubling of the camp form itself. For many volunteers, night was often the time when a freer sociality could be enacted, far from the strict gaze of organizers—which often meant sacrificing precious sleeping time to chat, laugh, drink, and get to know one another.

Equally, in the Grand Ghetto it was also by spending time in bars and restaurants that a sense of *proximity* with its inhabitants was forged, however precarious. Yet unlike the volunteers' living space, in the ghetto the radio tent and the space dedicated to the language school did in fact constitute an experiment for a countercamp, through the establishment of communal, open spaces that should foster horizontal relationships of mutual exchange. However, given the centrality of relationships and proximity in the process of composition, it could be equally argued that any trust relationship established was in an of itself a countercamp, regardless of the physical space where it could take place.

Thus, these experiences made evident the importance of physical presence and closeness in building relationships of trust and mutual understanding. Indeed, many workers remark on exactly this aspect when describing the process whereby they progressively approached militants and learned to make distinctions between their position and attitude and those of the myriad journalists, unionists, researchers, charities, and others that fleetingly transit through ghettos and camps, whose promises they have learned to dismiss. Of course, the school, as the radio, also represented a privileged moment of encounter, an attempt by militants to understand dynamics of work, to encourage a horizontal type of practice where teachers and students, whites and blacks, workers and militants would work and learn together, and to provide useful tools (e.g., bicycles and the skills to be able to fix them, legal advice) for workers to acquire strength vis-à-vis gangmasters and landowners—but also, more generally, to better navigate the hostile and alienating environment of a foreign country where structural and street-level racism heavily shape migrants' everyday experiences.

The whole project, and subsequent ones even more, was in fact a sort of social, anthropological experiment—or *experiencia*, as Colectivo Situaciones (2007) aptly condenses in the Spanish word the sense of experimentation with that of experience. Indeed, as several members of Campagne in Lotta would later articulate it, the foundations for the construction of a new "common language" were laid. Yet the possibility of a common language depends on something nonlinguistic, on a process of reciprocal contamination (where, of course, one has to "choose what to be contaminated by," as one of the network members put it) that operates at the affective, intersubjective, bodily level: "the affirmation of the experience (as a weave and experiential constellation) that causes the word to be spoken" (Colectivo Situaciones 2007, 80). "Composition defines relations between bodies. It does not refer to agreements established at a discursive level but to the multidimensional flows of affect and desire the relationship puts in motion" (77). It is accompanied and enveloped by feelings of "falling in love or friendship" (92n23). Especially in interactions between people with disparate origins, backgrounds, languages, habits, and understandings of the world, of power relations and of possibilities for action—as they were made possible through the presence of the network in migrants' ghettos and camps—trust and understanding, friendship and love, had to be built through physical proximity and presence. Such differences had to be somehow inserted in practices of translation that far exceeded the linguistic level, that did not rely on mediators, and that had the potential of undoing established identities to create an ever-changing, constituently open collective subject, the creation of a radical strike for political possibility as a relation at the site of incommensurability (Sakai 1997). Butler and Spivak (2007, 62) also describe plural acts and speech in translation as the creation of "a collectivity that comes to exercise its freedom in a language or a set of languages for which difference and translation are irreducible." However, what I am pointing to here are nonlinguistic practices of composition-in-difference, which in some way make those utterances possible.

The main result of the network's first collective project was the aggregation of a collective that, though continuously evolving in its makeup (indeed, composing and decomposing) and with varying degrees of individual participation and militancy, of harmony and conflict, would continue pursuing a common project in the months to come. A general meeting, informational and fund-raising nights across Italy, the creation of a website and the naming of the network as Campagne in Lotta, and a two-day self-training session followed. Then, alongside Italian militants a small group of African workers had started to gather, although at this stage a clear distinction between "us" and "them" was perceivable in the ways militants and workers referred to themselves and to one another, and silence often marked the presence of African workers in collective discussions. Common language was still far from articulate. It is only through a second intensive, collective experience that such distinctions and barriers began to become undone.

From the end of December 2012 until mid-March 2013, the network established a presence in Rosarno, in collaboration with local militants and the Africalabria association. This allowed the work of what was now Campagne in Lotta to start on a different footing, as African migrants and local militants there already met regularly to discuss issues to do with racism and exploitation and had thus created a ground for collective action. Conditions were, to some extent, much harder in the tent camp for militants to establish a countercamp, as they lacked the structured logistical support of missionaries and the large number of volunteers that could be recruited during the summer months. But this was counterbalanced by more independence in action and in communal living arrangements. After a general introduction of the network and its aims to the camp dwellers, whose consent was sought, and the distribution of flyers that explained the nature and purpose of our presence, we set up two tents in the shantytown adjacent to the camp, where language classes, discussions, and meetings with trade unionists, lawyers, and others were organized, as well as film nights and open-mic music sessions. Volunteers were housed by local supporters and could enjoy a much more flexible, self-organized living and work arrangement, and shared leisure time with Africans and locals—which was, again, crucial in terms of group building and creative action (though, of course, tensions were never missing).

Reflecting on his first experience with the network, Armando—a student in his midtwenties with little direct involvement with social movements—recalled his time in Rosarno thus:

> It's about creating relationships, understanding each other's position and doing things together. . . . There's not much need to say, "I am exploited too and therefore let's do things together," it's simply about establishing a relationship between two people, who know each other, know each other's positions and motivations and on that base do things together. . . . This is key, if you share an experience with people or not. I don't want to emphasize human relations too much but that's the thing that stayed with me most since Rosarno: in the moment you establish a relationship, if everything is in broad daylight it's easier to accept it for both parties. . . . A moment that stuck with me is when we were going to the tent camp in Rosarno, it was a Saturday and we should have shown a movie, the weather was shit, it was horrible, hailing, very cold, if it had been for me I would have stayed home. In a situation like that, it would have been easier to stay, also because we were going every day, but I remember that the others were adamant we should go, we had committed to do this, we said we'd do it, so we went to the camp, began to fix the tarpaulin with Africans helping us, and until the hail was so strong it destroyed it we resisted. . . . So it became clear that for us it wasn't like a holiday, an African safari, as some migrants thought. There is a minimum of sacrifice . . . and also the fact that we did things together, like setting up the tents. . . .
>
> Another episode was with this fifty-year old Tunisian man who lived in the camp, we had a connection also because I had been to Tunisia so we had things to talk about. He was owed benefits by the state, on which he had fantasized: he had already allocated different sums for different investments in his head. When we went to collect the sum he had shaved and dressed up, it was going to be his Big Day, but it turns out the sum he was entitled to was only seventy euros: a phenomenal blow. It was a moment when I began to understand that if they had told me this story . . . I mean, there was no pity from my part towards him, it was actual disappointment, I was really upset myself, but because it was something I was sharing with him in that moment, naturally, as when something bad happens to a friend: you are not sad because it happened to you, it happened to him, but you don't say "poor thing." . . . When one says, "Ah, poor thing," you are saying that if it had happened to me, yes, it would have been bad, but it happened to him . . . that is, automatically you are saying

you don't give a damn . . . but in that moment it was different. . . . We could get there because . . . we had shared things in the previous days, we had gotten to know each other, there was a relationship. This is not just to say I am happy I lived this nice experience of sharing, but that the way I was positioning myself vis-à-vis this situation was much more participating, "Why don't you do this, why can't you do that, have you thought about this?" I mean, we were on it together, trying to understand what could be done, something which in the moment you say "poor thing" you don't do, there is no such constructive side. And to broaden the issue this is valid in a more tangential sense, that maybe this isn't a situation you yourself are living, but when you share things with people, facing anger, the desire to change, frustration, in a difficult moment, you face this . . . you participate in others' anger, and you cooperate and share it, it comes natural for you to make some steps forward.

Despite all this, it was one series of events that more than any other marked a significant turning point in terms of composition. After months of silence, in early February the mayor of San Ferdinando (the municipality where the camp had been built) ordered the enforcement of a removal order that had been issued in December, after the shantytown had been erected. A new camp was ready a few hundred meters down the road to host both tent and shack dwellers, provided that they paid thirty euros a month each for the Evangelical association to manage the structure, as public funding was allegedly insufficient. At this point, resentment against the camp managers and general frustration for the lack of work and for living conditions had mounted, and relationships between camp dwellers and militants had been strengthening. Thus, the camp's inhabitants had several meetings during which they elected six representatives, one for each nationality present, and together with a couple of militants went to meet the mayor and police inspector in charge of the removal and relocation, on two separate occasions. Despite the paternalism and open racism with which they were met (the mayor spent most of the meeting with his eyes shut or his gaze turned), migrants finally obtained not paying for a place in the tents. Again, Armando used poignant words to reflect on this process:

Something I thought many times is that it's not necessary to find a definitive answer to the question what are our objectives, what are we doing, and if you find it, it's not necessarily a good sign. . . . This is a manager-like approach, performance-based. . . . One might need a direction, but in some context and circumstances you feel you have to do certain things, you have to be there, go, do things that you think are important even if you don't really know what will come out. . . . Like in life, you can ask yourself both "what do I want to do when I grow up?" but then also understand what makes sense doing at this time, seeing a direction without knowing where it's leading you. This is why I'm saying it's not necessarily a good sign to try setting concrete goals that might impoverish what your presence in a place is . . . The background idea behind the concept of self-organization is that people should be protagonists of all that concerns them, it's an idea that perhaps acts as a dial orienting all the activities. . . .

In Rosarno, the transition to the new camp for me was important, because what happened is that face to this transfer, that was decided behind closed doors between Prefecture, city council and the various camp-managing organizations, without even consulting with the Africans. . . . The fact that then, de facto behind their back (because it was Italians that asked for a meeting), perhaps they expected to talk with someone they knew, and instead they find themselves facing six Africans . . . that was something that in its small way was great, also because it was obtained with a trick, it was actually a cunning move.

It struck me because sometimes, when one looks at things on a more microscopic level, it always looks as if you are facing a superior mind, who already knows everything even before you do it, you have a small sense of impotence, but in a context where you are present, active, integrated, participating, you know the cards on the table, you can make your move. . . . This already struck me, as the fact we put Africans face-to-face with those that are called "strong" powers, even if actually they are wretches. . . . This generated a panic situation . . . something which went well beyond what might be "diplomatic" difficulties in managing the situation. . . . It was something that upset their ideas on how the world spins . . . and then . . . the fact that this thing was successful and they didn't have to pay those thirty euros. . . .

Now the question is: is the goal of the network that Africans don't pay those 30 euros? No, but all in all that thing made me say this is a thing worth doing, that I want to carry on doing, that putting in place different strategies you break certain equilibria and you get results that are very far from your utopia but they are concrete things. As far as I'm concerned I didn't have experience where I could be able to say I had contributed to change, allowing for events to take a certain direction instead of another in such a concrete manner. . . . It doesn't depend on you only, it also depends on the events but it is important, even if you are frustrated for a long time, in the moment when a window opens, something happens, you are there. Also for this reason I'm saying it's important to keep doing things even though at first you don't know what they are . . . the moment you wrong-foot them . . . *tac*! You do shift the balance. . . . That one was politics for me, that is, you make the move that stuns them. . . . They expected to find someone they knew with whom to chat, among Calabrian men, but you contribute to creating a situation that shakes things up.

After this collective success, one of the network's tents, the countercamp within the camp, was moved to the new site by workers and activists together, and progressively equipped with cushions, carpets, heaters, and posters for the school. It was used for classes, meetings, film screenings, and as a space of general sociability. More camp dwellers started coming to the Africalabria meetings in Rosarno, and by the end of the project a demonstration was organized in town to demand safer roads for (African) cyclists and pedestrians, who in more than one instance had lost their lives to reckless and even intentionally aggressive drivers. Once again, this may appear to be a small, even preposterous, claim in the face of a situation of extreme precarity, but like the meetings with the mayor and the police, it was nonetheless another act whereby African migrants established their presence in Rosarno and their "right to claim rights," as well as another step toward the constitution of a collective voice underscored by a principle of equality (see Butler and Spivak 2007, after Arendt's *The Origins of Totalitarianism*; Isin 2012). Victims were remembered and mourned, songs sung, humanity reclaimed once again. Furthermore, after the riots, and the aftermath of fear and suspicion they had left behind (artfully manipulated by local media and politicians in more than one occasion, to find scapegoats and avoid protest), a peaceful demonstration of African workers in Rosarno was an authentic breakthrough. Of course, claiming the right to have rights, defending and defining one's humanity, as Avramopoulou points out in her contribution to this volume, is never entirely devoid of ambiguities, insofar as it grants power and recognition to those subjects and institutions that are the root cause of oppression. At the same time, it might be argued that, at least for African farmworkers, the point was that of creating a relationship and thus authoring an intersubjectivity that simply was not there before. It meant going beyond what existed, opening up a new relational space—provisional and not entirely satisfactory or rid of power dynamics, to be sure.

In the following months, those workers who had become closer to the network continued to be in contact with militants, and after another general assembly and a self-training (*autoformazione*) held in Foggia, three different projects were set up in Foggia, Saluzzo, and Boreano (Potenza) in the summer. Here, the barrier separating workers and militants was further eroded, as some workers who had approached Campagne in Lotta in previous projects decided to join volunteers and actively commit to working with them. They were adamant that the paramount activity should be the spread of information among workers on basic labor rights, so flyers were designed and distributed across the province of Foggia. A shack was built in the ghetto to house the radio and provide sleeping space, and volunteers from different countries and continents shared the living space of a church a few kilometers uphill, on Mount Gargano. This experience allowed for a significant leap in compositional terms, as bonds of "friendship and love" could be consolidated and cemented, knowledge exchanged, and practices discussed and agreed on, on a continuous basis.

The most significant results of such projects were the numerous meetings held between militants and workers in Saluzzo, Boreano, and across the Foggia province and its many ghettos, which, together with the information campaign, in Foggia led to the creation of a self-organized workers' committee and to the stepping up of demands on the workers' part, for institutional commitment to end the gross and blatant exploitation to which they are subjected. In Saluzzo, after a meeting workers and militants (who themselves lived in a tent in the shantytown) reclaimed water provision for Guantánamo, autonomously connecting a pipe from a fountain a few hundred meters away. Once this was cut off by the municipality a few days later, they enacted a spontaneous protest, occupying the streets and erecting barricades, which ended with a meeting in the mayor's office and the promise that the water supply would be restored the following day.

Once again, these acts represented affirmations of rights and moments of aggregation, and they were just another step in a process of ongoing affective composition, of creative translation in difference, the momentary establishments of counterpowers that have to be continually reasserted. In subsequent years, some relationships would be cemented, new ones forged, and others collapsed, even violently—between militants and missionaries or representatives of associations and unions, among militants, between militants and some workers. New territories would keep being assembled out of continuously shifting intensities: demonstrations and pickets, at the local and national level, as well as small incidents in which individuals would strenuously fight for their right to recognition and for lives worth living. To be sure, disappointment and frustration, even hostility and mistrust, were never lacking. Many farmworkers accuse militants of empty talking, even of instrumentalization, expecting change to come from their initiative and leadership rather than from self-organized, collective action, or simply giving in to cynicism in the face of hardship. Between the lines, it appears that workers sometimes reproach militants for their lack of courage and persistence, while as militants we often feel frustrated by workers' tendency to delegate responsibility and by their cynicism. Political cultures meet and sometimes clash, but in such process new ones take shape. As Greenberg lucidly argues in her contribution to this volume, disappointment need not be the end; rather, it is the beginning of processes of pragmatic "epistemological activism," founded on a contingency of knowledge that suits, at least to some extent, the uncertain contexts I have described here, and which Armando's words emphatically crystallize. Albeit in a very different context and with different political aims and compositions, such processes resonate with what Ahmad describes elsewhere in this volume as a politics of the ordinary, which stretches the political to accommodate fragile and tentative contexts. At the same time, it might be argued that time cements certain ontologies and that even such pragmatic epistemologies have come to constitute a (provisional) militant ontology, built through conflicts and alliances.

* * *

In this chapter, I have traced the emergence and evolution of a militant network by highlighting the processes of composition that underscored them in relation to the fields of power in whose cracks they seek to insert themselves and to the claims and forms of representation to which such composition gave rise. Emergence designates "the introduction of incommensurability into social life," where incommensurability in turn represents affective potential (Dave 2011, 652). Affective composition as a matter of bodily proximity acts within already named and represented, structured yet always morphing subjectivities, to then lead to claims to rights and hence to the creation of new, if precarious, collective subjectivities. Discussing queer politics in India, Dave (2011) rightly points out that the constitutive ambivalence that characterizes the emergence of a new social form—as enhancing existence, action, and expression, but also as closure through its commensuration to existing social forms—is in fact not a matter of categorical opposition, for "closure is the condition of possibility for social invention and the emergence of new potential" (652). In the cases I have discussed here, migrants' and/as militants' claims can all be seen as pointing to already-existing social forms. Their demand to be considered part of the human community, their pressing of authorities to augment checks and enforce laws, their desire for "normal" housing or their need to access primary resources such as water can all be related to a desire to belong in something that is perceived to exclude them. And yet by inserting themselves cunningly in those realms from which they are banned, migrants/militants already transform such space and recalibrate the power struggles that shape it. The affective, as an eminently relational dimension, is crucial in this process of ontological insurrection as the potential immanent in the field of struggle.

Notes

1. For elaborations on the notion of migrants' struggles, see Peano (forthcoming) and Sandro Mezzadra, "L'Italia e vent'anni di fenomeno migratorio," talk delivered as part of the series of seminars *Autoformazione—Rivoluzione!*, organized by Network Antagonista Piacentino, December 21, 2014, https://www.youtube.com/watch?v=-Ncow9iTU-Y.

2. In addition, I would like to thank all those who read and commented on earlier versions of this chapter: Sandro Mezzadra, Ezio Puglia, Maple Razsa, Veronica, Maria, Gianandrea.

3. Given the extreme precarity I am describing here, and the irregular nature of much agricultural wage labor, it is extremely hard to provide reliable estimates of the number of workers involved. According to the Istituto Nazionale di Economia Agraria (2011), in 2010, 190, 000 nonnationals (a figure that includes migrants from both EU and non-EU countries) were employed in agriculture in Italy. Other estimates are much higher: according to the National Institute for Social Insurance (Istituto Nazionale di Previdenza Sociale), in 2013 around four hundred thousand foreign-born agricultural workers were employed in Italy (see Centro Studi e Ricerche IDOS 2014). Given the high degree of irregularity in this sector, figures are likely to be underestimated—one source estimates they should be at least 25 percent higher (ISFOL 2012).

4. Of course, current immigration laws, in Italy as elsewhere, create an especially vulnerable migrant workforce by tying certain kinds of permits to a labor contract, by making "clandestine immigration" a criminal offence, and more generally through the threat of detention and deportation (De Genova 2002). In Italy, migrants often obviate the difficulty of obtaining a regular work contract and their consequent illegal status by purchasing a fake one from willing employers, which is impossibly onerous when salaries are as meager as those received by agricultural laborers, who also have to support their kin networks back home or in the diaspora. Furthermore, given the recent developments, as far as migratory flows and in policies seeking to manage them are concerned, permits are less and less directly tied to possession of a labor contract and are increasingly granted on humanitarian grounds (for a more detailed account of the relationship between this kind of mobility governance and agricultural labor in contemporary Italy, see Dines and Rigo 2015). For this population, obtaining and renewing residence permits is often equally arduous on the ground of ever more restrictive interpretations of laws, requirements, and regulations. In parallel, the ever-growing presence of EU citizens among the hyperprecarious agricultural labor force has weakened the relationship between the institutional government of mobility, and in particular irregularization, and exploitation at work: regardless of legal status, migrant workers (as well as some Italians) endure heavy forms of precarity, while of course other mechanisms of "differential inclusion" (Mezzadra and Neilson 2013) remain in place, such as denial of access to residency rights.

5. In this respect, it is important to underline how ethnicization, as well as different migration patterns (only partly attributable to dynamics of mobility and labor control), also determine differences in the conditions of workers of different national origins. What I am describing, at least as far as the development of large, more or less institutionalized settlements goes, applies mainly (though not exclusively) to the sub-Saharan African population, as well as to Roma (Gypsy) communities—as opposed to, say, non-Roma Eastern Europeans, who make up the majority of agricultural laborers in some areas. Like Africans, Romany Eastern Europeans also live in concentrated ghettos. These groups usually undergo heavier forms of racism and segregation, although wages are comparable across the spectrum of migrant workers regardless of nationality or "ethnicity." At the same time, the spectacle of migration and misery (which also feeds a highly lucrative humanitarian machine) into which Africans are forced by media and institutions serves to screen the reality of widespread forms of segregation and exploitation that characterize "white" European workers too.

6. For an account of the struggle in Nardò from the perspective of the activists and migrants involved, see Brigate di Solidarietà Attiva and colleagues (2012).

7. All interview excerpts are my own translations from Italian.

8. All names are fictive to protect anonymity.

9. A collective account of this first experience was published in the journal *Gli Asini* 11 (2012): 96–102.

References

Agamben, Giorgio. 1998. *Homo Sacer: Sovereign Power and Bare Life.* Stanford, CA: Stanford University Press.

———. 2005. *State of Exception.* Chicago: University of Chicago Press.

Bojadžijev, Manuela, Serhat Karakayali, and Vassilis Tsianos. 2004. "L'enigma dell'arrivo: Su campi e spettri." In *I confini della libertà: Per un'analisi politica delle migrazioni contemporanee*, edited by Sandro Mezzadra, 125–141. Rome: DeriveApprodi.

Brigate di Solidarietà Attiva, Devi Sacchetto, Gianluca Nigro, Mimmo Perrotta, and Yvan Sagnet. 2012. *Sulla pelle viva. Nardò: La lotta autorganizzata dei braccianti immigrati.* Rome: DeriveApprodi.

Butler, Judith. 2004. *Precarious Life: The Powers of Mourning and Violence.* London: Verso Books.

Butler, Judith, and Gayatri Spivak. 2007. *Who Sings the Nation-State? Language, Politics, Belonging.* London: Seagull.

Centro Studi e Ricerche IDOS. 2014. *Dossier statistico immigrazione 2014. Rapporto UNAR: Dalle discriminazioni ai diritti.* Rome: Centro Studi e Ricerche IDOS/Immigrazione Dossier Statistico.

Colectivo Situaciones. 2007. "Something More on Research Militancy: Footnotes on Procedures and (In)Decisions." In *Constituent Imagination: Militant Investigations, Collective Theorization*, edited by Stevphen Shukaitis and David Graeber, 73–93. Oakland, CA: AK Press.

Corrado, Alessandra, and Carlo Colloca, eds. 2013. *La globalizzazione delle campagne: Migranti e società rurali nel Sud Italia.* Milan: Franco Angeli.

Dave, Naisargi. 2011. "Indian and Lesbian and What Came Next: Affect, Commensuration, and Queer Emergences." *American Ethnologist* 38 (4): 650–665.

De Genova, Nicholas. 2002. "Migrant 'Illegality' and Deportability in Everyday Life." *Annual Review of Anthropology* 31: 419–447.

Dines, Nick, and Enrica Rigo. 2015. "Postcolonial Citizenships between Representation, Borders and the 'Refugeeization' of the Workforce: Critical Reflections on Migrant Agricultural Labor in the Italian Mezzogiorno." In *Postcolonial Transitions in Europe: Contexts, Practices and Politics*, edited by Sandra Ponzanesi and Gianmaria Colpani, 151–172. London: Rowman and Littlefield.

Düvell, Franck. 2004. La globalizzazione del controllo delle migrazioni. In *I confini della libertà: Per un'analisi politica delle migrazioni contemporanee*, edited by Sandro Mezzadra, 23–50. Rome: DeriveApprodi.

Foucault, Michel. 1979. *Discipline and Punish: The Birth of the Prison.* New York: Vintage Books.

Hardt, Michael, and Antonio Negri. 2000. *Empire.* Cambridge, MA: Harvard University Press.

Istituto Nazionale Economia Agraria. 2011. *Rapporto sullo stato dell'agricoltura 2011.* Rome: Istituto Nazionale Economia Agraria.

Istituto per lo Sviluppo della Formazione Professionale dei Lavoratori (ISFOL). 2012. "Dimensioni e caratteristiche del lavoro sommerso/irregolare in agricoltura." http://isfoloa.isfol .it/bitstream/123456789/120/1/Iadevaia_Mainardi_Lavoro%20sommerso.pdf.

Isin, Engin. 2012. *Citizens without Frontiers.* London: Bloomsbury Publishing.

Mezzadra, Sandro, and Brett Neilson. 2013. *Border as Method: Or, The Multiplication of Labour.* Durham, NC: Duke University Press.

Milanesi, Franco. 2010. *Militanti: Un'antropologia politica del Novecento.* Milan: Edizioni Punto Rosso.

Neilson, Brett, and Neil Rossiter. 2005. "From Precarity to Precariousness and Back Again: Labour, Life and Unstable Networks." *Fibreculture Journal* 5. http://five.fibreculturejournal.org/fcj-022-from-precarity-to-precariousness-and-back-again-labour-life-and-unstable-networks/.

Ong, Aiwa. 2006. *Neoliberalism as Exception: Mutations in Citizenship and Sovereignty.* Durham, NC: Duke University Press.

Papadopoulos, Dimitris, Niamh Stephenson, and Vassilis Tsianos. 2008. *Escape Routes: Control and Subversion in the 21st Century.* London: Pluto Press.

Peano, Irene. (forthcoming). "Migrants' Struggles? Rethinking Citizenship, Anti-Racism and Labour Precarity through Migration Politics in Italy." In *Where Are the Unions? Organised Workers and Mass Mobilisations in the Arab World, Europe and Latin America*, edited by S. Lazar and A. Alexander. London: Zed Books.

Rahola, Federico. 2006. "La forma-campo: Appunti per una genealogia dei luoghi di internamento contemporanei." *Deportate, Esuli, Profughe* 5–6: 17–31.

Sakai, Naoki. 1997. *Translation and Subjectivity: On "Japan" and Cultural Nationalism.* Minneapolis: University of Minnesota Press.

Wacquant, Loïc J. D. 2001. "Deadly Symbiosis: When Ghetto and Prison Meet and Mesh." *Punishment & Society* 3: 95–133.

———. 2009. *Punishing the Poor: The Neoliberal Government of Social Insecurity.* Durham, NC: Duke University Press.

Wright, Steve. 2002. *Storming Heaven: Class Composition and Struggle in Italian Autonomist Marxism.* London: Pluto Press.

4 Cosmologicopolitics

Vitalistic Cosmology Meets Biopower

James D. Faubion

In the social thought of the past two decades, life has emerged as the chief leitmotif of the contemporary political imagination, of the prevailing frequency of the political present (see also Avramopoulou's chapter in this volume). Michel Foucault's articulation of what has since come to be known as biopower and biopolitics in the closing chapter of the first volume of *The History of Sexuality* (1978) and at greater length in his 1975–1976 lectures at the Collège de France (Foucault 2003) is illustrative. The ontological ground on which that articulation rests is neither an identity nor a community. It is instead the "mindful body" in all its fleshliness (see Scheper-Hughes and Lock 1987), whether individualized or represented as a statistical and demographic abstraction, a population, which is the representational vehicle that facilitates the translation of biopower into biopolitics as such. The same body is the ground of value, and the values it yields themselves are the grounds of the norms that justify biopolitics as a collective enterprise, an enterprise of the management of the health, security, and well-being of the population (Foucault 2003). Life politics may or may not be a disciplinary politics. As a distinctive modality of life politics, biopolitics is both totalizing and individualizing, but not in the manner of discipline. Its totalities are not disciplinary species. It justifies intervention into individual lives, but its interventions are neither wholesale nor uniform. They encompass only those cases deemed to deviate from and especially to put into danger the maintenance of established collective norms of proper health, security, and well-being severally or jointly.

Foucault's conceptualization of biopolitics is singularly seminal. It flowers into such bold mutations of life politics as Giorgio Agamben's ethically bereft camp (1998), Roberto Esposito's (2008) postulation of the promise of a politics of the flesh, and Michael Hardt's and Antonio Negri's multitudinous *Empire* (2000). Anthony Giddens contributes an analytical template at once more modest than and complementary to these Foucauldian variations in his 1991 *Modernity and Self-Identity* and has his most like-minded fellow diagnostician in Ülrich Beck (1994). If less a stable concept than a fuzzily magnetic key symbol, life serviceably draws into the same analytical orbit such ostensibly heterogeneous phenomena as the nineteenth-century outcry against masturbation, welfarist governmentality and the enthusiasms of Wilhelm Reich (for Foucault), animality and sovereignty (for Agamben), the politics of peace and the politics of continuous and continuously violent intervention (for Hardt and Negri), the distrust of science and the embrace of ecologism (for Giddens and Beck, among others). The reach of "life" and its politics is generous.

Even so, life as social thinkers now typically think of it is not exhaustive of the political present. What it typically fails to encompass is what Foucault (2000, 451), writing of the Iranian Revolution, characterized as the attempt "to inscribe the figures of spirituality on political ground," or what an increasing number of scholars call "religious politics." For the confident enlightener, the exclusion of the latter is only natural, since religious politics can only be an instance of superstitions properly and lawfully past casting their stain on what should be a more spotlessly secular present and future. For the less confident—in whose ranks I include myself—that exclusion seems suspiciously like another instance of the anthropological denial of the contemporaneity of what is experienced as Other (see Fabian 1983), the casting behind of what would be cast off and cast out. At the very least, the exclusion leaves an astonishing number of apparent anomalies unaccounted. At worst, it imposes a normative and aprioristic distinction between the political and the religious for which contrary matters of fact are of no consequence. Analysis looks poorly served in either case.

Odd Bedfellows? Religion, Vitalism, Politics

Take all the current versions of Islamist activism; add to them all the current Evangelical refractions of the Vision Thing that the elder president George Bush made so central to his now-dated presidency: even that prodigious total is far from exhausting the contemporary array of attempts to inscribe the figures of spirituality on the political ground of "life itself" (see Rose 2007). The initial examples of an explicitly religious or spiritual life politics that I have to offer capture only the sporadic attention of the press, but they remain anything but humble in their cosmological ambitions. Both are close to home (if one's home happens to be the United States), but neither is as purely local as at first sight it might seem.

Religious Biopolitics

The first of my examples derives from research that I conducted between 1994 and 1999 among certain of the members of the sectarian assemblage known to the broader public—if known any longer at all—as the Branch Davidians. The primary subject of my research was Amo Paul Bishop Roden, whom I'll designate hereafter as "Ms. Roden." She probably to this day remains convinced of her command of the hermeneutical and prophetic authority that she regularly asserted to me during our time together, but she seems to have ceased since the turn of the twenty-first century to press it upon her fellow Branch Davidians with nearly as much vigor as she had done during the middle and late 1990s. I cannot say with certainty; I have lost touch with her. I would, however, be much surprised were Ms. Roden to have abandoned those doctrinal elements of Branch Davidianism that she shared in the 1990s with her religious fellows, all of her more particular disagreements with them notwithstanding. Ms. Roden and her fractious fellows officially think of themselves as members of the Branch Davidian Seventh-Day Adventist Church—much to the consternation of the Seventh-Day Adventist Church itself, formally established in Battle Creek, Michigan, in 1863. They embrace most, if not all, of the central pronouncements of the church's founder, Ellen Harmon White, but their more proximate ancestor is Victor Houteff. At first an orthodox Seventh-Day Adventist, Houteff came to the conclusion in the 1920s that the church to which he belonged had betrayed White's teachings, accommodating itself too much to the ways of the material world and diluting White's own millenarian conviction in the imminence of the end-of-time forecast in the New Testament's book of Revelation. Houteff soon found himself disfellowshipped for his putative heresies, and shortly afterward moved from Los Angeles to Waco, Texas, to found the "Davidian" Seventh-Day Adventist Church, doctrinally predicated on the imminence of the reestablishment of the ancient Kingdom of David with the return of its most celebrated descendant, Jesus of Nazareth. Houteff rigorously declined to fix the specific date of the Christ's return—but after his death, his wife, Florence, was compelled to do so, and witnessed the effective dissolution of the Waco congregation in the aftermath of the date she proposed passing unredeemed. She removed the very small remnant of followers who remained with her to a tract of prairie some ten miles from Waco proper, but soon departed to the West Coast, leaving her followers behind. Among them were husband and wife Ben and Lois Roden. Ben claimed in due course that he had been blessed with the divine revelation that the true church of the End Times would be founded not by one of David's direct descendants but instead by a "branch." Not all loyal Davidians accepted the claim, but on the Texas prairie, at least, the Davidian Church acquired its further qualification. It was rechristened the Branch Davidian Church.

Lois received her own revelation in due course, a vision that the Holy Spirit was a feminine aspect of the Godhead. After Ben's death, she presided singly over the Branch Davidian Church, and it was under her suzerainty that the young man then known as Vernon Howell joined the resident congregation. The story thenceforth is well recounted in James Tabor and Eugene Gallagher's *Why Waco?* (1995) and needs only cursory synopsis as a result. Vernon Howell was visited with yet another revelation. He changed his name to David Koresh accordingly and gradually convinced an ever-increasing number of his co-congregants that his revelation established him as the Messiah returned, the very one. Lois seems never to have embraced his self-portrayal, not least because she seems to have continued to uphold her husband's deathbed pronouncement that George Roden, their son, was the Branch incarnate. After chasing George away from the church compound, and especially after Lois's death, Koresh emerged as a charismatic leader of near Weberian proportions. He dealt in guns, expecting an Armageddon in the very near future. He did not remit proper taxes for the guns he bought and modified. On February 28, 1993, brandishing a warrant, agents of the Bureau of Alcohol, Tobacco, and Firearms undertook to raid the church compound. Four agents and six Koreshites died in the shoot-out that ensued. After a protracted standoff, the compound caught fire; some eighty of those inside of it burned. Amo Roden was a Branch Davidian during Koresh's ascendance, but she was not a Koreshite. George Roden had recruited her to the church. She had married George. She was with him in exile when the standoff arose. She remained loyal to the legacy and—in some measure—to George throughout my research and, in her loyalty, a vigorous critic of the Koreshites themselves. The events of the standoff for their part retained their newsworthiness for a couple of years. They have lost it by now. After all, declarations of war and independence, calls to arms and account, are common parlance. World-historical visions of any number of stripes are available on the cheap, and violence and death their handmaidens. We have other sieges, other massacres to entertain us.

Slightly more pertinent to my purposes here is another of Ms. Roden's doctrines. Ellen White is its source, and the doctrine remains as central to the Seventh-Day Adventist Church today as it was during White's own lifetime. I have visited White's career at length elsewhere (Faubion 2001); here again a brief review will suffice. White was born in 1827 and grew up on a working farm near the town of Gorham, Maine. Her childhood and young adulthood were the decades of the Second Great Awakening, a Protestant revivalist movement especially active in the rural northeast. The most influential of the revivalists was the Adventist William Miller, a millenarian and biblical exegete of a Second Coming in the very near offing. His errors and his ecclesiastic fate were direct precursors of Florence Houteff's own. Well before his specification of the Christ's return on October 22, 1844, perpetuating what is known as the Great Disappointment, Ellen White had attended at least one of his previous exegetical sessions. She would come to adopt Miller's methods and amend his errors to her—and many others'—satisfaction. So the Seventh-Day Adventist Church would be born.

White wrote voluminously. She also copied voluminously (Numbers 2008), almost always without what academics would regard as proper citation, but no matter. Among the topics to which she gave especially copious attention were health and the healthy maintenance of the body. She was influenced by the moral physiologists of the eighteenth and of her own century. Her cardinal hygienist was, however, Sylvester Graham, a New Jersey minister whose flock ousted him for what they regarded as his overly zealous advocacy of abstention from alcohol. Graham moved on but did not abandon his hygienic commitments. In 1839, he published *The New Science of Human Life*, whose lessons were extracted (without citation) from the physiological writings of none other than François Broussais, disciple of the "empirical" vitalist Xavier Bichat and, with Bichat, a founding member of that primordial hotbed of biopolitical discourse, the Société de Santé de Paris, the Paris Health Society (Nissenbaum 1980; Sokolow 1983; Faubion 2011, 227). For Bichat, as for his epigone Graham, health in its entirety revolved around the intestinal tract.

White borrowed Graham's borrowed dietetic directives without revision and with the explicit approval of such eminent physicians as Dr. John Harvey Kellogg—an early member of the Seventh-Day Adventist Church and the father of the inventor of the cornflake. Seventh-Day Adventists continue to follow very closely in White's and so in Graham's hygienic footsteps, embracing a vegetarian diet rich in whole grains and eschewing both stimulants and sedatives. Ms. Roden follows (somewhat) faithfully in their train, seeking with special vigilance to "eat foods that provide all twenty-two amino acids to get . . . accelerated healing."

The position is not ascetic; it implies no advocacy of deprivation. It implies a therapeutics. Characteristically, Ms. Roden looks to the figures of the Old Testament for her precedents. As she puts it in one of many of her unpublished writings:

> Everything the Bible says you can eat is clean, and can be eaten. But if you look at the years before the Ark, before the flood, when they lived eight or nine hundred years, you will see that God gave them the herb of the ground, and right after the flood gave them all animals and the herb of the ground, and the difference in diet is particularly shown by Abraham, who lived to be a hundred and seventy-five. And Joseph, eating from the flesh-pots of Egypt, lived to be a hundred and ten. If you get away from animal foods, except perhaps for eating very young animals on ceremonial occasions, and that's your meat consumption, then you will live a lot longer.

The details of her justification are idiosyncratic. Roden's ethico-religious consequentialism and her quasi-transcendental hygienics nevertheless have many homologues. Seventh-Day Adventism is unusual among the "new denominations"—which include the Church of Christ, Scientist; the Church of Latter-Day Saints, and Jehovah's Witnesses—in its financing of hospitals and medical research. Not all new denominationalists maintain a diet as rigorously circumscribed as Roden's own. Biomedicine and biopolitical law have few admirers among either Christian Scientists or Jehovah's Witnesses, not least because the biomedical body borders on being purely material. New denominationalist bodies are of several sorts, but they are always godly bodies. Even so, the divide between the two is not absolute. As of their biomedical counterparts, the governmentality of new denominationalist bodies remains resolutely biopolitical in its worldly registers. Such values are first of all a "matter of conscience," not a matter of interests whose realization can or must be sought through public competition. They are not the foundation of a "politics"—and the policing of the boundary between church and polity in the United States and elsewhere often prevents them in fact from becoming one. This is so, however, only for the new denominations as institutional totalities. It is not so for the individual believer, who is perfectly free to go forth to try to transform the whole world into what he or she takes God's image of it to be. Ms. Roden for her part has by no means shied away from exercising that freedom.

Ecological Politics

The Internet yields my second example:

> Are you tired of namby-pamby environmentalist groups? Are you tried of overpaid corporate environmentalists who suck up to bureaucrats and industry? Have you become disempowered by the reductionist approach of environmental professionals and scientists?
> If you answered yes to any of these questions, then Earth First! is for you. (Earth First!, n.d.)

Earth First! is a notably international movement. Its representatives can be found in the United Kingdom, Belgium, Australia, South Korea, and Nigeria and widely elsewhere (Smith 2008). The fellow travelers that its current philosophical spokespersons—prominently, Bill Devall and George Sessions—count among their own include the Norwegian Spinozist and "ecocentrist" Arne Naess, who is credited with coining the term *deep ecology* (Devall and Sessions 2001; Naess 1973). Earth First! is "biocentric" and distinctly hostile to institutional routinization. It is also ecumenical (at least within limits):

> Earth First! is not an organization, but a movement. There are no "members" of Earth First!, only EarthFirst!ers. It is a belief in biocentrism, that life of the earth comes first, and a practice of putting our beliefs into action.
> While there is broad diversity within Earth First! from animal rights vegans to wilderness hunting guides, from monkeywrenchers to careful followers of Gandhi, from whiskey-drinking backwoods riffraff to thoughtful philosophers, from misanthropes to humanists there is agreement on one thing, the need for action. (Earth First! n.d.)

Here the composite (see Peano's chapter in this volume) speaks, unmistakably political in tone.

International, yes: but Earth First! has its distinctive American color and distinctly American roots. On the face of it, the roots are shallow. Its Wikipedia entry traces its official origin to April, 4, 1980, when environmental activist Dave Foreman and his friends jointly embraced the pledge "No Compromise in Defense of Mother Earth" as they were "traveling in Foreman's VW bus from the Pinacate Desert in northern Mexico to Albuquerque, New Mexico" (Earth First! 2016). The southwestern desert continues to prove a regular source of transcendentalist ("New Age") American inspiration. Be that as it may, the movement gained particular notoriety—not to say infamy—in the later 1980s. The founding editor of the movement's flagship journal (unsurprisingly titled *Earth First!*), Foreman was a fierce advocate of population control. In an interview he gave to Devall, published in the Australian journal *Simply Living* (Devall 1986), he entertained policies of enforced sterilization and the denial of aid to the victims of the famine in Ethiopia, insisting that "the best thing would be to just let nature seek its own balance, to let the people there just starve" (1986, 4). A year later, writing under the nom de plume Miss Ann Thropy (1987), fellow in arms and fellow editor with Foreman, Christopher Manes, contributed an essay to *Earth First!* that considered at length the ecological benefits of an AIDS pandemic.

Earth Firsters in the United States, past and present, can and do locate their precedents before 1980. Their most proximate ancestor is the environmentalist and anti-immigrationist author Edward Abbey, whose *Desert Solitaire* (1968), a polemical memoir of work as a park ranger (in the southwestern desert), would be followed seven years later by the semifictional *Monkey Wrench Gang* (1975), whose antics some Earth Firsters at least were determined to literalize. Especially as the author of *Desert Solitaire*, Abbey has himself been linked—and not without reason—to ancestors more historically distant. In a comparative review of William Eastlake's *Dancers of the Scalp House* and Abbey's *Monkey Wrench Gang* (both of which appeared in 1975), Larry McMurtry (often himself inspired by the southwestern desert) would conclude with a luminous diagnosis. "Eastlake," he wrote, "is the Kafka of the America desert; Abbey is its Thoreau." He adds that he considers *Desert Solitaire* Abbey's "masterpiece" (McMurtry 1975).

Born in 1817, ten years' Ellen White's senior, Henry David Thoreau is no American Adam. Ralph Waldo Emerson and Walt Whitman and their (aptly so-called) transcendentalist brethren are his spiritual companions and enough has been written about them all that a doctrinal reprise is unnecessary. I merely repeat the obvious in recalling the debt these naturalist supernaturalists (see Abrams 1971) owe to German and English romanticism, which is probably the common ancestor of the Earth Firsters as well as other currents of environmentalism on both sides of the contemporary Atlantic. What they add to the already incipiently biopolitical premises of eighteenth- and nineteenth-century moral physiology and the romantic critique of the debilitating aspects of civilized existence, however, is a recognizably American valorization of the self-sufficient individual, for whom a vital Nature serves in her own sublime self-reproduction as *magistra vitae*, at once a gymnasiarch and a spiritual adviser. If they were not yet ecologists, this is because neither the preservation of a pristine landscape nor the reduction or elimination of the pollutants of a clean environment were at the forefront of their this-worldly concerns. Liberty had pride of place. This is recognizably American as well, but had not itself yet reached the extreme of a libertarianism so self-centered as to permit indifference to the plights of others. The Thoreauvians were Unionists. They were abolitionists. They nevertheless established the footsteps that John Muir would extend west to California in the later nineteenth century. There, in an effort to "save the American soul from a total surrender to materialism" (Worster 2008, 403), Muir strove (successfully) to preserve the Yosemite wilderness (well, some of it) and western forests. In 1892, he founded the Sierra Club. No doubt the Earth Firsters generally regard the still thriving Sierra Club as much too mainstream for their ambitions and visions. They are nevertheless its spiritual cousins, however much collateral distance there may be between them.

The Life in Politics: Leading Analytical Variations

In the past two decades, and even well before that, social and cultural thinkers in Europe, the United States, and everywhere else have in fact had ample reason to devote increasing attention to the relation between the biopolitical and the vital, and between the two of those and the political, between living beings and political beings. Whether or not the topic is altogether new, the decline of the welfare state, the rise of global warming, rumors of free-roaming canisters of high-grade plutonium, and the prospect of bioengineering and bioterrorism conspire with a great many other looming specters to give it a contemporary ring. The topic of religious politics is not new, either, but if the ongoing conflict in the Middle East had not already done so, the specific events of September 11, 2001, served and continue to serve as a similarly emphatic reminder that it, too, is very much a topic of and in the present. The sociological dictionary of received ideas allows us readily enough to describe Ms. Roden's mission and the Earth First! manifestologist's paradigm shift as two expressions—if substantively quite distinct expressions—of the combination of two already-hybrid modalities of the political. Both are versions of a politics that derive from the ontological dictates of a vital and intrinsically "ethically ordered" cosmos (Weber 1946, 351). Or we might deploy the terminology of systems theory and characterize them instead as expressions of the de-differentiation of the biological, the religious (or metaphysical), and the political. Neither of these characterizations, however, does much justice to the biozoological vitalism that is at their imagistic and ideational center. We might hope that one or another of the conceptual programs that give pride of place to life in contemporary politics would do better.

If I take up critically only two such programs, this is not merely because they enjoy special prominence, but also because they seem to offer a more illuminating analytical framework than many other of their contenders. So, in *Modernity and Self-Identity*, Giddens (1991, 214) defines what he calls "life politics" as "the politics of a reflexively mobilised order—the system of late modernity—which, on an individual and collective level, has radically altered the existential parameters of social activity":

> It is a politics of self-actualisation in a reflexively ordered environment, where that reflexivity links self and body to systems of global scope. . . . [L]ife politics concerns political issues which flow from processes of self-actualisation in post-traditional contexts, where globalising influences intrude deeply into the reflexive project of the self, and conversely where processes of self-realisation influence global strategies.

Giddens gives every indication that he intends this definition to capture what is distinctive about the politics of what he joins many of his colleagues in calling the "new social movements." The latter include such more or less organized activist campaigns as gay pride, antinuclearism, neo-pacifism, patient and victims rights advocacy, and—of particular pertinence to Giddens as for my purposes—environmentalism and anticapitalist anticorporatism. Most analysts agree that at least two distinctive features render these movements "new" (or especially in the case of anticapitalist and anticorporate movements, "new new"; see Langman 2013). One is negative: unlike the major political movements of the first half of the twentieth century, they are not grounded in working-class interests alone; they are not labor (or labor-oriented) movements. The other is more positive: they are diversely concerned with "the quality of life," if not always of the entire planet, then of the self itself—as gendered or sexual or psycho-biological, potentially viable or potentially or actually of precarious vitality. Hence, for life politics, as the famous slogan has it, "the political is personal." Jean Cohen (1985, 669), among others, argues for a third mark of distinction: the new social movements are "nonfundamentalist," neither revolutionary nor totalizing; if radical at all, their radicalism is "self-limiting." Giddens's (1991) differentiation of life politics from a "politics of emancipation" implies much the same qualification (Giddens 1991, 210).

Should we agree with Cohen and Giddens, we must relegate Ms. Roden and her fellow travelers to the fundamentalist backwaters to which most other social theorists would readily assign them (see Giddens 1994, 100). We also seem to be constrained to regard the Earth First! call to arms as a transitional case at best, an incoherent anomaly at worst. On the side of the non-new social movements, the structural transformations at which it hints could not be more radical. The world it summons is nothing if not a world of emancipation. "Self-realization" is notably not among its prevailing motifs. On the other side, however, it is an expression of activist environmentalism and of an activist environmentalism that allows immediate, if not perfect, comparison to its less radical counterparts. It espouses doctrinal and practical positions that we could in fact treat as especially exemplary of the new social movements. The biocentrism it espouses is every bit as totalizing as the anthropocentric paradigm to which it accuses environmentalists of lower consciousness to be wed and links self and body to a system of (literally) global scope with such unambiguous reflexive immediacy that it could well serve Giddens—couldn't it?—as a textbook case.

The trouble is that Earth First! is not the rare exception that would deviate from an otherwise generally valid typological rule. It shares its anticorporatism and anticapitalism with a good number of the contemporary participants in antiglobalization movements. Its concatenation of nature, the earth, woman, and liberty is of a piece with the practical poetics of such eco-feminists as Riane Eisler (1987) and Dale Gruen (e.g., Gruen and Jamieson 1994). Its political imperatives are familiar if not in substance, then in their fundamentalist or (what I would prefer to call) categorical form to the imperatives, the frequent "nos" and "nevers," of the new peace activists, the antinuclear activists and the antiabortionists, the opponents of cloning and stem-cell research. As the manifestologist appropriately remarks, the doctrines of Earth First! also display a more systematic coherence, due in no small part to the ontological commitments that underpin and inspire them. If they recall Thoreau, this is not simply because they favor civil disobedience. It is also because they are vitalist and because the vitalism they presume is supraempirical, transcendent, and, in its metonymic figuration as natural land or wilderness, explicitly deemed sacred. In this respect as well, such doctrines are less a perversion than simply a version of the transcendentalism that links Ms. Roden to the eco-feminists and the eco-feminists to such odd and embattled bedfellows as former Miss America turned conservative activist Anita Bryant, whose campaign against homosexuals seems to have followed upon the realization that fellation might lead to the consumption of the inviolable seed of the Tree of Life. Lest I seem to be preoccupying myself only with the fringes, I would suggest that Roden and the Earth Firsters in fact stand at the opposite poles of a broad continuum of transcendentalist vitalisms in the United States that have their common roots in the fertile and fiery early third of the nineteenth century, many of them so "self-limiting" in their radicalism as to raise barely an eyebrow. I cannot argue adequately for that suggestion here. I can, however, recall briefly the more ecumenical horror that has greeted the announcement of the first successful experiments in animal cloning and stem-cell engineering, or the great unleashing of a sacred lexicon in the eleven states—not even to mention the other thirty-nine—in which voters considered and consistently rejected recognizing unions between couples of the same sex as "marriages" in the elections of November 2004 (things have since changed, of course—at least for the time being). Beyond the always rather frothy shores of the United States, it is worth noting the extent to which transcendental vitalism—if something of a crypto-Catholic sort— informs the spirituality that Paul Rabinow (1999) has brought to light in even the most official and policy-oriented of the opinions of the bioethical authorities in that great land of enlighteners and atheists, contemporary France.

Quite so many anomalies demand a more accommodating analytical housing than Giddens's life politics can provide. Nor is such housing idiosyncratically Giddens's own. Its designs echo those of the grand tradition of social thought and social theory more generally. With only rare exceptions, the carriers of and contributors to that tradition conform to what, in addressing the apparent improprieties of blending the political and the religious among Branch Davidians dead and living, I have called the principle of the separateness of estates (Faubion 2001). Though rarely, if ever, with one might consider due reflection, they tend toward treating as theoretically axiomatic the division of rights and duties and immunities that defined the separate spheres of clergy, aristocracy, and commerce in France and elsewhere in Europe before the champions of universal human (or rather, adult white male) rights sacrificed them to the flames of one or another revolutionary. The principle makes for odd bedfellows indeed: enlightened assassins of superstition with the later Max Weber, Marxists and many neo-Marxists with early and middle Émile Durkheim, Hannah Arendt with Jürgen Habermas. That conviction in such a principle (or any of its equivalents) should have gone hand in hand in Europe with the resolution of long centuries of strife between popes and kings and, after the Reformation, among an ever-increasing sectarian array of religious confessions is not surprising. That it endures as a presumption of social theory so long past the heyday of the charisma of Enlightenment reason and in the face of so many counterexamples is more than a bit puzzling.

Some of the pieces of that puzzle come at least partially to light in the ever more widely cited theory of the life that is in the contemporary political order that Agamben constructs most systematically in *Homo Sacer: Sovereign Power and Bare Life* (1998). Agamben (1998, 3) acknowledges as his immediate inspiration Michel Foucault's exegesis of "the process by which, at the threshold of the modern era, natural life begins to be included in the mechanisms and calculations of State power, and politics turns into *biopolitics*" (emphasis in original). He would, however, explicitly disagree with any suggestion—which is perhaps Foucault's—that the basic logic of biopolitics itself has no more historical depth than does the dominion of the bourgeoisie. From the middle of the eighteenth century forward, Foucault (1978, 124) discerns in the bourgeois preoccupation with "health, hygiene, descent, and race" a vector of problematization that will lead to the intensification of the policing of the family, the pathologization of every wasted and wasting sexual and hygienic practice, the statistical codification of populations and the statistical oversight of their self-maintenance and self-reproduction, and the proliferation of a vast and complex array of procedures and technologies designed to define, measure, effect, and sustain the normalization of the population as corpus and of the functionally critical mass of its constituent corpora. He discerns a vector of surveillance and regulation that nevertheless falls short and, because of the immense cost it would entail, must fall short of any actual Panopticon, that absolutely perfect apparatus of disciplinary subjection. In much the same phenomena, Agamben sees the unleashing of the paradox of a political exceptionalism that would culminate in the erasure of the distinction between norm and fact and in the reduction of politics to the politics of the concentration camp, in which the absolute sovereign and the absolute subject unveil themselves to each other as the binary couple they actually are. For Agamben, the camp is the nomos of modernity not because modern biopolitics is destined to fulfill itself in an Auschwitz writ grotesquely large, but because its exceptionalism is just as likely to lead to authoritarian and dehumanizing directions as it is to lead in their libertarian and anarchic (and perhaps similarly dehumanizing) opposites.

The logic of the exception, however, has much deeper historical roots than those that stop at "the threshold" of Agamben's "modern era." It is at least as old as *Homo sacer* himself—or so Agamben argues. A man judged in ancient Rome to have violated property boundaries, a son judged to have done violence to his parents, a counsel judged to have swindled his client, *Homo sacer* is the internal outsider, the exile or enemy whose fellow citizens are at exceptional liberty to put him to death without risking punishment for doing so. They must respect only one proscription: they cannot exploit him as a *sacrum*; *Homo sacer* must never be made the offering of a ritual sacrifice (Agamben 1998, 72). Agamben is surely correct in rejecting any construal of this long-debated figure as a "sacred" or "holy" man." He might instead be a "polluted" or "desecrated man." He could thus be as suitable a target of collective vengeance as he would be an unsuitable offering to the gods. The special resonance of his characteristic transgressions—all of which are violations of divinely sanctioned relationships or institutions—and the general semantic range of *sacer* support such a hypothesis. Nothing that we know of ancient Roman society excludes it. Agamben does not venture, however, even to entertain it. He proposes instead that *Homo sacer* carries us back to "an originary *political* structure that is located in a zone prior to the distinction between the sacred and the profane, religious and juridical" (Agamben 1998, 75, emphasis in original). *Homo sacer* is the "originary figure" of what might be thought of as the pure political subject, the figure of man reduced to being a mere living creature over whom "all men act as sovereigns" (84). This figure of bare, of "sacred life" reveals the sphere of the politically sovereign to be a sphere "*in which it permitted to kill without committing homicide and without celebrating a sacrifice*" (83, my emphasis). Similarly, Agamben's figure of the sovereign—an avatar in biopolitical guise of Carl Schmitt's (1985) sovereign, that quintessentially political agent and Hobbesian mortal god whose proper sphere is the sphere of exceptional conditions and whose sovereignty is enacted precisely in the decision to declare such conditions exceptions to the rule of law or the normal order—reveals the sphere of *Homo sacer* to be the sphere in which the distinction between citizen and outcast, a legitimate way of life (the Greek *bios*) and the mere living of life (the Greek *zoē*, at least in some of its pre-Christian usages), inviolability and vulnerability are all continuously in precarious suspense (see Agamben 1998, 83–84). The "modern era" must, for Agamben, thus be an era of the most radical sort of de-differentiation, an era in which the distinction not merely between norm and exception but also between sovereign and subject can no longer be drawn.[1]

To say nothing of his (notably epochal) characterization of modernity, Agamben's characterization of *Homo sacer* is itself much disputed. Yet few, if any, of his critics seem to have noted that it depends above all not merely on an interpretive but also on a logical sleight of hand. Whether or not polluted, *Homo sacer* could not be exploited as a sacrificial victim because this was not the Roman way. That he remained *Homo* was enough to disqualify him. In a thoroughly self-conscious contrast with certain "barbarians," Romans rejected the sacrifice of human beings under any conditions whatever. They constrained themselves exclusively to the sacrifice of domesticated—and ritually purified—animals. In defining *Homo sacer* as the categorical political subject, the precise binary inversion of the categorical sovereign, Agamben is forced to weaken the modality of the proscription under which he stands. The pitiful creature who might be killed with impunity but still not sacrificed becomes the even more pitiful creature whom the sovereign is "permitted to kill without committing homicide and without celebrating a sacrifice" (83). The latter phrasing preserves the absolute and unqualified character of sovereign liberty, but at the cost of what can be read only either as a contravention of the historical facts or (at best?) as a purely theoretical dismissal of them. It logically leaves the sovereign "permitted" to kill *Homo sacer* while also committing sacrifice. A prohibition becomes an option— but *pace* Agamben, a counterfactual exception that was available to a Roman autarch no more than it was available to a Roman slave.

One thus has little reason to accept Agamben's postulation that the "structure" of the "zone" that *Homo sacer* occupies is merely "political." The actual logic of that zone is the logic of liminality and of liminality of a simultaneously political and religious sort. As Agamben himself comes very close to recognizing, *Homo sacer* is politically liminal in his banishment to the neutered and neutral milieu that lies between the *urbs* and its barbarian enemies. But the same figure is simultaneously religiously liminal in his consignment to a status that falls below that of ritual fitness and yet hovers above that of the animal, which is also to say that of *zoē*. Perhaps we preserve a faint echo of his fateful sentence in our occasional pronouncement on the lost or the abject man, who is beyond all human succor and so can only be "in God's hands now," if in anyone's or anything's hands at all. *Homo sacer* is not thus reduced to being nothing more than "bare life" any more than those who might kill him with impunity are accorded the liberty to do with him whatever they might please. He is instead a man alive who can no longer trust his fellow men to sustain him. He is a man who must look to other powers for support. He is in a very precarious position, or she, as the case may be.

From Essences to Singularities

The structure of the zone of *Homo sacer* might in any event permit diagnosis as the structure of the intersection between the human and the divine (or, as some other traditions might have it, the visible and the invisible) arenas of a broader economy of power.[2] Those mere mortals who find themselves at that intersection are certainly structurally distinctive. The question remains whether their distinction is that of the anomaly of an undifferentiated blend of institutional orders—the political and the religious at the very least, though many more are involved—that by all right and reason are things apart. I can envisage only three ways of deciding this question. One is the way of simple fiat—but I think one might aspire to less sovereignty than that. Another is the way—Agamben's, but also that of all his predecessors in the grander reaches of political and social theory—of speculative generalization. That the latter proceeds and must proceed without the benefit of sufficiently determinative evidence goes without saying. As a process of the construction of models or—in a more old-fashioned vocabulary—ideal types, it is not constrained to be empirically accurate. It is likely to encounter and can survive any number of anomalies.

Speculation is, however, also always in danger of insulating itself too far from the force of anomaly in a cloak of putatively analytical but actually normative fabric. In light of our messy present, I think we have right to worry whether Agamben's effort to erase an already-articulate transcendental restriction on the absolute liberty of the political executive from the "originary" expression of the political and (so) to reduce modernity to the camp might belie an ardent secularism modulated (or disguised) by a certain Dostoevskian nostalgia for the very god it would displace. Indeed, Agamben—whether or not nostalgically—is often questing after the potential of a messianic disruption of the camp in which he thinks we nomically live (see Agamben 2003). I think we have right to worry whether that quest might simply be one of the most recent of a long cycle of a putatively analytical but in fact aprioristic resumptions of the principle of the separateness of estates. To put the matter as indelicately as possible (and to ally myself with Talal Asad's [1993, 2003] ruminations on similar subjects), I think we have right to worry whether the principle of the separateness of estates might actually be the normative leitmotif of the story that secularist agnostic moderns have been telling themselves about themselves since at least the eighteenth century under the pretext of distilling the essence at once of modernity and of social evolution as a whole.

I am an agnostic secularist modern, but having rebuked myself as such, I must turn away from speculation and pursue the third alternative to which I have alluded. It is the way not of theory but of diagnosis. Its leading assumption cannot be that the principle of the separateness of estates identifies the essential tendency either of modernization or of social evolution as a whole. It must depart instead from the moment at which the agents of the political and the agents of the religious first encounter themselves as such and proceed to explore the broader topology of what has unfolded as a result. Fortunately, it is a way already well and discerningly taken. Alessandro Pizzorno (1987) has effectively outlined its cartography in an essay appropriately entitled "Politics Unbound," now more than twenty years old. The essay has not earned the readership that it is due. Its analytical provocations might perhaps be lost beneath the distance of its historical focus. I suspect, however, that its untimeliness was until recently more thoroughgoing. In any case, Pizzorno's focus is the long eleventh- and twelfth-century battle over the distribution of the authority to confer and to hold political and church office, whose initial antagonists were Holy Roman Emperor Henry IV and Pope Gregory VII. In the later stages of that battle, the very idea of the separateness of political and clerical estates has its (explicitly normative, Western) advent. Put into practice, it established the pope alone (and no longer the emperor) as entitled to appoint and confirm his bishops. In his new "Gregorian" status, the pope was further entitled to exercise sovereignty over a spiritual community comprising all Christian Europeans—or all Europeans insofar as they were Christians. Most historians recognize the latter privilege as indispensable to the legitimation of all of the several Crusades that would follow on it.

Pizzorno, however, is more interested in the separation of political and clerical estates itself—not least because it did not last and remained unstable for many centuries. He concludes, and can only conclude, that what comes in the West (and so elsewhere) to be thought of as the political domain *as opposed to the religious* is simply one singularity, one determinate moment in the continuous dynamics of the distribution and redistribution of the control of the administration of proximate and ultimate ends (Pizzorno 1987, 44). The moment of the political as it comes to be thought of "as such" is just that moment in which the control of all and only proximate ends falls exclusively into the hands of the administrators of the "temporal" (the relatively short term, temporary, of this world). The moment of the religious as it also comes to be thought of "as such" emerges with all the simultaneity of binary opposition as just that moment at which the control of all and only ultimate ends falls exclusively into the hands of the administrators of the "spiritual" (the relatively long term, the eternal, the holy). What is enduringly at stake is thus the question of how managerial duties can and must be divided within certain of the earthly sectors of the economy of power. The question is ambiguous, not least because ambiguities tend to inhere in the reckoning of proximate and ultimate, temporal and spiritual. The actualization of the binarism, the mutual exclusivity, of the political and the religious domains may, moreover, be as rare in the past as it is at present. Indeed, Pizzorno describes the longer trajectory of their relationship as one of regular mutual encroachment. The opposition between those domains nevertheless remains axiomatic from at least Machiavelli to all of the (more) modern heralds of the principle of the separateness of estates. Hence, the tale that modernity consists as Habermas might put it in divesting politics of all its "metaphysical mortgages" is as familiar (if empirically as false) now as ever it was.

That the opposition in question has remained quite so axiomatic for quite so long and in spite of quite so many indications to the contrary suggests that beyond its secular and agnostic allure it serves crucial macrostructural functions. Perhaps none of the latter is so crucial as that of shielding the inevitably this-worldly ends of a technically rational capitalism from the transcendentalists and spiritualists who might otherwise feel it their right or privilege to censure them (which, of course, they do). In any event, it seems to have shielded the normative logic of a technically rational system from suffering the full force of frequent empirical contravention. The stimuli of those contraventions are quite diverse and different in many respects during the period of the Gregorian reforms from what they appear to be today. In accounting, however, for the former episode of what he calls the "politics of transcendence" (Pizzorno 1987, 46) or "absolute politics" (44), Pizzorno refers to the demographically driven dilution of the ties of kinship, descent, and personal loyalty that were the ground of territorial integrity among the German populations of Europe even well before they were colonized by the Romans.[3]

In this respect at least, the Gregorian episode appears to set a precedent for our own. Giddens (1994, 96) and Beck (1994, 13) accordingly write of the many contemporary processes pressing forward the "disembedding" of social relations. Alain Touraine (1995) points to their postindustrial "delocalization." Half-anticipating Pizzorno, Deleuze and Guattari (1983) write instead of "deterritorialization." All of these terms highlight the dilution of relationships that are finitistic in their scope, particularistic in their substance, and—whether ascribed at birth or established later—normatively permanent in duration. Kinship relations are one modality of such relations. So, too, are relations between the partners of any gift exchange; between friends and lovers and—so much in the news these days—marriage partners; and among the community of the divinely anointed, of the elect. All of these relations have a special affinity with the most intimately personal and ultimate ends. All of them have a critical role in the formation and maintenance of the actor as a social person. If such analysts as Jacob Pandian (1991, 87–88) are correct in emphasizing that anything or anyone that plays such a role is very likely to attract sacred symbols, it is a short step to the conclusion that the party or regime devoted to the protection and preservation of just such things and just such actors could hardly avoid attracting sacred symbols itself.

Yet its politics would not inevitably be a vitalistic politics. The latter sort of politics might draw fuel from any number of specific irritations. It might, for example, do so in resistance to the enclosure not merely of intimate and personal relationships but of life itself within the administrative universe of exclusively proximate ends. It might do so in the face of the possibility of the annihilation of all life in a nuclear holocaust. Though he (or she) is silent on the subject, the Earth First! manifestologist would very likely be opposed to the existence of nuclear weapons. After having a terrifying, nightmarish vision of a nuclear war, Ms. Roden for her part penned a letter to a Waco politician advising him to take and to organize precautionary measures. She received no direct response, but a brief confinement in a nearby psychiatric ward and the loss of the custody of her son were, after further dramas and traumas, in the offing. Such activists find themselves living in an economy of power whose earthly managers are not serving their vital interests. They have a good number of contemporary reasons to be champions of a regime that would free them from such neglect and from the threats that accompany it. Then again, so did anti-Lutheran peasant rebel Thomas Müntzer and so arguably have millenarians and other utopianists and vitalists throughout the centuries. I evoke them not to imply that the vitalistic politics of transcendence that we meet today is just another instance of the return of the suppressed or oppressed or of the past to the present. The similarities of circumstance that link peasants of the sixteenth century to the *paysans* of late capitalism (or whatever one wants to call them, and call it) permit the making of comparisons, but they do not establish continuity of any substantial sort. Nor do they preclude the possibility that what differences there are between the vitalistic politics of transcendence in the sixteenth century and the vitalistic politics of today are anything other than incidental—a matter of exploitative aristocrats back then, a matter of exploitative technocrats now. There is much that is not merely incidental in the shift from aristocrats to technocrats, of course, but the difference between a Müntzer and an Amo Paul Bishop Roden might have much more to do with singularities rather than with systemic business as usual even so. Does it?

Toward a History of the Religious, Vitalist Political Present (and Future)

The answer—which I can only sketch here—looks to be that it has most to do with singularities, which in accord with the prescriptions of the topological rendering of the real implies that it has much to do with the intersection of vectors arising and flowing as a matter of ordinary course in different systems, or at least systems different to some degree. Foucault's overview of the general topology of such intersections is entirely trenchant. Foucault is far more acutely aware than his epigones that what is at issue is not the principle of the separateness of estates. Instead, he traces the clinical and psychoanalytic pastoralism of the biopolitical "anatomo-politics of the human body" in large part to a Christian confessional that he characterizes as being in the seventeenth, eighteenth and nineteenth centuries and as still being "the general standard governing the production of true discourse about sex" (Foucault 1978, 139, 63). Yet in the course of becoming a properly biopolitical technology, reworked in the pedagogy of the eighteenth and the medicine of the nineteenth century, "it gradually lost its ritualistic and exclusive localization; it spread" (63). The confession became secular *as well as* religious and sex a secular *as well as* a religious concern along with it (116). The Reverend Wesley's teachings approach the threshold of the transformation. Beyond that threshold lies a coordinated array of discourses and practices that for the most part "escaped the ecclesiastical institution" if never entirely "the thematics of sin" (116). Their collective tenor is vitalistic, and so bears the mark of an ascendant bourgeoisie that gradually converted "the blue blood of the nobles" into the "sound organism and healthy sexuality" of those best suited to rule (126). The conversion in question has its most purely extraecclesiastic realization as a thoroughgoing medicalization of political and social legitimacy. The concepts, disciplines, and domains of intervention that Foucault includes within the broader Western European universe of biopower suggest that it has no more purely extraecclesiastic realization than in nineteenth-century France. Biopolitically normalizing physicians abound there, as (often in translation) do sexologists and psychoanalysts, from Richard von Krafft-Ebbing to Sigmund Freud and Wilhelm Reich. The church and its clerics are remarkable in Foucault's work for their absence.

Across the Atlantic, however, the technological realization of biopower as a biopolitics takes a different turn. Historically, the beginnings of the entrenchment of biopolitics in Europe and in America have roughly the same impetus—the cholera epidemic of 1832. In the United States, however, the great popularizers of biopolitical technologies at once of the nation and of the self are, with few exceptions, ardent Christians, though sometimes Christians very much of their own cloth. Religious biopolitics in the United States thus belongs to the history (and the anthropology) of the refractions of the modern apparatus of governmentality as it mingles with the voluntarism, sectarianism and pragmatic utopianism of an America that has long interposed between the individual body and the general population its ever fissile array of Protestant congregations.

The combination that results is, moreover, far more sustained and symbiotic in the New World than it is in the Old. Nor should this be unexpected. The United States has never been a land noted for the number and prominence of its enlighteners and atheists. On the contrary, it is a land in which, as Alexis de Tocqueville first noted, religious percepts and religious devotion can so deeply infuse the rest of thought and practice precisely because no single church can claim title to being the church either of the state or of its correlative regime of truth. In the United States, the dominant strands of religious biopolitics might heuristically be condensed into the two poles to which I have already alluded. One is Thoreauvian. To the other I could apply a number of particular names, but Whitean will do, after Ellen Harmon White. White is, however, only one of many prophetic and visionary spiritual adepts of the early and mid-nineteenth century to whose corporal and spiritual exercises substantial congregations were drawn and to whose exercises they continue to be drawn in ever-increasing numbers still today. Not alone but in the variety of their programs they articulate what can summarily be called a transcendental hygienics.

*   *   *

Two final observations are in order. The first is that the division between Thoreauvian vitalism and transcendental hygienics, however liable to mediation and collapse, points to a division of class, or rather of class fractions. It is well known that the majority of the participants in the new social movements have backgrounds that are comfortably middle class. They are in their majority also relatively well educated. They are social actors who are likely to see themselves as entitled and who are objectively capable of exercising an entitlement to a modicum of social power. They are likely to experience their social status as fairly secure even if age and such other variables as the short-term fluctuations of the career market may compel them to adopt programs of austerity (or as we're now speaking of it, "flexibility"). They have opinions. They vote, but their individuality is probably sufficiently cultivated to render them proud and jealous of their independence, at least of their independence of mind. If transcendental vitalists and practitioners of a politics of transcendence, they are likely to be Thoreauvian in their outlook. They are far more likely to be metaphysical or cosmicist New Agers than theological and ecclesiological new denominationalists. The Earth First! manifestologist is nearer to them than he or she is farther away.

If the new denominations are in fact quite diverse in their class composition, their doctrinal and pastoral credos still resonate most loudly with the frustrations and expectations of the members of a middle class less sure than the typical Thoreauvian of the security of either their status or their means and less confident of their individuality as well. If they are largely a petite bourgeoisie, they are in any case still a bourgeoisie; the new denominations do not tend to attract the majority of their numbers from the working class, much less from the underemployed or unemployed poor. Like the elite, the former and the latter are both more loyal to the older denominations. The elite may regard any too immediate or this-worldly promise of salvation as insufficiently sublime, insufficiently distant from necessity; the working classes and the poor appear to regard it as implausible.

My second observation is just this. The Greens are growing and so, too are the Seventh-Day Adventists. Indeed, with its fellow new denominations, the Seventh-Day Adventist Church is one of the most rapidly expanding of Christian churches today and is at the vanguard of a Christianization of the third world that, popular opinion to the contrary notwithstanding, is outpacing any Islamic rival. The contemporary topology of cosmologicopolitics thus looks as if it will remain contemporary for quite a long time to come. Neoliberalism does not wholly govern the world picture.

Notes

1. With what they would like to think of as the virtual substrate of as yet imperfectly realized but spectral tendencies, Michael Hardt and Antonio Negri (2000, 189, 217) conceive of our modern (or, in their eyes, somewhat beyond modern) present as the present of a biopolitical empire that thrives even as it seems to be crumbling on the effectuation and reproduction of "omni-crisis." The actual is for all of these worthy contributors to the grand and dangerous tradition of political theory at most a fragmented, a stuttering and a confused *eidōlon* of the real. There is no use here in the fieldworker protesting that his people aren't like that. Our theorists have no invested reason to listen.

2. Because I am pursuing a strictly diagnostic and strictly nominalistic mode of analysis in this chapter, I only allude here to the more speculative interpretation of the economy of power that I have previously ventured. I bother to allude to it, however, because it considerably and, I think, legitimately enlarges the context and the rationale of the vitalism that both Roden and the Earth First! manifestologist embrace. In brief, the economy in question is marked by a double duality, not just in this case but in every case: between powers human and suprahuman, between powers mundane and powers transcendent. It is everywhere an economy of continuous production and redistribution and consumption, an economy in which power has every appearance of being the telos of a considerable variety of exchanges—some strategic, as Clausewitz (1832) would have it, but others communicative and so at least partially semiological, still others of the promissory logic of the gift. Whether in its human or in its other-than-human arenas, this economy manifests yet another dualism, a bifurcation of positive and negative forces and agencies that very frequently attract if not the same, then at least very similar, terminologies. Hence, in its transcendent and positive valence, power might pass as "grace" or "sanctity"; in its negative valence, it might pass as "pollution" or "evil." In the

former valence, it is with remarkable consistency conceived as fertile and fecundating; in the latter valence, it is conceived with similar consistency as enervating and destructive. The transcendental arena of the economy of power is, in other words, ubiquitously a vitalistic arena and remains evincingly vitalistic throughout almost the entire gamut of its contextual variations. The rationale for such metaphysical stability is, moreover, the object of a distinguished tradition of analysis and philosopher José Gil's *Metaphors of the Body* (1998) simply its latest analytical installment. Gil is himself at least partially aware that his own treatise has numerous anthropological precedents. I would particularly underscore the precedent of Mary Douglas's *Natural Symbols* (1973), of Pierre Bourdieu's *Outline of a Theory of Practice* (1977), and of Claude Lévi-Strauss's *Mythologiques* (1969, 1973, 1978, 1981). Their many mutual incompatibilities aside, all these contributions to what I am happy to call our anthropological wisdom are in accord in their recognition that the human body—a sensuous and sensible body, a textural and rhythmic body, by no means least a living and dying body—is the most immediate and most ubiquitous matrix of our imagination of the cosmos itself.

3. The question is worth raising whether the phenomenon that Pizzorno analyzes here might just as appropriately be called "political religion" or "politicized religion." It seems to me that it could be, but I follow Pizzorno's usage throughout.

References

Abbey, Edward. 1968. *Desert Solitaire: A Season in the Wilderness*. New York: McGraw-Hill.

———. *The Monkey Wrench Gang*. Philadelphia: Lippincott Williams & Wilkins.

Abrams, M. H. 1971. *Natural Supernaturalism: Tradition and Revolution in Romantic Literature*. New York: Norton.

Agamben, Giorgio. 1998. *Homo Sacer: Sovereignty and Bare Life*. Trans. Daniel Heller-Roazen. Stanford, CA: Stanford University Press.

———. 2003. *Potentialities: Collected Essays in Philosophy*. Trans. Daniel Heller-Roazen. Stanford, CA: Stanford University Press.

Asad, Talal. 1993. *Genealogies of Religion: Discipline and Reasons of Power in Christianity*. Baltimore: Johns Hopkins University Press.

———. 2003. *Formations of the Secular: Christianity, Islam, Modernity*. Stanford, CA: Stanford University Press.

Beck, Ulrich. 1994. "The Reinvention of Politics: Towards a Theory of Reflexive Modernization." In *Reflexive Modernization: Politics, Tradition and Aesthetics in the Modern Social Order*, by Ulrich Beck, Anthony Giddens, and Scott Lash, 1–55. Stanford, CA: Stanford University Press.

Bourdieu, Pierre. 1977. *Outline of a Theory of Practice*. Trans. Richard Nice. Cambridge: Cambridge University Press.

Clausewitz, Carl von. 1832. *Vom Kriege*. Berlin: Dümmlers Verlag.

Cohen, Jean. 1985. "Strategy or Identity: New Theoretical Paradigms and Contemporary Social Movements." *Social Research* 52 (4): 663–716.

Deleuze, Gilles, and Félix Guattari. 1983. *Capitalism and Schizophrenia*. Vol. 1, *Anti-Oedipus*. Trans. Robert Hurley, Mark Seem, and Helen R. Lane. Minneapolis: University of Minnesota Press.

Devall, Bill. 1986. "Interview with Dave Foreman." *Simply Living* 2 (12): 40–43.

Devall, Bill, and George Sessions. 2001. *Deep Ecology: Living as If Nature Mattered*. Layton, UT: George Gibbs.

Douglas, Mary. 1973. *Natural Symbols: Explorations in Cosmology*. New York: Vintage Books.

Earth First! N.d. "About Earth First!" http://earthfirst.org/about.htm.

Earth First! 2016. https://en.wikipedia.org/wiki/Earth_First!.

Eisler, Riane. 1987. *The Chalice and the Blade: Our History, Our Future*. San Francisco: Harper and Row Publishers.

Esposito, Roberto. 2008. *Bíos: Biopolitics and Philosophy*. Trans. Timothy C. Campbell. Minneapolis: University of Minnesota Press.

Fabian, Johannes. 1983. *Time and The Other: How Anthropology Makes Its Object*. New York: Columbia University Press.

Faubion, James D. 2001. *The Shadows and Lights of Waco: Millennialism Today*. Princeton, NJ: Princeton University Press.

———. 2011. *An Anthropology of Ethics*. Cambridge: Cambridge University Press.

Foucault, Michel. 1978. *The History of Sexuality: An Introduction*. Trans. Robert Hurley. New York: Pantheon.

———. 2000. "Useless to Revolt?" In *Essential Works of Michel Foucault*. Vol. 3, *Power*, translated by Robert Hurley et al., edited by James D. Faubion, 49–53. New York: New Press.

———. 2003. *Society Must Be Defended: Lectures at the Collège de France, 1975–1976*. Translated by David Macey. New York: Picador.

Giddens, Anthony. 1991. *Modernity and Self-Identity: Self and Society in the Late Modern Age*. Cambridge, UK: Polity Press.

———. 1994. "Living in a Post-Traditional Society." In *Reflexive Modernization: Politics, Tradition and Aesthetics in the Modern Social Order*, by Ulrich Beck, Anthony Giddens, and Scott Lash, 56–109. Stanford, CA: Stanford University Press.

Gil, José. 1998. *Metamorphoses of the Body*. Trans. Stephen Muecke. Minneapolis: University of Minnesota Press.

Gruen, Dale, and Lori Jamieson, eds. 1994. *Reflecting on Nature: Readings in Environmental Philosophy*. New York: Oxford University Press.

Hardt, Michael, and Antonio Negri. 2000. *Empire*. Cambridge, MA: Harvard University Press.

Langman, Loren. 2013. "Occupy: A New New Social Movement." *Current Sociology* 61 (4): 510–524.

Lévi-Strauss, Claude. 1969. *Introduction to a Science of Mythology*. Vol. 1, *The Raw and the Cooked*. Trans. John Weightman and Doreen Weightman. New York: Harper Torchbooks.

———. 1973. *Introduction to a Science of Mythology*. Vol. 2, *From Honey to Ashes*. Trans. John Weightman and Doreen Weightman. New York: Harper Torchbooks.

———. 1978. *Introduction to a Science of Mythology*. Vol. 3, *The Origin of Table Manners*. Trans. John Weightman and Doreen Weightman. New York: Harper Torchbooks.

———. 1981. *Introduction to a Science of Mythology*. Vol. 4, *The Naked Man*. Trans. John Weightman and Doreen Weightman. New York: Harper Torchbooks.

McMurtry, Larry. 1975. "Fertile Fiction for the American Desert." *Washington Post*, September 8, C8.

Miss Ann Thropy. 1987."Population and AIDS." *Off-Road*. http://www.off-road.com/trails-events/voice/population-and-aids-miss-ann-thropy-earth-first-1987-16372.html.

Naess, Arne. 1973. "The Shallow and the Deep: Long-Range Ecology Movement." *Inquiry* 16: 95–100.

Nissenbaum, Stephen. 1980. *Sex, Diet, and Debility in Jacksonian America: Sylvester Graham and Health Reform*. Westport, CT: Greenwood Press.

Numbers, Ronald. 2008. *Prophetess of Health: A Study of Ellen G. White*. 3rd ed. Grand Rapids, MI: Eerdmanns.

Pandian, Jacob. 1991. *Culture, Religion, and the Sacred Self: A Critical Introduction to the Anthropological Study of Religion*. Englewood Cliffs, NJ: Prentice Hall.

Pizzorno, Alessandro. 1987. "Politics Unbound." In *Changing Boundaries of the Political*, edited by Charles S. Maier, 27–62. New York: Cambridge University Press.

Rabinow, Paul. 1999. *French DNA: Trouble in Purgatory*. Chicago: University of Chicago Press.

Rose, Nikolas. *The Politics of Life Itself: Biomedicine, Power and Subjectivity in the Twenty-First Century*. Princeton, NJ: Princeton University Press.

Scheper-Hughes, Nancy, and Margaret M. Lock. "The Mindful Body: A Prolegomenon to Future Work in Medical Anthropology." *Medical Anthropology Quarterly* 1 (1): 6–41.

Schmitt, Carl. 1985. *Political Theology: Four Chapters on the Concept of Sovereignty*. 1922. Trans. George Schwab. Cambridge, MA: MIT Press.

Smith, Rebecca K. 2008. "'Ecoterrorism'? A Critical Analysis of the Vilification of Radical Environmental Activists as Terrorists." *Earth First! Journal*. http://www.earthfirstjournal .org%2Fsection.php%3Fid%3D11:+1.

Sokolow, Jayme. 1983. *Eros and Modernization: Sylvester Graham, Health Reform, and the Origins of Victorian Sexuality in America*. London: Associated University Press.

Tabor, James, and Eugene Gallagher. 1995. *Why Waco? Cults and the Battle for Religious Freedom in America*. Berkeley: University of California Press.

Touraine, Alain. 1995. "Post-Industrial Classes." Translated by L. F. X. Mayhew. In *Rethinking the Subject: An Anthology of European Social Thought*, edited by James D. Faubion, 181–192. Boulder, CO: Rowman & Littlefield.

Weber, Max. 1946. "Religious Rejections of the World and Their Directions." In *From Max Weber: Essays in Sociology*, edited by Hans Gerth and C. Wright Mills, 323–359. New York: Oxford University Press.

Worster, Donald. 2008. *A Passion for Nature: The Life of John Muir*. New York: Oxford University Press.

5   Surreal Capitalism and the Dialectical Economies of Precarity

Neni Panourgiá

Friday, May 23, 2014

8:25 p.m.

We arrive at the Athens airport. My nephew can't pick us up because he is work-ing until late. We take two taxis to bring us home. On the way the driver is quiet, barely responds when I apologize for having taken him out to the countryside at night, but at least, I tell him, he will be rewarded as we will drive by the seaside. "After five hours at the airport seeing the sea is a real reward" is his response. I ask him if he really waited for five hours to pick up a ride. Yes, he did. He can't leave the airport without a ride, he tells me, because the cost of gas and tolls will eat up the day's earnings.

10:13 p.m.

My nephew has returned from work and the two of us go out to buy gyro sand-wiches. We buy three, along with three small shish kebabs. We pay thirteen euros; the extra pita is on the house. On the way there my nephew tells me that he picks up day employment—today installing awnings, other times installing aluminum doors and frames. He works eight to ten hours at the awnings, ten to twelve hours at the aluminum job. He makes twenty-five euros and thirty euros respectively, and pays twelve euros for gas. His girlfriend works close to the house at a café, eight- to ten-hour shifts, makes twenty-five euros a day but doesn't get paid if the café has no customers. On Tuesday she will be at commencement for her master's at the University of Athens in history and philosophy of science. My nephew has forgotten by now that he is a university graduate, too.

Saturday, May 24, 2014

8:30 a.m.

We take our car to the shop and the talk with the mechanic revolves around next day's Euro- and (run-off) municipal and local administrative elections. The neighborhood where the shop is, one that used to be full of car shops and garages, shows the effects of the crisis—most of them have closed and sit empty. A lowbrow restaurant that was sitting across from the garage is being refurbished: the owner burned it in order to collect the insurance money, we learn from the mechanic, and now a contractor and his team are busy painting it and replacing doors and windows. The mechanic points at them: "not one Greek worker," he says; "the contractor is Albanian and the workers from 'up there' [which can mean anything from Albania to Russia and the Ukraine]." Keeping in mind the daily wages that I have heard about last night, we all wonder why there are no Greeks working there. The mechanic offers no explanation but tells us about his two sons—the eldest (a university graduate with graduate studies in the United Kingdom) works at a bank on eight-month contracts on a salary that has been slashed five times in four years, making 920 euros a month; the youngest one is the regional manager for one of the European multinational retail companies—he works twelve-hour days and his salary has been dropped to 780 euros per month.

9:30 a.m.

While we wait for the car to be fixed, we make our way downtown. Jet lag hits and we need to have some breakfast. We sit at one of the new cafés that have opened in the periphery of Syntagma Square [see http://www.culanth.org/?q=node/432]. Two glasses of fresh orange juice and two filtered coffees come to 19.90 euros. It stings badly. Athens is almost empty because of the elections. I go to my favorite bookstore to buy books for my nephew and his girlfriend—books are on sale, and I buy a novel for 7.50 euros, Auguste Corteau's The Book of Katerina. I go to the hairdresser's—one of the oldest in Athens—where everyone is worried whether they will have a job come Monday, or in a week's time, or next month. I order a ham sandwich with mustard; I pay 2.30 euros.

4:30 p.m.

On the way back home, I stand on the platform waiting for the Metro to come. I am approached by a tall, lithe, well-dressed African man who asks me if this is the right Metro to the airport. I tell him that it is. At the transfer station we exit together. We've just missed the transfer train, we wonder when the next train will come, and he asks me if I am Greek. He starts telling me that he is in Greece because his brother was on the boat that capsized on May 6 [2014] carrying seventy immigrants mainly from Somalia, Eritrea, and Syria [see http://www.abc.net.au/news/2014 -05-06/migrants-drown-after-boats-capsize-off-greek-island/5432498]. His brother hasn't been located yet. He tells me that he works for a migrant organization in Malmö, Sweden, and asks me why Greeks are so glum and unfriendly. I try to talk to him about the Crisis, the sudden loss of everything, especially the sudden *loss of any prospect for the future, in addition to the loss of imminent livelihood. I catch myself realizing that I am talking to a Somali, and I say so. He tells me that precisely because he is a Somali he can tell me that Greeks should be more cheerful, that things will look up eventually. As time passes he decides that this crisis is a different thing from the one he knows from Somalia. "How so?" I ask. "Our crisis is long term, endemic, systemic," he says, "and we continue to smile through it."*

Sunday, May 25, 2014

5:00 p.m.

I am meeting an old friend for coffee at the Athens Hilton. We both decide to have fresh orange juice instead of more caffeine. My other nephew joins us toward the end. He is famished. He asks for a ham-and-cheese sandwich. It arrives, a large plate that includes a sandwich of immense proportions, salad, and fresh French fries. Our two juices cost 19.00 euros with tip. Exactly as much as his sandwich. I remember Willie Snow Ethridge complaining in 1947 that oranges were "ubiquitous" in Greece, and I am wondering what could cause a freshly squeezed orange juice in Athens to cost as much as a small meal.

6:30 p.m.

I go to the polling place to vote. Cutoff time is 7:00 p.m. There is a line and my nephew and I wait on it. The place is very familiar to me; it's my old high school. I map the place out for him: this is where I trained for gymnastics, I am voting in my old classroom (first grade of gymnasium), the big sheets of metal that block the view from and to the outside were installed in 1971 at the behest of my mother, who taught at the school, so that we, a girls' school, wouldn't flirt with the boys from the boys' school. As I am voting I hear the legal representative of the Supreme Court call out, "Please be quick, there are other people waiting to vote." I walk out from the voting booth, and I remind her that this is highly irregular, indeed illegal, because it can be taken as voter intimidation. We go back and forth for a few minutes until I go in again to vote on the municipal elections. As I am voting something hits me on the head. I turn to see that someone has crumpled up all the ballots that he didn't use and has tossed them straight on to my head. I exit the booth just on time to see him walk away.

Monday, May 26, 2014

2:30 a.m.

It is plainly clear by now that the Coalition of Leftist Forces, SYRIZA, has won the Euro vote with 26.7 percent of the vote. In sum, the antiausterity, anti-Troika, parliamentarian parties have won eleven of the twenty-one European Parliament seats. Adding the three seats won by the neo-Nazis, the anti-Troika antiausterity forces have won overwhelmingly. The government coalition of the right (New Democracy) and the center-socialists (PASOK, which has entered the race as Elia) have scraped together seven seats. The government spokesman tries to spin the unspinnable, but the truth remains that whether from the left or from the criminal extreme right, voters have positioned themselves squarely against the discourses of debt and the pragmatics of austerity.

* * *

There is a long-standing commitment that anthropology has to an ideal form of its subject. While the subject itself, ontologically, is never the same (in the sense that even the iconic "Nuer" are ontologically boundless), it is always an already-fixed epistemological object, an exercise in the dialectical dance of otherness initiated and effectuated by the anthropologist. Here and now I want to explore the process as I push the boundaries of production of anthropological knowledge in cases where the distance between the anthropologist and that epistemological subject is minimized as it, simultaneously, challenges the proxemics of that distance. I argue that this tension—not inevitably inherent in that relationship—is particularly salient and becomes apparent when viewed through the challenges presented in the case where research takes place under conditions of crisis, such as the recent political, social, and economic meltdown in Greece.

The specificity of these circumstances produces a constellation of methodological and epistemological queries: it depends on multi-sited research through various media, locations, discourses, and epistemic structures as it demands the ethnographic richness that can be attained only through long-term, in-depth engagement with the object of study.[1] It treads on dangerous and unsafe grounds as its object—"the crisis"—has an embodied materiality that is witnessed on the bodies of the citizens, while it is being wished away as soon as possible. What knowledges become possible under circumstances of crisis, especially a crisis that is itself the object of objections and suspicion as to what exactly constitutes it and what exactly it comprises? Analytically, experientially, structurally "the Crisis" is a different thing to the anthropologists than it is to political scientists, than it is to people on the ground, than what it is to the Troika and the Greek politicians.[2] The concept of the crisis might not help us analyze it, but it can certainly help us (with Jacques Rancière and Maria Kakogianni [2013]), to consider and change the way we think about *thinking*, provided (I would add) that we keep in mind Étienne Balibar's (2013) cautionary thought that we go about it dialectically (that is, thinking about the processes) and not metaphysically—and probably not against the grain of Janet Roitman's (2013, 9) crisis "as a transcendental placeholder because it is a means for signifying contingency." Can this contingency, I wonder, be shown if the crisis "on the ground" is shown?

Carolyn Nordstrom (2009, 36) has posited the following question: "Does a crisis . . . extend across the borders of sovereignty and temporality to flow into the personal lives, economic markets, and political systems?" I don't think that the answer to that question could be anything other than affirmative, but I am puzzled as to how this question could be articulated in the first place. What is there in the writing of crisis that has allowed such a discursive opening, or has even made it possible? But I think that there is a way in which the spirit of Nordstrom's question can be salvaged, which is not to ask whether a crisis spills out of the centers and structures of power that have created it, but rather to interrogate the ways the precarities that flow out of such crises can be written about. From the outside, "objectively," so to speak? From the within, offering perspectives that are otherwise inaccessible? Or from a third position still to be devised and defined? And what are the political and theoretical implications of such positionalities? The "outside" has been written, from the humanitarian point of view, from the economic, certainly from the political. But how does one give an account of one's own precarity without losing sight of the site of critique and responsibility? What sorts of formulations are available, cultural and political contingents that can speak the unspeakable and name the unnamable? And what does this precarity look like on the ground? What is the phenomenology of such an existence? The unrest of global youth since 2011 has ebbed and flowed and has been accused of having no direction, no leadership, no objectives, no plan, no structure. But is that really so? Or is it that the new global youth has actually found a way to both give an account of itself and demand accountability by means that are resolutely new and untried? If destruction and de-struction are the only identifiable positions today, what can they tell us about the position of the youth as the epicenter of precarity?

As a result of this precarity, new discourses of mourning and loss have appeared in Greece among the young who participate in these new formulations of being, as they are attempting to carve out a sense and an articulation of self out of the cinders of global capital, as the wake and the refuse of phatic accountabilities performed from the vacated spaces of real responsibilities.

But before we start looking at the crisis, we need to keep in mind the original meaning of the word in Greek: *crisis* and *critique*. And we also need to remember what Marx told us about the value of critique and crisis: that no critique can claim its name unless it is primarily and fundamentally *self-critique*. Therefore, if crisis and critique, as object and subject of the same political positionality and engagement, constitute and are constituted by a particular historical conjunction, can they also participate in the process of knowledge production? Roitman (2013, 49) stipulates that "crisis, in itself, cannot be located or observed as an object of first-order knowledge," even though "it is a term that permits one to think the 'otherwise,'" and she further complicates this stipulation by arguing that crisis cannot be looked at as an analytical concept that owes its articulation to formal structures of knowledge and routes of its dissemination (hence, the academy, the press, the political class) as if they were effectively separated from the experiential narratives that surround it. Hence, the analysts are not necessarily outside the circle of its immanence.

So, the haptic question is this: how do we write about this crisis as analysts when the unsafety of the ethnographic ground bleeds into and contaminates the safety of our text? How can we produce a safe text, one that can be read with a certain degree of certainty, that can produce an intelligible and legible narrative, that can create some of the comfort that is expected from the act of reading? And I won't even pose the question (as a student of mine did) of the possibility of creating a "timeless" (as she put it) text, a work that will be timeless because it will be telling the truth?

I had thought about writing something marginally funny or even (by today's standards) almost of minor significance—for instance, that at the beginning of the crisis in Greece, in the summer of 2011, while having dinner with American friends at a restaurant in the old part of Athens my bag was stolen. It would have been funny (I, an Athenian, was robbed in the heart of my city) if it was not traumatic—my bag contained items that belonged to my recently deceased parents: my father's wallet and cigarette holder and my mother's silver key chain, given to her by her father when she got her first job. A traumatic event that verged almost on being funny, especially when a month later our summer house was burglarized (the second of six burglaries over the course of five years).

Or I thought to relate something that had seemed really funny at the time: one week before that burglary a group of Romanian burglars had broken into a number of Albanian households in the area, and in one of those cases, the Albanian tenant took whiff of the burglar and yelled at him in Greek, while in another instance the family dog had grabbed the burglar by the foot as he was entering the house from the half-open window and had taken his flip-flop away. I thought at the time, "Burglars go to work wearing flip-flops?"

But hard as I try, it is impossible for me to find one instance that can bring some mirth to this situation that is called the Greek Crisis. Analyses are inadequate. Taking a position on this or the other side appear to be propelled by an internal need of the speaker to speak but without the ability for anyone to conceptualize or articulate the immense complex that has brought the country to this catastrophe. Every morning I wake up in agony for the future of the youth and deeply grateful that our elders—parents, grandparents, ascending and lateral kin—died before this unraveling.

In the past, before its entry to the then European Economic Community (EEC), Greece had a respectable level of manufacturing and production—nothing too grand, but of appropriate size. In 1980, upon entering the EEC, the country was self-sufficient in sugar production. Its tourism was manageable, as was its consumerism—meaning that there was a point at which one would not see three Porsche Cayennes parked at the main thoroughfare of a small, seaside vacation village. Schools were giving us an education that we could use, even in the haphazard and unsystematic way that they did, and they were handing us books for free from the previous years that we couldn't destroy when we were finished with them. Christmas shopping and the Saturday-night outing stood their ground because they did not happen every day. All this, though, when it happens can be the result only of a society that understands the dialectic between obligation and right—the right to a pleasant, if not always easy, quotidian life and the obligation to the social whole and the upcoming generations.

Every single stone that my father set upon another he did "for the girls" (for us, his daughters). The thought never crossed his mind to sell anything off in order to invest the money in hedge funds, or take a vacation, or buy a new car. He never oiled any part of the state machinery to expedite anything, to acquire something that was not legal, to find jobs for his children. And a few other million fathers and mothers did the same. But in these times of a global economy that cares only for its capital and has commodified human beings, such actions and such parents were not enough, and that's where we hit a snag.

And let's just say that the country starts anew, declares bankruptcy officially, and we start with new processual principles, new structures that index both interpersonal relations and the relationship of the citizen to the state; let's just say that something like this is possible despite everything that anthropology and sociology and political science have told us all along, that it is impossible. Let's play along and say that all this can be done: Grexit, bankruptcy, debt write-off: stopping the obliteration of the future generations, stopping the suicides of senior citizens who cannot feed themselves or take care of their spouses or their grown children, stopping the neo-Nazis of Golden Dawn. Will all those other millions of tax evaders whose evasion made them millions upon millions of euros start paying taxes?[3] Will those who have built illegally in burned forests, paying the requisite baksheesh (kickbacks and bribes) to police and building inspectors and civil engineers and urban planners—all of whom have accepted, if not demanded, it—will they accept the demolition of their illegal buildings for the good of the country? The corrupt politicians who ever since the restoration of democracy in 1974 (and a half-ass democracy at that) caressed and encouraged and goaded soccer as the speech of the national psyche exactly the way that the junta had done prior to them, so that they allowed hooliganism to spill out of all bounds and to contaminate all political demonstrations and dissent so that slogans such as "Burn, that whore the parliament" and "Prime minister, son of a whore" could appear as legitimate political language—all these politicians who have spent their political lives making money and turning citizens into compliant and complicit snitches instead of active citizens—will they put the gun in their mouth?

It would be easy to dismiss—or to critique—this position as nostalgic for a past that was never as it is remembered. But such a dismissal would miss the point of critique itself, namely that what is being described is not a golden past but, rather, the critical stance of the citizen toward affluence and its structures. What is being described is a self-discipline that did not foretell the absolute abandon of the latter years. And it is also a description of a different positionality toward poverty—in fact, a different conceptualization of poverty. And as Thomas Piketty (2013) has argued (and convincingly shown), the poverty of today is a different thing from the poverty of the early years of the twentieth century. But more important, this is a description of a capitalism tempered by the labor and social movements that produced the social welfare system of Europe, prior to the legitimation of greed and the culture wars of Ronald Reagan and Margaret Thatcher. In 2010 and 2011 the narrative that the government and the Troika had introduced to the public discourse was one of neoliberal absolutism: the crisis was the fault of a profligate citizenry that had brought the country to the point of being unable to meet its obligations and asked the citizens to own their responsibility, all draped in the language of the accountability of the self. But by 2012 the crisis had acquired its correct dimensions and its place in the catastrophic global financial system, and the new narratives that started being produced by citizens themselves, narratives that involved both a new engagement with politics and the development of solidarity networks (see Rakopoulos 2014), prefigured the different forms of resistance that appeared to the hegemonic narratives of the Troika and its local representatives.

Crisis

Reinhart Koselleck (1988, 161) has afforded to the concept of crisis a "diagnostic and predictive meaning," a meaning that allows crisis to become "the indicator of a new awareness," an awareness that came to philosophers of history who could correctly see "the turning point" when it happens in the circularity of history, something that, Koselleck argues, eludes the philosophers of the state who believed in progress and, hence, could not recognize crisis as such. But what progress can be born of a crisis that is experientially split between the state and the citizens, where the two are positioned at the diametrically opposite ends of its event? Or, as Roitman (2013, 10) correctly echoes this question: "How can one *know* crisis in history? And how can one *know* crisis itself?" Where can any sense of stability be located in the spectrum that constitutes this experience? And how to write about it?

There Is No End to Mourning Here

For the first time in my life I find myself unable to say anything that would be of any help to anyone, anything that would be able to elucidate anything, that would extend a hand of recognition, understanding, even a partial explanation. Analysis fails me daily, or I fail analysis. "There is no end to mourning in Athens" my nephew's girlfriend wrote to me in 2011, as Athens was burning once again by yet another demonstration turned violent by the soccer hooligans who coincide with the politics hooligans who coincide with the neo-Nazis, who manage to disorient a youth that is politically innocent—no, not just innocent but also ignorant, easily manipulated, a youth that is handed an expedient way to scream its desperation without being given a means to organize its anger—and that is precisely what one of these demonstrators asked for: a way to organize his anger. Stones get picked up and thrown at "powers that be"—whatever they be: the police, the special forces, politicians; the marble steps of Constitution Square and the surrounding luxury hotels are broken into pieces, dislodged, and hurdled. The graffiti on them in 2011, the summer of the Indignados movements throughout Europe, read sternly: "no more luxuries" (τέρμα στα λούσα).[4] In 2014 graffiti, in gallows humor, read: "We are the last generation that saw the radiators working." Education and employment—the motors that integrate youth into society—have been dismantled, thus evacuating the social space of any signification. How can this desperation, this anger be organized? Who will organize it? Who will narrate it when it stubbornly resists any narration? "Cultural silence," Renato Rosaldo has offered in his reading of Le Roy Ladurie's *Montaillou* (1985). Cultural silence—when the women of Montaillou refused to say anything to the interrogators, nothing that would be of any use to the inquisitor, Fournier. This is where we are then? At the point where nothing can be said anymore, nothing can be articulated, there is nothing that could drown out the lies that are being told, give a hand to the desperation, offer even a patched-up logos, a patched-up way of seeing?

Therefore, right now, in this crisis that is not "becoming," is not "progressive," a crisis that came from the specificity of hypervalue and hypercommodification of the crudest capitalism that we have seen since the days of Manchester at the beginning of the Industrial Revolution, in this crisis that does not take us anywhere, that does not carry us out of anything into anything, in this crisis that has replaced "the most remotely occluded and transparently mediating figure" that Gayatri Spivak (1985) identified as "woman," now that this "woman" figure has become the migrant, the refugee, the student, the pensioner, the university graduate, the daily worker, the precariat?

Who is now the "woman" of whom Spivak writes as remotely occluded and transparently mediating? The 65 percent of unemployed youth in 2014 (53 percent in November 2012)? The 29.5 percent of the unemployed in the general population? Maybe those who commit suicide: in 2010 there was a 40 percent hike in the rate of suicides over all previously recorded years in the history of the country. In 2011 there was a 40 percent hike over that of 2010. In the first four months of 2012 the rates rose by more than 33 percent against the same period for 2011, with some seven hundred people taking their lives within those four months (Economou et al. 2011; Karanikolos et al. 2011; Branas et al. 2015).[5] Before the financial crisis began, Greece's suicide rate was only 2.8 per hundred thousand inhabitants, according to the European Union's statistics agency Eurostat (quoted in Branas et al. 2015), while in 2014 the German news magazine *Der Spiegel* wrote, "Most of the suicides were among members of the middle class and, in many cases, the act itself was carried out in public, almost as if it were a theatrical performance."[6]

But, one could argue, is not the face of this crude capitalism precisely its recurrent face each time that it appears at the new locations where the capitalist forms of production are becoming entrenched, now in Manchester, then in Detroit, then in Shanghai, now in Brasília? Isn't that what Marx meant, that new forms of labor and production relations rise up where capitalism deconstructs and destroys the already-existing ones, provided that this is indeed Koselleck's intended conceptualization of crisis, as the inevitable, teleological end product of the modernization of industrial capitalism.

Here, though, we are not faced with a crisis of a productive industrial capital, but rather with a crisis of an inherently nonproductive one; we are not at the beginning of capitalism (at Manchester, at Detroit, at Chicago) but at what Marx saw as its end (even if whether he did so rightly or wrongly is debatable). We are at the point where capitalism has become a simulacrum of itself, as if looking itself in the mirror gesticulating with the opposite hand, a surrealist capitalism. Therefore, we find ourselves at this point fighting again for rights and privileges that need to be restated as self-evident—the basics: education, pensions, health care, the right to assembly, and the right to strike.

Old industrial capitalism took it for granted that its products would be produced and consumed ad infinitum. That cars, railroads, pins, and pens would be constantly in production and on demand. That industrial capital would expand its reach. That a global economy would safeguard such production through the creation of ever-expanding and demanding markets. But all of us—namely industrial capitalism and its attendant labor alongside us, the consuming public—received a crash course in reality. And this is a market reality that bespeaks the biopower exercised by the sovereignty of politics and economics.

The biopower that is being exercised by the European Union, the International Monetary Fund (IMF), and the World Bank proceeds from the molar to the molecular in ways that become visible only when we consider Joan Scott's (1991) "evidence of the experience," on the micro-level of what is on the surface invisible (i.e., poverty doesn't "show" yet, either in the upper or in the lower so-cioeconomic strata). In the small village where we spend our summers there is a family that has always been of limited means—the father was a tailor, the mother a greengrocer. When the children grew up, the son acquired a job as a municipal employee, collecting the garbage, servicing the equipment for the water treat-ment plant, and being the occasional handyman for the vacation homes in the area. The daughter married twelve miles away to a bank teller and, as she spoke English and French, worked as a concierge in a hotel in Delphi. The father died many years ago, and the mother had already closed the greengrocery and was living on her husband's pension, with some support from her unmarried son. They were always pulled together, their clothes clean and well made, even if not fancy or extraordinary; food was always at their table, plentiful but not wasted; the daughter's kids had extra tutoring in English and in French; and the mother chipped in to augment her own mother's meager pension.

When the crisis struck and the bottom fell out of everything and public-sector salaries and pensions were slashed, and slashed again, and then again, and once more—four times in total in the course of eighteen months—the mother's pension was brought down to 400 euros a month, the son's salary was cut from 1,400 euros a month to 1,200, then to 800, then to 600, and the daughter lost her job and her husband lost all his bonuses. This extended family of four adults and two children, one of whom away at college, subsists on less than US$2,400 a month, $400 per person, without help from anywhere. But this is a poverty that doesn't show on the outside. The family—precisely because of the social struc-tures that have made Greece, Greece—owns their homes. They own a plot of land with a small olive grove from which they source their olive oil. The son goes hunting for boar and migratory birds, and the mother has entered into the barter economy that sprung up the moment that the IMF walked in—just as in Argen-tina and other places before that. She collects the oranges and lemons from the trees in our garden and exchanges them for fish or a chicken or flour. She expertly mends the family's clothes, meticulously shines their shoes, and puts less, much less, food on the table.

Or consider the food kitchen at Kolonaki, the very affluent neighborhood of Athens, where apartments are being valued (but not sold) in the millions of euros, where a year's rent for the stores also used to go in the millions before the crisis, but where now stores one after the other remain empty. Elderly women and men who have lived in the area for a few generations, very well dressed, in their old but well-kept cashmere and lambswool sweaters, in their hats and watch chains, line up for food at the soup kitchens. Or they go secretly into the night to rummage the rubbish in search of discarded food. Outside of that line, seen in the streets of Athens, they would never cause anyone to think that the crisis has touched them.

Let Me Tell You about a Drilled Well and Its Pump

There is a certain olive grove in the northern Peloponnese that dates back a few hundred years. The grove had been all but abandoned by the descendants of the original owners, initially as a result of emigration to the United States and Australia in the turn of the twentieth century. After their return from the United States in 1922, brokenhearted and despondent after a series of personal losses—deaths, stillborn children, depression, melancholia—the grove fell into complete disrepair. At some point in the mid-1970s the husband of the surviving daughter of the (by now) deceased repatriates, as a response to middle-life crisis, decided to revive the grove. Being a chemical and mechanical engineer specializing in PVC watering systems, he approached the entire enterprise methodically, scientifically, and with an open budget. In 1975 he drilled for water (and we know the exact date because he inscribed his initials along with the date on the platform of the well). The entire affair was so immense that in the summer of 2013, some forty years later, a friend of his said that what he had done was the equivalent of having anchored a sailing yacht at a place that didn't even have a marina ("έφερε μιά θαλαμηγό και την αγκυροβόλησε στην Ακράτα"). The drill had to be brought from the town of Argos, about a hundred kilometers away. The mechanic who drilled had brought along his son, who, thirty years later, met one of the helping hands for the grove and still remembered the expedition. This being a drilled well it required a pump, and the engineer bought the best made, most reliable, with a lifetime guarantee for parts and repairs. It was a pump made in Wisconsin (figure 5.1).

Throughout the years, with the supervision of the owner, the grove was tended for its everyday needs by a local farmer who wanted to supplement his income. And supplement he did. With the income that he received for tending the grove, he was able to send both of his children to Athens for higher education. Around the late 1980s the caretaker, too old and fragile and egged on by his grown children, resigned his duties, leaving the grove without immediate and daily supervision. A few replacements came and went as Greece was on an upward financial and social spiral, helping hands were scarce, and expertise and dedication to agricultural production were gone—both in search of a life easier than that of the farmer's and aided by the catastrophic decision of successive Greek governments to turn the country from agricultural economy to service economy, primarily and specifically tourism.

The beginning of the 1990s brought along not only a galloping global economy but also a galloping migration movement. During the 1980s Greece had itinerant migrants who came from Yugoslavia in the summer months and settled primarily in the southern Peloponnese as pickers for the summer crops. There were also Filipino nannies and domestic workers who came at the same time, and

Figure 5.1 Pump registration plate noting the unit was manufactured by STA-RITE Industries Inc. in Delavan, Wisconsin.

a small number of Pakistanis brought by the dictatorship of 1967–1974. But all of these were the result of bilateral governmental agreements that were very strictly regulated. The Filipinos are still a presence in upper-class Greek households, the Pakistanis have created a community, but the itinerant pickers from Yugoslavia were temporary and all but disappeared with the collapse of the Soviet economy.

In Greece, the 1990s were the years of the Albanian immigration. Albanian men, initially, started arriving in Greece over the Epirus mountains in numbers that Greece had not seen before. Actually, Greece had not seen such immigrants before. At least not since the Albanian migration of the 1300s. The Albanians came as the result of the breakdown of Albania and the old socialist republics, in general, and settled primarily in the countryside, looking for work in the fields or in construction. One of them made his way to the village where the olive grove is and was immediately scooped up for work, first by our engineer. The Albanian was young and capable, smart and willing, and within a few years he had learned the ins and outs of the grove, of olive oil production, the particulars of polyculture and (reluctantly) of organic farming, and was on the lookout for anything untoward. That is, until the owner died, and (within two years) the bottom fell out in Greece. And this is precisely where the crisis shows in covert but detrimental ways. Money became scarce for everyone, and the Albanian caretaker—whose Albanian name is Taufik but whom everyone knows by his Greek name, Spyros—started slacking off. Sensing a vacuum of power among the heirs of the grove, he started slowly abandoning his duties. As a result, he burned the pump. He announced in April 2013 that the pump was not working. "I don't know why," he said. The owners live in Athens, 150 kilometers away, but until mid-May they didn't have the gas money to go to the farm and inspect the damage. When they scraped together the hundred euros needed, they went to assess the damage and decide how to proceed. One of the neighbors, an electrician, who was a teenager when the original drilling took place, volunteered to help. He and the owner's grandson took the pump out to check whether it was burned or simply broken. That would take about a week, and the grandson couldn't stay that long, as he had been told that he could perhaps find a summer job at one of the tourist islands in the north. He put all the money he had into getting himself and his girlfriend there. It all proved for naught, but he had already spent the money. June came and went, and then July, when, finally, the entire family managed to get together to discuss what could be done with the pump, as the grove hadn't been watered since the last rains of March. Phone calls upon phone calls to companies that sell this type of equipment led to nothing. No one could identify the pump; no one could say anything about it more than that such a pump could not be had nowadays. One of the heirs to the grove looked up the company in Wisconsin and called them. The person who answered the phone knew and remembered the particular model. It had started been produced two years before he got there in 1975. Don't waste time and energy, he said. We don't make these pumps any longer. You are better off buying an Italian one. Will it be comparable? was the question. Nothing will be comparable, he said. On your pump I can tell you exactly how each one of its components worked, how strong it was, how it fit in with the rest. Now, he said, to sell these pumps to Japan we make the motor and the pump as one unit, not separate as before, we buy the thrust bearing from Italy, the thrust collar from Japan, and then we sell the pump back to Japan as a finished product. Buy a Tesla one, he said. It won't be the same, but it will be close to it. And so it was done, everyone finding themselves in the thick of a globalized market that had promised greater equity in the balance between production of goods and distribution of wealth and had failed even in maintaining the rudiments of industrial production. Surreal capitalism.

The operation of installing the pump took an entire week, working from early in the morning until midnight, with floodlights and the glare of cell phones. The knowledge that the grandson had was almost nonexistent besides what he had read on the Internet and had been told by the person who sold him the new pump. The electrician remembered parts of the original operation, but inevitably each day they hit a snag in their knowledge. Why did the pump have that particular output? What was the sound or running water coming from inside the well? Why did the pump start and stop and start and stop? The men of the neighborhood who were young teenagers when the original drilling took place and the first pump was installed remembered the operation, but only in fragments. One of them remembered that the drill had hit water at seventeen meters, much higher than the final bottom of the well at sixty meters. That explained the running water sound. Another one remembered that the owner never watered the grove straight from the well but filled the cistern he had built and watered from there. These bits of fragments, nested knowledges in essence, produced the rounded knowledge that was needed for the successful installation of the new pump. In its turn this rounded knowledge was produced by the combination of two factors. One was the impression this enormous project had on the memory of the young men, itself the result of an affective economy differently aligned. A second one is that the tight specialization, professionalization, and compartmentalization of knowledge that we see now as a result of the extreme tightening of capital relations was not present yet outside of the centers of capitalist production.

Poverty That Refuses to Speak Its Name

The grandson of the owner, this owner who, to install the pump in 1975, had paid the astronomical sum of 1,800,000 drachmas (the equivalent of US$42,000 in today's money, where the average salary in Greece is four hundred euros) and who in 2007 paid fifty thousand euros for a week's care in a private intensive care unit (ICU) in Athens, money that was but a drop in his financial bucket, this grandson now uses the free Social Solidarity Clinic in his neighborhood for a surgery that he needs to undergo, as he is out of a job, out of health insurance coverage, and out of the care of his parents (Papantoniou 2015).[7] When asked about poverty, the grandson was adamant. "We are not poor," he said. "We are still not starving and we have a house, we are not out in the street." How about the immigrants, I asked. "They are not poor; they are destitute," he replied.

Survival

These are modalities of survival well known to Greeks who enjoyed financial amplitude only during the past thirty years, even the disavowing of poverty is part of that modality. But that's what they are: modalities of survival. But they also echo two other locations of being, both of them in this volume: what Jessica Greenberg calls "ontological activism" and what Eirini Avramopoulou describes as an "overwhelming life." These strategies of survival manage to effectuate such survival precisely because their actors figure resistance to the overwhelming life that has been refashioned for them from the outside through the engagement with an ontological activism that manifests itself by becoming constitutive of this new on, this new ontology, that acts up against the refashioned, deactivated originary self.

In 2010 I was writing and speaking about the ICUs in Athens where my current research has taken me since 2007. These units do not exist any longer because the first sector that the "crisis" hit (meaning, the first sector where the "Troika" demanded cuts) was precisely this one: the sector that makes the social welfare state possible. Not because the Troika (and the local Greek politicians who have supported its measures and demands) do not consider such services as needed, but because they want these services to be turned over to the private sector.

In this chapter I have endeavored to create a cartography of the visuality of the crisis and the precarity that it has engendered, a critical visuality, if you wish, of what this phenomenon, this event, this moment, really looks like on the ground, not unlike the mapping of crisis in the urban context produced at crisis-scapes.net, and along the lines that Jessica Greenberg is following (in this volume). I have done so by looking not only at the structural changes and damages that this crisis has incurred but also at actual micro-level descriptions of its appearance. I have asked what the rise of unfathomable poverty and its seepage into all strata except for the famous top 1 percent look like. But more is needed, work that shows in equal ethnographic detail the presence of the deadly neo-Nazi formulation of Golden Dawn with its anti-immigrant, anti-leftist, anti-intellectual, antigay, antiwomen, antipolitical mobilizations. Work that gives both the coarse and the fine textures of the faces of the uninsured, of the pensionless, of the underemployed. Work that documents and analyzes the immense explosion of drug abuse, visible in broad daylight in the middle of the city, in parks, at street corners, and the explosion of the new phenomenon (for Greece) of human trafficking, and the illegal prostitution that has developed of the trottoir kind, not of the housed, inspected, legal trade that has existed in Greece thus far. We need more work like Heath Cabot's that engages the stories of the immigrants and of the organizations that help them—the impossibility of survival, the impossibility of leaving, the impossibility of staying, the impossibility of employment, the beatings, the lashings, and the killings by Golden Dawn and by the police. Work that shows and engages with the astronomical rise in crime—petty, as I mentioned earlier, but also far more serious: murders, kidnappings, torture, trafficking of guns, trafficking of humans, trafficking of goods, and the human beings trapped therein. With such research we will be able to engage in the production of a radical genealogy of the crisis, hopefully even a Foucauldian archaeology of it. And finally we will be able to effectuate a new definition of it, which at the moment remains elusive and unstable.

And then maybe we can start writing about it in infinitely unsafe texts, texts that will destabilize the secure placement of debt and crisis, that will not allow us to think of financial debt as a moral category; texts that will force us to encounter the spectrality of poverty as a political project; texts that will not allow us to walk away from considering the materiality of the crisis to the bodies of the human beings it wrecks; texts that will force us to undertake the responsibility of *logon didonai* as the obligation of all to give an account of and reasons for their actions, as Cornelius Castoriadis (1997, 109) has reminded us; texts that will insist on saying that ultimately "crisis" means living in a world of privatized wealth and socialized debt.

In the Search of an End

I have decided to keep this chapter within the temporality that initially produced it, namely the years of the first two *Mnemonia* (memoranda of understanding, 2011–2014) signed by the coalition government formed by the Greek neoliberal right wing and centrist-left parties of New Democracy, the Panhellenic Socialist Movement (PASOK), and the Democratic Left (DIMAR). The developments that have occurred between the time of writing and its printing are of immense importance, and they would require the addition of dozens of pages to do them justice. The leftist coalition SYRIZA was voted to power in January 20, 2015, and carried out intense negotiations with the Troika, with an eye to renegotiating the debt. When it became clear that the country's European creditors (the European Central Bank and the European Commission) had no intention of engaging in negotiations with a leftist government, Prime Minister Alexis Tsipras brought the negotiations to the citizens. Tsipras announced a referendum that would posit to citizens the question of whether the government ought to sign the agreement presented by the European Central Bank and the European Commission, an agreement that the creditors had framed within Margaret Thatcher's (in)famous "There Is No Alternative" (TINA) doctrine.[8] For reasons that are far too complex to analyze here, the county overwhelmingly voted "No" (62 percent), in a vote that mapped not only class divisions,[9] but also a landscape of fear, hope, and frustration. Two weeks later the government signed a third memorandum, an act that was met with disappointment and a deep sense of disenchantment in the country. Two months after that, primarily responding to gestures from the left flank of the party that clearly aimed to destabilize the government, Tsipras announced the dissolution of the government and scheduled new elections, to take place within five weeks. The change in the social and political conditions in the country during the SYRIZA government have been palpable, with a dramatic decrease in acts of police brutality and the presence of Golden Dawn in the streets, an affect of hope present in the public sphere, and a heightened sense of regained dignity as a result of the government efforts to renegotiate the debt and the terms of the agreement, even if the financial situation of individual citizens and migrants might not have changed. But this chapter cannot address the dramatic changes that have occurred since January 2015; it is much too soon to engage in anthropological analysis that would have any longevity or that would be ethically justified.

Notes

This chapter, in a much shorter form, was published in 2014 at the invitation of David Palumbo-Liu as "Unsafe Texts: Interiority and Knowledge at the Time of Crisis" in *Arcade*. I wish to thank *Arcade* for permission to include some portions of it here. I also thank Kostis Karpozilos, Sofian Merabet, David Nugent, Dimitris Papadopoulos, Katherine Stefatos, Kathleen Stewart, and Kamala Visweswaran for their valuable comments. In its various forms, this text has been circulating since 2011, when I was invited to submit early thoughts on the crisis to a Greek online journal, and this form is its last iteration.

1. I use multi-sited research as George Marcus defined it in 1995, where the intensity of the singular field site becomes even further pressurized and saturated with information and meanings that flow from its outside, from assemblages and constellations that constitute it in these ethnographic times that are formed differently, through rapidly transmitted communications, through collages of experience and the reverberations of existence located outside of the spatial and territorial confines of the geographical site itself. Multi-sited ethnography does not imply (only) the ethnographic encounter of a transnational ethnographic subject, but it demands acknowledgment that the subject engages with multiple modalities of encounter, all of which are not necessarily bound by the physical presence of the body.

2. In 2014 the "Troika" was the common way of reference in the Greek press to indicate the triad of creditors to the Greek state, namely the International Monetary Fund (IMF), the European Central Bank (ECB), and the European Commission (EC). Since then, Greece has paid off its debt to the IMF, and its role as a player in the Greek crisis has been somewhat more peripheral and under negotiation.

3. Balibar (2013) points out the connection that Habermas has made between democracy and taxation. Habermas reminds us that the American Revolution was fought precisely on the slogan "no taxation without representation." But Balibar brings up the ways in which this economy between taxation and democracy has been superseded by late capitalism, so that the slogan should now be reversed to "no representation without taxation."

4. The meaning of the movement of the Indignados, taken from Stéphan Hessel's 2011 pamphlet *Indignez Vous!*, was reformulated in Greece as "We are not indignant, we are determined."

5. On the issue of crisis-related suicides, see Economou et al. (2011); Karanikolos et al. (2011); http://www.statistics.gr/portal/page/portal/ESYE/BUCKET/General/A12_ETHSIA_EKTHESH_AXIOLOGHSHS_STAT_PROGRAMMATOS_en.pdf.

6. For a more complicated analysis, see Branas and colleagues (2015).

7. One of the effects of the collapse of the social welfare state in Greece as a result of the austerity measures brought about by the memoranda is the dual destruction of the public health system (i.e., public hospitals) and the insurance system (especially since funds of the different public insurance programs have been raided over the years by the various governments), bringing about a health crisis that has been unprecedented for the country. There have been arguments, most notably brought forth by Sarah-Luzia Hassel-Reusing (2012), that regard the collapse of health care as a human rights violation and have brought the case to the International Criminal Court. The Social Solidarity Clinic of Hellenico conducted research asking people whose health has been adversely affected by the crisis to provide testimonials for use by the International Criminal Court (see the newspaper *Avgi*, September 2, 2015, http://www.avgi.gr/article/5810893/ekklisi-gia-marturies-pligenton-tis-oikonomikis-krisis).

8. In an article about TINA published in *Eutopia*, Zygmunt Bauman (2014) argued that with the fall of the Berlin Wall, TINA became globalized rather than remaining a doctrine that concerned the old colonial and postcolonial nations. Bauman saw TINA appearing in the newly independent and capitalized former Soviet republics and Eastern European countries, such as Lithuania and Poland, where the introduction of capitalist forms of economic exchange engendered the complete erosion of the social welfare state. In a curious twist Bauman, reading and quoting Ivan Krastev, reproduces Krastev's position that elections under the current conditions of crisis and actualized TINA are useless, as they fail to bring about governments willing and capable of challenging and changing the balance of power effectuated by capitalism (what recently is called neoliberalism). Obviously, when both articles were written, all indentured countries of the European South (also known as PIIGS, for Portugal, Italy, Ireland, Greece, and Spain) were under governments completely aligned with the political demands of their creditors—SYRIZA had not won elections yet, and in Spain Podemos was not yet a sizable possibility. But what is interesting is that the robust opposition to latter-day TINA performed by the citizens of Greece, Italy, Spain, and Ireland (Portugal is in a different position in terms of resistance movements) seems to have eluded both Krastev and Bauman not only in its actuality but even as a possibility.

9. In this late-stage capitalism and, more specifically, since the beginning of the crisis, the classic Marxist and Leninist understandings of social classes as existing in a historically antithetical and agonistic relationship to each other (Marx) and as being historically determined through the experience of where each stands in history, their historical relationship to the means of production and relation to labor, and their position in the distributive scale of wealth (Lenin), along with the understanding of a shared class project (à la Althusser through Marx), have been severely muddied, as the crisis has produced an economic base of destitution that increasingly absorbs the detritus of the previously clearly defined and practiced socioeconomic classes. The vote was cast along these lines—the economic elites of the northern and southern suburbs of Athens and the other cities voted yes, while the no vote became a map of the effects of the crisis and the devastating results of the memoranda, as it included every other social marker, from the previously affluent to the historically laboring.

References

Balibar, Étienne. 2013. "How Can the Aporia of the 'European People' Be Resolved?" *Radical Philosophy* 181 (September–October): 13–18.

Bauman, Zygmunt. 2014. "TINA: A World without Alternatives" *Eutopia Magazine*, November 8. http://www.eutopiamagazine.eu/en/zygmunt-bauman/issue/tina-world-without-alternatives #sthash.3czFkeVR.XUxOvQgD.dpuf.

Branas, Charles C., Anastasia E. Kastanaki, Manolis Michalodimitrakis, John Tzougas, Elena F. Kranioti, Pavlos N. Theodorakis, Brendan G. Carr, Douglas J. Wiebe, et al. 2015. "The Impact of Economic Austerity and Prosperity Events on Suicide in Greece: A 30-year Inter-rupted Time-Series Analysis." *BMJ Open* 5 (1). http://bmjopen.bmj.com/content/5/1/e005619.

Castoriadis, Cornelius. 1997. "Anthropology, Philosophy, Politics." *Thesis Eleven* (49): 99–116.

Economou, M., M. Madianos, C. Theleritis, L. E. Peppou, and C. N. Stefanis. 2011. "Increased Suicidality amid Economic Crisis in Greece." *Lancet* 378 (9801): 1459.

Hardinghaus, Barbara, and Julia Amalia Heyer. 2012. "Troubled Times: Wave of Suicides Shocks Greece." *Der Spiegel* (Spiegel Online International), August 15.

Hassel-Reusing, Sarah-Luzia. 2012. "Letter to the ICC." *justiceforgreece* (blog). https://justicefor greece.wordpress.com/complaints/sarah-luzia-hassel-reusing-στον-εισαγγελέα-του-δπδ -icc/.

Hessel, Stéphane. 2011. *Indignez-vous!* Montpellier, France: Indigène Éditions.

Karanikolos, Marina, Philipa Mladovsky, Jonathan Cylus, Sarah Thomson, Sanjay Basu, David Stuckler, Johan P. Mackenbach, and Martin McKee. 2013. "Financial Crisis, Austerity, and Health in Europe." *Lancet* 381 (9874): 1323–1331.

Koselleck, Reinhard. 1988. *Critique and Crisis: Enlightenment and the Pathogenesis of Modern Society*. Boston: MIT Press.

Marcus, George. 1995. "Ethnography in/of the World System: The Emergence of Multi-Sited Ethnography." *Annual Review of Anthropology* 24: 95–117.

Miller, Barbara. 2014. "Migrants Drown after Boats Capsize off Greek Islands." ABC News, May 6, http://www.abc.net.au/news/2014-05-06/migrants-drown-after-boats-capsize-off-greek -island/5432498.

Nordstrom, Caroline. 2009. "The Bard." In *Anthropology off the Shelf: Anthropologists on Writing*, edited by Alisse Waterston and Maria Vesperi, 35–46. Malden, MA: Blackwell.

Papantoniou, Kostas. "Έκκληση για μαρτυρίες πληγέντων της οικονομικής κρίσης." *Avgi*, http:// www.avgi.gr/article/5810893/ekklisi-gia-marturies-pligenton-tis-oikonomikis-krisis.

Piketty, Thomas. 2013. *Le capital au 21ᵉ siècle*. Paris: Ed. du Seuil.

Rakopoulos, Theodore. 2014. "Resonance of Solidarity: Meanings of a Local Concept in Anti-austerity Greece." *Journal of Modern Greek Studies* 32 (2): 313–337.

Rancière, Jacques, and Maria Kakogianni. 2013. "A Precarious Dialogue." *Radical Philosophy* 181 (September–October): 18–26.

Roitman, Janet. 2014. *Anti-Crisis*. Durham, NC: Duke University Press.

Rosaldo, Renato. 1985. "From the Door of His Tent: The Fieldworker and the Inquisitor." In *Writing Culture. The Poetics and Politics of Ethnography*, edited by James Clifford and George Mar-cus, 77–98. Berkeley: University of California Press.

Scott, Joan W. 1991. "The Evidence of Experience." *Critical Inquiry* 17 (4): 773–797.

Spivak, Gayatri Chakravortry. 1985. "Scattered Speculations on the Question of Value." *Diacritics* 15 (4): 73–93.

PART II

AGENCY AS ETHICAL CONDITION

6 Intolerants

Politics of the Ordinary in Karachi, Pakistan

Tania Ahmad

> Put simply, my point is this: if the ability to effect change in the world and in
> oneself is historically and culturally specific (both in terms of what constitutes
> "change" and the means by which it is effected), then the meaning and sense of
> agency cannot be fixed in advance, but must emerge through an analysis of the
> particular concepts that enable specific modes of being, responsibility, effectivity.
> Viewed in this way, what may appear to be a case of deplorable passivity and
> docility from a progressivist point of view, may actually be a form of agency—but
> one that can be understood only from within the discourses and structures of
> subordination that create the conditions of its enactment.
>
> —Saba Mahmood, *Politics of Piety* (2005, 15)

IF RESISTANCE IS ANCHORED in a concept of agency, then the question of how we recognize resistance always drags behind it the unwieldy issue of how we identify agency, like an empty can on a rope, noisily clanging around corners with nothing like grace. As Saba Mahmood notes in the epigraph to this chapter, the meanings of change and action are contingent on the historical and cultural contexts that give them a specific form. In urban Pakistan, a long history of violence in the name of politics leads me to ask if institutions, movements and organizations have a monopoly over political agency. This question becomes especially pressing if we consider the very limited contemporary practice of public protest, particularly in cities where urban space is emphatically territorialized through turf politics. What do we lose if we dismiss the experiences of Pakistanis who are not formally affiliated with either political or activist organizations as depoliticized? What do we forgo if we disregard tentative accounts that narrate an alternative in oblique terms? We risk mistaking the affective intensities of fearlessness for conservatism and subjection instead of perceiving the hint, or potential, for a recognition of shared experiences and, perhaps, an emergent collectivity. There is nothing radical about this contention; it merely strives to locate the political in new ways in urban Pakistan.

Violence is part of the fabric of everyday life in Karachi. Nonetheless, an important aspect of public discourse in the city—through gossip, rumors, mass-media commentary, and Internet blogs—focuses on the rejection of violence, specifically of politically motivated conflict.[1] That many Karachi residents routinely talk about the possibility of living without urban violence does not suggest that they reject politics altogether, or that they do not identify or sympathize with particular political parties. More than this rejection talk itself, it is important to consider, first, what constitutes rejecting violence in popular discourse, and second, what alternatives residents posit. In this chapter, I argue that residents of Karachi's middle-class neighborhoods, which were especially imbricated in a recent history of political turf wars and urban unrest, locate their rejection of violence in a discourse of respectability. This respectability combines sensibilities for pious morality with leisure activities, consumer practices, and the authority of a kinship-based domestic order. All of these aspects are cast as normative, even as interlocutors acknowledge that they have gained this status—if not their moral authority—only in recent memory. As such, the position of rejecting political violence in the name of respectability engages a politics of the ordinary, where a claim to banal, everyday activities itself becomes a political stance.

To consider the ordinary as a locus of politics, it is necessary to stretch the political to accommodate fragile and tentative contexts.[2] Here, the question is less about power and effective action and more about the possibility of articulating intentional practices through affective belonging. As discourses of respectability interpellate normative others, their idiom of pious morality conjures an emergent collectivity. Talk of rejecting violence suggests a shared experience of ordinary, everyday ethics, where positing alternatives, however limited or ineffective, articulates critique. Elsewhere I have discussed how violent events render this conjunctural sense of shared morality especially palpable (Ahmad 2011, 2014), but here I would like to focus on a longer temporal frame of neighborhood history and everyday practice.

Three critically interconnected points help to explain why such highly contingent forms of agency through affect might be considered a political stance. First, Lauren Berlant (2008, 5), in her book on women's insistently vague sentimental publics, reminds us that "one of the main utopias is normativity itself." Karachi residents who assert normative morality as an alternative to politically motivated violence are also making a utopian claim, expressing a hope for hegemonic social norms. Second, Berlant notes that such utopian visions construct insistently vague *senses* of collectivity, in which participants "*feel* as though it expresses what is common among them," but ultimately "cultivate fantasies of vague belonging as an alleviation of what is hard to manage in the lived real—social antagonisms, exploitation, compromised intimacies, the attrition of life" (5).[3] The feeling of the ordinary that Karachi residents invoke, circumscribed by respectable morality and leisure practices, expresses a generalized and imprecise sense of belonging that is powerfully situated by political animosities played out through street violence, alongside a lived real that has included decades of uncertainty and vulnerability. Berlant's suggestion that this vagueness alleviates rather than mobilizes those who participate in a utopian normative sense of belonging simultaneously disregards and acknowledges the fragility of its claim to both belonging and critique. Being delicate and tentative, however, does not make it less agential, only less organized, less defined, and more contingent on a shared sense of ordinariness. Third, Berlant (2008, 10) identifies such critiques of politics, which foreground emotional attachment located in fantasies of normativity, as "juxtapolitical": next to or adjacent to politics, they mark the sense of a shared emotional world, a shared historical burden, and "an aesthetic and spiritual scene that generates *relief from the political.*" She implies that the juxtapolitical does not constitute an active antagonism, and is thus not political, but she neglects to mention that, despite its imbrication in normativity and a vague sense of belonging, it formulates not only a critique but also an affectively grounded alternative to existing political possibilities. Still, Berlant's term allows us to envision an agency that takes on the form of relief, where resistance— complex, vague, fantastical—occurs through claims of shared feelings around respite, leisure, and normative morality. The middle-class Karachi residents I worked with explicitly connected their rejections of violence to forms of relief, expressly formulating alternatives to politics as usual through vague critiques and oblique allusions to the possibility of shared subjection.

The contributors to this volume provide a vital reminder that political action is not limited to effective challenges to social hierarchy. Resistance is shaped by affective intensities, with circumscribed agency as a starting point and modes of belonging as an open question, not to mention methodological circumstances providing the conditions of possibility for representation and analysis. Jessica Greenberg's (this volume) astute focus on disappointment as the impetus for political engagement in post–Cold War Serbia draws attention to the affective intensities of enacting a practical political alternative that begins with a rejection of politics: Milena locates her pragmatic activism in a critique of backdoor formal politics. Greenberg's broader argument about the affective structure of pragmatism is intertwined with moral orientations toward uncertainty, albeit where a mutable framework is considered the best way to maintain ethical principles under changing conditions. Whereas the middle-class Karachi residents I describe here are neither activists nor avowed pragmatists, and thus do not participate in organized transformational social justice initiatives like Milena, their rejection of political violence also responds to a moral orientation toward historical upheaval, but along a distinct tack: they develop an affective structure of relief, respite, and leisure. Eirini Avramopoulou (this volume) asks how political presence can become vocal, and her answer is located not in effective social transformation, but in the flip side of "agency's impossibilities" that prevent any easy solution: making a rights claim, sitting in a police station with Bariş, waiting to file a report about being physically assaulted that never materialized "felt *as if*" they were working toward justice. Avramopoulou maintains, however, that the violently "unfulfilled desire for recognition and justice" leads to a continual melancholic embodiment of loss that produces an affect of being overwhelmed. While the Karachi residents' accounts provided here take place in an aftermath of prolonged political unrest, rather than in the moment of a direct assault, I argue that their political presence is equally located in the limits to their agency and that their resort to relief and respite draws on equally powerful historically unfulfilled desires for nonviolent ordinariness. Moreover, their interpellation of others, who reject political violence and find some respite, "feels as if" shared experiences can generate a sense of belonging, which raises difficult questions about its status as a collectivity.

Spatiality is also critical to the limits and possibilities for transformation. Irene Peano (this volume) emphasizes the processes of encounter and intersubjectivity that contribute to overcoming divisions through the term *affective composition*. She notes that in the case of the countercamps of laborers and activists in Italy, spatial proximity developed relationships, however precarious, that operated across difference through the affective intensities of friendship. While Peano's focus on composition, and the countercamp participants' awareness that collectivity was always in formation, critically slows down assumptions about solidarity, her findings about spatially proximate encounters provide a telling counterexample to middle-class Karachi residents, who consider their absence from public space evidence of respectable morality. How can composition operate in a context where encounters with unknown others through proximity is considered inappropriate, if not reckless? This question prompts me to consider the articulation of a sense of belonging anchored by respite and the rejection of violence. The question of spatiality builds on Cymene Howe's (this volume) discussions of negative space or ethnographic moments of apparent unmovement that work to "reveal the finer contours of the political ecologies of activism and transformative social action." The Karachi residents I discuss here locate their relief and respite precisely in the ordinariness of ostensible unmovement; it is their platform, utopia, and the basis for a sense of shared experience and a fantasy of belonging anchored in normative morality. For them, what seems like nothing happening is the substance of their alternative and their fragile, tentative critique of political violence.

In retrospect, I conducted research in Karachi during one of the most peaceful periods in recent memory, from about 2004 to 2007. They felt like years of promise, featuring a bustling public sphere, wild consumer fantasies, and mushrooming leisure destinations for residents of modest means. They were the early years of new private television channels catering specifically to local audiences, advertising that targeted ever-lower income demographics, and dramatically increasing inflation. The government of president General Musharraf boasted economic growth, which peaked in 2005, while residents complained about stagnant wages that couldn't keep up with rising costs. At the same time, Karachi was slowly recovering from over a decade of turf wars, when a new and perhaps unruly political party that had once enjoyed broad local support was forcibly contained by federal, military, and paramilitary forces through the 1980s and 1990s, but reemerged as a mainstream political entity in the 2000s.

The party, known by its acronym as the MQM, which then stood for the Muhajir Qaumi Movement but changed its name to the Muttahida Qaumi Movement in 1997,[4] not only was regarded with hostility by the state and political enemies but also was internally factionalized. The rise of violent turf-based politics, combining territoriality with protection rackets (*bhatta khori*), occurred in the late 1970s and early 1980s, when overseas remittances and easily available weapons generated the possibility of armed political animosity. Hardly confined to the emergence of the MQM, reports of a "Kalashnikov culture" were initially attributed to the enmity between the university student wings of the Jamaat-e-Islami (JI) and the Pakistan Peoples Party (PPP). The campus hostilities coincided with the beginning of the military dictatorship of General Zia (1977–1988), when a familiar narrative states that the federal government none-too-covertly allowed the US support of the Afghani mujahideen, funneling large quantities of arms through Karachi, Pakistan's largest port city, and thus making semiautomatic weaponry both available and affordable to new demographics. At the same time, a quota system designed to bring a form of affirmative action to university admissions was implemented by the government preceding Zia, Z. A. Bhutto's PPP.

This change was welcomed by underrepresented groups, whose sympathies the PPP relied on to garner support in the province of Sindh, but the historically Urdu-speaking migrant groups who made up the majority of Karachi at the time experienced the quota system as a direct threat to their ability to acquire government employment or be admitted to university. A group of discontented students are credited with founding the student wing of the MQM, and later the party itself, with the object of rectifying the loss of privilege suffered by the loosely defined identity of Urdu-speaking descendants of Partition-era migrants, or *muhajirs*. The accounts elaborating alternatives to political violence below are all by the descendants of *muhajirs* living in neighborhoods considered the turf or particular strongholds of the MQM. Nonetheless, while they do not condemn the MQM directly, they do posit alternatives to political strife and street violence that cast ordinary, respectable pursuits, often in public space, as morally righteous ground. This form of agency points to its limited claims, expressed through a tentative sense of collectivity and a shared utopian vision of ordinariness. Its efficacy is imagined through shared emotional worlds of relief and respite.

Troubles and Respite

In his portion of the extended family bungalow in Nazimabad, Munir Sahib obliquely described the recent history of his neighborhood in the preceding five years. He used the term *sukun*, which is sometimes translated as "peace" but also carries connotations of respite or relief, in addition to meaning "rest," "tranquility," and "contentment" (Platts 1884, 665). In the past five years, Munir Sahib said, *sukun* has come. This vague-sounding assertion slowly takes on force in the context of his wider narrative, the history of the neighborhood, the city, and the particular moment of the interview, in late 2006. Munir Sahib, a middle-aged man in his early fifties, lived with his wife in the heart of Nazimabad Block 1, on a pleasant street with closely packed concrete homes, a few trees, and a conspicuous metal barrier gate that could block the entry of cars from the bigger street but was usually propped open in the daytime.

Nazimabad was in western Karachi, established by government initiative in the 1950s to house some of the hundreds of thousands of migrants who had traveled to Pakistan at Independence in 1947. Many among them had been Urdu-speakers from Uttar Pradesh in India (then, the United Provinces). According to Munir Sahib and his neighbors, family patriarchs had bought land at subsidized rates and had homes built. Many came to Nazimabad after having lived in long-term refugee camps upon arriving in Karachi, and the population of those camps had more than tripled as they accommodated migrants in the first five years following Pakistan's independence. This trajectory differed significantly from my own extended family, who had had enough capital to obtain homes in an existing and more affluent area, from the government employees who sold or rented out the properties they had been officially allocated. Nazimabad residents I spoke with prided themselves on the cultural capital of the neighborhood residents in the 1950s and 1960s; they described intellectuals, professional musicians (*ustads*), and engineers, all Urdu speakers, they said, from Uttar Pradesh. These migrants and their descendants across Karachi adopted the conspicuous label of *muhajir*, figuring their travel from India in the terms of the *hijrat*: Prophet Muhammad and the early Muslims' journey from Mecca to Medina to avoid persecution. The term *muhajir* simultaneously referred to migrants as refugees on a journey to avoid religious persecution, as traveling to defend or protect their beliefs, and as a privileged location of sacrifice by the people who had given up their homes, relationships, and livelihoods to establish Pakistan.[5] The meanings of the term changed over time (see Verkaaik 2004; Nichola Khan 2010), both socially and politically, but it is telling that two generations and fifty years later, Munir Sahib sat in the house his father had built, describing Nazimabad as "belonging" to Urdu speakers.

Part of Munir Sahib's narrative articulated neighborhood belonging through the implicit *muhajir* category by complaining about the new, ethnically marked "others" who had recently moved into the area. He cited their lack of etiquette and discretion by using a term indexing respectability in an Urdu-language cultural complex; they did not have the same *tameez* as previous residents. In another part of his narrative, however, Munir Sahib was much more oblique about *muhajir* belonging. He referred to troubles (*buraiyan*) in the neighborhood that had improved over the previous five years. These troubles had subsided, leading to more *sukun*. A more recent historical context of Nazimabad reveals that rather than disconnected instances, Munir Sahib's references to ethnic discrimination and local troubles are intertwined at the site of residential mobility. Many of the ethnically marked newer residents moved into the neighborhood when euphemistic "troubles" had led to longtime residents moving out of Nazimabad.

The troubles to which Munir Sahib referred invoked over a decade of politically motivated turf wars and government intervention. Following the state imposition of quotas on government jobs and university admissions in the 1970s, intended as a form of affirmative action for underrepresented ethnic minorities, the Urdu-speaking migrants who experienced this change as social disenfranchisement founded a political party explicitly aimed at defending *muhajir* interests: the Muhajir Qaumi Movement, meaning the Muhajir Nationalist Movement, also called the MQM.[6] Established in 1984, and based nearly exclusively in the cities of Karachi and Hyderabad in the southern province of Sindh, the MQM developed a platform aimed expressly at a broadly conceived "middle class," providing a secular and nonintellectual alternative to the parties that the *muhajir* community had supported in the past, notably the Islamic modernist Jamaat-e-Islami. The MQM addressed *muhajirs* as an ethnicity, but despite their rhetoric about a politicized *muhajir* collectivity, the descendants of Independence-era migrants in Karachi are politically, religiously, and socioeconomically diverse. Although in the early years of the party's history, beginning in the late 1980s, the MQM enjoyed overwhelming support, over the long term, how Urdu speakers identified with the category of *muhajir*, as it was mobilized by the MQM, has been highly variable.

Nazimabad and the area immediately adjacent to it, Liaquatabad, were particularly known as strongholds of the MQM.[7] In the 1980s and 1990s, the party prided itself on its involvement in and knowledge of local affairs at the neighborhood level, aggressively recruiting young men and eventually developing a subsection specialized in targeted violence, known as its terror wing. Widely available weaponry, factional intraparty violence, and gruesome target killings, as well as competition over territorial rights to collect revenue from protection rackets, escalated the street violence associated with the area in this period. The party was subjected to active government animosity for more than fifteen years, during which the MQM was declared a terrorist organization. Certain neighborhoods, including Liaquatabad but not Nazimabad, were declared "no-go areas" by the police. This meant both that police would not guarantee security within specific boundaries and that in these spaces police and military would regularly impose curfews, round up groups of men on the often-feeble suspicion of being militants, and engage in extrajudicial killings, allowing them to eliminate "street nationalists" with impunity.

The most significant instance of street violence and government intervention targeting the MQM occurred between 1992 and 1994. During Operation Clean-Up, military and paramilitary forces occupied the city for twenty-nine months with the objective of purging Karachi of alleged antistate and antisocial elements (see Bakhtiar 1992, 26). The operation followed several years of MQM electoral victories and alliances with established parties. In 1987, the party had won municipal elections in Karachi and Hyderabad. In the general elections of 1988 and 1990, the MQM had won the majority of Karachi's seats, establishing itself as a new political presence in the southern urban centers of Sindh. These victories were shortly followed by the factionalization of the party into two groups. The MQM-Altaf, remaining loyal to party leader Altaf Hussain, was the majority faction, while the MQM-Haqiqi splintered off as a group with a more militant agenda. It was widely believed that the minority MQM-Haqiqi was intentionally established by government and military intelligence in order to provoke intraparty animosity and justify state intervention, despite the MQM-Altaf's support of then prime minister Nawaz Sharif's party.[8]

Dissent between the two MQM groups manifested as turf wars and, reportedly chaotic street violence. As a result, Operation Clean-Up cracked down with special force on the MQM. Party members were rounded up en masse and interrogated. Torture cells allegedly used by the MQM were shown to journalists under heavy military cover. In addition, street battles between the soldiers and armed civilians took place regularly (Jafri 1992). The MQM-Haqiqi was widely assumed to be allied with the military operation, and government officials broadly characterized their political rivals, MQM-Altaf members, as "terrorists" (Verkaaik 2004, 75). The MQM-Altaf immediately withdrew its support from Prime Minister Nawaz Sharif's coalition government, and federal as well as provincial representatives resigned from their respective assemblies in protest (Jafri 1992).

Casualties were inflicted by a combination of intraparty factionalism and the government-sanctioned onslaught. The second year of the operation, 1993, was marked by street battles between members of the two MQM factions, and the MQM-Altaf fought over the turf it had lost to the MQM-Haqiqi in the initial months of Operation Clean-Up (Verkaaik 2004, 86). Meanwhile, Benazir Bhutto's Pakistan Peoples Party, or the PPP, won the general elections in late 1993. The MQM boycotted elections at the federal level but won a significant number of seats in provincial elections, officially entering into an alliance with Bhutto's PPP in Sindh. Nonetheless, under Bhutto, the crackdown as well as the street violence seemed to be infused with new gusto. Hasan Mujtaba, writing for the magazine *Newsline*, reported that official army sources claimed that one thousand dacoits and terrorists had been killed in the operation up to August 1993 (cited in Verkaaik 2004, 85). In addition, MQM chairman Azim Ahmad Tariq was murdered. Mutual accusations by the two MQM factions were accompanied by months of gunfights in the streets and struggles over territorial control. Leading up to the withdrawal of the army in late November, in 1994 "565 people were gunned down" in Karachi alone (Bakhtiar 1994, 32). Despite the abrupt withdrawal of the military, between 1,500 and 2,000 people are estimated to have died in the aftermath of military withdrawal. These casualties were officially accounted for in the euphemistic terms of "police encounters" and "extrajudicial killings" (Abbas 1995; Verkaaik 2004, 58), suggesting unofficial obfuscation. In 1995, Bhutto's government began arduous negotiations with, rather than violent repression of, the MQM. Although the street violence and street politics that dominated Karachi between 1985 and 1995 supposedly quieted down, significant casualties and target killings continued. Particularly famously, the murder of former provincial governor, renowned philanthropist, herbal medicine entrepreneur, and local Nazimabad celebrity Hakim Saeed in late 1997 led to the imposition of Governor's rule in the province of Sindh. Then prime minister Nawaz Sharif directly accused the MQM, his party's provincial coalition partner at the time, of terrorism and established short-lived military courts, later deemed unconstitutional, to attempt to control crime (read: militant violence associated with the MQM) in Karachi.

I arrived in Karachi to stay with my relatives for a couple of months shortly after Governor's rule was imposed at the end of 1997. I have vivid memories of gruesome spreads on the pages of newspapers, featuring rows of images of the heads of corpses, published so they could be identified. The morbid display was occasionally printed in color, with bloody flesh wounds contrasting against the grungy tones of hair and skin and street. A decade later, during field research in 2006–2007, I heard occasional references to the extended period of urban unrest that had engulfed entire neighborhoods in Karachi. After an episode of citywide political violence, including shootouts in the streets, I was repeatedly told by several Karachi residents that "this was nothing compared to 1992," after which I was promptly regaled with stories of prolonged gunfire and cowering at home, waiting for the worst to be over. I had intended to focus on a growing consumer culture, but ultimately I traced the social trajectories of former Nazimabad residents who had moved to other parts of the city as violence had escalated, as well as those of the longtime residents who had lived through what Munir Sahib so obliquely referred to as "troubles."

By then, the party and the city had changed substantially. The MQM had modified its platform, attempting to broaden its support base. To do so, in 1997 it changed its name to the Muttahida Qaumi Movement, meaning the United Nationalist Movement, thereby dropping the explicit ethnic signifier in favor of a more general moniker of solidarity. That the party continued to be identified with Urdu speakers and descendants of Independence-era migrants to Pakistan was clear, for example, as MQM officials were consistently elected into office only in the urban areas of Sindh. For example, in the 2013 general elections, more than five hundred MQM candidates ran for federal and provincial office across Pakistan, but the party won seats only in urban Sindh, elected in nearly twenty constituencies and securing almost all the National Assembly seats in Karachi (MQM 2013; Pakistan Elections 2013a, 2013b). In the interim, under the local government scheme implemented by president General Musharraf, the charismatic MQM mayor Syed Mustafa Kamal was elected into municipal office in 2005. Under the party's leadership, a number of infrastructural initiatives improved traffic and drainage systems, buttressing the widespread sense that the MQM had become a more moderate and "mainstream" political entity (see Baig 2008). The Karachi residents I conducted research with, however, had different opinions. While some asserted that MQM workers had stopped collecting protection monies, others maintained that they continued to do so. While some still spoke about the MQM only discreetly, others lauded the initiatives to alleviate traffic and replace sewerage drains, and still others cynically regarded the municipal projects as merely cosmetic. Overall, however, a broad sense of optimism about the future of the city, and its administration by the MQM government, remained in effect throughout 2006, overlapping with Munir Sahib's account. It began to subside after May 2007, when the party was accused of escalating political violence (Ahmad 2014), and in the targeted violence represented in a familiar and explicitly ethnic, *muhajir*-versus-Pashtun register in late 2008, which escalated to a large-scale ethnopolitical turf war in the summer of 2011.[9]

Besides the official change in the party's name and the efforts to address a wider constituency, a few Karachi residents explained that the MQM had disbanded its militant wing.[10] In a particularly memorable conversation during my field research, two male university students described how police had arrested, convicted, or eliminated in extrajudicial encounters key militants working for the MQM. They continued to narrate an account I had heard before, about how the responsible police officers had eventually been knocked off over the course of five or six years. They were interrupted when my research assistant at the time, a man in his late thirties, entered the room, and they immediately fell silent, sitting poker-faced until I rallied to change the subject. Months later, another young man maintained that the leaders of the militant wing had been imprisoned but continued to be active from jail, holding regular meetings with party workers at the jail. He knew this, he said, because one of his friend's brothers, who was apparently involved with the MQM, attended those meetings. Thus, although the street violence associated with the party seemed to have subsided, and although municipal governance initiatives had improved the MQM's image, a wealth of speculation and rumors about the party continued to circulate.

In 2006, Nazimabad carried both the markers of MQM history and the evidence of the party's power in the current municipal government. Party flags adorned roundabouts painted in party colors, territorializing party turf.[11] Local parks were named after MQM martyrs (*shaheed*), activists killed in police and military crackdowns. A colleague pointed out the railroad tracks, which were nearly buried in dust and litter, asserting that a low level of violence persisted; every year, one or two corpses of Jamaat-e-Islami activists were found near the tracks.

And so, when Munir Sahib sat in his living room reflecting on the troubles in his neighborhood that had improved over the previous five years, he referenced a long and complicated history of political conflict, violence, and state repression. He repeated that *sukun*—peace, respite, relief—had come. I asked him how it had come. In his response, Munir Sahib elaborated on the notion of *sukun* to encompass words like *sahulat*, meaning "ease" or "convenience"; *ilaaj*, meaning "remedy" or "cure"; and *abaadi*, meaning "cultivation" or "prosperity." His account meandered, following his train of thought. It referred to government intervention, violent animosity, and negotiations, but I believe his emphasis was not the most repressive moments of the military operation, but rather the local point of view of factionalism and turf wars that took place in the streets outside Munir Sahib's home. Moreover, his narrative moved between multiple scales, most noticeably between the state and local actors, perhaps initially anticipating what he thought I may have wanted to hear; vacillating among general, metaexplanations and more targeted, yet often more oblique, ones was a common feature in the interviews I conducted.

Initially, Munir Sahib attributed the *sukun* to government involvement. *Sukun* came, he said, because some changes in government happened in order to improve the situation; some *ilaaj* was needed so that the situation would get better. It got better; it got better for the whole country. The increased disturbances or unrest (*garbar*) that was happening had done damage all over Pakistan. As a result of this, as a result of the fighting, no one took control. Munir Sahib went on to say that the government recognized its responsibilities and its way of doing things (*andaaz*), taking steps so that the situation got better. The fighting has decreased a lot, he added. Instead, they try to talk things through. Both recognized their responsibilities to make the situation better. This is how the dealings (*moamalaat*) ended, so that some *sukun* could come.

Before this *sahulat* came, Munir Sahib continued, a dead body would be found lying in the neighborhood, creating an uncomfortable atmosphere of fear. Implicit in his stark memory was that the corpses were not anonymous but literally close to home. Families in this area may have lost friends, sons, or relatives through the events that preceded the five years during which *sukun* had come.

As he reflected on his own account, Munir Sahib repeated his narrative of transformation on a more immediate scale, referring more directly to turf wars and factional infighting, as if to provide an alternate explanation of the changes that had taken place. Maybe the people from this area, he speculated, met and mixed with some people from outside and said, "These people are different from us. They have some *tameez* and don't fight." Maybe that is why *sukun* suddenly happened. I mean, this change didn't happen suddenly. It seemed to happen suddenly, but a lot of sacrifices were made and there were considerable losses—poor things, they just wanted to show some responsibility. Meeting and sitting together, people reasoned with one another, expressed sorrow about the losses they had sustained, and agreed to take responsibility, rather than revenge, to stop the violence, because ultimately, we are all the children of one land. In the previous five years a lot of good things have happened. Things have gotten a lot better, and people know it. Before, a person's life was nothing, it would be easily knocked off. Now people come here every day and Nazimabad has become a better place, more developed. There is more education, more people are hospitalized; that is, there are more hospitals. We have achieved *sukun*. There are fewer problems in the center of Karachi, in our area. Inside people a lot of ease (*sahulat*) has come. Prosperity (*abaadi*) is here.

Munir Sahib's account may sound vague to a reader expecting clear references and direct explanations, backed up with precise facts, names, and dates. I found, however, that many of the residents who had experienced the period of urban unrest most closely, remembering corpses lying in their streets or hearing gunfights outside their doors, spoke most obliquely and euphemistically about what they had lived through. It was as if subtlety was crystal clear enough, or as if being explicit might conjure dangerous memories. Rather than dismiss the indirect quality of his narrative as a failing, I urge readers to consider that Munir Sahib is not an expert informant, a former party activist, or an intellectual. He is, like tens of thousands of Nazimabad residents, a bystander subjected to politically motivated street violence, even though the activists were likely his friends or classmates or neighbors. It is imperative that we consider multiple relations to legacies of urban violence not limited victims and activists. And yet the position that Munir Sahib constructs as he narrates an account of the political violence in his neighborhood in the 1990s, as a fearful nonactivist finder of corpses, precisely describes both the limits to his agency and the "structures of subordination that create the conditions of its enactment" (Mahmood 2005, 15). By invoking an atmosphere of fear, he indicates it was a shared emotional experience of that time, conspicuously counterposing it to *sukun*, or respite, as a guiding trope of the comparatively peaceful present.

To locate how Munir Sahib articulates *sukun*, it bears considering his use of terms signifying order. For example, he uses the metaphor *ilaaj*, which refers to a medical remedy, alongside terms referring to style (*andaaz*), dealings (*moamalaat*), ease (*sahulat*), etiquette (*tameez*), responsibility (*zimidari*), and prosperity or cultivation (*abaadi*). He refers to verbal negotiation, through meeting and reasoning with each other, as being more conducive to allowing *sukun* to come, implicitly referencing not only the government but also the warring factions in the protracted turf war.[12]

Most interesting, however, is the way that the respite of the recent past is attributed to an orderliness entrenched in good manners and moral obligation. Although the medical metaphor refers to a cure, all the other terms refer to conduct, as markers of a specifically moral refinement. It is at this point that alternatives to urban unrest are mediated by respectability. At the end of his comments about government involvement, Munir Sahib explains that the negotiations between the government and the parties that battled each other—exactly which two he means is unclear—ended because they recognized their responsibilities, thus emulating a moral priority on duty.

This comment spurs his emphasis on cultivation based in acquired, rather than intrinsic, practices. Especially striking is his speculation that the perpetrators of violence may have undergone a moral transformation attributed to the influence of outsiders. This explanation relies on a logic of malleable selves—in this case, impressionable and possibly misguided—who benefit from keeping good company. I find it fascinating that this emphasis on learning to be well mannered is critically geographical. Superior moral cultivation is described as an internal transformation of people from one neighborhood by people who live in another, or at least, in a nebulous "outside." In an interesting twist on Veena Das (1995, 2007, 2008) and Naveeda Khan's (2006, 2012) emphases on internal enemies, or "outsiders within," Munir Sahib evokes the insiders without, where the moral ideals he espouses are emulated by influential people in a geographically removed social location. He continues this focus on becoming cultivated and thereby prosperous, building on an idiom of social indicators—development, education, hospitals—before asserting that ease and convenience (*sahulat*) has come. On its heels is *abaadi*, which combines the connotations of cultivation, prosperity, and urban inhabitation—the quality, then, of being occupied by a morally informed humanity.

The emphasis Munir Sahib places on moral transformation draws clearly on a vision of normative, respectable ideals of decency, duty, and orderliness. Moreover, his suggestion that the verbal negotiations, that ostensibly enabled peaceful resolution, were anchored in the acquisition of etiquette completely by-passes the questions of grievance and marginalization in favor of a moral logic of implicitly pious respectability. A vague sense of generalized respite just manages to allude to the complex history of "troubles," only obliquely articulating a fantasy of belonging through the emotional worlds of ease, prosperity, and relief in the aftermath of political turf wars. Circumscribed and tentative as it is, Munir Sahib's narrative is shaped by the social, historical, and political conditions of his subjection and the possibilities that it enables. His understanding of change through a moral transformation constitutes Munir Sahib's stance as a political location, embracing the ordinary as a lens of historical interpretation and a mode of articulating an alternative to turf wars and street violence.

Intolerants

A particular sentiment was generally repeated by those who were old enough to remember the fear (*khauf*) that had pervaded the 1980s and 1990s: "Nowadays, people don't heed hooliganism" (*aajkal log badmaashi nahin maante*). The verb for "to acquiesce"—*maanna*—was the same one used to describe relations between subordinates and authorities: children listening to or obeying parents and teachers, or young people doing what elders told them to. Not complying indicated fearlessness, recklessness, and an indignant refusal to tolerate the paranoid expectation of threats and blackmail. The *badmaashi* to which they referred was a euphemism for *garbar*, harassment, and violent tactics associated with political party workers during previous decades, as made clear in Munir Sahib's narrative. In addition, allusions to fearlessness were couched in quiet voices and oblique references—those who spoke loudly and frankly were most often considered simultaneously careless, brave, and naive.

Despite the clear limitations of its scope, the very repetition of this intolerance invoked a rejection of the recent history of urban unrest in Karachi. More important, it conjured an emergent collectivity, the idea of a public and a sense of shared experiences and belonging through the generalized subject—"people"—which imagined alternatives to "hooliganism." Still vague, still oblique, tentative, fragile, and perhaps ultimately ineffective, the claim nonetheless rallied around a morally righteous transformation positing ordinary, respectable conduct as an alternative to violent street politics, as the content of sukun. A form of resistance built on very limited agency that might slip entirely off the analytical radar if we were looking only for effective challenges to social hierarchy, the conspicuous reiteration of an affect of fearlessness points to a fantasy of belonging, rather than organized mobilization, through the normative moral ground of ordinariness. Nonetheless, I heard this sentiment, which connected a demand for respite with the alleged power of indignant moral righteousness, echoed by middle-class men and women of varying ages, divergent occupations and residing in disparate neighborhoods that had all been affected by the turf politics and government operations of earlier decades.

Munir Sahib was one of many who made this assertion, locating it temporally, in parallel to *sukun*, as something that had developed over the past five years. He implicitly connected the affective relief of *sukun* to the moral high ground of intolerance. It buttressed his description of the changes that had occurred, and his claim that a lot of good things had happened, and people knew it. In another part of his neighborhood, two men in their fifties expressed a similar view, asserting that people nowadays did not tolerate *badmaashi*, even as they were in the midst of telling me indignantly how young armed party activists enforced curfews in the area, or how the local parks were named after MQM party members killed by the police and military. Evoking a vague collectivity of "people" who insisted they would no longer be complicit with so-called hooligans suggested that political violence had already subsided, and the conditions of Karachi residents' subjection to violent turf politics had already transformed, providing the space of respite that allowed them to imagine that they could reject the immorality of armed political unrest.

Another version was presented by Nadia Baji, who was in her early thirties and lived with her husband and two small children in an apartment building near her workplace. She extended the statement of a generalized rejection of *badmaashi* to insolence, or *badtameezi*. Although she began by describing how political violence would no longer be tolerated, her account moved quickly to domestic relations, higher incidences of divorce, and how women no longer put up with husbands and families-in-law unquestioningly. She immediately linked euphemistic turf politics to personal, household relations of power and patriarchal structures of gendered and generational inequality. Nadia Baji's narrative trajectory begins with a vague sense of belonging achieved through the shared fantasy of intolerance, first among the nebulous "people" she invites to share her sentiment, which is seamlessly extended into an equally imprecise reference to the shared emotional worlds of women. Who were these "people"? Who are these women? Nadia Baji makes a tentative and yet powerfully felt assertion that fantasizes about not one, but two, distinct collectivities.

Both, however, nonetheless potentially recognize shared experiences, albeit in ways that are shaped by critically significant histories and structures of subjection.

A third, and conspicuously less moralizing, version was presented by young people in their twenties. Farid Bhai, a university student, good-naturedly narrated how he was able to attend the rallies of enemy parties the MQM and the JI without having to succumb to the pressure to join either. This stance was enabled by social capital: his friendship with a JI student leader and a former neighbor who had become prominent in the MQM. Bushra, a college student, explained that the solution was to stop being afraid and go outside. Her perspective, confidently brandished under the worried and fidgety gaze of her mother, was also enabled by social capital: a local MQM politician lived on their block and had installed security barriers at both ends of the street. Both Farid Bhai and Bushra suggested that they elided the pressure to affiliate or identify with a particular political organization, albeit in decidedly conditional ways that depended on whom they knew, where they lived, and a resolute confidence in their own fearlessness and the relative serenity of the current political climate.

Though clearly fragile and highly contingent, the shared sense of avowed fearlessness seemed to be embedded in an idiom of denunciation and indignation. A particularly significant conjuncture was after political rallies devolved into three days of citywide violence in May 2007 and, buttressed by live news television broadcasts, gave way to a brief period of explicit accusations leveled directly at the MQM (see Ahmad 2014). The political conflict and street violence mobilized a moralized discourse that not only singled out one instigator but also used indignant denunciation as an idiom of differentiation. Specific references to compassion and respectability underscored the vocal othering of political violence, thus contrasting the reports and images of unrest against the implicitly middle-class decency that invoked itself as normatively unmarked. For example, an elderly Partition-era migrant who was ethnically Pashtun, had been involved with the PPP three decades earlier and now lived with his sons in a northern neighborhood adjacent to an area of actively contested political turf, spat out a familiar sentiment in the days after the violence: "there are no politics in this country, only hooliganism" (*is mulk men siyaasat nahin hai, ṣirf badmaashi*). He went on to exclaim that "they" used guns to deal with each other, invoking a "they" consisting of delinquent hooligans who engaged in armed confrontation. By implication, his narrative conjured a normative, more cultivated "we" who could envision politics without resorting to armed encounters. His critique nonetheless relied on generalized and vaguely identified groups that mobilized a sense of belonging animated by the shared emotional world of righteous respectability. This powerful sentiment of a morality of restraint drawing on manners and decency was even more explicit in a comment on an English-language blog entry about the same events:

One bullet is fired and then nobody knows who is on whose side. Every political confrontation devolves into a gang-fight and people wanting a political change stay at home to watch the massacre in their city. In all honesty, ask how many *shareef* [respectable] Karachiites actually went outside to support one party or the other? Our *sharaafat* [implicitly pious, respectable strata] stayed at home, in *purdah* [veiled, concealed by a curtain, segregated, usually women from men]. (May 12, 2007, comment on Najam 2007)

The idiom of respectability operationalizes terms associated with piety and modesty, *sharaafat* and purdah, to contrast politicized violence, and even political action more broadly, with the moral position of being subjected to staying at home, waiting for the worst to be over. Of course, this comment could also be read as a satire of subjection rationalized as implicitly pious decency. More important, however, its double-edged and ambivalent quality points to the emergence of a political sensibility that is expressed through a discourse of nonparticipation in political violence through domestic confinement, where staying at home is both an action and a compulsion.

Figuring the respectability of retreating from public space in contrast to the "hooliganism" of political violence that supports political parties and the use of firearms posits a normative order subordinated to domesticity. As Lubna Chaudhry (2004) and others have emphasized, "multileveled" relations of power situate the possibilities of agency and critique in urban Pakistan (see also Chaudhry and Bertram 2009; Nichola Khan 2010, 2012; Verkaaik 2004). Nested hegemonies of generational and gendered domestic authority position young men who act without morally normative restraint, by engaging in street violence or aligning themselves with party objectives, as uncontrolled or uncontrollable rather than directly within familial, patriarchal hierarchies. Thus, the complex individual relationships young male activists negotiate in relation to their families and militancy, whether asserting generational independence (Verkaaik 2004) or the possibility of self-transformation (Nichola Khan 2010, 2012), are obscured in popular discourses that frame them as hooligans and denounce their involvement in urban unrest, by virtue of not staying at home, as a moral failing. The scolding tone assumed by critics of political violence in the aftermath of May 2007 subsumed street tactics to a privatized familial order that located a moral political alternative in the shared experiences of denunciation and domestic confinement.

The tentative, delicate, and ultimately minimally effective sentiment that hooliganism and political violence would no longer be tolerated by ordinary and respectable people in the name of normative pious morality suggests an emergent collectivity, albeit as yet only as a fantasy and a sense of belonging. It would be a mistake to disregard this set of discourses as a misrecognition by the powerless and depoliticized, masking their mere subjection. I contend that it articulates something more radical: the hint of that subjection as a shared, and potentially contested, experience. Locating grievance in a primarily moral register not only conjures a classed sensibility but also generates a normative imaginary. As Mahmood reminds us in the epigraph to this chapter, imaginaries of change and the potential for action are critically shaped and limited by the conditions of subordination that structure and inform the possibilities of agency. As Avramopoulou reminds us in her contribution to this volume, the limits of effective action alert us to how a political presence can become vocal despite violently unfulfilled political desires.

Middle-class Karachi residents' discourses of indignantly righteous ordinariness were eventually, though fleetingly it seems, mobilized into an organized political platform. In subsequent years, I believe that their accounts of moral normativity were aligned with the rise of a new party, the Pakistan Tehreek-e-Insaf (PTI). Founded by former cricket star Imran Khan in the late 1990s, the party was appreciated by a very small group, largely consisting of elites, until a decade later. Khan's moralizing, and often vague, narratives about truth and justice, and his equally abstract denunciations of corruption and inefficiency, suddenly and almost inexplicably enjoyed a massive following, largely by young people.[13] A key turning point was precisely the violent events of May 2007 mentioned earlier, when Khan contributed to the circulating discourses of indignation by recklessly stating that he would press criminal charges against the leader of the MQM, who lived in self-imposed exile in London. This was the first time I heard middle-class Karachi residents say anything positive about Khan and his party. I watched as my younger informants, who used to refer to Khan only in vitriolic terms, slowly became staunch supporters over the course of a few years. In the 2013 general elections, the PTI won significant seats, especially in Khyber-Pakhtunkhwa, but also in Punjab and Karachi. It has emerged as the third-largest party presence at the federal level.[14] I would attribute the PTI's success precisely to its leader's invocations of normative, respectable morality as an alternative to all that young, urban middle-class Pakistanis rejected as being distasteful about their government and politics.

Shauq

How is this moral alternative articulated? What does it espouse? Here, accounts reveal that leisure activities and consumer practices are enabled by the effective rejection of political violence. Conversely, these pursuits are marked by not being feasible, available, or possible in the same way during periods of widespread urban unrest. Leisure and consumer practices were often expressed through the term *shauq*, meaning "inclination" or "predilection" (Platts 1884, 736), but more colloquially used to indicate pleasure or activities that gave pleasure, akin to hobbies. Significantly, the *shauq* Karachi residents described was outdoors, often in public spaces like streets or parks, and thus precisely in those locations that protracted turf wars had rendered inaccessible. In the vague, albeit hopeful, visions of normativity, where ordinariness becomes a political position, leisure and consumer pursuits posit a morally respectable alternative to political grievances.

Leisure, pleasure, and consumption are intertwined with assertions about relief, respite, and ostensibly fearless indignation in the aftermath of extended street violence. Karachi residents describe them as what becomes possible when tactics of political violence subside, although they phrase this as their elective rejection of hooliganism. I must emphasize that their claims about normative morality are decidedly optimistic, conspicuously vague, and grounded in structures of feeling; theirs is a vision of the potential for change and a sense of belonging rather than an organized group or even a movement. Emphatically emergent, the shared emotional, sensory, and aesthetic experiences of pleasure and consumption articulate what respite feels like, how it is accessed, and how it constitutes an alternative to the forms of politics that middle-class Karachi residents suggest, ineffectually as it turned out, they would no longer tolerate.

One of the newly possible pastimes that people in Nazimabad and nearby neighborhoods were most excited about was taking evening walks in local parks. Family picnics were a close second. The presence of women in both of these spaces was especially noted; "family" was also a euphemism for groups including women. In parks and restaurants, the family section was where only men accompanied by women were permitted. They could also include groups with only women, but groups of men alone had to sit in the regular section. This was supposed to provide a safe space, free from the intrusive gazes and potential harassment of "Eve teasers." It effectively contributed to public areas that were much more accommodating to women. Several parks in Nazimabad also had family sections for women and children, separated from where men could spend time together by a signpost and an invisible, socially enforced line.

Munir Bhai explicitly connected respite and pleasure through the terms *sukun* and *shauq*. In his account of *sukun* in neighborhood politics and the concomitant decrease in street violence, he mentioned that tending birds on his roof was his *shauq*. Almost immediately, Munir Bhai related this hobby to back the term *sukun*, shifting its significance from a general scale to a personal one. When I was younger and my life became difficult, he said, I would find *sukun* by spending time with the birds, feeding them, watching them. It was my *sukun*, he added. I still do it for *sukun*. The connection between the scales of *sukun* and the pursuits that bring *shauq* are importantly connected, not only literally in the course of Munir Sahib's account but also causally, where subsiding urban unrest and the respite it provided open up the possibility for leisure activities. For Munir Sahib, tending birds was also a consumer practice. He told me that he sold the birds as an additional source of income, and my research assistant mentioned that he had a relative who had once bought a pair of birds for twenty-eight thousand rupees, which at that time was about the same price as a brand-new Chinese-made motorcycle. According to Munir Sahib, leisure and consumption on his rooftop were made possible by what he understood as the moral transformation that had brought about *sukun* from political violence in urban space.

I asked Munir Sahib what other people did for *shauq* or *sukun*, reproducing the link he had drawn between the terms. Well, he said, they spend time with their friends and families. They go on outings together (*ghumna*). He added that many parks had been built in the past few years, and he rattled off the names of parks in Block 1 and in Nazimabad generally. In parks, he said, mostly you see "families." Families go on picnics together in the park or at the seaside. That was one thing that had changed over the past few years: families can sit in the parks together. He continued, saying that they went mostly in the evenings, but also on Sundays. That didn't used to be possible, he said, up until five years ago it wasn't possible. In the past five years there has been some *sukun* and now you see families on picnics in the park. That's a good thing I have noticed.

The parks, walks, and family picnics Munir Sahib described are a new possibility. Respite from turf wars and ongoing street violence enabled alternative pursuits: leisure activities in public spaces, especially inside the neighborhood, that were deemed safe, as well respectable enough, for women and children. Moreover, Munir Sahib noted that many of the local parks had been built only recently, within the past few years, in the aftermath of decreasing urban violence, in tandem with the coming of *sukun*. Apparent in his account was that local residents relish these new spaces and new opportunities. The moral transformation Munir Sahib described earlier is indelibly linked to *shauq* by the "family" unit; perhaps intergenerational, cohabiting kin groups that form a domestic order, but also, euphemistically, groups that include women and may also include children or men. The contrast of leisure, gender, and generation marked the earlier "troubles" as having masculinized such nondomestic spaces, but more literally, these opportunities for public leisure were made possible when the troubles subsided.[15]

The enthusiasm for leisure activities accessible to the middle classes abounded. Parveen Baji, a middle-aged widow and notable personality on her street, continually talked about how much she enjoyed evening walks with her female friends. She observed how much fun it was to people watch and occasionally told anecdotes about her walks with gusto. Parents described taking their young children to Aladdin Park to have their faces painted. Newspapers, billboards, and television commercials advertised new restaurants and sprawling adventure parks on the new superhighway. Meanwhile, editorials complained about how gluttonous Karachi residents jostled for seats, parking, and a place in the buffet line at fast-breaking restaurant events during the holy month of Ramadan.

Young men joyously described the infamy of Safari Park, where the naughty but self-righteous would go to harass young couples on simultaneously reprehensible and titillating "dates." University faculty at a woefully underattended event lamented that their occasion had unfortunately coincided with an open campus picnic sponsored by the student wing of a political party. Leisure had become so powerful that party organizations mobilized it to attract a following, albeit often consisting of smilingly good-natured, self-proclaimed freeloaders.

Shauq, it seemed, had become paramount, perhaps because of its novelty in the aftermath of extended political violence. Pleasure through leisure and consumer practices was the moral alternative to turf wars and urban unrest. Residents embraced these pursuits as "ordinary" and respectable, thus constituting them as normative within a middle-class framework. This ordinariness, which finds articulation in both *shauq* and *sukun*, becomes a tentative, fragile, and admittedly vulnerable political position that begins with a rejection of street violence. Rather than a depoliticized or apolitical stance, when espoused by the very people who live in the politically territorialized neighborhoods of Karachi that carry the memories of sustained state repression and militant violent conflict, the quality of the ordinary as a shared experience allows the recognition of a collectivity and the potential, however slight, for contestation.

Oskar Verkaaik (2004, 118) notes how the English term *fun* was used by MQM activists not only as an expression of the pleasures that "gave party members and supporters a sense of agency that enabled them to identify with the movement," but also as a ludic form of transgression that overlapped with violence. Munir Sahib and others' emphasis on the pleasures of leisure activities, described through the term *shauq*, also gives the middle-class Karachi residents I spoke with a sense of agency and belonging akin to fearlessness, but in contrast to Verkaaik's findings, their everyday playfulness takes place in relation to memories of being subjected to, rather than participating in, turf wars. The fear and domestic confinement they remember combines with the self-conscious novelty of leisure practices in public spaces and oblique rejections of violent politics to critically generate relief, or as Munir Sahib maintained, *sukun*. None of this directly challenges an established social hierarchy, but it does point to a growing fantasy, hope, and potential for what Peano describes in this volume as the composition of a movement that can overcome divisions, perhaps precisely through the vague and general allusions to a moral ordinariness that work against the grain of identity politics, experimenting with untested senses of belonging.

Conclusion

The ordinariness of everyday life, as Veena Das (2007) reminds us, is an achievement, the outcome of ongoing processes of enfolding that incorporate as they remake past ruptures into the renewed temporalities of daily experience. Das focuses on the recuperation of the everyday in the aftermath of a space of violent devastation, where lives and relationships are remade precisely through the "descent into the ordinary." The fragile alternatives of *shauq* and *sukun* that middle-class Karachi residents invoke as they reject political violence produce the ordinary as a juxtapolitical category, as described by Lauren Berlant (2008, 10): proximate to a political elsewhere, occasionally crossing into political alliance, but also bound to the sense of an emotional world that has "more than survived social negativity by making an aesthetic and spiritual scene that generates *relief from the political.*" As such, they point toward ordinariness as an affective structure of relief, as well as a platform for imagining belonging and the possibility for change. In Karachi, this figurative mode of relief was inflected by respectability, more specifically, by casting peace as the result of a moral transformation, by indignantly rejecting violence as something that would no longer be tolerated by "respectable" people, and by locating alternatives to political conflict in leisure and consumer practices that reclaimed public space.

The changes that a politics of the ordinary can bring about, when grounded in respectable morality, are decidedly limited. Rather than advocate or form a grievance through institutionalized party politics, indignant voices avoided the activities that they condemned and pleaded for party affiliates to be transformed, to dispense with the violence that has constituted "the political" in Karachi. The political presence of the middle-class residents I worked with resided in the limits to their agency, which cast historically situated relief and respite as "feeling as if" a sense of belonging and an emergent collectivity could be built up through oblique, disparate, and tentative narratives of moral ordinariness.

The formalization of this moral agenda through the meteoric rise of Imran Khan's PTI party is a very recent development. The party won a small but not insubstantial number of seats in selected urban centers in the 2013 elections, after having boycotted the 2008 elections and, in 2002, having its leader win its only seat in the National Assembly in his home constituency of Mianwali, Punjab. In Karachi, a landmark rally was held on December 25, 2011, at the Mazar-e-Quaid, the national monument and mausoleum commemorating the death of Pakistan's founder, Muhammad Ali Jinnah. The site was significant because, while not exactly public space—the site usually charged admission and other parties generally held rallies in the streets—it was appropriated as public space for the duration of the rally. More than two hundred thousand people, many of them youth from both elite and nonelite backgrounds, milled about the site, which was located at an important historical nexus of turf politics. Not the monument grounds themselves, but the roads immediately adjacent on their northwestern side, were used for rallies by other parties, and moreover were the conspicuous turf of the MQM. In the events of May 2007 described earlier, the nearby intersection of

Gurumandir had been the site of a prolonged gunfight between workers of rival political parties. The peaceful denouement of a huge rally in the area seemed contingent on the secure enclosure of an available, fenced-in space. Rather than vying for the popular, and potentially confrontational, aspect of street politics, the PTI rally occupied a designated location, away from residential or commercial space, with clear boundaries that asserted "politics happens here." By confining political activity to a specific site, the PTI event embraced the respectable alternative of rejecting, avoiding, and perhaps protecting itself from turf politics.

The rise of the PTI mirrored an important relapse of urban violence in Karachi, most notably since 2007. After the violence of May 2007, political animosity through target killings was increasingly figured in a familiar *muhajir*-Pashtun register, mimicking the ethnicized politics of the MQM's early years. Sustained turf wars among political party rivals resumed, escalating between 2009 and 2011. They grew into a large-scale ethnopolitical turf war in the summer of 2011. These more familiar turf politics continue but have been increasingly complemented by sectarian and political violence on a less local scale. Since 2011, events attributed to the Pakistani Taliban have altered the terrain of urban unrest in Karachi. Leading up to the 2013 general elections, political rallies held by a range of parties with historically strong representation, some of whom were each other's enemies, were bombed in series, allegedly by the organization of the Pakistani Taliban. In Karachi, this included the MQM (see Kazmi 2013). The shared experience of being targeted may prompt the parties to do what I have argued many middle-class Karachi residents have done: recognize a sense of belonging and articulate a rejection of violence on the grounds of moral transformation, and in the name of respectability, enacting a form of agency shaped by the very structures of their subjection.

Notes

1. For perspectives on the rejection of violence in Karachi, see Ahmad (2011, 2014), Baig (2008), Chaudhry (2004), Chaudhry and Bertram (2009), A. Khan (2003), Nichola Khan (2010), and Ring (2006).

2. Anthropological interventions mobilizing the "ordinary" draw on the philosophical legacies emphasizing complex contextual descriptions of everyday life in the work of Austin, Cavell, and Wittgenstein. Notable efforts to grapple with this term include Veena Das's (2007) astute observations that the everyday is an achievement engaging the experiential uncertainties of skepticism and Michael Lambek's (2010, 3) anthology exploring how everyday ethical sensibilities "draw on and are drawn into the ordinary."

3. Berlant's (2008) work focuses on textual relations and gender-marked North American popular culture, but the theoretical basis of her argument about women and feminine belonging in the United States addresses parallel issues of tentative critique articulated through a feeling of belonging that was prominent in my ethnographic findings among middle-class Karachi residents.

4. A more detailed account of the MQM appears in the following section of the chapter.

5. Sarah Ansari (2005) provides a historical account of Partition-era migrants in Sindh and the growing mobilization of the term *muhajir* as a category of identity in the early years of Pakistan's Independence. Tahir Naqvi (2012) and Vazira Zamindar (2007) examine the ambivalent construction of the *muhajir* migrant refugee from the non-agreed areas for "population transfer" in official government discourse, and Naqvi elaborates the trope of sacrifice that critically shaped *muhajir* claims to privileged Pakistani belonging.

6. For a more detailed history of the MQM, see, for example, Nichola Khan (2010) and Verkaaik (1994, 2004). For an explanation of how *muhajir* experiences of exclusion through the quota system were exacerbated by language politics in the province of Sindh, which just preceded the introduction of the quotas and built momentum for politicizing muhajir belonging, see Rahman (1996, 120–128) and Nichola Khan (2010, 33–34).

7. Many Nazimabad residents were also Jamaat-e-Islami (JI) supporters, but Nichola Khan (2010, 38) notes that party affiliation included a socioeconomic dimension: the parts of Nazimabad that had remained JI bastions were more affluent and less affected by unemployment than the areas that supported the MQM.

8. At the time of writing, following the general elections of 2013, Nawaz Sharif is again the prime minister of Pakistan and the MQM again won the majority of National Assembly seats in Karachi. Now, however, the MQM is part of the official opposition.

9. Violent events attributed to the Pakistani Taliban since 2011 have altered the terrain of urban unrest in Karachi, departing from the sustained turf wars among political party rivals, which escalated between 2009 and 2011. For example, leading up to the 2013 general elections, political rallies held by multiple parties with historically strong representation were bombed, allegedly by the organization of the Pakistani Taliban. In Karachi, this included the MQM (see Kazmi 2013). The targeted violence followed a series of sectarian bombings in early 2013, also attributed to the Pakistani Taliban.

10. Nichola Khan (2010) documents the memories and experiences of violence of former members who have since "retired."

11. The previous municipal government was led by the Jamaat-e-Islami from 2002 to 2005. In a lively argument between Munir Sahib's neighbors, two middle-aged men argued about whether the new MQM government had actually modified a problematic local roundabout or whether they had just painted over the previous party's colors, limiting their intervention to a symbolic territorial claim.

12. It is clear that Munir Sahib is referring to the period of negotiations with the government that followed Operation Clean-Up; neither I nor my research assistant interpreted Munir Sahib's account as in any way condoning the government-sanctioned occupation of the city.

13. For my knowledge of Khan's early moralizing narratives, I thank my father, who persistently inundated my inbox with his writings throughout the 2000s.

14. It bears mentioning that the 2013 election of a PTI-led government in the province of Khyber-Pakhtunkhwa has been followed by repeated scandals accusing Khan and the PTI leadership of corruption. It is not yet clear, at the time of writing, what the implications for the PTI support base will be, but the young Karachi residents of my acquaintance who were once fervent supporters have been decidedly more cynical about the PTI's claims since 2013.

15. I do not mean to suggest that leisure activities in public space emerged only after the late 1990s, but rather that in the particular neighborhood strongholds or contested turf of the MQM, fifteen years of active state repression and factional interparty conflict intensified the novelty of literally new parks and a new peace, made possible in part by remade political priorities and relationships to local government under General Musharraf. Young people

marveled disbelievingly and older residents reminisced wistfully about leisure pursuits in the 1970s, before the Islamization campaign of General Zia. The recent history urban unrest has fundamentally transformed how Karachi residents relate to being in public—or open (see Chakrabarty 1991)—space.

References

Abbas, Zaffar. 1995. "Karachi: Benazir's Waterloo?" *Herald* (Karachi) 26 (6): 24–31.

Ahmad, Tania. 2011. "Bystander Tactics: Life on Turf in Karachi." *South Asia Multidisciplinary Academic Journal* 5. http://samaj.revues.org/3537.

———. 2014. "Socialities of Indignation: Denouncing Party Politics in Karachi." *Cultural Anthropology* 29 (2): 411–432. http://www.culanth.org/articles/744-socialities-of-indignation-denouncing-party.

Ansari, Sarah. 2005. *Life After Partition: Migration, Community and Strife in Sindh, 1947–1962.* Karachi: Oxford University Press.

Baig, Noman. 2008. "From Mohallah to Mainstream: The MQM's Transformation from an Ethnic to a Catch-All Party." M.A. thesis, Department of Political Science, University of Victoria, Canada.

Bakhtiar, Idrees. 1992. "Operation Sindh: Can the Army Deliver?" *Herald* (Karachi, Pakistan) 23 (6): 24–29.

———. 1994. "What Does the MQM Really Want?" *Herald* (Karachi, Pakistan) 25 (5): 26–33.

Berlant, Lauren. 2008. *The Female Complaint: The Unfinished Business of Sentimentality in American Culture.* Durham, NC: Duke University Press.

Chakrabarty, Dipesh. 1991. "Open Space/Public Place: Garbage, Modernity and India." *South Asia: Journal of South Asian Studies* 14 (1): 15–31.

Chaudhry, Lubna Nazir. 2004. "Reconstituting Selves in the Karachi Conflict: Mohajir Women Survivors and Structural Violence." *Cultural Dynamics* 16 (2–3): 259–290.

Chaudhry, Lubna Nazir, and Corrine Bertram. 2009. "Narrating Trauma and Reconstruction in Post-Conflict Karachi: Feminist Liberation Psychology and the Contours of Agency in the Margins." *Feminism & Psychology* 19 (3): 298–312.

Das, Veena. 1995. *Critical Events: An Anthropological Perspective on Contemporary India.* New Delhi: Oxford University Press.

———. 2007. *Life and Words: Violence and the Descent into the Ordinary.* Berkeley: University of California Press.

———. 2008. "Violence, Gender and Subjectivity." *Annual Review of Anthropology* 37: 283–299.

Jafri, Hasan M. 1992. "MQM: A Fight to the Finish?" *Herald* (Karachi, Pakistan) 23 (7): 24–30.

Kazmi, Imran. 2013. "Attacks on MQM, PPP in Karachi; Five Killed." *Dawn*, April 28. http://www.dawn.com/news/1025539/attacks-on-mqm-ppp-in-karachi-five-killed.

Khan, Ayesha. 2003. "Gendering War Talk." *International Feminist Journal of Politics* 5 (3): 448–455.

Khan, Naveeda. 2006. "Of Children and Jinn: An Inquiry into an Unexpected Friendship during Uncertain Times." *Cultural Anthropology* 21 (2): 234–264.

———. 2012. *Muslim Becoming: Aspiration and Skepticism in Pakistan.* Durham, NC: Duke University Press.

Khan, Nichola. 2010. *Mohajir Militancy in Pakistan: Violence and Transformation in the Karachi Conflict.* New York: Routledge.

———. 2012. "Between Spectacle and Banality: Trajectories of Islamic Radicalism in a Karachi Neighborhood." *International Journal of Urban and Regional Research* 36 (3): 568–584.

Lambek, Michael. 2010. *Ordinary Ethics: Anthropology, Language, and Action.* New York: Fordham University Press.

Mahmood, Saba. 2005. *Politics of Piety: The Islamic Revival and the Feminist Subject.* Princeton, NJ: Princeton University Press.

Muttahida Qaumi Movement. 2013. "MQM Candidates for Elections." http://www.mqm.org /englishnews/2017/mqm-candidates-for-elections-2013.

Najam, Adil. 2007. "Karachi Burning: Clashes, Violence, Firing, Deaths." *All Things Pakistan* (blog), May 12. http://pakistaniat.com/2007/05/12/karachi-burning-civil-war-firing-dead -violence-mqm-aaj/.

Naqvi, Tahir. 2012. "Migration, Sacrifice and the Crisis of Muslim Nationalism." *Journal of Refugee Studies* 25 (3): 474–490.

Pakistan Elections. 2013a. "Candidate List." http://elections.com.pk/candidatelist.php.

———. 2013b. "Pakistan Elections 2013 Results." http://elections.com.pk/results.php?elecID =6&start=651.

Platts, John T. 1884. *A Dictionary of Urdu, Classical Hindi, and English.* London: W. H. Allen & Co.

Rahman, Tariq. 1996. *Language and Politics in Pakistan.* Karachi: Oxford University Press.

Ring, Laura. 2006. *Zenana: Everyday Peace in a Karachi Apartment Building.* Bloomington: Indiana University Press.

Verkaaik, Oskar. 1994. *A People of Migrants: Ethnicity, State and Religion in Karachi.* Amsterdam: VU University Press.

———. 2004. *Migrants and Militants: Fun and Urban Violence in Pakistan.* Princeton, NJ: Princeton University Press.

Zamindar, Vazira Fazila-Yacoobali. 2007. *The Long Partition and the Making of Modern South Asia: Refugees, Boundaries, Histories.* New York: Columbia University Press.

7 Negative Space

Unmovement and the Study of Activism When There Is No Action

Cymene Howe

Bars and Corners

The sandbar of Santa Teresa arcs across lagoonal waters. On its shores cluster mangrove stands, and its aquatic surroundings are alive with fish and shrimp, a reservoir of subsistence for many of the fishing families who live near the *barra* in Mexico's Isthmus of Tehuantepec. The *barra* is also the place where a barricade has prevented the installation of what would have been Latin America's largest single-phase wind park. A handful of people—women, men, and sometimes a child or two—have occupied a small stretch of road near the village of Emiliano Zapata and the hamlet of Álvaro Obregón in order to prevent the wind-park developer, Mareña Renovables, from entering the sandbar and beginning construction on the 132-turbine park slated to be erected across the windswept curve of the *barra*. The fisherfolk of these two villages are worried about the impact the wind park will have on their fishing grounds, and they are concerned for the future of their towns and their children's lives. Using their bodies as tactical instruments, they have prevented company trucks from laying tires on the sandbar. However, early on a November morning in 2012, those at the barricade faced a heated confrontation with company contractors that ended in a violent standoff with the state police, jailed protestors, and two hijacked trucks. But as the women on the barricade explained in very clear and concise terms that morning, "Ellos no pasarán" (They won't get through). The occupiers at Álvaro Obregón, as well as others in the "anti-Aeolic" resistance, are resolute about the moral importance of their cause, and they are committed to maintaining their position against what they believe is an exploitative form of renewable energy development.[1] But they do not call themselves a "movement."

Managua's main thoroughfares are home to congested intersections, swollen with taxis, trucks, and repurposed school buses competing for space with street vendors hawking everything from tabloid newspapers to exotic animals. In June, many of the intersections in Nicaragua's capital city become more colorful still when they are decorated with rainbow flags and posters bearing pink triangles, the signature emblems of lesbian and gay rights movements. With people holding banners reading "Los derechos de homosexuales y lesbianas son derechos humanos" (the rights of homosexuals and lesbians are human rights), acts of queer visibility and publicity appear to be sure signs of a vital lesbian and gay movement. Until recently, however, Nicaragua held the dubious honor of maintaining the most repressive antisodomy law in Latin America. Despite legal prohibitions from 1992 to 2008 that could incur jail sentences, sexual rights activists in the country have annually hosted an entire week dedicated to "sexuality free from prejudice." They have organized queer film screenings, delivered research reports on HIV prevention and gay and lesbian mental health, held teach-ins at the local university, and published magazines such as *Fuera del Closet* (Out of the Closet), among other things. Given the reach of the antisodomy law and Nicaragua's place as the second most impoverished country in the Western Hemisphere, the depth and scope of sexual rights activism in Nicaragua has been impressive. And yet my friends and interlocutors insisted time and again, "No hay movimiento gay aquí" (There is no gay movement here). "What we have," they said, "is a *lucha* [struggle]."

* * *

This chapter is a meditation on two social movements that are not social movements. It is a reflection on social justice interventions with different means and objectives, as well as distinct physical and temporal locations, in Nicaragua more than a decade ago and in Mexico, now, in an ongoing conflict. At the barricade in Álvaro Obregón and on the streets of Managua, the people with whom I have worked have exercised various forms of resistance, and they have accomplished some of their objectives—including overturning Nicaragua's antisodomy law and preventing the installation of the massive Mareña Renovables wind park.[2] However, those who have engaged in these social justice interventions do not describe their actions in terms of a "social movement"; instead, they speak about cultural struggles and the collective power of assemblies to confront long-lasting inequalities. With its ontological orientation toward motion, the term *movement* projects a future horizon, a goal, and a resolution imagined to be ahead of us. Instead, and in practice, transformative political action is often borne out in vacillations, backsliding, disagreement, contradiction, and sometimes failure. Participants in these struggles may be devout ideologues or committed advocates; but they may also be unaware and unsure: accidental activists rather than intentional actors. The question of what precisely constitutes a social movement, coupled with the inherent ambivalences and oscillations that make up social justice work, brings us, in a roundabout way, to the second purpose of this chapter and its methodological proposition: to reflect on the significance of those instances when—in the context of ongoing collective action—there is seemingly nothing happening. For many of us, myself included, documenting the complex relationship of resistance actions, political contexts, and collective processes has been critical to better understanding how social justice operates. However, it is also true that ethnographic life doesn't always reflect the signature events associated with movements, struggles, and political outcomes; rather, we are often in a place of "adjacency"—a critical distance and untimeliness to the action of social activism (Rabinow 2011; Rabinow and Marcus 2008). This chapter offers an exploration of possibilities afforded by untimely adjacency through the terms of "negative space." For the visual arts, "negative space" denotes the empty space adjacent to the form and outline of the subject. As a methodological metaphor for the study of resistance, negative space focuses analytic attention where there is no action: when nonhappening, nil events, quiet, calm, and ostensibly little movement are, in fact, the most vivid. Put another way, this chapter poses a series of questions about how *un*movement may in fact reveal the finer contours of the political ecologies of activism and transformative social action.

From the proletariat struggles of the nineteenth century to the new social movements starting in the 1960s (Laclau and Mouffe 1985; Melucci 1989; Touraine 1988), to a contemporary third wave of activist interventions—taking place on the street and on the screen, on keypads and corporate doorsteps (Juris 2012; Juris and Khasnabish 2013; Razsa and Kurnik 2012)—the study of social movements has sought to illuminate multiple dimensions of social action, both in terms of practical organizing and in terms of their theoretical presuppositions (see Faubion in this volume). The anthropology of activism, as a subdiscipline and to its credit, has had an abiding interest in understanding the role of researchers, often as activists and participants in social movements themselves (Calhoun and Hale 2008; Dave 2012; Graeber 2009; Howe 2013). The self-reflexivity of activist anthropology has produced an extensive history of definitional exercises as to what constitutes a social movement in terms of its etiology, aims, and constituency (see Edelman 2001). While each social movement is innately contingent and contextual, the measure of a movement's success, or failure, is very often predicated on its capacity to mount mass mobilizations and foment public protest (see, e.g., Warren 1998, 41). Analytic attention often—perhaps always—centers on a suite of signature events that, in turn, serve to qualify a set of actions as social justice activism. These are the moments when major confrontations occur, when impactful decisions are made, when demands become articulated, and when some victory is achieved: the spectacular moments of concentrated protest.

Great accounts of activist worlds pivot upon one's "being there" (Geertz 1989) and capturing the ethnographic life of the movement, if from a particular vantage point (see, e.g., Juris and Khasnabish 2013, 3). In this sense, the epistemological center of social movement analysis is not so distinct from the event-rich orientation of anthropology more generally. Think of Geertz's cockfight, narrating in dramatic microcosm the dangerous "deep play" of Balinese masculinity and kinship. Or consider the spectacular proposal to scale a 180-foot cliff in chemical jumpsuits, gas masks, and foam rubber padding in David Graeber's (2009, 1–4) *Direct Action*. In each of these accounts, the edges of the event are also crucially important: the daily life practices in the village, the minutiae of consensus agreement in activist campaigns. Labors of planning and solidarity building, coupled with dramatic confrontations, actions, and publicity, are an enduring point of contrast in ethnographies of activism, providing an implicit foil between organizing and the intricacies of "social changing" (see Postill in this volume). While taking very seriously the importance of both events and process for the study of activism, here I propose to take a slightly different approach by asking, in very broad terms: How do we know a movement when we see one? Or, more exactly, how can we observe and analyze ethnographic moments that are, apparently, absent of movement in order to render more depth and scope to our understanding of resistance actions and political interventions? In this chapter I first describe the ways that social struggles in Nicaragua and Oaxaca, Mexico, have been defined by their unmovement qualities. This involves, probably unsurprisingly, resorting to a handful of epochal events, challenges, and actions in their respective political fields. Following the logic of the unmovement counternarrative that activists in Mexico and Nicaragua have each articulated, I then spend some time in the adjacent spaces of "unaction," occupying the counter-"intensities" (Alexandrakis this volume) of political formations and oppositional actions. Rather than a resolution, I pose a series of questions throughout about how seemingly uneventful times may speak to how we define, represent, and imagine social justice and collective dissent.

Nicaragua: Insurrections

Nicaragua has a certain fame as a place of insurrection. During the 1980s the country was renowned for its challenge to US imperialism, cultivating socialism in the "backyard" of the United States. The Sandinista Revolution was one of the few Latin American revolutions to successfully overthrow the state, utilizing a blend of liberation theology, Marxian principles, and a robust and avowed nationalism. Nicaragua's notoriety as a nonaligned state leveraging collectivist politics in the midst of the Reagan-era Cold War was a warranted fame. But the glory of insurrection was tarnished and eventually destroyed, in large part, because of the US-sponsored war against the country. Ultimately the Sandinistas were voted from power. A short two years later, in 1992, Nicaragua's National Assembly voted to intensify the country's antisodomy law and increase the penalties and scope of its reach. Article 204 mandated up to three years of imprisonment for "anyone who induces, promotes, propagandizes or practices in scandalous form sexual intercourse between persons of the same sex." It threatened to incarcerate, potentially, anyone who wrote about, spoke about, or putatively propagandized the subject of homosexuality in any way. In response, the *lucha* began.

Sexual rights activists who have tirelessly labored to overturn article 204 have been a diverse group. Some are grassroots advocates, and others are activists employed by nongovernmental organizations (NGOs), health clinics, or other social service agencies. During my fieldwork working within the *lucha* in Nicaragua from 1999 to 2006, I spent time with street protestors and feminist thinkers, university students and HIV-prevention educators, viewers of queer cinema and hosts of LGBT radio shows. My *compañeros* were participants in lesbian and gay discussion groups, Pride-party attendees, soap opera screenwriters, and attorneys who were well versed in the vicissitudes of human rights, sexual identity, and Nicaraguan law. Many sexual rights advocates were longtime Sandinista *militantes*, and others were neoliberal converts. Most were Nicaraguan, but a handful of advocates were foreign nationals and expatriates, some of whom had lived in Nicaragua since the revolutionary era. I also spent much of my time in Nicaragua with people who were known around the neighborhood as a *cochón* (fag) or a *cochona* (dyke) and who were increasingly referring to themselves as *gay* and *lesbiana*. Helping to plan the weeklong Sexuality Free from Prejudice events, joining lesbian discussion groups, attending HIV/AIDS-prevention events, and assisting in the creation of a Latin American database of gay and lesbian organizations all came to inform my understanding of the *lucha* for sexual rights in Nicaragua. There were days when I shared *pinolillo*, a traditional drink made of corn and cacao, with my Nicaraguan friends and coworkers, but most of my conversations occurred over well-sugared lukewarm coffee. I was also more likely to hear the best anecdotes and the bawdier details after the bottle of Flor de Caña rum had gone around the table a couple of times and the Shakira song had subsided on the speakers at the *disco gay*. During the time that my field research took place, it was illegal to promote, propagandize, or practice homosexuality in Nicaragua. However, this is precisely what many activists were doing.

Sexual rights began to emerge in Nicaragua in part because Sandinismo offered opportunities to question the status quo. Yet during the revolutionary period, both gender politics and sexual rights were, officially, suspected of being deviations from the true revolutionary path. A combination of political openings and, ironically, closures ultimately offered a template for future struggles. For activists whose political skills were honed during the Sandinista period, the communitarian ethos of revolution was a constant provocation; it inspired them to imagine social transformation in national dimensions and, at the same time, highlighted the arenas of discrimination that were unresolved by the revolutionary project. Indeed, some activists who would become involved in and committed to sexual rights were compelled by the Sandinistas' refusal to do so during their tenure. Several Nicaraguans who identified themselves as lesbian or gay told me that they became reinvested in sexual rights activism precisely because they had been prohibited from doing so, openly, during the Sandinistas' reign. Like many feminists in the wake of the revolutionary period, proponents of sexual rights were able to devote their activist energy to issues of sexual equality when the revolution ceased to be the priority. Draconian changes to the anti-sodomy law also inspired them to do so. The demise of the revolutionary regime in 1990 signaled the end of a particular ideological epoch, but it also inaugurated an era of growth among Nicaraguan NGOs, increased civil society activism, and greater global networks for advocates (Keck and Sikkink 1998). By this time, too, closet doors were opening around the world and Nicaraguan activists were beginning to see themselves as part of a growing network of transnational movements for sexual rights (see Adam, Duyvendak, and Krouwel 1999; de la Dehesa 2010; Gould 2009).

For my friends and interlocutors in the Nicaraguan sexual rights *lucha* there were substantial differences between social movements and their particular struggle. From their experiences through the revolutionary period, either as actors in that process or as closely aligned with those that were, they enumerated many differences. First was the question of size. In a country in which mass mobilization had resulted in national upheaval and an overthrow of the state, the term *movement* had a particularly massive quality, involving tens of thousands of participants. While many individual activists, coalitions, groups, networks, and organizations were promoting sexual rights in Nicaragua, by local standards of scope and scale, these interventions did not quite reach the magnitude of a movement. Second, and perhaps most important, sexual rights activists explained that some challenges, such as overcoming machismo, were more cultural than policy oriented. The social circumstances that they named—such as sexism and suspicions about sexuality more generally—actually served to sustain conditions of machismo and heterosexism (*heterosexismo*). These were cultural conditions, they explained, that at times seemed intractable, and thus they required the laborious and quotidian remediation that activists equated with struggle.

Commentaries such as these reiterated a debate within social movement scholarship, namely how a particular social movement could be designated as either "cultural" or "political" (see Alvarez, Dagnino, and Escobar 1998; Fox and Starn 1997). The node of distinction within these debates, in truncated form, was whether a particular new social movement was primarily motivated by "identity" concerns—and thus subscribed to a post-Marxist emphasis upon the transformation of culture—or, conversely, if it was more emphatically political economic in orientation and its pursuit of collective action, protest, or policy change. The tension between political and cultural movement forms was partially resolved with the concession that ultimately "[all] protest necessarily involves struggle over ideas, identities, symbols, and strategies within and across regional and national borders" (Fox and Starn 1997, 3). However, the fact that sexual rights activists highlighted the cultural dimension of their activities as central to their definition of struggle, one that fundamentally distinguished it from a movement, suggests that there continues to be an epistemological gravity to culture as a tool of social transformation. Activists' commitment to the cultural basis of the *lucha* was in fact instrumental to their policy objective of overturning the law, a "political" goal. With the aim of abolishing the antisodomy law firmly in mind, sexual rights activists found novel ways to deepen their struggle in a stereotypically cultural domain, the television soap opera.

La Telenovela Nicaragüense

Wearing spaghetti-strap tank tops and trendy jeans, "Vicki" epitomizes the gendered ideals of Nicaraguan girlhood, except for the fact that she is a *lesbiana*. *Sexto Sentido* (Sixth Sense) debuted in 2001 on the country's most popular commercial television station. According to polling data, 80 percent of the show's target audience (thirteen- to seventeen-year-olds) tuned in to watch the program, and it had some of the highest television ratings in the overall national market, claiming 70 percent of the *entire* Nicaraguan viewing audience. Produced by a Nicaraguan NGO that has had a leading role in the country's sexual rights struggle, *Sexto Sentido*, like other telenovelas, never wanted for melodrama. But it was not simply another beloved TV show; rather, it was a social justice soap opera with very specific aims to transform Nicaraguan culture. I sat for many hours on the set of *Sexto Sentido* watching the show's taping. Two cameramen with MiniDV cameras captured the show's drama, and the director, Iliana, very carefully scrutinized the performances taking place on the set. She would often praise the actors who assiduously sought to perfect their characters, and she would, occasionally, encourage them to try to make their performances "more real." I began to wonder, in the context of this social justice production, what the "real" was for the woman who portrayed the *lesbiana* character.

Jacinta, the actress who played Vicki, explained to me as we sat backstage waiting for her next scene, that she had been excited when she was told during her audition that the character she would be playing was a lesbian. "I liked it," she said, laughing:

> It made me really happy . . . to break with all the *normal*. This is something that I had never done, and I was interested in doing it as a personal goal—to break with my own prejudices and do something public like this and to go

out in the street and say, "Look, this is the work. Watch it. Analyze it. Take in the message, and if you can't do that, at least take away something." This is what made me really excited about doing it. If I had been some other way, then maybe I wouldn't have been so interested in it.

Jacinta's reaction to discovering her new character, like the ideological aspirations of the show's producers, follows a pedagogical curve in which new identity forms are seen as challenging older conventions around sexuality and gender. In good activist form, the actress is up for the challenge of facing her own prejudice. Jacinta was also convinced that her character would have a social impact:

> Commentaries, yes, we're going to hear those from people here on the street. [When they see these characters] on TV, these lesbian or gay roles are difficult. The people take it like this [she exhaled loudly and threw her hands up, mocking a reaction of being scandalized]: "This girl is a dyke or I don't know what!" But it also so happens, on the flip side, that this is positive, because people are learning, with these little details and examples, about how to handle this.

Jacinta enthusiastically performed the role of a TV character that would teach people "how to handle" the subject of lesbianism. Although her performances take place on the screen, it is noteworthy that Jacinta sees her work as taking place, if only metaphorically, on the "street" of Nicaraguan public consciousness. She has, in one sense, gone from actress to activist.

As she reflects on her introduction to the show and, in turn, to the sexual rights struggle of which it is a part, Jacinta describes her interest in performing Vicki as a "personal goal." However, Jacinta's subjectivity, more generally, raises a series of questions about participation and who becomes defined as an activist in social justice struggles. While her performance was integral to the televised drama, Jacinta was, essentially, contracted into the struggle. She was an actress looking for work in a country with no theater or film industry to speak of. She auditioned for a role, but she did not join the struggle as an avowed proponent of sexual and gender rights. Rather, she became "composed" into both roles, as activist and as actress through a series of relations, flows, and encounters (see Peano this volume). Inhabiting the character of Vicki meant balancing between gender conventionality and sexual difference, and it was through this carefully managed performance that Vicki's character was meant to change the way that Nicaraguans thought about, spoke about, and judged homosexuality. Jacinta expertly executed a set of gestures and words conceived by other activists (producers, directors, and scriptwriters) who are themselves deeply committed to the struggle. However, does Jacinta's "role"—whether performative or political—make her a true activist in the struggle? Perhaps. Although she may have originally become involved because of professional aspirations, she now voices explicit support for the cause itself. If it is sometimes unclear who counts as an activist, this should encourage us to question how social movements are differentially populated, and to consider how particular participants, whether intentional or accidental, shape social justice struggles.

Sexto Sentido broached many controversial issues over the course of eighty episodes, including sexual identity, abortion, family violence, sexism, racism, classism, and homophobia. The scriptwriters, directors, and NGO staff who produced the show noted that they were able to address these issues "without sacrificing entertainment value." Entertainment was the path to fascination and this was, in turn, the path to social justice. Engaging audiences in their homes was the explicit goal of *Sexto Sentido*'s "edutainment" programming. It was meant as a mechanism to encourage dialogue and conversation within and among Nicaraguan families. It also seemed to be succeeding because nearly everyone in Nicaragua appeared to be enthralled with *Sexto Sentido*. One Sunday afternoon, for example, while the family I lived with gathered around the household television for an anticipated episode, I walked to the nearest *pulpería* (convenience store) in a working-class neighborhood in Managua to gather cold drinks for everyone. *Sexto Sentido*'s theme song and the actors' dialogue spilled from every open window of the cinderblock houses I passed along the way. As an explicitly dialogic forum for advocacy, the TV program was intended to transform how Nicaraguans thought about, and talked about, the controversial issues being aired in the show's plotline.

It was, of course, impossible to be in each of those living rooms every Sunday afternoon and to listen in on all the conversations that were unfolding and, supposedly, changing the sexual culture of Nicaragua. Other than a handful of families with whom I was able to meet and share a screen, many of these conversations were lost, ethnographically nonexistent. From the point of view of understanding the greater cultural impact of the *lucha* for sexual rights, these conversations behind cinderblock walls were fundamentally important. And yet they were events that were unobservable, or maybe better put, inaudible and unavailable to representation. Without rehashing old debates about whether media's "impact" on audiences can ever be fully grasped, it is clear that some elements of any *lucha*, or movement, will always be out of reach. The issue is not simply how to account for the television show's impact, its transformational potential within a wider rubric of sexual rights struggle, but rather how we can be attentive to what impacts, events, or actions must be present for a movement, a struggle, or a collective action to exist. This is an epistemological question of what can be, and must be, documented in order to render the full scope and shape of movement politics. This is also a deeply methodological issue because it conditions how our narrative analyses of social movements and their kindred struggles are shaped by particular inclusions and deletions.

Banner Moments

In the late afternoon, the streets of Managua are often crowded and thus a good place for a protest. On a fading afternoon in late June 2001, a local HIV/AIDS prevention organization decided to take advantage of the streets' evening bustle by rallying a coterie of twenty young men to commandeer the sidewalks. Carrying banners proclaiming "Everyone Has a Right to Their Sexuality" and chanting "Human Rights Are Our Rights," the troupe made its way down a traffic-laden boulevard toward the Nicaraguan National Assembly and the Office of the President. Armed with yellow balloons that read "No al artículo 204" (No to article 204), the protesters managed momentarily to fill the skies with their demands. The group then found its way to an iconic figure in Managua: the hypermasculine statue of a revolutionary soldier that towers above one of the city's main thoroughfares. Erected by the Sandinistas, the statue honors Nicaragua's fallen soldiers in the Contra war. Although his official designation is *el guerrillero sin nombre*" (the unknown soldier), he is commonly referred to as "Rambo." The public sculpture was meant to stand in opposition to the kind of US-centered imperialisms that the original Rambo represents, but his figure embodies much more than one description alone can capture. In an effort to ensure a more durable message for their cause than was possible with balloons and banners, the protestors decided to plaster the base of the statue with stickers that read "No al artículo 204." Rambo's raised AK-47 cast an imposing shadow over the endeavor, but the young men were committed to affixing their message here because it was, as they put it, *un mensaje simbólico* (a symbolic message). It was a way to make their opposition to the antisodomy law very visible and to provide a subtle rebuttal of machismo and the masculine prerogative that protesters believed bolstered the antisodomy law.

Marching through Managua is a sweaty endeavor at almost any time of year, and so it was more than kind that the group who had organized our visit to Rambo came prepared for the aftermath with cold Coca-Cola and bags of chips. Sitting in the shade of a tree near the presidential palace was, in some ways, the moment that everyone was waiting for. The action was done, and it had been good. But now it was time to refresh and relax and in all truth, to just share some *chisme* (gossip). One could argue this was a moment of everyday solidarity building, or maybe it was just reward for hard work in the *lucha* on the streets of Managua. In either case, one wonders what to make of these quiet nonmovement moments. For what do they count and how might they contribute to a greater arc of social struggle? The Coke and chips followed a dramatic and demonstrable act of collective protest, replete with banners and chanted refrains. But this was the afterglow, not the climax.

The following day, the quiet continued. Everyone on our march was now back at home, back at work in the outdoor market, back to school. The media was silent too, having decided that the protest was not worthy of recognition or coverage. The action in the middle of Managua was spectacular, for its scale at least; it was a public and very clearly articulated message to advance the goals of the sexual rights *lucha*. For the arbiters of content in the daily news, it was, however, a nonevent. Was the march a small victory for the *lucha*, or was it effectively lost to history in the same way that the Coke and chips remained unrecognized and unwritten in the ethnographic account of the sexual rights *lucha* in Nicaragua (Howe 2013)?

It would be an impossible task to chart every intervention or political oscillation that shapes a movement, a struggle, or a set of resistance actions. But from a position of adjacency one has to wonder about the role of unrecognized moments, whether in ethnographic accounts, popular media, or political deliberations. How do these apparently empty spaces and times of nonmovement inform instances where social action and activism are so clearly defined and so clearly evident? Or, taken a step further, how do nonevents and the mundane hours of nonmovement in fact allow us, or seduce us, to unproblematically understand social struggles in particularly concentrated and spectacular forms?

Mexico: Depletions

Oil is faltering in Mexico, but there are ambitious plans afoot to power the country in new ways, utilizing the forces of wind, sun, and water. Mexican heavy crude extraction dropped by nearly 50 percent from 2004 to 2012, and the supergiant oil field in the gulf of Mexico, Cantarell, is beginning to run dry. The nationalized oil company Petróleos Mexicanos (PEMEX) may not be able to continue to contribute the immense revenue stream it has provided to the Mexican nation state—at times as much as 43 percent of the federal government's operating budget. In light of these petro-resource declines, and in an attempt to partially staunch greenhouse-gas emissions and slow the growth of global warming, Mexico has instituted some of the most aggressive climate change policies in the world. While the Kyoto Protocol did not demand emissions reductions for the country, Felipe Calderón (2006–2012) instituted legislation that made Mexico one of only two developing countries in the world to enshrine long-term climate targets into federal law.[3] The 2008 Renewable Energy and Energetic Transition law requires that 35 percent of electricity come from non-fossil-fuel sources by 2024. Hydropower has been a long-standing part of Mexico's energy portfolio, but new investments in wind and solar are likewise increasing. The advent of renewables and carbon mitigation targets, however, have also raised questions about how renewable energy megaprojects disenfranchise local populations and limit local autonomy. How ecological spaces and environmental resources are to be used and managed have become a cornerstone of debates in Mexico's renewable turn.

The wind that blows across the Isthmus of Tehuantepec in the state of Oaxaca has been a particularly coveted *energía limpia* (clean energy). Renewable energy producers and state officials alike have looked to the winds of the isthmus because of their profit potential as well as their possibility to reduce greenhouse gases. A study sponsored by the US Agency for International Development and conducted by the US National Renewable Energy Laboratory concluded that the isthmus has some of the best wind in the world for electricity generation: consistent, strong, and—following apertures in Mexican law that facilitate international investment in Mexican energy resources—available.[4] The "wind rush" has begun.[5] Or, in more critical terms, as many in opposition voice, the isthmus has become the site of a *nueva conquista* (new conquest). Dominated by Spanish renewable energy corporations, the wind sector seems to reiterate a politics of colonial exploitation in the form of transnational capital that has financed the installation of hundreds and hundreds of turbines that many *istmeños* have come to call "the white giants." The initial contracting for wind parks took place under somewhat suspicious conditions with select corporate sponsors given exclusive negotiation rights over prime land that, in turn, prohibited landowners from seeking competitive bids on contracts. Circulating throughout the isthmus, in addition, are stories of local authorities being manipulated and "bought" at the expense of communities to which they are supposed to be accountable. Critics of wind development readily claim that exploration and usufructuary rights were ill gotten, often through bribes paid to *presidentes municipales* (mayors) or *comisariados* (collective land commissioners).

For those who oppose how renewable energy has proceeded in the isthmus, the way in which land has been conscripted into the service of renewable energy has been an enduring problem. Some tracts of territory where parks have been planned, or placed, are located on land federally designated as *ejidos* or *bienes comunales*. Each of these tenure systems confers members (*ejidatarios* or *comuneros*, respectively) with the right to collectively decide the fate of their shared land. Development, however, has followed a much more neoliberal and individualized economic logic. In general, land that is privately owned (with owners receiving a direct rental payment) has been less contentious, although this appears to be shifting too. The industrial development model in place in the isthmus is largely predicated on a corporate self-supply model, *autoabastecimiento*. *Autoabastacimiento* engineers partnerships between private wind developers and large industrial clients (e.g., Walmart, Coca-Cola) over a period of many years. Corporate consumers are able to secure below-market prices for their electricity and benefit from *bonos de carbono* (emission reduction credits); meanwhile, the state receives infrastructural assistance (in the form of substation construction for instance) at no, or low, cost. In the discourses of clean energy development, local communities are also often portrayed as profiting from the *autoabastecimiento* model because landowners receive rents. However, many *istmeños* have begun to wonder about the true benefits of wind development. Not everyone owns windy land for rent, and some claim that the promise of jobs did not materialize in the ways they had expected. Others describe being pressured into signing contracts by government agents or developers, and, following a longer political tradition in the Isthmus, there are concerns about megaprojects in general, even those that are supposed to be clean and green.

Asambleas Istmeñas

Climate change mitigation measures and renewable energy projects have, as some analysts have predicted, fomented new opportunities for environmental consciousness and activism (Hulme 2009, xxvii). However, in the case of the Isthmus of Tehuantepec it has not been the sort of environmental response that renewable energy companies, or the state, have hoped for. Protestors involved in anti–wind park activism do not designate themselves as a movement; they are instead a collective "resistance" with a strong sense of their political genealogy. They connect their activist practices to ideological links with the Zapatistas and the Coalición Obrera, Campesina, Estudiantil del Istmo (COCEI, or the Isthmus Coalition of Workers, Peasants, and Students),[6] before the latter was corrupted and institutionalized. Like other contemporary protests against the status quo, from antiglobalization movements to Occupy, the *resistencia* is invested in collectivist, nonhierarchal organizational models (Graeber 2009; Razsa and Kurnik 2012). Drawing from ideals of neo-indigenous horizontal organization, members of the resistance are very clear about their specific opposition to megaprojects and the foreign financial intervention that characterize them (Howe, Boyer, and Barrera 2015). The *resistencia* has found political purchase, it is important to point out, not because it opposes renewable energy but because it has voiced concerns about the potential environmental and social consequences that may result from massive wind park installations (see Nahmed Sittón 2011). The size of the Mareña Renovables wind park, and its siting on the *barra*, so near to the fishing grounds of the lagoon and the sea, resulted in wind park protests that were unprecedented in scale (figure 7.1).

The office of the Asamblea de los Pueblos Indígenas del Istmo de Tehuantepec en Defensa de la Tierra y el Territorio (Assembly of Indigenous Peoples of the Isthmus of Tehuantepec in Defense of Land and Territory) is readily identified on the streets of Juchitán; it is the one with the anti-turbine art on its facade. Our meeting with two of the founders of the *resistencia* took place in a tiny room decorated with images of past victories and heroes from Che to "el Sub" (the Zapatista leader Subcomandante Marcos). Roberto began our conversation and proceeded to detail a vast historical narrative of the *resistencia*. Roberto

Figure 7.1 Opposition to the installation of a wind park on the *barra de Santa Teresa.*

is one of the primary voices of the resistance; he does not, however, like to be called a "leader." This is a designation that he associates with several hierarchical, vanguardist, and ultimately corrupt political forms in Mexico that began as movements. The *resistencia* to Mareña, Roberto explained, began with a group of teachers, of which he is one. He also emphasized that the anti-Aeolic resistance must be understood through a longer genealogy that spans many decades and locations. Roberto linked the *resistencia* to a series of insurrections: the student movement in Mexico City in 1968 and a guerrilla *foco* in Chihuahua before that; the Chiapas rebellion of the Zapatistas beginning with NAFTA and a battle over the development of an airport in San Salvador Atenco, outside of Mexico City, in the early 2000s; the teachers' strike and state violence in the capital of Oaxaca in 2006 guided by the Popular Assembly of the Peoples of Oaxaca (APPO)—which has seen a dramatic revival in 2016. Finally, he turned to Maoism itself with its agrarian peasant insurgencies and challenges to first-world imperialism. Roberto's carefully crafted genealogy drew from multiple sources of inspiration and acts, tracing a timeline through resistances near and far, temporally proximate as well as distant (see Postill as well as Peano, both in this volume). His cartography of responses to foreign domination, urban hegemony, and rebellions against neoliberal development brought us to the origins of the anti-Aeolic resistance in 2005. He and others had protested against the installation of a wind park next to the town of La Venta in the 1990s, noting that Subcomandante Marcos himself showed up and spoke in solidarity with them. Beyond symbolic gestures by the Zapatista leadership, the *resistencia* also claimed several significant victories of its own. These included nullifying contracts across the region and "rescuing" 1,200 hectares of land from being contracted and thus turned into wind parks.

Roberto gives credit where credit is due; he is faithfully citational in his rendering of the *resistencia*'s insurrectionary lineage. Originally, the Juchitecan arm of the resistance worked under the name Frente de Pueblos en Defensa de la Tierra y del Territorio (People's Front in Defense of Land and Territory). However, the designation *frente*, Roberto explained, is encumbered by vanguardism, hierarchical leadership, and a military etymology—all qualities that he and others hoped to surpass. By consensus it was decided that *asamblea* (assembly) better captured their ethos. An *asamblea* evokes, as Roberto put it, "a more indigenous notion, that of community." Roberto explained that with an egalitarian order and a rejection of hierarchical leadership the *resistencia* had proceeded with their platform in place:

> That is how we began and how we have preserved the shape of this struggle. . . . Since then, and in a concrete way, we have defined the line we have held until now, and that is, legal defense, direct action, mobilization, constant information for the communities, and founding *asambleas*.

Roberto reiterates the heritage of the *resistencia* as well as their innovations, explaining, "We have traversed the entire historical process of the Left in Mexico in order to be able to offer an alternative." The *resistencia*'s communitarian spirit of lateralist leadership and collective consensus is emphasized both in name, *asamblea*, and in spirit, rejecting leaders and, implicitly, a flock of followers. Dedication to the collective model is also manifest in the deeds of the *resistencia*, which has prioritized founding more *asambleas* as a central part of its mission. *Asambleas generales* have since multiplied across the isthmus in towns and villages, in support of the anti-Mareña resistance. These working forms of *autonomista* protest and process call for collective decision making in a reinvented use of *usos y costumbres* (literally, "practices and customs")—indigenous legal and social systems operating in parallel to state governance. *Usos y costumbres* have generally been regarded as a counterbalance to indigenous people's marginalization in elite national projects throughout Mexico and in other Latin American countries. The *resistencia* has evoked similar neo-indigenist ideals in their organizational forms as well as discursively in their materials and pronouncements, retooled to articulate with the anti-Mareña resistance.[7] Lauding indigenous knowledge and evoking autochthonous environmental stewardship has been a

176 | *Cymene Howe*

powerful and proximate logic for the struggle, even as they risk certain essential-ist interpretations (Dove 2006, 195–198; Jackson and Warren 2005; Tsing 2003). Claims to environmental wisdom and indigenous sovereignty have also been tai-lored to a very specific, and novel, alliance between Binnizá (Zapotec) and Ikojts (Huave) communities (Howe and Boyer 2016).

The *resistencia* has fomented and fostered collaborations that traverse histor-ical divisions between local indigenous populations, but they have also managed to navigate political party lines. Given the historical strength and chauvinism of party politics in Mexico it is rare for *priístas* (members of Mexico's long-reigning Institutional Revolutionary Party, or PRI) to share common ground with the left-ists of the Partido de la Revolución Democrática (PRD) and COCEI. Since the po-litical parties, left and right, have, for the most part, been in favor of the Mareña project, the parties themselves have lost favor in the eyes of *istmeños* in the resis-tance. The anti-Mareña resistance has, in further bids for autonomy, summarily questioned the inherent validity of political parties as legitimate democratic enti-ties. Antonio, one of the founders of the *asamblea* and one of the key voices in the *resistencia*, speaking to a crowd gathered in Álvaro Obregón, affirmed, "Today is a declaration of war against the political parties, against the government, against Mareña Renovables, against everyone who is allied with or affiliates with Mareña Renovables." Antonio and others also publically announced that no political party candidate would be allowed to campaign for political office in the upcom-ing municipal elections in Álvaro Obregon. In June 2013 they made good on this pronouncement by prohibiting the installation of voting machines. The parties and the park had become a combined menace for those in the resistance, and so both were given a directive and a direction: *fuera* (out).

Field Trips with Jesús

Jesús is a man with a long lineage in the isthmus. He lives in San Dionisio del Mar, where the Mareña park was slated to be built. His family has been there for generations and Jesús's father was known as the local community historian. His father was even visited once, Jesús told us one afternoon over a bowl of fish soup, by an anthropology student hoping to learn about Ikojts culture and tradition. Another of Jesús's family, his uncle, was the presiding *comisariado* back in 2004, when the ill-fated land use contract was signed with Mareña Renovables. But now, unlike then, his uncle is opposed to the construction of the wind park. It is clear in the way that Uncle Sosa winces when "*el famoso* 2004" is mentioned that he feels implicated in the wind park conflict in ways that few others do. We are here in San Dionisio, in a somewhat far-flung corner of the isthmus, to talk more with Uncle Sosa and Jesús, both of whom are now key representatives (though not leaders) of the *inconformes* (protestors). Uncle Sosa is there when we visit the site of the municipal hall that the *inconformes* have occupied for the last several months. A banner hangs from two rusting wires inside the *palacio municipal,* "La nación ikojts en resistencia contra el megaproyecto eólico" (The Ikojts nation in resistance to the Aeolic megaproject). We recognize the big cloth banner immediately; it has an eminence of its own having appeared several times in local press accounts about the anti-Aeolic resistance. Painted with an image of a man standing in his wooden canoe, surrounded by lagoonal waters, it does make for a good photograph. We hear many stories at the *palacio* about the fissures that have deepened in the community since the battle over the wind park began. We learn a lot. However, most of our time in San Dionisio is not spent at the *palacio,* the iconic site of resistance for the *inconformes.* Instead, Jesús has taken us on a field trip.

Jesús teaches at the high school in San Dionisio. He is, in true form to the teacher-dense origins of the *resistencia,* an educator by trade. His school is hosting an important event, a regional gathering of students from neighboring towns who have come to learn about the history and culture of San Dionisio. The day begins early at the school with eighty or so students in crisp blue and white uniforms obediently listening to the formal introductions of the teachers who will lead the pedagogical work for the day. We are then broken into smaller groups of students and make our introductions before we are guided through our lesson on Ikojts history by a local teacher. His mastery of the subject is better than most could claim, even if it resembles an encyclopedia entry in its factual narration. We hear from an aging fisherman who tells us about the "olden days" when fishing and shrimping were done with hand-sewn nets, repaired by careful hands stitching by gas light. This is the morning session; there is lunch to come, tiny dried and salted shrimp served with as many corn tortillas as you like. In the afternoon we are off again, this time in a caravan of trucks out to the *faro* (lighthouse), where there are boats awaiting the students and their teachers for a trip across the lagoon to the *barra* of Santa Teresa. By the time our truck arrives over dirt roads, potholes, and one missed turn, the boats are already afloat on the lagoon. It is late in the afternoon, and as Jesús had worried out loud to us, the winds are high. The waves blowing across the lagoon are sloshing and tipping the little metal boats filled with teenagers and so, disappointed, they will have to return to shore before landing on the *barra.*

Jesús shares several anecdotes that afternoon of the failed field trip. We hear histories about the town, about the conflicts that have preceded the wind park protests, and about deep divisions that have grown since "the arrival of the political parties and the wind parks." Although it was information rich, the day itself could not be described as dense with social movement. There were no momentous events, no decisive revelations, no notable ethnographic moments to illustrate a particular angle on the form of the anti-Aeolic struggle. No strategic planning took place, and it would stretch the truth to call the students' educational sessions "consciousness raising"; they were more akin to a social studies lecture than oriented toward transforming political awareness. This day—and one might select many dozens of others over the course of sixteen months of fieldwork that were yet more "eventless" in terms of active protest—was not meaningless in an ethnographic or epistemological sense; it contributed to a broader context and set of meanings, if only to explicate a longer historical view of the *resistencia* and the usually quiet lives of the *inconformes*. And yet it was noneventful from the perspective of action and activism. Times like these, in Oaxaca and elsewhere, do, however, provide a provocation as to how and whether eventlessness such as this has a place in the portraits and processes of social movements, struggles, and resistances that we hope to better understand.

The unmovement is undoubtedly part of "the social," or a cultural chronicle of a kind, but the question remains as to how these somewhat mundane times figure in the composition of social justice struggles. There is no causal moment to note, no particular tension between the status quo and the aspirations of activists to denote, describe, or theorize as "part of" the struggle. How, then, do we, as ethnographers of activism, incorporate the unremarkable events and contexts that are undoubtedly part of the larger dynamics in which social activism, struggle, and collective action take place? This is perhaps an unsatisfying question in place of a resolution, but this is, in part, the point. It is to unsettle assumptions about the unmoments, the nonevents, the absence of organizing, educating, planning, and performing protest, and to wonder how and whether they inform resistances, movements, and struggles. In shedding the fetishization of spectacular resistances—the clash in the street, the policy victory in the courtroom, or the poignant retreat of one's foes—we might also come closer to rethinking the temporalities of the moment when, supposedly, everything changes for the better.

Sleeping

In the capital city of Oaxaca we meet another Jesús, the secretary-general of the state of Oaxaca, the second in command. He appears somewhat exhausted, and on his desk is the evidence for why, a thick manila folder with "San Dionisio del Mar" written across it in ink. Despite the artifact filled with documents, he explains to us, "After two or three months of watching this conflict we still do not have all of the information we need as a government . . . and we still have many competing interests." The governor has tasked Jesús's office with resolving the blockade in Álvaro Obregón and wading further into the San Dionisio–Mareña debacle. He is pleased that we describe his role as that of mediator; he does seem to be making a real effort to understand all of the social dynamics as well as the legal and political implications. The secretary is meeting with at least one of the parties involved, the Mareña executives. We know this not only because of his statement to that effect but also because when we arrive for our meeting with him, we share the lobby for a few minutes with key corporate officials who we recognize from earlier street protests against the company in Mexico City.

Since the police and community stand off in November in Álvaro Obregón, a federal judge has issued an *amparo* (injunction) that prevents the company from doing any work on the project. The *barra* is, for now, off limits. The secretary thinks the *amparo* will soon be overruled in Mexico City. And he is convinced, at least rhetorically, if not in his affective demeanor, that the conflict will be resolved soon despite how many "mistakes," as he puts it, the company has made and despite the involvement of "outside" organizations that he believes are compelling people in Álvaro Obregón to action. He notes that his office has spoken with the fisherfolk in the region and that they have faith in the government, though not in the company. The secretary is not willing to trample the rights of indigenous people in the isthmus, and he is seeking a compromise, if he can find one. Today, after our meeting he will speak to the company about conducting further environmental clean up in the waters surrounding the lagoon which are already contaminated by sewage run off from the neighboring towns. This is one piece of the solution. But the other, from the secretary's point of view, will have a more direct and immediate impact. The government, he explains, is going to create jobs for the people of Álvaro Obregón: short term, hard labor, decently paid, and beginning soon. The task will be to clear the overgrowth from irrigation canals on agricultural tracts around Álvaro Obregón and Zapata. The secretary assures us that providing payments to the resistance, in the form of a daily wage rather than bribes, will bring the confrontation to an end. He predicts that the matter may be resolved within the week. But it is not.

Back near the barricade at Álvaro Obregon, some weeks later, we are talking with some of the older men from Zapata and Álvaro Obregón who have positioned themselves in the shade of the crumbling brick walls of the former hacienda that the *resistencia* has appropriated as its headquarters (figure 7.2). We are catching up, and they are, even after all this time, still a little curious about us, where we come from and what languages we speak. We inquire about the canal-clearing jobs, and they nod in recognition. "Yes, some of our people from the resistance are doing that work now, and getting paid too. Which is good." "So does that mean that they have agreed to the Mareña park, the men who are doing the canal work?" we ask. Absolutely not. "They may work for the daily pay," one man assures us, "but at night, they sleep here, with us, in the hacienda, to protect the barricade."

A most unlikely act of protest, a predictable resignation to the end of the day, sleep did more than one might think.

Figure 7.2 Men waiting at the crumbling hacienda that is the headquarters of the resistance.

Notes

This research, a collaborative ethnographic project conducted by Dominic Boyer and the author, was made possible by a grant from the National Science Foundation (#1127246). Our sincere gratitude goes to all of the people of the Isthmus of Tehuantepec, as well as the many people in Oaxaca City and Mexico City who took the time to share their perspectives on the challenges facing renewable energy transitions. Even in their critiques of the ways that renewable energy has been developed, we heard in equally clear terms about the need to move away from the contaminative logics of carbon and its climate-damaging externalities. Our work has tried to surface the tensions involved in the politics of renewable energy while still aiming for a future that refuses subscription to carbon modernity.

1. *Energía eólica* translates as "wind energy," and *parques eólicos* are "wind parks"; the English-language equivalent is the adjective *Aeolian*, "produced by or related to the wind." The term *anti-eólico* is a term describing those in opposition to wind park developments.

2. My field research in Nicaragua took place primarily in Managua among a variety of sexual rights activists, as described in the text here (see Howe 2013). The research on renewable energy transitions in Oaxaca, Mexico, is an ongoing collaborative project with Dominic Boyer, beginning in 2009.

3. In May 2007, President Felipe Calderón announced the National Climate Change Strategy, instituting climate change mitigation as a central part of national development policy.

In 2012, before leaving office, Calderón signed the General Climate Change Law that formalizes targets in previous legislation, inaugurates the National Institute of Ecology and Climate Change, and coordinates federal offices to develop holistic mitigation and accommodation planning.

4. NAFTA, the Agrarian Law Reform, and the program PROCEDE—coupled with the 1992 Electric Energy Public Service Law—allowed local landholders to more easily sell and contract their land to private interests and gave private sector companies the ability to participate in electric power generation in public-private partnerships.

5. Wind power has expanded exponentially from two parks in 2008, producing 84.9 megawatts, to fifteen parks producing 1.331 gigawatts by the end of 2012, making Mexico the second-largest producer of wind power in Latin America after Brazil.

6. COCEI was established in Juchitán, the gravitational center of the isthmus, in the early 1970s on a platform of agrarian reform and workers' and indigenous peoples' rights. They won municipal elections that ushered in the first socialist city council in Mexico, defying the hegemony of the country's ruling party, the PRI (see Rubin 1997).

7. Although they are understood to be a pre-Columbian inheritance, *usos y costumbres* have been modified over time and have undergone a resurgence throughout Mexico (see Stephen 2002; Rubin 1997).

References

Adam, Barry D., Jan Willem Duyvendak, and André Krouwel, eds. 1999. *The Global Emergence of Gay and Lesbian Politics: National Imprints of a Worldwide Movement*. Philadelphia: Temple University Press.

Alvarez, Sonia, Evelina Dagnino, and Arturo Escobar, eds. 1998. *Cultures of Politics/Politics of Cultures: Re-Visioning Latin American Social Movements*. Boulder, CO: Westview Press.

Calhoun, Craig, and Charles R. Hale, eds. 2008. *Engaging Contradictions: Theory, Politics, and Methods of Activist Scholarship*. Berkeley: University of California Press.

Dave, Naisargi. 2012. *Queer Activism in India: A Story in the Anthropology of Ethics*. Durham, NC: Duke University Press.

de la Dehesa, Rafael. 2010. *Queering the Public Sphere in Mexico and Brazil: Sexual Rights Movements in Emerging Democracies*. Durham, NC: Duke University Press.

Dove, Michael R. 2006. "Indigenous People and Environmental Politics." *Annual Review of Anthropology* 35: 191–208.

Edelman, Marc. 2001. "Social Movements: Changing Paradigms and Forms of Politics." *Annual Review of Anthropology* 30: 285–317.

Fox, Richard G., and Orin Starn, eds. 1997. *Between Resistance and Revolution: Cultural Politics and Social Protest*. New Brunswick, NJ: Rutgers University Press.

Geertz, Clifford. 1989. *Works and Lives: The Anthropologist as Author*. Stanford, CA: Stanford University Press.

Gould, Deborah B. 2009. *Moving Politics: Emotion and Act Up's Fight against AIDS*. Chicago: University of Chicago Press.

Graeber, David. 2009. *Direct Action: An Ethnography*. Oakland, CA: AK Press.

Howe, Cymene. 2013. *Intimate Activism: The Struggle for Sexual Rights in Postrevolutionary Nicaragua*. Durham, NC: Duke University Press.

Howe, Cymene and Dominic Boyer. 2016. "Aeolian Extractivism and Community Wind in Southern Mexico." *Public Culture* 28 (2): 215–236.

Howe, Cymene, Dominic Boyer, and Edith Barrera. 2015. "Los márgenes del Estado al viento: Autonomía y desarrollo de energías renovables en el sur de México." *Journal of Latin American and Caribbean Anthropology* 20 (2): 285–307.

Hulme, Mike. 2009. *Why We Disagree about Climate Change: Understanding Controversy, Inopportunity and Inaction*. Cambridge: Cambridge University Press.

Jackson, Jean E., and Kay B. Warren. 2005. "Indigenous Movements in Latin America, 1992–2004: Controversies, Ironies, New Directions." *Annual Review of Anthropology* 34: 549–573.

Juris, Jeffrey S. 2012. "Reflections on #Occupy Everywhere: Social Media, Public Space and Emerging Logics of Aggregation." *American Ethnologist* 39 (2): 259–279.

Juris, Jeffrey S., and Alexander Khasnabish, eds. 2013. *Insurgent Encounters: Transnational Activism, Ethnography and the Political*. Durham, NC: Duke University Press.

Keck, Margaret E., and Kathryn Sikkink. 1998. *Activists beyond Borders: Advocacy Networks in International Politics*. Ithaca, NY: Cornell University Press.

Laclau, Ernesto, and Chantal Mouffe. 1985. *Hegemony and Socialist Strategy: Towards a Radical Democratic Politics*. London: Verso.

Melucci, Alberto. 1989. *Nomads of the Present: Social Movements and Individual Needs in Contemporary Society*. Philadelphia: Temple University Press.

Nahmed Sittón, Salomón. 2011. "El impacto social del uso del recurso eólico." Oaxaca City, Mexico: Centro de Investigaciones y Estudios Superiores en Antropología Social (CIESAS), Unidad Pacífico Sur.

Rabinow, Paul. 2011. *Marking Time: On the Anthropology of the Contemporary*. Princeton, NJ: Princeton University Press.

Rabinow, Paul, and George Marcus, with James Faubion and Tobias Rees. 2008. *Designs for an Anthropology of the Contemporary*. Durham, NC: Duke University Press.

Razsa, Maple, and Andrej Kurnik. 2012. "The Occupy Movement in Žižek's Hometown: Direct Democracy and a Politics of Becoming." *American Ethnologist* 39 (2): 238–258.

Rubin, Jeffrey W. 1997. *Decentering the Regime: Ethnicity, Radicalism, and Democracy in Juchitán, Mexico*. Durham, NC: Duke University Press.

Stephen, Lynn. 2002. *Zapata Lives! Histories and Cultural Politics in Southern Mexico*. Berkeley: University of California Press.

Touraine, Alaine. 1988. *Return of the Actor: Social Theory in Postindustrial Society*. 1984. Trans. M. Godzich. Minneapolis: University of Minnesota Press.

Tsing, Anna Lowenhaupt. 2003. "Agrarian Allegory and Global Futures," In *Nature in the Global South: Environmental Projects in South and Southeast Asia*, edited by P. Greenough and A. L. Tsing, 124–169. Durham, NC: Duke University Press.

Warren, Kay B. 1998. *Indigenous Movements and Their Critics: Pan-Maya Activism in Guatemala*. Princeton, NJ: Princeton University Press.

8 What Should Be Done?

Art and Political Possibility in Russia

Petra Rethmann

How do we imagine struggle for political agency today? What kinds of political possibilities do exist? These are the questions that drive the Russian art collective *chto delat'* (what needs to be done). Founded in 2003 by visual artists, philosophers, and writers from St. Petersburg and Moscow, *chto delat'* draws its name from social revolutionary Nikolai Chernichevskii's 1863 novel *What Needs to Be Done*, written while he was imprisoned in the Peter and Paul Fortress in St. Petersburg.[1] Generally considered the most important radical novel in nineteenth-century Russian literature, Chernichevskii's fiction revolves around questions of collective communitarianism; the overthrow of social, sexual, and economic hierarchies; and freedom. While it is the radical utopian impulse of Chernichevskii's vision that most deeply resonates with *chto delat'*, the collective's name also self-consciously places it within a social history of radical thought that ranges from Tolstoy's 1886 *What Then Must We Do?* to Lenin's 1902 tract also entitled *What Needs to Be Done?* Among activists and critical analysts, answers to this question remain subjects of debate. In this chapter, I trace some of the answers specific to *chto delat'*, especially those that are related to temporality and art.

I first became acquainted with some members of *chto delat'*, especially Alexei Penzin and Dmitrii Vilenskii, when in the summer of 2007 I participated in a two-week workshop on the idea of *alternativnost'* at the University of St. Petersburg.[2] By and large, the workshop had been designed to bring together young scholars and faculty from Eastern Europe and Russia to think about modes of political critique and dissent in the Warsaw Pact countries during the era of the Cold War, to understand the legacy of those modes, and to discuss if and how they still exercised some force today. In looking at cultural themes and productions that ranged from illegal reproductions of censored literatures (*samizdat*), dystopian views of Russian writer Andrei Platonov, dissidents who had been involved in Russia's 1960s artistic and political underground scenes (*shestidesiatniki*), and Eastern European and Russian avant-gardes, participants debated the values of and possibilities for political critique. Diverse as the topics might seem, in St. Petersburg discussions were held together by an understanding that—whatever *alternativnost'* was—one of its distinguishing markers was that it served as a term of critique of normative culture and art. In the contemporary Russian context, *chto delat'* has emerged as one visible and activist collective interested in alternative formulations of politics.

One way in which especially Dmitrii as one representative of *chto delat'* introduced himself at the workshop was through his affinity with Russian constructivist practice and art, especially as it emerged in the early 1920s at the Moscow Institute of Artistic Culture (INKhUK, by its Russian abbreviation). Organized in Moscow in March 1920 by the painter Wassily Kandinsky, the state-sponsored art institute was set up for the sole purpose of conducting research on the very processes of art making. In Russia's then-revolutionary culture, it also constituted a hotbed of vigorous discussions centering on the purposes of art and the aesthetics of art objects. In particular, the constructivists called for artists to abandon the nonobjective (*bezpredmetnyi*) paintings that a Russian avant-garde had pioneered in the preceding decade to enter Soviet industrial production. In seeking to dilute the boundaries between art and everyday life (*byt*), the idea was that artists should use their artistic expertise in material and form to produce useful objects for new socialist collectives. As Dmitrii described it at the workshop, one reason constructivism was so important for him and, by extension, for *chto delat'* was that it sought to sublate art in life.[3] That is, while the fact that the constructivists critiqued the very institutions of bourgeois art (the academy, museum, gallery, and dealer) was important for *chto delat'*, what deeply resonated for the collective was constructivism's promise to open up spaces for alternative imaginings of the world that might produce new social relations.

As mentioned already, in this chapter I trace this sense of possibility through the registers of temporality and art. In centering on the question of what *chto delat'* has to offer to the question of activism and resistance—the question that is also at the center of this book—I first examine some of the reasons Dmitrii might be interested in Russia's constructivist avant-garde and how it might inspire him. In looking at Arvatov's notion of the "thinglike" (*dinglich*) commodity, Rodchenko's Workers' Club, and Dmitrii's Activist Club, I seek to understand how constructivism might inspire the search for activist approaches and subjectivities. Once I have established constructivism's importance to *chto delat'*, I move on to discussions of temporality and time. In interviews and talks members of *chto delat'* tend to point to the political necessity of rethinking the relations between the tenses to find modes of temporality that allow them to think about how change can be imagined (for a similar argument, see also Postill's chapter in this volume). In this regard, *chto delat'* tends to invoke the writings of Walter Benjamin to point to the political possibilities of nonlinear conceptions of time.

In recapitulating why Benjamin is so important to *chto delat'*, I ask about how imaginations borrowed from the past can enable but also constrain visions of the future. I end by asking about the agentive possibilities of art, especially in relation to the possibilities of agency and resistance that are also so important to *chto delat'*.

A caveat might be in order before the analysis begins: while *chto delat'* forms by no means a monolithic entity, all members proceed from the conviction that intellectual histories and movements are crucial for understanding how political possibilities are structured in this now. Anthropologists concerned with questions of possibility and activism, however, tend to pay more attention to the experiential dimensions on the ground: for example, the possibilities and difficulties of organizing and the challenges of direct action (Graeber 2009; Juris 2008). Consequently, one challenge in writing this chapter has been the representation of *chto delat'*. Given the philosophical and artistic tendencies of *chto delat'*, at times this chapter evinces the tendency to shift from "the ground" to the text—not to emphasize the theoretical tendencies of *chto delat'* but to think with the collective about the ways resistance might be configured. Here thinking with is an exercise in listening not just to what *chto delat'* presents or says, but also to what their thinking might open in terms of possibility. It is for this reason that in this chapter configuring resistance also entails a deliberate strategy of theoretical analyzing to capture the logic of *chto delat'*. To analyze in such a way means not suspending critical evaluation but acknowledging that we who want to imagine alternative futures have much to gain by thinking with *chto delat'* about the ways political imaginations are structured—if, admittedly, not always lived.

Workers' Club and Activist Club: The Thing as Coworker and Comrade

In his pivotal essay "Everyday Life and the Culture of the Thing" ("Byt I kul'tura veshchi"), Boris Arvatov (1925; see also Kiaer 1997) attempted to imagine a new way of being for "the thing" (*veshch'*): as a "coworker," or what Kiaer (2005) signifies as "comrade." In being concerned with understanding how socialism might help transform passive capitalist commodities into activist socialist things, Arvatov imagined objects and things as alive—that is, as endowed with the ability to produce new experiences, new social relations, and new human subjects. Especially if liberated from the oppressive labor and class conditions of capitalism and reinvented as agentive, "the thing" (in particular the industrial thing) is capable of transforming social and political relations. While based in Marxist thinking about the commodity fetish, in which the commodity is severed from the realm of production to transform relations between people into social relations between things, Arvatov thus sought to reformulate the "thinglike" character

of commodities and objects. In working hard to recuperate the thinglike relation between humans and objects, as well as between objects and objects, for the
benefit of socialist culture, he actually argued that relations between people and
objects should be not less thinglike, but more so. For Arvatov, the problem was
not with the way the commodity structured social relations, but with the actual
material qualities of the things produced. What he imagined with Marx was the
fact that the relations of productions needed to be restructured and rethought;
where he differed was in arguing that not only social relations but things themselves need to undergo formal transformations.

Although at the workshop in St. Petersburg, Dmitrii introduced Arvatov as
one important reference point for his thinking and that of *chto delat'*, this reference was by no means self-evident. One reason Arvatov was integral to Dmitrii's
thinking was that in the early 1920s, Arvatov assumed a leading role in Moscow's
Institute of Artistic Culture; another is that in 1925 the Soviet Union decided
to contribute to the Paris exhibition *Internationale des arts décoratifs* by giving
pride of place to avant-garde theater designs, graphics, and architectural projects.
Aleksandr Rodchenko, who agreed with Arvatov that one goal of the object was
its functionality and expediency (*tseleoobraznost'*), was hired to travel to Paris as
artistic executor of the Soviet exhibits, and to build his proposed Workers' Club
on-site. In one letter that he wrote from Paris to his partner Varvara Stepanova
in Moscow, Rodchenko described how "the light from the East is not only the
liberation of workers but . . . the new relation to things. Our things in our hands
must be equals, comrades, and not these black and mournful slaves, as they are
here."[4] As if to answer Arvatov's call to transform both social relations and objects, his 1925 Workers' Club sought to translate this assessment into practice by
establishing the socialist object as "coworker" (Arvatov's term) and "comrade."

By all accounts, at the Paris exhibition Rodchenko's Workers' Club installation in Konstantin Melnikov's Soviet pavilion was a success. As a highly visible symbol of the new political structures and forms of everyday life that the
constructivists sought to invent, the Workers' Club constituted a lucidly spare
and geometric arrangement. In refusing all material ostentation (a move that was
also assured by the small budget allotted to the project), the club's interior was
constructed out of cheap, lightweight wood to eliminate excess weight and bulk.
While the objects in the club—a movable table and chairs—had the function of
materially organizing the leisure time in the everyday lives of workers, the club
could also be used for activism and agitation. This idea was best symbolized in
the speaker's platform of the club, where aesthetic forms took on an utilitarian
purpose—for example, in the foldout screen for projecting slides and the con-
tractible bench and speakers' stand. Other objects in the Workers' Club also operated like the speaker's platform: the side flaps of the long central table could be
lowered for a more comfortable reading position; the chess ensemble in the back

of the room, under a poster of Lenin, consisted of two chairs separated by a nifty revolving chessboard on hinges; and above it, the case for the "wall newspaper" allowed for the recording of daily changes.

In his own installation also titled Activist Club, Dmitrii approximates Rodchenko's installation in color, material, and form. The interior of Activist Club is marked by a monochromatic color palette of red, white, and black. Its material—cheap wood—is hard and resistant, and where the Workers' Club had areas for games and reading, Activist Club emphasized viewing films and listening to talks. There is graffiti on the walls of the Activist Club that insists that "we need our own cinema" and "cinema, for us, states the importance of art." As slogans reminiscent of, for example, May 1968, the slogans also assume a political meaning as invocations, as statements of desires. While the desires are not specified, they point to the power of the creative arts to imagine things in keys, which Elizabeth Povinelli (2011) has marked as "otherwise." In St. Petersburg and in other meetings in which I participated with members of *chto delat'*, Dmitrii expressed the hope that art and film might trigger fresh imaginations to think about and address a number of social ills that are currently plaguing Russia: Putin's authoritarianism, the erosion of social welfare programs, and the curtailment of free speech. Yet at the same time, to Dmitrii the point worth making is that it might behoove activists and others to use the intrinsic value of objects and art to build new social relations and imaginations. As Dmitrii sees it, the goal of Activist Club is not so much to determine what should be imagined or—to say it with *chto delat'*—what should be done, but to use art as a resource to imagine what could be done.

Temporality and Time

While Dmitrii imagined Activist Club as capable of raising questions about new ways of being and subjectivities, others considered Dmitrii's installation as outmoded and dated. For example, at the workshop in St. Petersburg participants charged *chto delat'* with using an approach that is obsolete and passé, one more attached to the preservation of historical memory than to the possibilities of overcoming it. From such a perspective, a project such as Activist Club is marked by a nostalgic relation to a once-revolutionary past that has outlived its potential and can no longer inspire. However, in inadvertently casting Activist Club as not only of its time but as only of its time, such assessments make it hard to grasp the future-oriented dimensions of the *chto delat'* project. In situating historical temporalities within limited horizons marked by origins and closures, they also remain attached to linear understanding of time. Even when conceived as a living legacy rather than as a dead relic, the future remains more of a historical artifact than a project.

It is largely for this reason that for *chto delat'* Walter Benjamin has emerged as a central figure. In casting Benjamin—as Dmitrii and Alexei put it at the workshop—"as the philosopher of possibility," his thinking assists them in bringing together the present and the past in ways that helps them move beyond interpretations that mark their interest in constructivism and Rodchenko just as an interest in an odd curio from the archives of the socialist past. In particular, Benjamin allows *chto delat'* to imagine how the past might be brought to bear on the present and its possible future. Especially Benjamin's interest in constellating "what has been" with "the now" to develop an understanding of temporality as a political mode of interruption has become important for the collective because it assists them in rejecting conventional conceptualizations of time as linear and historicist ideas of the present in terms of "transition."

As for so many anthropologists and critical analysts of time (Wilder 2015; Coronil 1997), Benjamin's (2003a, 396) aim "to blast a specific era out of the homogenous course of history . . . to blast open the continuum of history" itself is particularly decisive here. Benjamin (2003b, 402) also famously described change—he uses the term *revolution*—as "an attempt by the passengers of the train [of world history] to activate the emergency break." In other words, part of what for *chto delat'* and others is at stake in Benjamin's thinking is his concern not with memory but with the "explosion" of conceptions of linear progress. "Time," as Benjamin (2003b, 403) wrote, "must be brought to a standstill."

However, Benjamin's recognition that the path to an open future is mediated by what has been is attractive to *chto delat'* because it presumably justifies a return to the past and also because of the way the past itself is understood and thought. As Benjamin (2003a, 397) argues, the critic articulates the past historically, not to recognize it, like a positivist historian, as "the way it really was," but to grasp the revolutionary possibilities of the present political situation. In claiming that "the historian is a prophet facing backward," Benjamin (2003b, 405–407) argues that "the historian [must] turn his back on his own time, and [direct] his seer's gaze towards [the efforts] of earlier generations as they sink further and further into the past." Paradoxically, then, the task of the critical historian—and, by extension, critical inquiries into temporality and time—is to maintain a prophetic relation to the future buy turning to the past. Or, to paraphrase Benjamin's words, the critical historian perceives the contours of the future in the past, even as it moves away from him. From such a point of view, Benjamin affirms the conviction of *chto delat'* that politics is obliged to act in the present and also to imagine a future.

Benjamin's insights into the workings of temporality and time are important for *chto delat'* because it allows them to center on constructivism as one punctual (and ephemeral) moment of disruption within a world marked by historical continuity, not because it permits them to maintain social solidarity and continuity with the past. That is, while the charge of nostalgia with which *chto delat'* continuously struggles is based on linear conceptions of time that assume a progressive relationship between the present and the past, Benjamin assists them in pointing to those "revolutionary energies" that are crystallized within existing but temporally "outmoded" models. In exchanging a political for a historical view of the past, in essence Benjamin proposes a method (Pensky 2004) for achieving politically irreverent illuminations. However, instead of appearing in the form of a ready-made imagination or political blueprint, such illuminations appear as fragments: as "a flash" of recognition that potentially becomes and enables political action. Precisely because for Benjamin every historical moment carries within it a revolutionary chance—a chance grounded simultaneously in a given historical situation and in the ways this historical moment is or can be positioned vis-à-vis the past—he has become the "philosopher of possibility" in a world in which, according to Benjamin (2003b, 402), "possibilities are closed and locked."

Figuring Resistance: Activism and Art

To some of those who participated in the workshop in St. Petersburg as well as for activists, the claim by *chto delat'* that art, and in particular an arts-oriented imagination, can assist in opening up thinking about political possibilities does not always come easy. This is not only so because the practices of Dmitrii and, by extension, *chto delat'* can quickly come across as hopeful but empty thinking or as a nostalgic return to the socialist past, but also because activists tend to consider the collective's practices as too art oriented and ineffective. One issue, then, is that the focus of *chto delat'* on art strikes activists as dated, as out of touch with our times. Another problem is that activists consider art as "just aesthetic," out of touch with the real needs of political activism and movement, and incognizant of the ways activists actually engage with struggles on the ground.

For *chto delat'*, one issue has been that in the eyes of many activists and friends who move in their orbit, they are rapidly becoming part of the star system of celebrity radicals, a system that not only serves a stabilizing function but also exists as one in which an oppositional rhetoric of radicalness is rather academic and formulaic. At the workshop, one speaker forcefully expressed a version of such an assessment by describing the efforts of *chto delat'* as self-interested and vain, as an expression of an "egotistical narcissism" and an "elitist brain." From the perspective of some, if not all, of the collective's critics, it is certainly the case that the practices of *chto delat'* have brought the group considerable prestige and several of its members the opportunity to travel. It is also for this reason that a number of activists have asked *chto delat'* for an admission of complicity, by which they mean the supposed fact that the collective's practices are driven by self-interest rather than a desire for protest and change. Especially for some of the activists who tend to prefer the materiality of direct action, the collective's focus on art can constitute a problem.

Collectively, all members of *chto delat'* are aware of such indictments and seek to address them in various ways. First, although the collective does not directly address issues related to, for example, the wars in Chechnya or Afghanistan, populist nationalism and the rise of a political right, increase of homelessness and police busts, and curtailments of free speech, it has participated in protests against the G8 summit in 2007 in Heiligendamm, fascism in Russia, and the reduction of public funds in the realm of education. Second, if *chto delat'* does not directly address these questions, it is not to ignore them but rather to situate their politics in a different field. In valorizing art's facility with imagining forms of protest and temporal structures that many activists may find counterintuitive, they wish not to situate themselves in opposition to those more steeped in the material of direct action, but to suggest that the "creative arts" are capable of maintaining a space outside hegemonic constructions of politics and history, and that art can grasp heterodoxies that other approaches often cannot. It is part of the conviction of *chto delat'* that, at the very least, mindfulness to the potentialities of art can deepen our commitment to justice in the present, so that what remains artistic for now may still show its material effects in the future.

The best way to understand *chto delat'* is perhaps as an integral part of an artistic and philosophical tradition that argues for the power of the utopian imagination. In this sense, part of *the collective's* political strategy is to entice a shift in the political terrain that marks the political dispiritedness that Greenberg (2014; see also Greenberg's chapter in this volume) has described. By introducing art as part of the political imagination to the registers of activism and resistance, they seek to provoke reflection and desire. Yet producing desire in condition marked by political hopelessness and disappointment is not an easy thing to do: it is not an easy thing to be in time this way, to straddle past, present, and future, to nurture both critical and affirmative investments in art and a political imagination ostensibly attached to the past but potentially capable of generating different futures. What's important to recognize is that the imagination of *chto delat'* may require us—to draw on James Scott's (2012) description—"to squint": to strain our visions and analytical convictions in such a way that we might be enticed in terms of what Elizabeth Povinelli (2011) has described as "otherwise."

Notes

1. Within a Russian and politically insurgent context, Lenin called *chto delat'* a novel that showed what a revolutionary should look like, and the philosopher Nikolai Berdyaev called it *the* textbook of the Russian intelligentsia.

2. In Russian, *alternativnost'* signifies an awkward term, and is perhaps best translated as "alternative culture."

3. The constructivists sought to reintegrate art into life by designing objects—furniture, utensils, fabrics, clothing, and advertisement—with a view to their purposefulness and functionality. Margolin (1997) and Lodder (1983) have eloquently written about constructivist history and art.

4. In her analysis of the constructivist avant-garde, the art historian Christine Kiaer (2005, 1, 211–220) gives this excerpt from Rodchenko's Paris letters a prominent place.

References

Arvatov, Boris. 1925. *Byt i kul'tura veshchi: Al'manakh proletkul'ta*. Moscow: Proletkul't.

Benjamin, Walter. 2003a. "On the Concept of History." In *Selected Writings*, vol. 4, *1938–1940*, 389–400. Cambridge, MA: Belknap Press of Harvard University Press.

———. 2003b. "Paralipomena to 'On the Concept of History.'" In *Selected Writings*, vol. 4, *1938–1940*, 401–411. Cambridge, MA: Belknap Press of Harvard University Press.

Coronil, Fernando. 1997. *The Magical State: Nature, Money, and Modernity in Venezuela*. Chicago: University of Chicago Press.

Graeber, David. 2009. *Direct Action: An Ethnography*. Oakland, CA: AK Press.

Greenberg, Jessica. 2014. *After the Revolution: Youth, Democracy, and the Politics of Disappointment in Serbia*. Stanford, CA: Stanford University Press.

Juris, Jeffrey. 2008. *Networking Futures: The Movements against Corporate Globalization*. Berkeley: University of California Press.

Kiaer, Christina. 1997. "Boris Arvatov's Socialist Objects." *October* 81: 105–118.

———. 2005. *Imagine No Possessions: The Socialist Objects of Russian Constructivism*. Cambridge, MA: MIT Press.

Lodder, Christina. 1983. *Russian Constructivism*. New Haven, CT: Yale University Press.

Margolin, Victor. 1997. *The Struggle for Utopia: Rodchenko, Lissitzky, Moholy-Nagy, 1917–1946*. Chicago: University of Chicago Press.

Pensky, Max. 2004. "Method and Time: Walter Benjamin's Dialectical Images." In *The Cambridge Companion to Walter Benjamin*, edited by David Ferris, 177–198. Cambridge: Cambridge University Press.

Povinelli, Elizabeth. 2011. *Economies of Abandonment: Social Belonging and Endurance in Late Liberalism*. Durham, NC: Duke University Press.

Scott, James. 2012. *Two Cheers for Anarchism*. Princeton, NJ: Princeton University Press.

Wilder, Garry. 2015. *Freedom Time: Negritude, Decolonization, and the Future of the World*. Durham, NC: Duke University Press.

9 The Multilinearity of Protest

Understanding New Social Movements through Their Events, Trends, and Routines

John Postill

Recent contributions to the study of temporality in anthropology and neighboring fields have stressed the need to attend to the heterogeneity of time. For instance, in her anthropological work on cultural production, Georgina Born (2010, 195) follows Foucault's lead in distinguishing "three modalities of difference" when tracing cultural genealogies, namely synchronic, diachronic, and analytical modalities. Born argues that we should "read the ethnographic material for its encapsulation of currents or dynamics of different temporal depth" in order to effect, quoting Foucault, "a sort of multiplication or pluralization of causes . . . a multiplication [that] means analysing an event according to the multiple processes that constitute it" (195). In a similarly plural vein, the political scientist Anna Grzymala-Busse (2011) calls for analyses of temporality in relation to causal processes and mechanisms. Basing her discussion on research into institutional change in former communist regimes, she argues that aspects of temporality such as tempo, timing, acceleration and duration "allow us to predict which causal mechanisms can unfold and to differentiate causal sequences" (Grzymala-Busse 2011, 1267).

These works are but two examples of promising recent forays into a more complex, multidimensional theorization of temporality and human life than has been the norm in the past. At the same time, they pose a serious challenge to social theorists, including anthropologists, steeped in traditions that have long had troubled relationships with history, time, and social change. These are traditions in which one key dimension of modern temporal heterogeneity, namely its ubiquitous mediation by clock-and-calendar time, has been all but ignored (Postill 2002). Take, for example, the strangely ahistorical case of the anthropology of time. In a much-cited review essay, Nancy Munn (1992, 109–111) examines how certain "calendric and related time shifts" reach into "the body time of persons" by grounding them and their daily activities in "a wider politico-cosmic order" (Postill 2002, 254). Munn provides three historical instances to explore these shifts (or trends): the Gregorian calendar introduced into the Solomon Islands by European missionaries, the secular calendar of the French revolutionaries, and the diffusion of industrial time in nineteenth-century America. As I have argued elsewhere,

> these examples exhibit a common social/cultural anthropological feature: they are not presented in any coherent world-historic frame. We do not get a sense of scale, or an idea of how those "wider politico-cosmic orders" may have inter-locked with other orders as the European powers and the United States expanded beyond their shores. What came first, missionising in the Pacific or the French Revolution? How did U.S. economic and military expansion in the twentieth century transform time notions and practices in the Pacific, including the Solomons? How do these three country-specific "time shifts" fit into the common history of humankind? (Postill 2002, 254)

This lack of fit between anthropological theory and world history extends to the study of social change. Although anthropologists have been concerned with matters of social change for many decades, most have to date paid far more attention to "social changing" than to social change. In other words, they have tended to discuss how matters were changing at the time of fieldwork rather than how they actually changed, say, in the late 2000s, or in 1939–1945, in any given locale. In this respect they are no different from most scholars who study contemporary lifeworlds. This is no doubt partly an artifact of the ethnographic genre in its current incarnation. While earlier generations of anthropologists denied their research participants coevalness by writing in the ethnographic present simple (Fabian 1983; Postill 2006, 31–33), the current generation writes in the ethnographic present continuous as it strives for an "anthropology of the contemporary" (Rabinow and Marcus 2008; Budka 2011).

To further complicate matters, most anthropologists today exhibit an aversion to the idea of temporal linearity, preferring received invocations of "nonlinear," "contingent," or "ad hoc" time. The reasons for this aversion are complex, but we can assume that they are partly related to the firm rejection of the notion of teleological progress, a rejection deeply set in the field's discourse, and partly to the field's 1980s postmodern turn. For instance, Estalella (2011) has studied "passionate blogging" in Spain through the prism of actor-network theory. His Latourian approach works well in a number of places (e.g., when defining blogs as databases), but it runs into difficulties when broaching the temporality of blogging. Although rightly dismissing fanciful—and dated—notions of cyberspace as a paradoxical realm of "timeless time" (Castells 1999) and identifying some of the clock-and-calendar aspects of blogging (not least the folk definition of blogs as diaries displayed in reverse chronological order), he then follows Latour into a world in which time and space are the ad hoc products of agents and actants constituting one another. To borrow an insightful remark by Gell (1992, 315) about the anthropology of time, this Latourian world is a fantasy, "engendered in the process of scholarly reflection."

In fact, as we all know from personal experience, modern life is fully mediated by clock-and-calendar time—arguably the most universal of all human codes (Postill 2002). Granted that in recent decades most of us have experienced an "acceleration" of social life (Eriksen 2001; Wittel 2001), the fact remains that our worldwide standard of time reckoning and scheduling has not changed at all. Our days still have twenty-four hours, and there are still seven days in a week. Governments, markets, protest movements, and digital technologies may come and go, but this ubiquitous code remains firmly in place around the globe, with no signs of a replacement code being needed.

It follows that clock-and-calendar time is integral to the planning and coordination of modern socio-technical practices and "assemblages" in our increasingly digitized world, including collective actions such as protests. With this fundamental premise in mind, in this chapter I explore the heterogeneity of protest-related time through three concepts borrowed from the historian and social theorist William H. Sewell (2005), namely events, trends, and routines, in the context of Spain's Indignados (or 15M) movement. Rather than deploying these concepts synoptically, I do so diachronically, drawing a separate protest timeline (or set of parallel timelines) for each concept. This multilinear approach will allow me to explore the highly diverse temporality of digitally assisted protest, yet without overlooking the ubiquity of clock-and-calendar time.

The Temporality of Social Movements

Scholars working on the question of social movement temporality have approached it from three main angles. First, there is a growing literature that locates social movement temporality at the meeting of individual or collective life histories and the history of a particular movement. Thus, Bosi (2007) asks when and why individuals became involved in the Northern Ireland civil rights movement of the 1960s, arguing that researchers must pay more heed to the timing of involvement. Bosi found that in the early stages of a movement, most individuals were moved primarily by instrumentality. Later on, however, their involvement had more to do with ideology and identity. Similarly, Lorenz-Meyer (2013) investigates the "timespaces" of activism through the "trajectories, encounters and timings of Czech women's NGOs," including the life course timing of their incorporation. For her part, Vaillant (2013) discusses the "politics of temporality" among contemporary leftist activists in Uruguay, revealing a problematic relationship with "significant generational others," namely leftists from an earlier "revolutionary" generation.

Second, a growing number of authors focus on the microtemporality and momentariness of protest movements. For instance, Lee (2012, 159) points out that theories of social movement temporality have so far emphasized medium- and long-term processes, not the "micro-dynamics of protest." Taking the 2008 anti-US-beef protests in South Korea as the case study, Lee tracks "the political and discursive opportunities for protests to develop" over a period of 121 days, arguing that we must measure the effect on political processes of short-term protests by studying "how they develop in interaction with their external environment every day" (159). Kurzman (2012) also looks at the microdynamics and opportunities to protest, in his case with reference to the Arab Spring and the phenomenology of protest. Kurzman investigates "how actors changed as they perceived the possibility of protest," zeroing in on those "twists of history that confound social scientific explanation" (377) (see also McAdam and Sewell 2001). For instance, the sudden surge of bravery is best understood not as a causal variable but as "a disposition that may appear and disappear with the vagaries of the moment, altering the micro-flow of events and making a noticeable, if tiny, difference in the course of mass protests" (Kurzman 2012, 377). Also in the context of the Arab Spring, Howard and colleagues (2011) found that a spike in revolution-related conversations online often signaled major developments on the ground.

A third group of scholars add an explicit spatial dimension to their temporal analyses. Thus, Andrews and Biggs (2006, 752) track the "dynamics of protest diffusion" in the 1960s struggle for racial equality in America's South, finding three main channels of diffusion: social networks, the mainstream media, and movement organizations. In my own research in Spain, I have called for a "media epidemiography" of protest that can monitor and analyze the "viral" circulation of digital contents (Postill 2014a). Other studies have highlighted the simultaneity of protests across locales aided by new networked technologies. Davies (2009) examines the relation of ethnography, politics, and space in regard to the Tibetan freedom movement, suggesting that the global-local dichotomy plays down "connections, disconnections and process[es] that occur between places" (19). Along these lines, Monterde and I have tracked the simultaneity of connection across squares aided by smartphones, aggregator sites and social media in the 2011 wave of international protests (Monterde and Postill 2014; see also Gerbaudo 2012; Haug 2013; Kornetis 2009; Panelli 2007; Panelli and Larner 2010).

Absent from all of these studies is an explicit theorization of the part played by clock-and-calendar time in the birth, growth, and decline (or demise) of social movements, or indeed in their tactics and strategies, including the emergent convention of naming the new movements by means of a Twitter calendrical shorthand (e.g., #jan25 for Egypt, #feb17 for Libya, #15M for Spain, #15O globally). To rectify this problem, in the following section I make clock-and-calendar time a necessary, but not sufficient, part of my proposed model.

A Theory of Multiple Timelines

The working theory of new social movement temporality that I am proposing elaborates on Rinke and Röder's (2011) synthesis of the media ecology, communication culture, and spatiotemporality of protest. I do so with reference to a dynamic version of field theory (Postill 2011, 2015) as well as to Sewell's (2005) conceptual trinity of events, trends, and routines, both of which I explain below.

Basing their model on preliminary research in Cairo during the early phases of the 2011 uprising, Rinke and Röder (2011, 1274) describe their approach as consisting of three centerpieces:

> (a) The media ecologies of the anti-authoritarian uprising—that is, the availabilities of different forms of communication to different actors involved in the revolutionary processes at different points in time; (b) the cultural specificities of the Arab world with regard to what and how communication is socially acceptable, conducted and furnished for social change; and (c) the dynamics of how the anti-authoritarian movement unfolded over time and across distances within the nucleus of protest—the capital—and beyond.

Critical of academic and media hyperbole surrounding the role of "new media" in the Arab Spring, Rinke and Röder argue that earlier forms of communication should not be ignored when studying the day-by-day unfolding of a protest. This may include a consideration of "the multiple functions a single medium and different media may have at different points in time during the regime-changing process for different groups of actors" (1274–1275; see also Monterde and Postill 2014). Their point b refers to the need for an awareness of cultural difference, specifically in the context of communication. While careful not fall into the trap of cultural essentialism, these authors rightly contend that "the communication cultures of the Arab world generally differ from those in the Western world in some notable ways" (1275), for example, the part played by Friday mosque gatherings in political communication. The third, and equally cogent, point is to advance the analysis beyond the current focus on "prominent individual events taking place within a narrow spatial and temporal frame" in order to trace the entire arch of the protest movement from its inception to its "final outcome"—in the Egyptian case, regime change.

In the present chapter I wish to expand on this powerful model by understanding protest movements as special kinds of fields that differ from those traditionally studied by Bourdieu and his followers. In my 2010–2011 anthropological fieldwork in Barcelona (Spain), I observed firsthand the dynamic, dialogical nature of interactions taking place both within the Indignados "movement-field" (Juris 2008) and with external actors such as the police or the press. In an earlier work among Internet activists in the Malaysian suburb of Subang Jaya,

I introduced the concept of field of residential affairs, to refer to the domain of contention in which residents, politicians, journalists, civil servants, business-people, and other local political agents struggle over local issues through a global technology—the Internet (Postill 2011). Here my aim is rather to scale up the analytical level to investigate the multilinear temporality of what we might call Spain's field of national affairs, a domain in which the struggles are over national, not local, issues. This is a field whose establishment players witnessed in shock the sudden irruption of new actors onto the political scene in mid-May 2011 as tens of thousands of "indignant" citizens peacefully occupied the country's main squares demanding "real democracy now."

So far scholars and activists linked to the Indignados movement have pro-duced a number of timelines to chart its birth and development through either its main events or trends (e.g., Vallina-Rodríguez et al. 2012), but to my knowledge no multilinear account has yet been written for this or comparable protests in other countries. As said earlier, to this end I incorporate Sewell's (2005) temporal typology of events, trends, and routines into my protest field model. Sewell (2005, 273) argues that the temporality of any historical sequence is complex, for it is invariably a combination of "many different social processes with varying tem-poralities." Out of these various temporalities he singles out three:

1. *Events*. These are not merely notable incidents, but rather "temporally con-centrated sequences of actions that transform structures."
2. By contrast, *trends* are those "directional changes in social relations" that historians typically mark with terms such as "rise," "fall," "decline," "prolif-eration," and so on.
3. Finally, *routines* are "practical schemas that reproduce structures," whilst institutions are "machines for the production and maintenance of routines."

Sewell's historical case study is Marseilles's dockworkers in the 1814–1870 period, a golden age of high wages and political privileges for these proletarians. This situation can be explained, he suggests, as "an outcome of the specific trends, events, and routines that made their detailed control over work on the docks ac-ceptable to Marseilles' merchants and municipal authorities" (280). For Sewell this episode exemplifies the "uneven development" of capitalist temporality, as argued long ago by Lenin, Trotsky, and others, a temporality in which profit-making opportunities vary hugely across time and space and as the capitalist order itself evolves over time (277–278). By analogy, I am suggesting that Spain's Indignados movement, which is still evolving five years after its inception, can be explained as an outcome of the specific protest-field events, trends, and routines that make its demands appealing to the majority of the Spanish population. To flesh out this working assumption, I turn now to each of those temporalities in turn, starting with some of the field's main events to date.

Protest Field Events

Adapting Sewell's (2005) definition to the case at hand, we can provisionally define protest field events as those temporally condensed sequences of actions that transform a protest field (see also McAdam and Sewell 2001). This definition makes a field event distinct from a media event, as normally understood in the literature (Dayan 2010).

Although protest field events are sometimes media events as well, this is not always necessarily the case, much to the disappointment of publicity-seeking activists. In the Spanish context, we can single out three main events that transformed the field in the middle of 2011, only one of which—the square occupations—was undoubtedly a media event as well. These three events are the May 15 pro-democracy marches, the mid-May to mid-June occupations of squares across Spain, and the vacating of the squares in mid-June.

The choice of Sunday, May 15, 2011, as the date of the marches was no accident. This was a carefully chosen date, as it fell exactly one week before the local and regional elections to be held in many parts of Spain on May 22. Here we see clearly the importance both of timing (remarked upon by a number of protest scholars) and of clock-and-calendar time (a taken-for-granted universal code ignored by protest scholars). The proximity of the elections lent the May 15 demonstrations a mirror quality, creating the desired effect of contrasting peaceful marches by outraged citizens with a discredited political system. From a media event perspective, the marches were, however, a disappointment to activists who had hoped for wider mainstream media coverage, although many celebrated the fact that the marches generated a great deal of social and citizen media buzz (Postill 2014a). Nevertheless, from a field theoretical perspective, the marches can indeed be regarded as an event in that they transformed the protest field. After several months of intense online and offline planning in small groups, these had finally morphed into on-the-ground multitudes traversing highly visible public space.

That same night, some forty protesters, inspired by the occupation of Tahrir Square in Cairo earlier that year, decided to spend the night at Madrid's iconic Puerta del Sol square, Spain's geographical, temporal, and symbolic center (it is from here that the New Year is traditionally ushered in via a television broadcast to the whole nation). For the hacktivist group Isaac Hacksimov, this action was "a gesture that broke the collective mental block" (quoted by Sánchez 2011). Concerned that the police may seek to evict them, as eventually came to happen, the pioneers sent out calls for reinforcements through their smartphones. They were soon joined by others who had learned about the sit-in not on television but through Twitter and other social media sites. By May 17 there were two hundred campers in Puerta del Sol, and by May 20 their numbers had risen dramatically to nearly thirty thousand. As argued by Nanabhay and Farmanfarmaian (2011) in the case of Tahrir Square, these occupations constituted a "media spectacular" that globalized Puerta del Sol through both social media streaming and traditional broadcasting (Monterde and Postill 2014). By then numerous cities around Spain had their own encampments and the fledgling movement had become a global media event.

The encampments and assemblies reconfigured the young protest field, transforming not only its demographics but also its relationship to urban Spain's existing spatiotemporalities:

> While the encampment [*acampada*] is organized as a parallel city (with its own allotment, clinic, cleaning services, library, etc.), the assembly transforms the square from a place of passage into a meeting point and a space for discussion and deliberation—[in other words], it transforms it into an agora. The open-air assembly is part of the appropriation of the city; it breaks the urban rhythm and foregrounds the bodies of its participants. (Martín Rojo 2012, 279, my translation)

The third event I wish to highlight is the abandoning of the squares in June 2011. By the middle of June, most *acampadas* across Spain had been dismantled after exhausting deliberations. The stated aim was now to take the movement from the central squares to the neighborhoods (*barrios*), but not before informing the authorities that they reserved their right as citizens to reoccupy the squares in future. As a result, neighborhood assemblies mushroomed throughout the country, albeit with highly uneven levels of attendance and engagement (Corsin and Estalella 2011). At the same time, the protests "returned to the Internet," a realm where some of the leading activists and networks felt more at home than in the unwieldy assemblies. Energies were focused on elaborating concrete goals such as the right to a home, a fairer distribution of work, or stripping the political class of its privileges (Castells 2011). This relocation constituted another reconfiguration of the protest field, namely a move from the anchoring of the struggle in large physical spaces (the squares) to a more scattered, mobile universe of practices and actions. This protracted phase of civic dispersal was followed by the current phase of ongoing political institutionalization with the creation of 15M-derived parties such as Partido X, Podemos, and Barcelona en Comú in 2013–2014 (Postill 2016).

As we can see, protest field events are instructive both in their own right and as temporally condensed sequences of collective action and communicative praxis that mark the transition from one phase of the movement to another. In the Indignados case (and parallels can be drawn here with the Arab Spring, Occupy, and others) these key foundational events took place over the relatively short period of a month. They are proof of the naturalized predominance of the clock-and-calendar code across the entire media ecology, from "old" media such as radio, TV, and newspapers, to "new" platforms such as Menéame, Facebook, and Twitter, in the latter case through the ubiquitous hashtag device applied to dates of particular significance to protesters (e.g., #15M, #27M, #15O).

At this juncture, it is important to reiterate that not all field incidents, however dramatic or meaningful to participants at the time, can be fruitfully regarded as events as I am defining them here. For instance, many Indignados remember to this day the violent eviction of peaceful demonstrators from Barcelona's Plaça de Catalunya by the regional police. News media and citizen videos of these incidents were widely shared and caused outrage, but they did not usher in a new phase in the field's evolution. Similarly, the harassment of Catalan parliamentarians by irate protesters on June 15 attracted huge social media interest, but along with a peaceful counterdemonstration that took place shortly thereafter, this incident only served to reaffirm the participants' commitment to a nonviolent strategy in the face of police brutality (Postill 2014b). In sum, they did not transform the field.

I should also note that there is a great deal about the 15M movement and comparable movements elsewhere that an exclusive focus on events would leave unexamined. To recall a point made earlier, it is not sufficient to stay at the site of momentous historical events; we must follow the unfolding of social upheavals across other sites and over a period of time (see also Postill 2012). With this crucial point in mind, I turn to some of the field's main trends and routines over time.

Protest Field Trends

The study of trends has been popular in fields such as finance, fashion, crime, or sport for many decades. Indeed, in 2013 the Nobel Prize in Economics was won by three American economists specializing in the study of trends in asset markets (*Telegraph* 2013). In social movements research, this is also an area of growing interest. Thus, Valenzuela, Arriagada, and Scherman (2012) have tracked the "time dynamics of the social media-protest relationship" in Chile's youth mobilizations of 2009–2012, conducting a "trend study of social media and protest behaviour" (299). Weber, Garimella, and Teka's (2013) Twitter investigation of political hashtag trends in the United States is also a trend study, in this case from a computer science perspective.

In the context of Spain's 15M movement, García Canclini, Cruces, and Castro Pozo (2012) highlight the emergence of a new research area focused on the relationship between Twitter trending topics (the most popular Twitter topics at any given point in time) and events such as the square occupations of May 2011. These authors contrast the current tweet-driven age of a "perpetual now" with an earlier age in which the mainstream media set the news agenda in an orderly, scheduled manner. The Indignados' "real time," they add,

> is a vertiginous, heteroclite, fragmentary chronotope in perpetual motion. It gathers around it a human collective with diffuse contours whose link is the present in the strict sense of the term, [a collective] lacking territorial boundaries, history or a common project. Pure present. (García Canclini, Cruces, and Castro Pozo 2012, my translation)

This view of the 15M movement is held by other Spanish observers, such as the leftist rapper Nega (2011), who dismisses the Indignados as "slaves to the ephemeral" forever attentive to the latest fad. It also echoes moral anxieties around the world about the rise of a superficial "viral culture" marked by the acceleration of news cycles—what Wasik (2009) terms, in the context of US political campaigns, an age of nanopolitics. To be sure, there is some truth to these reports of the ephemerality of shared contents in the digital age, but they are far too reductionist to help us understand the significance of trends in today's social movements. Adapting once again Sewell's (2005) terminology, I define protest field trends as those directional changes in techno-political relations that protest scholars and participants typically mark with terms such as *rise, decline, fall, acceleration*, and so forth.

Just as soap opera researchers study these genres over a period of time—at least a season or two (see Mankekar 1999)—social movement scholars cannot but regard protest-related trending topics as episodes in a series rather than as isolated phenomena. For example, a study of the most popular hashtags (keywords) employed by Twitter users in Spain from March to May 2011 discovered

> a shift from a general political vocabulary (with terms such as "politics," "corruption" or "elections" being commonly used) to what today we recognize as a distinctive 15M language ("streets," "Sol," "real democracy"). Thus Spain's "trending topics" for the 10–15 May period included hashtags such as #15M, #15Mfacts, #tomalacalle (#takethestreet), #15Mpasalo (#15Mpassiton) and #spanishrevolution. (Monterde and Postill 2014)

Leading 15M activists are not merely caught up in trends not of their own making; they have actively sought, so far with a large degree of success, to set the country's civil society trends and to reverse what they regard as pernicious trends, such as an increase in protest-related violence. First, over the years 15M activists have learned how to "game the algorithm" so that their campaigns will trend on Twitter and reach wider publics, both through the mediation of journalists and directly to fellow citizens (Postill and Pink 2012). But to say that they are so immersed in this activity that they are unable to see past the horizon of the next trending topic would be a gross misrepresentation. In fact, as we will see,

15M activists combine in their praxis a diverse suite of orientations toward the future, from the here and now of a trending topic to the long-term dream of a truly democratic Spain.

Second, core activists keep a watchful eye on field-specific trends and seek to warn one another of any deviation from the movement's aims and objectives. For example, in November 2012 the author Isaac Rosa (2012) published a piece in an online newspaper warning fellow Indignados about the trend toward the "normalization" of police brutality in Spain through the habitual sharing of violent videos on social media. Another example would be the collective displays of nonviolent behavior following incidents that may be construed by the mainstream media—and especially by the more conservative press and TV stations—as signaling a trend toward an increase in violence by the Indignados, a worrying prospect that they have managed to keep in check for five years now.

Elsewhere I have written about the Indignados "perpetually transient temporality," an orientation toward the future whereby "the immediate and ephemeral are accorded the same weight as the enduring and long-term" (Postill 2014b):

> On the one hand, the indignados borrow from Mexico's Zapatistas the idea that "We walk, not run, because we are going very far" (Sitrin 2005). . . . On the other hand, indignados' personal and collective actions are characterised by an "inevitable and attractive aesthetic of the urgent and fleeting" (Albeida 2011: 98). In the occupied spaces, new forms of popular action arose that did not require to be expressed "through lasting artistic manufactures, but rather through a common creativity that emerged spontaneously out of the need to be there and to protest" (Albeida 2011: 97). (Postill 2014b)

On reflection, the situation on the ground is more complicated. At least four temporal horizons coexist in the Indignados' imaginary: the present moment (e.g., trending topics, Facebook threads, assembly meetings), the short term (e.g., preparing an action two weeks in advance), the medium term (e.g., planning a mobilization a year in advance), and the long term (e.g., changing Spain's political system). It is at the intersection of these different time scales that trends are set, observed, encouraged, and checked. Again, as with the vast majority of modern practices (Postill 2002), Indignados' trend-related practices would be unthinkable without the fully normalized mediation of clock-and-calendar time.

Protest Field Routines

While the concepts of events and trends would seem to possess a logical affinity with the diachronic approach to the theorization of protest fields I am advocating here, that of routines appears at first sight to jar with it. After all, aren't routines, by their very logic, recursive phenomena that help maintain a social field rather than to change it? How, then, can routines be studied diachronically, as distinct lineages in a multilinear model? What can they actually tell us about the collective life course of a rapidly changing social movement?

As it happens, field routines can tell us a great deal about both continuity and change in the internal and external dynamics of a protest field over a period of time. Like any social life form, routines have their own individual and collective biographies. They may reproduce social fields such as the Indignados movement, but that does not mean that they remain frozen in time, impervious to the waxing and waning of collective action. Concretizing yet again Sewell's (2005) general definition, I define protest field routines as *practical schemas that reproduce the field*. Additionally, instead of Sewell's notion of institutions, I use the Giddens-inspired term *field stations* to refer to those sites of socio-technical intercourse where protest routines are regularly produced and maintained, which in turn help sustain the station (Giddens 1984; Postill 2011). Examples of Indignados' stations include key "meme factories" such as the free culture centers Conservas in Barcelona or La Tabacalera in Madrid; high-traffic social media sites such as Facebook, Twitter, and Menéame; and pro-15M news sites like *Público* or *El Diario*.

Not all field stations, however, are as long lived as these examples may suggest. A multiple-timeline approach requires that we consider the continuities and changes in the 15M web of routines before and after major events such as the May 15, 2011, marches, the subsequent May and June square occupations, or the mid-June vacating of the squares—and that we do so in chronological order. Let us consider, therefore, the occupied square routines. How did they differ, if at all, from pre-occupation routines? What new routines emerged in the squares that were not in existence prior to the encampments, and which routines were carried over from an earlier phase? With what consequences for the future development of the protest field? The following passage provides a first step toward an answer:

> The encampments rapidly evolved into "cities within cities" governed through popular assemblies and committees. The committees were created around practical needs such as cooking, cleaning, communicating and carrying out actions. Decisions were made through both majority-rule vote and consensus. The structure was horizontal, with rotating spokespersons in lieu of leaders. Tens of thousands of citizens were thus experimenting with participatory, direct and inclusive forms of democracy at odds with the dominant logic of political representation. (Postill 2014a)

In other words, the protesters re-created three conventional civic formations (the encampment, the popular assembly, and the committee) in unconventional places—Spain's main squares. The committees were an early by-product of essential day-to-day routines such as cooking, cleaning, and communicating. Occupiers took it in turns to act as spokespersons, another practical schema that reproduced the protest field during its square-centric phase. As always, clock-and-calendar time was the universally shared temporal code both online and offline:

> "These assemblies are open 24 hours a day, seven days a week." This is how Olmo Galvez, one of the social network stars of Democracia Real Ya, explains the online assembly process. "The information is constantly being updated, the ideas keep coming chaotically, but it works, it produces results. It's as if the networks had their own thinking brain. Proposals are put forth, an agreement is reached, and then it's back to work." (Elola 2011)

However, after four weeks of grueling collaborative work both on- and offline, the transient universe of square-focused routines came to an end, as protesters reached the conclusion that the encampments were not sustainable:

> On a tactical level . . . a very simple problem arises: the squares can reproduce everyday life on a small scale but they are not everyday life. The encampment is not the world. In the long run the "tent cities" become unsustainable, which is why in many cases (such as in Puerta del Sol), it was the campers themselves who decided to dismantle their small settlements. (Moreno-Caballud 2013, 125–126)

After taking apart the encampments, many Indignados became active participants in neighborhood (*barrio*) assemblies. Again, these assemblies exist not in a postmodern realm of timeless time, but in the familiar worldwide code of clock-and-calendar time. The anthropologists Adolfo Estalella and Alberto Corsin (2013) provide evidence of this chronometric logic in connection to the 15M assembly of Lavapiés, in central Madrid:

> During its first year of life, the Lavapiés assembly has met regularly every week. The assembly has been held in different squares across the *barrio*, except during the winter months, when it took up residence in two self-managed centers [*centros autogestionados*], one of which is a squat [*okupado*]. (70, my translation)

These meetings are not random encounters where anything goes but rather highly routinized affairs "ordered through formulas that repeat themselves like litanies":

> During the first months there are almost ten people taking care of the meetings, each responsible for a specific function: moderation, facilitation, turn taking, and minute taking. The shared responsibility of all [participants] is to maintain a dialogical and respectful atmosphere in the assembly space. There are other regulated aspects of the assembly besides the roles. A language of hand gestures has the purpose of promoting participation and generating an atmosphere of conviviality. There is no clapping; instead, hands are raised and

waved about. When someone takes up too much time and repeats herself, forearms begin to spin like windmills to indicate: "You're jabbering on" [*te estás enrollando*]. (Estalella and Corsin 2013, 71, my translation)

As we can see from this ethnographic snippet, assembly routines show both continuities and changes with regard to the square routines that preceded them. Among the continuities we can single out the fact that the *barrio* assemblies still occupy the same region of the protest field, namely the citizen sector, as opposed to the state and industry sectors occupied by social agents such as politicians, journalists, financiers, and the riot police. This location lends the assemblies their horizontal and homophilic (or "birds of a feather") character. These are spaces in which participants have learned over time to contribute to the joint effort through skilled embodied practice, quintessentially modern "third places" where conviviality is paramount, places that are neither the home nor the workplace (Oldenburg 1989).

Among the breaks (or discontinuities) with the square assemblies we can highlight their unique chronological position as immediately post-square practices (with some overlap) at a time of intense debate about the uncertain future of the movement, and the markedly different character lent to them by their much smaller scale and location within neighborhoods. Thus, although many of the *barrio* routines and subroutines (e.g., the nonverbal forms of communication) were inherited from the square phase of the movement, their social import and meaning underwent significant changes as they were reembedded in a new environment.

This account of the relationship between field routines and events over time would be incomplete without at least some mention of field agents other than assembly participants. How did field players such as journalists, politicians, financiers, spies, academics, and others adapt their day-to-day routines to the changing trends and configurations of the 15M protest field, if at all? The evidence on this matter is still scant, but two recent studies offer us some clues. In my own social media research practice during the prehistory and early stages of the Indignados movement, I developed five main digital subpractices (or routines), namely catching up, sharing, exploring, interacting, and archiving. Although these routines ran through the entire period of fieldwork in 2010 and 2011—with some modifications as time went by—there were also times of great upheaval when my habitual day-to-day activities, like those of my research participants, were overturned. As recounted in Postill and Pink (2012, 130):

Fieldwork often shifts between periods of relative calm and periods of intense activity, even turbulence. Thus, following the 15 May 2011 demonstrations across Spain, in which John marched through the streets of Barcelona with tens of thousands of protesters, Spain's social media landscape underwent a prodigious transformation as countless citizens rushed to share digital contents across blogs, microblogs, social networking sites, and a myriad of other platforms. . . . Under such conditions, social media research is anything but routine!

To my knowledge, little has been written about changes and continuities to journalistic and other professional routines as the 15M movement gathered momentum, but the following passage does suggest an important shift related to the mid-2011 explosion in social media uses by activists and the general population, at least in some sectors of Spain's journalistic field:

The contributions of the indignados eventually entered the traditional news media, signaling a change in the routines of news production and a reconfiguration of news making. Although some voices, perhaps many voices, criticized the excessive, uncontrolled use of social media linked to an inability to tell apart rumors, truths and falsities, there is no doubt that social media are today an integral part of the news media landscape. (Fundación Telefónica 2013, my translation)

Even less is known about how Spain's powerful elites, the country's 1 percent, adjusted their daily routines, if at all, in response to the popular uprising of May 2011 and its aftermath. This is a crucial area of investigation in need of urgent research (Postill 2013b).

Conclusion

In this chapter I have explored the multilinearity of protest, that is, the idea that a protest movement is made up of countless timelines. I have argued that we must overcome our reliance on single, event-driven protest timelines and develop instead accounts of the new protest movements that bring together multiple concurrent timelines, such as those of trends and routines. This multilinear approach, I suggest, can help us produce accounts of the protests that foreground the continued centrality of clock-and-calendar time worldwide, as well as allowing us to track the dynamic coevolution of protest practices and actions across time and space.

This emphasis on linearity does not commit us to a Whig version of history as the relentless march toward greater progress (Stocking 1968). On the contrary, it provides us with a robust analytical methodology to track the often meandering paths taken by movement fields as they move through time. While the passing of world historical time is a linear, non-recursive process (i.e., the year 2011 will never return), social protests and other forms of collective action are open ended, nonteleological processes. We can be certain that 2018 will follow 2017, but we have no way of predicting the birth or shape of protest movements that will unfold that year, if any.

What did this analytical experiment teach us about the temporalities of the new protest movements? First, we learned that while it makes sense to draw a single timeline of protest field events (in the sense of transformative moments in the life course of a movement), this is not the case for field trends and routines, for which we need to draw a larger set of partially concurrent timeliness. We saw, for example, how a distinctive vocabulary emerged on Twitter in the April–June 2011 period, a vocabulary we now recognize as distinctively 15M or Indignados. But this was not, of course, the only trend at work during that period. Other trends included the sharp rise and fall of public space participation in the protests by Spain's general population; the roughly concomitant growth and decline of social media sharing of 15M-related contents; and the ongoing politicization of geeks, hackers, online journalists, digital rights lawyers, and other "freedom technologists" (Postill 2013a, 2016). Second, we found that protest movement trends do not just happen—they are *made* to happen by committed activists using a range of techno-political tools, including Twitter's trending topics facility. Here I took issue with those commentators who have taken the ephemerality of Twitter to represent Indignados' seeming obsession with the here and now. In fact, 15M's informal leaders are highly adept at juggling a number of temporal horizons in their day-to-day activities, and more than capable of realizing that a long sequence of fleeting trending topics adds up to a grand narrative of popular struggle against an unjust system (on social media and national narratives, see Lim 2013). Third, there appears to be a close link between protest field events and routines, more precisely, between the specific stage of a protest movement and the social meaning of routines found within it. Thus, we saw how a range of assembly routines survived protesters' relocation to the *barrios*, such as the use of a basic sign language, but under radically different conditions that changed the routines' social meanings and outcomes. Many other square routines did not make the transition and fell into disuse.

Future research could develop this chapter's core idea of the multilinearity of protest. This could be taken in new directions through interdisciplinary collaborations among qualitative and quantitative scholars, comparative studies in different national and regional contexts, further theoretical work on the interrelations between the three key temporal concepts (events, routines, and trends, such as on the hybrid notion of routinization), on the spatial dimensions of these heuristic devices, or on the part played by the 1 percent in the multiple timelines that make up a protest movement.

References

Andrews, Kenneth T., and Michael Biggs. 2006. "The Dynamics of Protest Diffusion: Movement Organizations, Social Networks, and News Media in the 1960 Sit-ins." *American Sociological Review* 71 (5): 752–777.

Born, Georgina. 2010. "The Social and the Aesthetic: For a Post-Bourdieuian Theory of Cultural Production." *Cultural Sociology* 4 (2): 1–38.

Bosi, Lorenzo. 2007. "Social Movement Participation and the 'Timing' of Involvement: The Case of the Northern Ireland Civil Rights Movement." In *Research in Social Movements, Conflicts and Change* 27: 37–61.

Budka, Philipp. 2011. "From Cyber to Digital Anthropology to an Anthropology of the Contemporary?" Paper presented at the 38th e-seminar of the European Association of Social Anthropologists Media Anthropology Network, November 22–December 6. http://www.media anthropology.net/index.php/e-seminars.

Castells, Manuel. 1999. "An Introduction to the Information Age." In *The Media Reader: Continuity & Transformation*, edited by Hugh Mackay and Tim O'Sullivan, 398–410. London: Sage.

———. "#Wikiacampadas." *La Vanguardia* (Barcelona), May 28. http://www.lavanguardia.com /opinion/articulos/20110528/54160922879/wikiacampadas.html.

Corsin, Alberto, and Adolfo Estalella. 2011. "#spanishrevolution." *Anthropology Today* 27 (4): 19–23.

Davies, Andy D. 2009. "Ethnography, Space and Politics: Interrogating the Process of Protest in the Tibetan Freedom Movement." *Area* 41 (1): 19–25.

Dayan, Daniel. 2010. "Beyond Media Events: Disenchantment, Derailment, Disruption." In *Media Events in a Global Age*, edited by Nick Couldry, Andreas Hepp, and Friedrich Krotz, 23–31. New York: Routledge.

Elola, Joseba. 2011. "El 15-M sacude el sistema." *El País*, May 22. http://politica.elpais.com/politica /2011/05/21/actualidad/1305999838_462379.

Eriksen, Thomas H. 2001. *Tyranny of the Moment: Fast and Slow Time in the Information Age.* London: Pluto Press.

Estalella, Adolfo. 2011. "Ensamblajes de esperanza: Un estudio antropológico del bloguear apasionado." PhD diss., Universitat Oberta de Catalunya, Barcelona.

———., and A. Corsin. 2013. "Asambleas populares: El ritmo urbano de una política de la experimentación." In *Orígenes y retos del 15M*, edited by M. Cruells and P. Ibarra, 61–80. Madrid: Icaria.

Fabian, Johannes. 1983. *Time and the Other: How Anthropology Makes Its Object.* New York: Columbia University Press.

Fundación Telefónica. 2013. "Gobiernos en la calle y ciudadanos en las redes sociales: Nuevas exigencias para el periodismo." *Telos: Cuadernos de Comunicación y de Innovación* 94 (January–April 2013). http://sociedadinformacion.fundacion.telefonica.com/seccion =1266&idioma=es_ES&id=2013021317570002&activo=6.do#.

García Canclini, Nestor, Francisco Cruces, and Maritza U. Castro Pozo, eds. 2012. *Jóvenes, culturas urbanas y redes digitales.* Barcelona: Ariel and Telefónica.

Gell, Alfred. 1992. *The Anthropology of Time: Cultural Constructions of Temporal Maps and Images.* Oxford, UK: Berg.

Gerbaudo, Paolo. 2012. *Tweets and the Streets.* London: Pluto Press.

Giddens, Anthony. 1984. *The Constitution of Society.* Cambridge, UK: Polity Press.

Grzymala-Busse, Anna. 2011. "Time Will Tell? Temporality and the Analysis of Causal Mechanisms and Processes." *Comparative Political Studies* 44 (9): 1267–1297.

Haug, Christoph. 2013. "Organizing Spaces: Meeting Arenas as a Social Movement Infrastructure between Organization, Network, and Institution." *Organization Studies* 34 (5–6): 705–732.

Howard, Philip N., Aiden Duffy, Deen Freelon, Muzammil M. Hussain, Will Mari, and Marwa Maziad. 2011. *Opening Closed Regimes: What Was the Role of Social Media during the Arab*

Spring Project on Information Technology and Political Islam? Seattle: Department of Communication, University of Washington.

Juris, Jeffrey. S. 2008. *Networking Futures: The Movements against Corporate Globalization.* Durham, NC: Duke University Press.

Kornetis, Kostis. 2009. "'Everything Links?' Temporality, Territoriality and Cultural Transfer in the '68 Protest Movements." *Historein* 9: 34–45.

Kurzman, Charles. 2012. "The Arab Spring Uncoiled." *Mobilization: An International Quarterly*, 17 (4): 377–390.

Lee, Jung-eun. 2012. "Micro-Dynamics of Protests: The Political and Cultural Conditions for Anti-US Beef Protests in South Korea." *Sociological Perspectives* 55 (3): 399–420.

Lim, Merlyna. (2013). "Many Clicks but Little Sticks: Social Media Activism in Indonesia." *Journal of Contemporary Asia* 43 (4): 636–657.

Lorenz-Meyer, Dagmar. 2013. "Timescapes of Activism: Trajectories, Encounters and Timings of Czech Women's NGOs." *European Journal of Women's Studies.*

Mankekar, Purnima. 1999. *Screening Culture, Viewing Politics: An Ethnography of Television, Womanhood, and Nation in Postcolonial India.* Durham, NC: Duke University Press.

Martín Rojo, Luisa. 2012. "Paisajes lingüísticos de indignación: Prácticas comunicativas para tomar las plazas." *Anuari del Conflicte Social*, 275–302.

McAdam, Douglas, and William H. Sewell Jr. 2001. "It's About Time: Temporality in the Study of Social Movements and Revolutions." In *Silence and Voice in the Study of Contentious Politics*, edited by R. R. Aminzade, J. A. Goldstone, D. McAdam, E. J. Perry, W. H. Sewell Jr., S. Tarrow, and C. Tilly, 89–125. Cambridge: Cambridge University Press.

Monterde, Arnau, and John Postill. 2014. "Mobile Ensembles: The Uses of Mobile Phones for Social Protest by Spain's Indignados." In *Routledge Companion to Mobile Media*, edited by G. Goggin and L. Hjorth, 429–438. London: Routledge.

Moreno-Caballud, Luis. 2013. "Desbordamientos culturales en torno al 15-M." *Teknokultura: Revista de Cultura Digital y Movimientos Sociales* 10 (1): 101–130.

Munn, Nancy D. 1992. "The Cultural Anthropology of Time: A Critical Essay." *Annual Review of Anthropology* 21: 93–123.

Nanabhay, Mohamed, and Roxane Farmanfarmaian. 2011. "From Spectacle to Spectacular: How Physical Space, Social Media and Mainstream Broadcast Amplified the Public Sphere in Egypt's 'Revolution.'" *Journal of North African Studies* 16 (4): 573–603.

Nega. 2011. "Cultura y estética del 15-M: De eslóganes y falsos profetas." *Kaos en la red*, July 2. http://old.kaosenlared.net/noticia/cultura-estetica-15-m-esloganes-falsos-profetas.

Oldenburg, Ray. 1989. *The Great Good Place: Cafes, Coffee Shops, Community Centers, Beauty Parlors, General Stores, Bars, Hangouts, and How They Get You through the Day.* New York: Paragon House.

Panelli, Ruth. 2007. "Time-Space Geometries of Activism and the Case of Mis/placing Gender in Australian Agriculture." *Transactions of the Institute of British Geographers* 32: 46–65.

Panelli, Ruth, and Wendy Larner. 2010. "Timely Partnerships? Contrasting Geographies of Activism in New Zealand and Australia." *Urban Studies* 47 (6): 1343–1366.

Postill, John. 2002. "Clock and Calendar Time: A Missing Anthropological Problem." *Time and Society* 11: 251–270.

———. 2006. *Media and Nation Building: How the Iban Became Malaysian.* Oxford, UK: Berghahn.

———. 2011. *Localizing the Internet: An Anthropological Account.* Oxford, UK: Berghahn.

———. 2012. "Digital Politics and Political Engagement." In *Digital Anthropology*, edited by H. Horst and D. Miller, 165–184. Oxford, UK: Berg.

——. 2013a. "The Uneven Convergence of Digital Freedom Activism and Popular Protest: A Global Theory of the New Protest Movements." Melbourne: RMIT University. http://rmit.academia.edu/JohnPostill.

——. 2013b. "We Are the One Percent: Rethinking National Elites as Protest Participants." *Reviews & Critical Commentary (CritCom)*, November 26.

——. 2014a. "Democracy in the Age of Viral Reality: A Media Epidemiography of Spain's Indignados Movement." *Ethnography* 15 (1): 51–69.

——. 2014b. "Spain's Indignados and the Mediated Aesthetics of Nonviolence." In *The Political Aesthetics of Global Protest: Beyond the Arab Spring*, edited by P. Werbner, K. Spellman-Poots, and M. Webb, 341–367. Edinburgh: Edinburgh University Press.

——. 2015. "Fields: Dynamic Configurations of Practices, Games, and Socialities." In *Concepts of Sociality: An Anthropological Interrogation*, edited by V. Amit, 47–68. Oxford, UK: Berghahn.

——. 2016. "Freedom Technologists and the Future of Global Justice." In *State of Power 2016*. Amsterdam: Transnational Institute.

Postill, John, and Sarah Pink. 2012. "Social Media Ethnography: The Digital Researcher in a Messy Web." *Media International Australia* 145: 123–134.

Rabinow, Paul, and George E. Marcus (with James D. Faubion and Tobias Rees). 2008. *Designs for an Anthropology of the Contemporary*. Durham, NC: Duke University Press.

Rinke, Eike M., and Maria Röder. 2011. "Media Ecologies, Communication Culture, and Temporal-Spatial Unfolding: Three Components in a Communication Model of the Egyptian Regime Change." *International Journal of Communication* 5: 1273–1285.

Rosa, Isaac. 2012. "Violencia policial: ¿Qué tiene que pasar para que alguien tome medidas?" *El Diario*, November 15. http://www.eldiario.es/zonacritica/represion_huelga_general_policia_6_69353080.html.

Sánchez, Juan L. 2011. "Los primeros 40 de Sol." *Periodismo Humano*, May 26. http://periodismo humano.com/temas-destacados/los-primeros-40-de-sol.html.

Sewell, William H., Jr. 2005. *Logics of History: Social Theory and Social Transformation*. Chicago: University of Chicago Press.

Stocking, George W. 1968. *Race, Culture, and Evolution: Essays in the History of Anthropology*. New York: Free Press.

Telegraph. 2013. "Nobel Prize for Economists Robert Shiller, Eugene Fama, and Lars Peter Hansen for Study of Asset Markets." October 16.

Vaillant, Gabriela G. 2013. "The Politics of Temporality: An Analysis of Leftist Youth Politics and Generational Contention." *Social Movement Studies* 12 (4): 377–396.

Valenzuela, Sebastian, Arturo Arriagada, and Andres Scherman. 2012. "The Social Media Basis of Youth Protest Behavior: The Case of Chile." *Journal of Communication* 62 (2): 299–314.

Vallina-Rodriguez, Narseo, Salvatore Scellato, Hamed Haddadi, Carl Forsell, Jon Crowcroft, and Cecilia Mascolo. 2012. "Los Twindignados: The Rise of the Indignados Movement on Twitter." In *SOCIALCOM-PASSAT '12: Proceedings of the 2012 ASE/IEEE International Conference on Social Computing and 2012 ASE/IEEE International Conference on Privacy, Security, Risk and Trust*, 496–501.

Wasik, Bill. 2009. *And Then There's This: How Stories Live and Die in Viral Culture*. New York: Viking.

Weber, Ingmar, Venkata Rama K. Garimella, and Asmelash Teka. 2013. "Political Hashtag Trends." In *Advances in Information Retrieval: Proceedings of the 35th European Conference on IR Research*, ECIR 2013, Moscow, Russia, March 24–27. Berlin: Springer, 857–860.

Wittel, Andreas. 2001. "Toward a Network Sociality." *Theory, Culture & Society* 18 (6): 51–76.

10   Whose Ethics?

Negotiating Ethics and Responsibility in the Field

Marianne Maeckelbergh

How does one do "ethical" anthropological research among social movements? The same question could also be phrased as more of a directive: what are the rules that should guide researchers' behavior when they are doing research within social movements? The directives approach to ethics, however, helps very little in either anthropological research or research within social movements. While some of the more experimental sciences resolve their ethical responsibility to the research subjects through the means of consent forms and guidelines for experiments on humans and on nonhuman animals, approved by ethics boards that ensure all the necessary boxes are ticked, anthropologists often reject the tick-box approach to ethics embodied in rules and administrative approvals, preferring instead to view ethics as an ongoing reflection on our responsibility to assess and reassess the multiple ethical positions we continuously embody as we navigate the field. We rarely have a clear set of ethical principles with which to make the most important ethical assessments. In fact, most commonly, anthropologists find themselves in the position that they have to negotiate many different sets of ethical frameworks at once. At times, these multiple ethical frameworks even contradict one another. Sometimes, the ethical choice is obvious to the researcher; other times, however, the choice is not at all clear. This chapter explores some of these tensions for anthropological research in general and for research within social movements specifically, but it does not presume to know how, or even if, "ethical" research can be done within social movements.

This chapter stems from a skepticism about the usefulness of, and an unease with, the power of ethics within academic research, especially when embodied by a tick-box approach to ethics. I believe that it is not so simple to identify what is unethical and what is not, and that perhaps academic value systems may not be the best value systems to apply when assessing what is ethical and what is not, given that academic knowledge is produced within institutional contexts that have their own sets of interests and that operate within a dominant paradigm of knowledge that shapes and produces notions of what is and is not ethical. Lakoff and Collier (2004, 420) argue that "configurations of ethical reflection and practice" can be understood as "regimes of living." The choice to include the word *regime* is important here, as it "suggests a 'manner, method, or system of rule or government,' characteristic of political regimes, systems of administration, or modes of techno-scientific intervention" (420). Through such an analysis of ethics, the political power of any given ethical framework quickly becomes apparent. Any researcher, therefore, who is trying to behave ethically, is also trying to behave within a "manner, method or system of rule or government." Ethical behavior is therefore never a universal or neutral act. Understanding which systems of rule we are embodying, and how to navigate these systems and perhaps at times transgress them from one context to the next, is an important skill for the ethnographer.

Although one might not encounter the phrase "regime of living" in an introductory anthropological textbook, the idea that underlies this concept, that "ethical configurations in diverse situations" take "diverse actual forms" (Lakoff and Collier 2004, 420) is prevalent in disciplinary discussions of ethics. Disciplinary ethics are largely based on what Castañeda (2006) calls nonmoral principles. He argues that morals refer to a "normative and rule-driven framework of principles," whereas nonmoral ethics "is a situational, context-driven, relativist approach" (Castañeda 2006, 123). Such an approach to ethics requires that we evaluate each ethical situation in context and act differently depending on the circumstances. Just as "regimes of living" are context dependent, each field situation is deemed unique and the ethical choice within each situation is not set in stone. This evaluation of ethical choices does "not involve knowledge of a fixed set of moral rules, nor [is] it a purely abstract form of rationality. It [is], rather, a capacity for reasoned *choice*—a practical wisdom—that allowed an individual to act on the basis of 'the requirements of virtue in each fresh context'" (Lakoff and Collier 2004, 423, citing Taylor 1994, emphasis added). This approach to ethics implies that "a given regime provides one possible means, and always only one among various possible means, for organizing, reasoning about, and living ethically" (Lakoff and Collier 2004, 426). The acknowledgment that a given regime of living is only one among many possible regimes, among which the anthropologist may have to choose, is the starting point of this chapter in which I reflect on the question of how to navigate multiple ethical regimes, especially when these regimes come into contradiction with each other. I first briefly explore certain characteristics of social movements to emphasize which types of ethical considerations are important for ethnographic fieldwork among social movements specifically and why. I then turn to the question of ethics within anthropology as a discipline, to highlight the situated nature of ethics as embodied in the discipline's Code of Ethics. In the third section, I turn to the question of multiple ethical frameworks and the problem of negotiating these when two or more ethical frameworks contradict each other. I draw on examples of ethnographic fieldwork that have brought researchers into a position where the various ethical frameworks came into conflict in a way that forced the researcher to choose which ethical framework to adhere to and which to violate. Finally, I reflect on the question of multiple ethical frameworks from the point of view of social movement research. The focus here is on the practice of ethnography in the field, not on the complex questions of representation involved in writing about the "other" from an "authoritative" position (see Chesters 2012; Gillan and Pickerill 2012). While there are, as always, ethical considerations built into the process of writing and representation, I emphasize here the ethical dilemmas that arise in the field during ethnographic fieldwork, as these are less often addressed and are equally important. I also intentionally leave out any discussion of right-wing or fascist movements, as I think choosing to do research among these movements raises many larger ethical questions that are, luckily, beyond the scope of my knowledge.[1]

The movements I have worked with and with which I am familiar are grassroots movements on the left (although they might not describe themselves this way), ranging from small-scale campaigns to large international convergences such as protests against the G8, World Trade Organization, World Bank, and International Monetary Fund, and the World and European Social Forums of the alterglobalization movement. I have been active within these movements since the 1990s and have been doing research within them since the early 2000s. Most recently, I have also been researching the wave of uprisings post-2011, primarily in Spain and the United States, but with visits to Bosnia and Herzegovina, Egypt, Greece, Portugal, Turkey and the United Kingdom as well, as part of a film series called Global Uprisings (http://www.globaluprisings.org). I base my reflections in this chapter on my experiences within these movements. While some might find it preferable to come up with universal ethical guidelines for all social movement research, I do not believe this is possible, and the situated perspective I offer here is situated for a reason. If other movements had been taken as the backdrop for this reflection about the ethics of ethnographic fieldwork within social movements, then I imagine very different ethical concerns would emerge.

Ethics and Social Movements

Understanding ethical practice as a "regime of living," and ethics more generally as implicated in a regime of rule, strikes me as especially important for the study of social movements, since quite often social movements are explicitly challenging the ethical codes and the manner of rule or government within which they find themselves. Furthermore, social movement actors are often, even when not ideological per se, organized and guided by strong morals. The very reason for becoming part of a social movement, or for the existence of the social movement in the first place, is often tied to a particular normative notion about how society should be organized. Almost by definition (although there are certainly exceptions) these normative notions about how society should be organized contradict the system of rule that prevails in the context in which the social movement operates. Social movements, then, often embody multiple alternative systems of ethics, and these ethics are part of their daily practice and at the very heart of their raison d'être. Understanding the multiple ethical frameworks of social movement actors, therefore, is an important component of understanding the movement. Since movement ethics are often counter to or in some way challenging the dominant "normative and rule-driven framework of principles" (Castañeda 2006, 123). Ignoring movement actors' ethical practices becomes, perhaps inadvertently, an act against these practices and in favor of dominant ethical paradigms.

Second, social movement actors, by going against dominant norms, ideals, and institutions of power, sometimes through illegal action, often put themselves at risk. Part of every implicit or explicit ethical code developed by social movement actors addresses the question of how anyone participating in the movements must treat and act toward others in the movement and how to respond against powerful actors that target movement actors through repression, arrest, physical attacks, smear campaigns, counterinformation, surveillance, and so on. The ethical practices that exist within social movements to protect movement actors, while not necessarily clearly articulated, have high stakes attached to them, and a researcher who, even inadvertently, violates these ethical practices runs the risk of endangering movement actors.

Very mundane practices like writing down people's names can at times put people in danger, keeping basic ethnographic data about who is friends with whom, how they know each other, where and how people meet, and how they are all connected to one another is exactly the kind of standard ethnographic information that can be dangerous in the wrong hands. However, many people involved in movements are public figures with their own theories and arguments and political projects for which they want to be recognized and credited. Not naming people who want to be remembered for their role in creating history also serves to obscure their hard work and accomplishments, to erase them from the historical record, in a way that would be disrespectful. The problem, then, is knowing the difference between those who want to remain anonymous, those who don't care, and those who would be insulted if they were not recognized. This is not a dilemma to be addressed in the "writing up" phase of the research, when the researcher decides whom to name and whom to give a pseudonym; this is a question for the field—what to note down and what not to note down in the first place, and how to get to know the field well enough so that the researcher can correctly assess each person's ethical desires from one context to another without having to ask every few minutes. Attaining this knowledge is tricky, especially when we consider that the same person may want credit for some things they say and to remain anonymous for others.

While these concerns are likely relevant for research among other groups of people as well, they are especially important when gathering data on social movement practices—and especially considering that anthropologists often gather information informally and at times when people are not fully aware that they are being researched. Even if the movement actors officially know that you are an anthropologist doing research, the ethnographic method always involves a lot of casual conversation, and the more of an inside position one holds (the more one moves, as I do, between being an activist at some times and a recording device at others), the more important it becomes to be able to filter for oneself what information can and cannot be shared or stored and in what way the information can be shared or stored, as this is usually a crucial component of the ethical practices of the movement actors themselves. There are many precedents for this, and gathering information, especially as an activist, is not per se a violation of the movement actors own ethics. The activists I have worked with are often their own movement historians and analysts. Even as movements reject mainstream media, for example, they often allow for "our media" to cover actions and meetings, even seek this kind of media out, at times to ensure that there is an independent activist media to publicize events, issues, and movement perspectives. These media activists are usually trusted because they understand and share the ethical framework of the movement actors who are seeking them out.[2]

For researchers a similar dynamic might apply: perhaps the best way to navigate the complex, fluctuating, and multiple ethical positions of social movement actors is to apply the ethical framework of the person with whom you are speaking to all of the information you gather through that person. This ethical framework might very well be different for each person you speak to; people might shift their own ethical framework depending on where they are and in which capacity they speak (as an individual, as a member of a group, as a media spokesperson, or as a representative for a political organization). The two crucial questions for ethnographic fieldwork within social movements therefore become these: What are the sets of morals being developed and pursued through the various groups and individuals, and how can I ensure that my research at the very least does not impede these? And what are the ethical practices that each movement actor expects from the others, and how can I be consistent with these practices during my research?

Ethics in Anthropological Research

There are at least four or five sets of ethical frameworks that anthropologists, or field workers in general, are negotiating in any given field setting. First is the ethical framework of the researcher's own "home" country or community. Whether we realize it or not, we enter the field with a set of inherited assumptions about right and wrong that give shape to the way we see and interpret events around us. Even when researchers go into the field with a very open heart and mind, the frame of reference is inevitably the researchers' previous life experiences, complete with explicit and implicit lessons about ethical and unethical behavior. The second ethical framework is very closely related to the first, which is the researcher's personal ethics. To a certain extent, researchers' personal ethics will be a reflection of the context from which they come, where they grew up, family, friends, religious or political background, but perhaps a researcher intentionally rejects certain ethical values of his or her own background, intentionally embracing others values, by for example, being an avid egalitarian despite living in a highly hierarchical society. These two types of ethical frameworks then come into contact with at least three other sets of ethical practices that the researcher is confronted with through the act of doing ethnographic fieldwork: the disciplinary ethical code (e.g., the American Anthropological Association's Code of Ethics); the ethical demands of the institutional setting or employer, be it a university or another private or public entity; and finally, and certainly not least, a series of ethical practices within the everyday lives of the people who are being "researched." Rarely do all of these ethical frameworks completely coincide.

Despite the lack of a unified disciplinary stance on ethics (Shore 1999, 124), anthropology has two ways in which ethics appear in a slightly more structured and proscriptive form. First, through text books and teaching. Here the story tends to be that there are at least five important dimensions of ethics within anthropological research: "informed consent, privacy, harm, exploitation and consequences for future research" (Hammersley and Atkinson 2007, 209), usually presented with all of the necessary caveats about how difficult it is to really get informed consent in anthropological research because we have no definition of either *informed* or *consent* and about how hard it is to predict what kind of harm might come from your research and to whom. Even these seemingly more structured dimensions of ethical research are often presented as domains to think about and consider rather than as a set of rules to follow. The second way anthropology attempts to guide the ethics of research is through disciplinary norms, currently encapsulated in the creation of a code of ethics. These codes are inventions that emerged over time and were not a part of anthropology from the start. Pels (1999, 101) shows that "a historical approach would soon indicate that the present interest in ethical codes is only one way of institutionalizing moral

standards and ethical guidelines in anthropology and a very recent and fairly unusual one at that." Pels also traces the history of disciplinary ethics further back
to the colonial era and describes the rise of a "folk epistemology of professional-
ism" and argues that, "in this professional ideology, ethical codes are meant to
ensure the competence and honour of the professional, that is, to help discipline
the members of the profession so that its clients can trust the technical and moral
quality of the service rendered" (102). Berreman (2007, citing Carr-Saunders and
Wilson 1933 and Taeusch 1933) described in detail the history of how the American Anthropological Association's Code of Ethics came into being, emphasizing
especially controversies over anthropologists involved in various forms of warfare and counterinsurgency.

This history starts with Franz Boas, who "became the only member of the
[American Anthropological] association ever to be expelled" (Berreman 2007
[1991]: 299, citing Stocking 1968: 273) for reporting that at least four anthropologists "had served as spies under cover of scholarly research during World War I"
(Berreman 2007, 299, drawing on Boas 1919, 729, and American Anthropological
Association, or AAA, 1920, 93–94). Then, after World War II came the adoption
of the "Resolution of Freedom of Publication," which insisted that all "sponsoring
institutions . . . guarantee their research scientists complete freedom to interpret
and publish their findings without censorship or interference, provided that the
interests of those studied are protected" (AAA 1949, 370, in Berreman 2007, 299).
In 1967, the AAA adopted the "Statement of Problems of Anthropological Research and Ethics," which was the forerunner to the Principles of Professional
Responsibility (Berreman 2007, 299), which the American Anthropological
Association (AAA) devised in the period 1969–1971 in response to outcry over
anthropologists involvement in Project Camelot, a US counterinsurgency operation (Fluehr-Lobban 1991, 23). At the time the idea that anthropologists would
allow their research to be used in strategic warfare and counterinsurgency was
considered by some to be scandalous enough to warrant the creation of ethical
and professional guidelines for researchers (Jorgensen 1971).

Contradictory Ethical Frameworks

Disciplinary and Institutional Ethical Frameworks

Despite outrage over the involvement of anthropologists in counterinsurgency
initiatives in the 1960s, there remain to this day no clear boundaries as to what
kind of research anthropologists can undertake and with which motives. Ethical practice remains a situational and relativist construct within anthropology,
and if we examine how the disciplinary ethical codes have been constructed, as
Berreman (2007) does, we see how the multiple ethical frameworks that the ethnographer negotiates can at times come into conflict with each other. Berreman's

history of ethical practice within anthropology is specifically aimed at addressing the proposed changes to the Code of Ethics that were put forth in 1984. These changes, he argues, were the result, in part, of anthropologists increasingly working in the public and private sectors for employers who made their own demands of anthropological conduct, in some cases even claiming ownership over the data produced through the anthropologists research. This shift in the "reality" of anthropological research meant that the Principles of Professional Responsibility needed to be rewritten to better reflect the institutional contexts of professional anthropologists (Berreman 2007).

Berreman's (2007) specific critiques of *how* the guidelines were going to be rewritten are relevant here because he highlights how the ethical frameworks of the companies and governments for which anthropologists were working collided with the ethical principles of the AAA. Berreman argues that "the recent impetus for redefinition of anthropological ethics comes clearly from those outside of academia who find the Principles of Professional Responsibility to be inconsistent with the demands of their employment" (314). These changes, he argues, were being made to accommodate the practical demands of anthropologists careers and were at the expense of four key ethical considerations captured in the Principles of Professional Responsibility: first, the removal of the assertion that "the anthropologists' paramount responsibility is to those they study." Second, the removal of the claim that secret or clandestine research is a violation of anthropological ethics. Third, removal of the principle of accountability of the anthropologist for violations of ethical principles. And finally, the deletion of assertion that the anthropologist has a positive responsibility to society at large to convey their findings openly (Berreman 2007, 306, 315).

Although the Code of Ethics has since been rewritten to once again include many of these important points, the specific deletions that were being proposed are important in that they represent a conflict between disciplinary ethics and institutional ethics. While we can view both of these ethical frameworks as equal to each other, or perhaps even think that the disciplinary ethical framework should take precedence, in practice the ethical frameworks that have more power behind them, which is inevitably the institutional ethics, are the ones that have a higher likelihood of prevailing. Institutions, be they corporate, governmental, or even academic, can make many demands of researchers that researchers have little choice but to comply with, especially if quitting their jobs and dropping their research agenda entirely is not an appealing option for them. When research becomes a career and not merely an intellectual pursuit, we become more limited in the range of ethical decisions we can make and often find ourselves negotiating conflicting interests and divergent scientific paradigms in such a way that may, if ethics continues to become institutionalized, make it hard to do research on social movements at all.

It is one thing to gain the trust of social movement actors when you are an independent researcher and when you can claim control over the data gathered, how it is stored, and with whom it is shared. It is an entirely different matter when the data gathered is not yours or will be demanded to be seen by others as part of an institutional practice of "ethics" that places primary value on bureaucratic notions of accountability and transparency—an ethical framework that is based on either a lack of trust of the researchers themselves or ownership regimes in which the employee researcher gathers information that legally belongs to the employer. Under these types of institutional ethics, the social movement actors, and anyone being researched, would need to have trust not only in the researcher but also in the institution for which the researcher works. This type of trust is much harder to build and would often be deemed impossible, for good reason. I can't imagine having to encourage everyone I do research with that they have to not only trust me but also to trust everyone I work with at the university, including the administration of the university, the legal liability officers, the public relations staff, and so on. Never can all of those people even begin to understand the multiple ethical frameworks of the social movement actors, much less commit themselves to respect these ethical frameworks. Consequently, asking social movement actors to trust the institution I work for, which compared to many other possible institutions anthropologists might work for is relatively harmless, would be in and of itself ethically questionable given that the institution—including its ethics review board, if it has one—is unlikely to understand what is or might be at stake for movement actors in relation to the research being carried out.

If we use Lakoff and Collier's (2004, 420) approach to think about ethical frameworks as "configurations of ethical reflection and practice" that are "regimes of living," in which regime is "a 'manner, method, or system of rule or government,' characteristic of political regimes, systems of administration, or modes of techno-scientific intervention,'" then we see the danger more clearly of the choices researchers make when negotiating multiple ethical frameworks in the field. As we see in Berreman's (2007) example, the regime of institutional ethics can outweigh the regime of disciplinary ethics, and as we shall see in the next section, both regimes can easily outweigh the regime of personal ethics, unless actively challenged.

Personal or Human Ethical Frameworks

An anthropologist who has repeatedly placed the "politics of ethics" centrally in his research, asking difficult questions and making difficult choices, is Philippe Bourgois. His research began among Salvadoran refugees in Honduras at a time of political turmoil. Later he moved into East Harlem in New York City to do research among crack dealers, and later still, he turned his attention to drug users.

While he is not always researching social movements, many of the ethical dilemmas Bourgois has encountered are highly relevant for an anthropology of social movements, especially his work among revolutionary peasants. Bourgois (2007, 289–290) argues that anthropology has a "narrow" definition of ethics that does not consider "the larger moral and human dimensions of the political and economic structures ravaging most of the peoples that anthropologists have studied historically" and that most North American anthropologists "do not include the political or even the human rights dimension confronting the people they research in their discussion of 'anthropological ethics'" (290). He concludes that "the problem with contemporary anthropological ethics is not merely that the boundaries of what is defined as ethical are too narrowly drawn, but more importantly, that ethics can be subject to rigid righteous interpretations which place them at loggerheads with overarching human rights concerns" (290).

Bourgois (2007, 290) argues that the "moral imperative to anthropology" is to take unequal power relationships seriously and to challenge and expose these whenever possible. He argues that since anthropology is methodologically based on participant observation and often carried out among disadvantaged groups, "ethnography offers a privileged arena for intensive contact with human tragedy" (290). In his own fieldwork he encountered many moments when he was confronted with the need to violate institutional protocol, national laws, and anthropological ethics in order to defend the human rights of the people he studied. Bourgois (2007, 293–294) describes when he was in Honduras at the Salvadoran refugee camp and was offered the chance to accompany a group of peasants planning to cross back into El Salvador. He intended to join them for forty-eight hours, but the journey quickly turned into a "fourteen day nightmare when the Salvadoran military launched a search and destroy operation against the region." The human tragedy that he experienced firsthand and witnessed was dramatic, and he immediately took his story to the media and to human rights lobbyists on Capitol Hill.

What he discovered is "that anthropologists are not supposed to document human rights violations if it involves violating a host country government's laws or contravenes the informed consent and right to privacy of the parties involved" (Bourgois 2007, 295). After being accused of violating anthropological ethics and risking that future research in the region would be more difficult due to his having angered the government, he argues that within the anthropological framework of ethics, "most political economy studies can be potentially unethical. A fieldworker cannot obtain important information on unequal power relations by strictly obeying the power structure's rules and laws," and he asks the poignant question, "did I have an obligation to obtain informed consent from the Salvadoran government troops firing at us before photographing the children they wounded?" (296). So while Bourgois felt that his "personal sense of moral responsibility obliged [him] to provide public testimony" (295), this choice led him to violate the ethical framework of the discipline.

This example is relevant to social movement research because it highlights how many of the seemingly harmless and self-evident ethical assumptions within disciplinary ethical frameworks actually stem from a very specific regime of ethics, one that takes dominant power structures as given and that operates within the same paradigm of authority and acceptability that attributes a certain degree, if not a great deal, of respect to these power structures. This may be practically necessary for the discipline, but it is not always in the best interest of those studied, especially when those being studied are positioning themselves specifically against these power structures or when those being studied are being targeted by these power structures—both of which can often be the case in the study of social movements. Which ethical frameworks to apply and when to adhere to them becomes slightly more complex when researching social movements. Researchers might need to be willing, as Bourgois was, to place their personal ethics, or the ethical framework(s) of the movements, above those of the institution for which they work and above those of the discipline within which they operate, in order to protect and defend the people with whom they are doing research.

Social Movement Ethical Frameworks

From these examples we can see that the various ethical frameworks the anthropologist operates within can often diverge from one another, leading to difficult choices for the anthropologist. Whether researchers honor their work contract and the demands of the institution for which they work, or whether they remain as close as possible to the guidelines of the discipline or whether researchers ultimately choose to follow their personal ethics, there are no simple solutions to ethical problems encountered in the field. In none of these discussions so far, however, have the people being studied appeared as agents with their own sets of ethics. And while the anthropologist has the responsibility to respect and do no harm to those being studied, rarely are the ethical frameworks of those studied considered more important than the ethical frameworks of the anthropologist.

Much has been written about the need for engaged anthropology, or even militant anthropology, especially when doing research among social movements (Hale 2006; Juris and Khasnabish 2013; Maeckelbergh 2009; Scheper-Hughes 1995; Speed 2006). Within the framework of engaged anthropology or militant anthropology, the anthropologist contributes to the political project being pursued by social movements in the field through an "ethics of solidarity" (Khasnabish this volume). This task can often be carried out perfectly in accordance with one's personal ethics, the ethics of the researcher's own background, the ethics of the discipline, the ethics of employers, and the ethics of the movements, but the difficult questions arise when these ethical frameworks collide. Given that the movement actors being studied are unlikely to share a singular ethical framework, it is not merely enough to assume the position of the engaged anthropologist. Taking in a specific subject position, which may be politically important for reasons similar to those described by Bourgois, does not necessarily ensure that the researcher can or will respect the ethical frameworks of the movement actors.

Social movements often have similar dilemmas to those presented in Bourgois's research. Social movement actors have reasoned arguments about the necessity of breaking unjust laws, and in some cases have developed complex critiques of legal systems. They often refuse to adhere to laws placed upon them that primarily benefit rich and powerful others. To name just a few examples that I have encountered in my own research, activists and residents often take over houses or buildings illegally in order to meet the greater human rights need of shelter for people being evicted from their homes. There is no question that entering and occupying private property is illegal, but for some movements it is fully legitimate because they see it as part of the moral responsibility that we as human beings have to one another. Other forms of illegal action might involve blockading a public highway, refusing to leave public property when told to do so by the police, smashing windows, building barricades, stealing supplies, and so on. The dynamics of violating national laws during research (described as sometimes necessary by Bourgois) become even more controversial in the eyes of employers and disciplinary codes when the research is not carried out in a faraway country with a "corrupt" regime but at home, or in Europe and North America.

The more legitimacy the dominant regime of government has, the more controversial it becomes for the anthropologist to argue that the permission of the powerful should not be a prerequisite to doing research among the powerless. As the government's legitimacy goes up, so too does the challenge of explaining why and how illegal action is deemed legitimate by movement actors and why the researcher should protect even people who violate the very legitimate law and order of the very legitimate democratic government. The gap between the imaginary that institutions and academics often can have about how democratic governments function and the lived reality that social movement actors experience of how "democratic" governments function on the streets, in courtrooms, and in jails can be enormous. This gap between institutions and movements informs the ethical frameworks they each hold, often creating a fundamental disconnect between notions of ethical behavior between institutions who experience the government and its laws as legitimate and fair and movement actors who experience them as illegitimate and violent.

Quite often this gap between social movement and institutional assumptions about how democratic institutions function can go unnoticed, but from time to time these two ethical frameworks collide. One such collision for me was after I had been arrested at a protest and held by the police overnight. I was arrested at the same time as other people who I did not know. The police officers who held us were violent: hitting us, kicking us, spitting on us. They handcuffed us to radiators in the main office space of the police station where all the police officers were sitting at their desks working (surreal), and every time they walked past us they would threaten us, or in the case of the young man chained to the radiator by the door, they would beat him until he could hardly scream anymore. When I returned to work the next week, I had a meeting with a legal representative of the university, who among other things, was brainstorming about ways I might protect myself in the future. One suggestion he had was that in the future before going to do research with activists, I should contact the police so that they know I am there and that they should not arrest me or beat me. It was just an off-the-cuff suggestion and not a university policy, but in that moment I was confronted with the realization that this legal representative and I lived in two very different worlds with two completely different senses of reality. Not only did we have very different assumptions about how the police and legal systems work, not to mention how protests work, but we also clearly had different ideas about research ethics. Striking a deal with people who violently attack me and my research subjects is not my personal idea of an ethically sound choice.

The reality that public institutions, including universities, are embedded in moral discourses of law and order that don't match the experience of those who try to exercise dissent, is important because it is not just a question of divergent experiences—it is a question of which discourses inform our sense of moral responsibility. Pels (1999, 114) argues that "ethnographers have always been sandwiched between the conflicting moralities of (neo)-colonial 'law and order' and the rights of the oppressed." For many people involved in social movements the choice to ignore law and order through various forms of illegal action is linked to ideas about moral responsibility. The argument usually goes that there is a moral imperative to stop a far greater evil, a worse crime, that the corporations or the government are carrying out. The institutional and disciplinary frameworks fit (unwittingly?) within the regime of ethics shared by governments and corporations. Even when the institutions might be critical of government or corporate power in specific ways, the basic ethical framework will match this power in some important ways. One such match might be the belief that activists cannot just go ahead and decide for themselves what is right and what is wrong, but that there are legitimate channels (i.e., the government) through which to make such appeals. This version of institutional ethics is condescending toward the movements who make intelligent and considered moral decisions, and it ignores the reality that many of the values that institutions hold to be inalienable (human rights, nondiscrimination policies, freedom of thought and expression, the eight-hour workday) were originally brought about because social movements fought for them when it was considered wrong to do so.

But the choice itself is not simply a matter of choosing between two otherwise equal ethical frameworks—the choice is between a dominant ethical framework that has the weight of legitimacy and social institutions behind it and the marginalized ethical frameworks of individuals and groups that are going against the grain. This unequal power relationship has two important consequences: first, it means that when these ethical frameworks collide, the easier choice will almost always be to adhere to and follow the institutional or disciplinary ethical framework. This framework is usually more clearly articulated, perhaps even written down and ready-made, and has the weight of institutions behind it. Second, it means that choosing the easier option of institutional and disciplinary ethics runs the risk of further disadvantaging those being researched by placing the researchers (who possess a great deal of information and authority) within the paradigm of the mainstream ethical frameworks that those being studied are actively challenging and rejecting.

Reinforcing this power inequality, however, might not be so bad if it were only a question of impeding the moral agenda of the movement actors, or in other words, if it were merely a question of not actively supporting the aims and ideals of the movement actors. Then it would be a matter that would fall squarely in the debate on engaged anthropology, which is an important discussion that has been developed extensively elsewhere (see references earlier). As I have already highlighted, however, the stakes are a bit higher than merely perpetuating or inhibiting the aims of the movement. When doing ethnographic fieldwork, the researcher gathers a great deal of data, some of which may be incriminating either directly, or in combination with other pieces of information that the researcher may not have but that are out there. This means that even seemingly harmless information can become incriminating in ways the researcher cannot predict. In most social movement research, the number of these cases is small, I imagine, but one never knows, and even one such case is enough to warrant serious consideration. At the current historical moment, when government repression of social movements is on the rise and surveillance practices are at unprecedented levels, when antiterror legislation is being used against activists for minor infractions and even people who hand out leaflets are labeled "extremists" by their governments, a statement that may not be incriminating today may become so tomorrow. Caution is therefore essential.

Paranoia, in contrast, is not necessary. There are simple ways to ensure that the data gathered are relatively safe for those being studied. As mentioned already, the main task is to get to know the field well enough to be able to assess the risks yourself as a researcher and to assess for yourself which people have which ethical frameworks and when: people's own willingness to have what they say written down and included in a study shifts from one setting or topic of conversation to the next. Having someone agree to be part of a study or someone knowing that you are a researcher is not nearly as important an ethical frame as the careful consideration by the researcher of whether or not each thing someone says should be included in the research based on the content of the statement. Anthropologists build strong relationships of trust over time with the people in the movements they are researching, and so as an anthropologist you may find yourself quickly in the position of knowing more than what is meant for public consumption. And there is no objective way to know the difference.

For example, a person might make a public speech at a general assembly that is being recorded with a video camera, live-streamed, and tweeted in real time. This could lead one to think the person is a public figure and doesn't mind everyone knowing what he or she thinks and who he or she is. Certainly a quote from such a speech could be recorded, and given the sheer amount of recording going on, it seems unlikely the researcher would do harm by writing it down. If the reason for live-streaming and tweeting the meeting is tied to an ethics of transparency, as it often was at the Occupy encampments in 2011, then recording this information is also in line with the ethics of the movement. The example of live-streaming, however, shows the internal diversity of ethical values within the movements themselves. While some people insisted on live-streaming meetings and actions because they believed the movement should be 100 percent transparent, many other people within the movement warned that live-streaming or uploading footage of actions could lead to the arrest of people who could easily be identified in the footage. As an ethnographer who also produces films of mobilizations, my coproducer and I take this latter concern seriously, and we either embargo footage that is sensitive or black out faces in footage before we upload it, usually a combination of both. And there are many things that we simply have not filmed at all.

This question of ethical recording of information is perhaps heightened when filming, but it is important for written notes as well. The same person who made a public statement at the general assembly might take off the public persona after the meeting, at the pub, or at home and discuss different topics that are not necessarily meant for public consumption (although this person might say things at home that he or she would just as well say in public). This is a far more difficult matter, and it becomes a question of the anthropologist's ability to asses the person they are talking with and the content of what the person is saying. My rule of thumb is usually that if the comment is a general one that anyone could have said, and which is rather representative of opinions many people have expressed, or is an abstract analysis, it is probably okay to note these down anonymously. If, however, the comment is one about a specific action the person was involved in, or especially if it is about the planning of future actions, then I treat it as confidential and not for the record.

When the planning of actions takes place at open meetings, however, this rule of thumb gets more complicated. Open discussion of action plans is common, and I am often at meetings as an activist and not just an anthropologist, so knowing when these meetings can be included in ethnographic field notes and when they should not be is a sensitive matter. If a meeting is large, open, in public, and being recorded as the Occupy meetings described earlier, even if future action plans are being made, most things can probably be written down (though again, if someone says something incriminating, even if publicly, there is no need to increase the chances of the quote getting used against him or her by writing it down). When the meeting is open, but smaller and not being recorded, more caution is needed, but some things can certainly be included in notes. When a meeting is closed, and the action being planned is clearly not "public," then, so far, I have always opted to engage only as an activist and not include these meetings in the field notes. I might make notes about the action itself after it has happened, but the planning process for the action falls outside of my notion of field notes. For example, during the anti-G8 summit mobilization between 2003 and 2008, I participated as an activist and researched the decision-making procedures of the movement. At the large assemblies in the camps that anyone could attend, I took notes. I did not write down everything people said, but I took notes about the procedure of the meetings and the way people presented information, as well as some of the specific comments made. When my affinity group and I sat together around a map of the region planning our highway blockade, I did not take notes, because I considered this space of movement activity as one that fell outside my "field" of research.

How public a meeting or action is can be a good guideline for researchers who are wondering whether the information they are receiving should be written down or not. Still, even taking notes of quite public meetings can be risky, especially when action planning is involved. During the anti-G8 camp in Japan, there were several times when the camp was under threat of a police raid, and so I kept my notebook tucked into the back of my pants so that if the camp were raided, and my tent searched, the notebook would not be found (I had been told that body searches were illegal and highly unlikely). My notebook had no names in it, and only information that would make little sense to anyone that did not know the context, but it was very important to me that the notebook be kept out of the reach of anyone but me, especially the police. On the opposite end of this spectrum, when I researched the European Social Forum, meetings were taking place in municipal government buildings, with complete access to government officials, but not always to activists, making it far less important to guard, even politically useful to share, notes from meetings.

There are no fixed rules here; every comment, every meeting needs to be evaluated in context. Most of the time these matters are of no consequence, but caution is needed nevertheless. A good approach might be to treat information the way another activist would. In other words, take the ethical responsibility for those being studied that those being studied would take for each other. But even this does not lead to any clear conduct since movement actors themselves have many different ethical practices. For example, when some of the protestors react against others as a result of internal disagreements, as often happens, the researcher has to choose between the ethical frameworks that arise. One such common disagreement in the movements I study is when one group is mad because windows have been smashed at a demonstration, and they are trying, based on their sense of moral imperative, to identify those who smashed the windows to bring them to the police. At the same time other activists argue that calling the police at all, for any reason, is a violation of movement ethics. What does it mean in this case to follow the movement actor's own ethical framework?

In this case, when the multiple ethical frameworks of the movement actors themselves collide, the researcher needs to consider how their own ethical position may or may not lead to people coming to harm, including, perhaps especially, those being accused of crimes. In such a case applying the ethical framework of the activists that are accused or in danger is probably the better choice than applying the ethical framework of the activists that are not in danger. In some cases, this might require that the researcher violate their own personal ethics or the ethical guidelines or demands of their employer when these ethical frameworks uphold the rule of law or disavow the use of tactics that are perceived to be violent. In liberal democratic contexts especially, the use of confrontational tactics by social movements often comes coupled with strong moral responses from those who believe in the potential for social change through established channels. It is important to recognise this personal or institutional moral response as part and parcel of powerful moral discourses, as part of a dominant regime of living, and to recognize this outrage itself as one way through which dominant ethical frameworks are reproduced. While a researcher can always decide to privilege personal ethics above ethics of the activists that they do not agree with, this choice should be done with an understanding of the consequences. An alternative option to the researcher who disagrees with actions taken by activists, rather than taking a moral stance, is to do what other movement actors would do: bring these disagreements directly into the field in discussions with other movement actors to engage in a concerted dialogue.

Navigating the complex and multiple field of ethical frameworks held by social movements therefore requires, on the one hand, a willingness on the part of the researcher to take these ethical frameworks seriously, and on the other hand, it requires an acute knowledge of the many conflicting ethical frameworks that are employed by the movement actors themselves. Finally, it also requires an awareness of the consequences of each ethical choice made by the researcher—in other words, it necessitates an analysis and awareness of the political and economic structures in which these movements are operating and in some cases a refusal to act in accordance with institutional guidelines and disciplinary codes when these codes ignore or reinforce the power of the economic and political structures the movements are resisting, even if it means withholding data, not recording certain data, and not publishing. This kind of in-depth knowledge may take some time to build for someone who is not already a part of the movement being studied, but it is nevertheless important.

Conclusion

Navigating the multiple and conflicting ethical frameworks encountered during ethnographic fieldwork is a challenge for all anthropologists, especially since anthropology as a discipline has the tendency to research groups of people who are marginalized and in positions of relative powerlessness, meaning that the stakes are high for any group being researched. I have tried to highlight five ethical frameworks that are present during ethnographic fieldwork and have explored specifically four key ethical frameworks: the interaction between institutional and disciplinary ethical frameworks, the interaction between personal ethics and disciplinary or institutional ethics, and finally the interaction between the multiple ethical frameworks of social movements and disciplinary or institutional ethical frameworks. Each of these ethical frameworks ought to be viewed as embedded within specific regimes of power, and they should therefore be engaged with critically and not simplistically. I have shown how these ethical frameworks can contradict each other and create a situation in which the researcher has a "divided loyalty" (Nader 1999, 121) that they must navigate, usually on the spot, in the field.

Acknowledging that "configurations of ethical reflection and practice" are part of "regimes of living" suggests that ethical frameworks are tied to "a 'manner, method, or system of rule or government,' characteristic of political regimes, systems of administration, or modes of techno-scientific intervention" (Lakoff and Collier 2004, 420). These systems of rule are part and parcel of many ethical frameworks that researchers inherit from their predecessors. For research of social movements, this can be problematic, especially if the movement being researched places itself in opposition to these systems of rule, as many of the movements I have researched do. Given that there is therefore potentially a tension between the dominant ethical frameworks and the multiple ethical frameworks present within social movements, the researcher has to be all the more aware of what all of these tensions are and if and when the ethical frameworks collide, the researcher must be prepared to choose.

The stakes attached to this choice are high, especially in social movement research, for two reasons. First, because social movements are often organized around or united by moral considerations—thereby making ethical frameworks an essential and important part of the movement's survival and success. Second, because social movements often blur the line between legality and legitimacy and take actions that are considered fully legitimate by participants, perhaps even morally necessary, but that are nevertheless technically illegal. This illegality and the challenge that many movements pose to the legitimacy of the status quo can make social movement actors vulnerable and can lead to them being harmed. As repression of a movement increases, so too do the risks for those involved. These changes in the level of risk can happen rapidly, and so the researcher needs to have deep knowledge not only of the movement actors and their ethical frameworks but also of the political and economic structures in which the movement is operating, to (try to) ensure that the data he or she is gathering will not later become incriminating or damaging. A tall order to say the least. Is it possible? I don't know.

Notes

The writing of this chapter was supported by a Marie Curie International Outgoing Fellowship within the 7th European Community Framework Programme and a portion of the research based on the film series http://www.globaluprisings.org was funded by the Foundation for Democracy and Media.

1. One way in which this kind of research might be relevant here, however, is in as far as it exemplifies a conflict between academic values and ethics and specific activist values and ethics. Within academia, research on right-wing movements and fascism is deemed in and of itself valuable because knowledge is by definition valuable. If we then add anthropological ethics specifically, the research would also have to ensure the safety of fascists, because by choosing to research them, the anthropologist pledges to do no harm. From within anthropological ethics, therefore, this research would be considered highly valuable and the researcher would be obliged to protect, defend, and explain the interests of those studied. From within the ethical frameworks of many of the activists I have worked with, however, it would be considered entirely unethical to defend fascists and ensure their safety at all costs (including, presumably, by ignoring racist violence).

2. This gets even more specific and complicated in practice—in the movements I have worked with (primarily the alterglobalization movement, its precedents, and most recently to a lesser extent Occupy and the Indignados in Spain), it was not just an activist-nonactivist media distinction, but all the different groups and networks involved in these umbrella movements had different ideas about which people from independent media groups could be trusted and which could not, since media activists also have diverse set of ethical practices and political notions that influence the way they represent movements and are often critiqued when they represent the movement one way and not another.

References

Berreman, Gerald. 2007. "Ethics versus 'Realism' in Anthropology." 1991. In *Ethnographic Field-work: An Anthropological Reader*, edited by Antonius C. G. M. Robben and Jeffrey A. Sluka, 298–315. Malden, MA: Blackwell.

Bourgois, Philippe. 2007. "Confronting the Ethics of Ethnography: Lessons from Fieldwork in Central America." 1991. In *Ethnographic Fieldwork: An Anthropological Reader*, edited by Antonius C. G. M. Robben and Jeffrey A. Sluka, 288–297. Malden, MA: Blackwell.

Castañeda, Quetzil E. 2006. "Ethnography in the Forest: An Analysis of Ethics in the Morals of Anthropology" *Cultural Anthropology* 21 (1): 121–145.

Chesters, Graeme. 2012. "Social Movements and the Ethics of Knowledge Production." *Social Movement Studies* 11 (2): 145–160.

Fluehr-Lobban, Carolyn, ed. 1991. *Ethics and the Profession of Anthropology: Dialogue for a New Era*. Philadelphia: University of Pennsylvania Press.

Gillan, Kevin, and Jenny Pickerill. 2012. "The Difficult and Hopeful Ethics of Research on, and with, Social Movements." *Social Movement Studies* 11 (2): 133–143.

Hale, Charles. 2006. "Activist Research v. Cultural Critique: Indigenous Land Rights and the Contradictions of Politically Engaged Anthropology." *Cultural Anthropology* 21 (1): 96–120.

Hammersley, Martyn, and Paul Atkinson. 2007. *Ethnography: Principles in Practice*. New York: Routledge.

Jorgensen, Joseph. 1971. "On Ethics and Anthropology." *Current Anthropology* 12 (3): 321–334.

Juris, Jeffrey, and Alex Khasnabish. 2013. *Insurgent Encounters: Transnational Activism, Ethnography, and the Political*. Durham, NC: Duke University Press.

Lakoff, Andrew, and Stephen J. Collier. 2004. "Ethics and the Anthropology of Modern Reason." *Anthropological Theory* 4 (4): 419–434.

Maeckelbergh, Marianne. 2009. *The Will of the Many: How the Alterglobalisation Movement Is Changing the Face of Democracy*. London: Pluto Press.

Nader, Laura. 1999. "Comment on Pels, Peter 'Professions of Duplexity.'" *Current Anthropology* 40 (2): 121–122.

Pels, Peter. 1999. "Professions of Duplexity: A Prehistory of Ethical Codes in Anthropology." *Current Anthropology* 40 (2): 101–136.

Scheper-Hughes, Nancy. 1995. "The Primacy of the Ethical: Propositions for a Militant Anthropology." *Current Anthropology* 36 (3): 409–440.

Shore, Cris. 1999. "Comment on Pels, Peter 'Professions of Duplexity.'" *Current Anthropology* 40 (2): 123–124.

Speed, Shannon. 2006. "At the Crossroads of Human Rights and Anthropology: Toward a Critically Engaged Activist Research." *American Anthropologist* 108 (1): 66–76.

11 Within, Against, Beyond

The Radical Imagination in the Age of the Slow-Motion Apocalypse

Alex Khasnabish

THIS CHAPTER IS ABOUT politically engaged research with social movements and, more broadly, the value of academically based research in times of crisis. Knowledge work, particularly in its academic formation, has lived a complex and compromised relationship with systems of power and privilege (Lal 2002; Smith 1999; Wallerstein 1996). As someone trained in the anthropological tradition, I am bound up in a discipline shaped by imperial and colonial ambitions. I will not delve into this troubled history and anthropology's relationship to empire building, colonization, and genocide. Neither do I want to suggest that anthropology is simplistically reducible to this and only this. But such realities cannot be ignored, and if they give us pause then the advancing weaponization of anthropology and other disciplines should certainly be cause for urgent action today (Network of Concerned Anthropologists 2009; Price 2011). Rather than dwelling on the profoundly compromised history of anthropological knowledge production, I want to acknowledge it and use it as a starting point for further exploration. In what follows, I explore what engaged social science research might offer to struggles for social change and the construction of a more just, democratic, dignified, liberated, and peaceful world. Drawing on a decade of work with radical social justice activists across the north of the Americas and particularly with the Radical Imagination Project, an ethnographically grounded and politically engaged project focused on radical social movements and the radical imagination in Halifax, Nova Scotia, I attempt to chart what prefigurative solidarity research—that is, social research capable not simply of documenting what is but of participating in collectively bringing something into being—might look like and what it can offer.

While I discuss the Radical Imagination Project at length in the second half of this chapter, I briefly sketch its contours here to ground the argument that follows in a concrete example of solidarity research. In August 2010, funded by a Social Sciences and Humanities Research Council standard research grant, a four-person research team consisting of two research assistants from the local activist community, my project codirector (Dr. Max Haiven), and myself began the Radical Imagination Project in Halifax, Nova Scotia. The project's aim was to "convoke" the radical imagination—that is, to call something that is not yet fully present into being—in collaboration with activists self-identifying as "radical." For us, the term *radical* names movements or approaches that understand the social problems that concern them to be irresolvable within the current political system and so seek systemic change. In particular, both as researchers and political actors, we are interested in radical social movements that have emerged in the wake of the so-called antiglobalization movement and that stress values of participatory democracy, radical equality, anticapitalism, and antioppression in pursuit of social, economic, and ecological justice (Day 2005; Dixon 2014; Graeber 2009; Juris 2008; Khasnabish 2008; Maeckelbergh 2009; Sitrin 2012; Walia 2013; Wood 2012). The project's first active research phase concluded in 2012, but since then my project codirector and I have maintained our focus on convoking the radical imagination while extending our original scope beyond the activist milieu to include diverse constituencies in struggle in Halifax, especially those seeking alternative forms of development capable of maintaining robust and resilient communities in the face of gentrification—a term better unpacked as a process of capitalist accumulation by the displacement and dispossession of marginalized communities. As I write this, the second phase of our research is ongoing and incomplete and so it is the first phase of our research with radical activists that I focus on later in this piece.

Key Words

By way of introduction a few words about this chapter's title are warranted, beginning with the triumvirate of "within, against, beyond." In one sense, "within, against, beyond" evokes the familiar modernist pathways to sociopolitical change: reform, resistance, revolution. This is important not least because the notion that these terms designate different kinds of political action was fundamentally problematized by the rise of a new, radical, and distinctly anarchistic ethic in the last decade of the previous millennium but whose roots lie in struggles that extend far beyond that (Day 2005; Dixon 2014; Holloway 2002a; Walia 2013). It is also significant because in the wake of movements from global justice to Occupy some activists and observers have called for a turn away from this ethic and toward a more centralized, structured, and politically pragmatic orientation—what Jodi Dean (2012) has called "the communist horizon." The tension between these political imaginaries is a live one in many radical milieus today and bears exploring not in the vain hope of definitively identifying "effective" forms of political action (as if such an assessment could be arrived at independently of the context in which struggle occurs) but, more important, to critically explore what each of these imaginaries illuminates, makes possible, and obscures in terms of systems of oppression and exploitation and the pathways to collective liberation beyond them (see Katsiaficas 2006; Selbin 2010; Sitrin 2012).

In another sense, the "within, against, beyond" trio also alludes to the positionality of the craft of research in relation to the conflicting interests at work within the neoliberal academy as well as its relationship to collectives struggling for radical sociopolitical change. What is the role of the academically based researcher in the age of austerity? What does a call to practice "public" research mean? What alternative visions of the university of the future lie beyond the well-worn liberal tropes of an educated and engaged citizenry and neoliberal notions of the university as the publicly subsidized research, development, and training wing of capital? Other chapters in this volume take up the question of ethics, the academic vocation, and promises and pitfalls of politically engaged research (see Maeckelberg as well as Panourgiá in this volume), and my own efforts resonate with them. But my central concern here is not ethics or anthropological research and its outcomes, but rather what social research conducted from the unjustly, weirdly, and only partially autonomous site of the university can do *with* social justice movements that they cannot or do not do for themselves. How can academically based researchers working within the space of the university make use of university resources (understood in the most expansive sense) in collaboration with grassroots movements for social justice and social change, in order to push back against the predations of the dominant order and, ultimately, build liberated alternatives beyond it?

The concept of the radical imagination has seen wide circulation in recent years in academic and activist circles alike. Here I utilize it in accordance with the way we have developed it in the context of the Radical Imagination Project. Rather than a clearly defined "thing" possessed by singularly gifted or inspired individuals, we have argued that the radical imagination is most appropriately understood as a reference to an always collective process of figuring out from where we have come, where we are now, and toward what time and place we want to go (see Haiven and Khasnabish 2010). Such imaginations are given form in dialogic encounters between those engaged in struggles for social change, and they serve as the spark animating radical struggles for social change. Rather than the more formal, codified realm of ideology, the radical imagination is a horizon toward which social movements walk. Like all horizons, the radical imagination is a powerful orienting force even as it recedes as one moves toward it. Amorphous and intangible it may be, but without it we lack the capacity to imagine how the world might be otherwise, a critical element in the dynamics propelling powerful and resilient social change movements (see Selbin 2010).

I borrow the term *slow-motion apocalypse* from Patrick Reinsborough, an activist whose work focuses on the power of meaning making in struggles for social change (see Reinsborough and Canning 2010). Situated against the horizon of the "ecological end game" driven by global capitalism and industrial civilization, Reinsborough's (2010, 69–70) explanation of the slow-motion apocalypse is far from another recapitulation of an "end-is-nigh" catastrophism that so preoccupies the popular imagination today. Describing the slow-motion apocalypse as "the gradual unraveling of the routines, expectations and institutions that comfort the privileged and define the status quo," Reinsborough mines the Greek root of the word *apocalypse* and tells us that it literally means "to take the cover away . . . to reveal something that has not been seen." Reinsborough challenges us to understand the ways in which our attempts to make meaning out of the world buttress or challenge existing systems of domination and exploitation and advance or inhibit grassroots alternative building. In advancing the potentially revelatory capacity of crisis, Reinsborough evokes the Marxist narrative of capitalism's internal crises setting the stage for proletarian revolution without the assurances that high-modernist moments seemed to offer.

The slow-motion apocalypse that Reinsborough illuminates and that I borrow also intersects with much recent climate change research that not only positions humanity—and particularly its most powerful and privileged strata—at the heart of looming climate catastrophe but also posits humanity as a world-changing force unto itself, unlike any other living species on this planet. The increasing popularity of the informal geologic chronological term *Anthropocene* that serves to mark the evidence and extent of humanity's impact on Earth's ecosystems is another rhetorical confirmation of this growing realization. Indeed, in a provocative column published in the *New York Times*, Roy Scranton (2013) deploys the term and mines its significance by asserting that the biggest problem posed by the Anthropocene is not one of periodization or even figuring out ways to mitigate drastic, irreversible climate change; rather, "the biggest problem we face is a philosophical one: understanding that this civilization is *already dead.*" He urges us to "learn to die"—civilizationally—in the Anthropocene so that we can get on with the business of learning to live anew. Peter Linebaugh (2014) adds an important corrective to this narrative line: to focus on *Homo sapiens sapiens* as a species and geological time reduces "history to biology" and obscures the fact that we are, in fact, not all equally responsible for the eco-social crisis manifesting as global warming and climate chaos. The point is not that life on Earth is doomed or that humanity's time on the planet has come to an end, but that nothing we can do now will save the civilizational engine—properly understood as a patriarchal, racist, capitalist engine—driving globe-spanning systems of oppression and exploitation (see Moore 2015). We don't inhabit the Anthropocene; we inhabit the Capitalocene. Implicit in this is the understanding that the challenges of the slow-motion apocalypse are far from merely technical or reform based, they require a radical reimagining of what is possible and necessary socially, politically, and economically. Where are we to look for such radical imagination? Where does the spark of such innovation lie? One place we might begin to look is at people's grassroots movements for radical social justice and social change.

Expect the Unexpected

My own academically grounded work with social movements emerged out of the deep affinity I felt with the Zapatistas—a radical social change movement that began as an armed insurgency initiated by the Ejército Zapatista de Liberación Nacional (Zapatista National Liberation Army, EZLN) in the Mexican state of Chiapas on January 1, 1994 (see Khasnabish 2010). On the first day of the new year in 1994, several thousand indigenous Mayan insurgents—some armed with semiautomatic weapons, many others with nothing more than sticks—emerged from ten years of clandestine organizing and five centuries of resistance and persistence in the face of genocide, colonialism, and imperialism, and declared war on the federal executive of the Mexican Republic and the Mexican army (Muñoz Ramírez 2008). In statements issued during those first days of the new year, the insurgents of the EZLN declared that they had risen up in arms not to seize the state but to smash a corrupt, violent, and illegitimate system so that Mexicans could freely and democratically govern themselves (Marcos 2002). They called the North American Free Trade Agreement (NAFTA) a "death sentence" for the indigenous peoples of Mexico, but more than a rebellion for or against a particular kind of economic model, the Zapatistas articulated the rationale for their uprising in terms of justice, dignity, liberty, and democracy.

The Zapatista uprising did not topple the government of President Carlos Salinas, nor did it manage to defeat the Mexican army, but in many ways the rebellion initiated by the Zapatistas would accomplish something as revolutionary—and far less predictable—as these goals. Indeed, as the dream of state-sponsored socialism lay for so many buried beneath the rubble of the Berlin Wall, what began as an armed uprising in the far southeast of Mexico would radically expand the horizon of political possibility on a global scale and spark a transnational direct action, anticapitalist, radically democratic "movement of movements" for an alternative globalization (Callahan 2004; Khasnabish 2008; Kingsnorth 2004; Klein 2002; Midnight Notes Collective 2001; Notes from Nowhere 2003). It is no exaggeration to say that without the Zapatista uprising and the dynamic and complex movement that emerged in its wake, the contours of radical politics on a global scale would look dramatically different today. For example, People's Global Action was the transnational network of communication and coordination at the heart of the Global Days of Action and many of the summit convergence protests, and it emerged directly out of the Zapatista *encuentros*. In this same vein, the World Social Forum process owes a great debt to the Zapatistas—even if they remain excluded from the forum process as a result of their status as an armed force. As I came to understand through my research with activists in Canada and the United States, the Zapatistas' initiation of a protracted dialogue with dissidents on a global scale reshaped the very logic and ethic of radical political practice and possibility for many (see Khasnabish 2008).

How do we measure the nonlinear effects of the circulation and resonance of a radical political imagination? What are the rhizomatic effects this resonance leaves in its wake? Cognizant of the risks of romanticizing and commodifying radical struggles that always seem to be happening "elsewhere," the radical imagination and its relationship to powerful and resilient social movements cannot be cynically reduced to them. Of course, transnationalized Zapatismo is certainly not the first example of a rebel or revolutionary movement in one part of the world sparking the imaginations of activists located elsewhere. Indeed, as Silvia Federici (2003) and Peter Linebaugh and Marcus Rediker (2000) so powerfully demonstrate, the circulation and proliferation of powerfully liberatory and revolutionary ideas, and the human beings and social relationships that gave them form, were central—if all too often hidden or ignored—features of the rise of capitalism, the colonial enterprise, and the emergence of the modern world system. What is so striking about the circulation of these powerful revolutionary ideas is that they were carried throughout the Atlantic World by those whom history has so often forgotten and despised—sailors, slaves, market women, laborers, criminals, pirates, indentured servants, and commoners. Propelled by processes of enclosure, criminalization, exploitation, resistance, and exodus and by traveling the emerging pathways of the nascent Atlantic capitalist economy, this motley, unruly multitude carried with it radical political imaginations that would persist despite the consolidation of the modern nation-state and the rise of capitalism by the early eighteenth century. The radical imagination today owes a great debt to these struggles and the radical sociopolitical horizons they aspired to, even if many activists and organizers remain only dimly aware of their implication in this enduring legacy.

To return to Zapatismo, its transnational resonance among communities of activists around the world produced effects as diverse as they were powerful and unpredictable (see Khasnabish 2007). While the Zapatista uprising would elicit familiar solidaristic responses from activists throughout Mexico and around the world, it also provoked a rethinking of the logic and horizon of radical politics that broke from conventional modernist socialist revolutionary ideologies (Holloway 2002b). Zapatismo disavowed the seizure of the state as the fulcrum of revolution and emphasized direct democracy and action, autonomy, dignity, a living rather than theoretical anticapitalism, and a belief in a multitude of revolutionary subjectivities rather than a singular privileged subject. Amid the ashes of modernist revolutionary imaginaries that seemed almost impossible at the turn of the millennium, Zapatismo's transnational resonance intersected powerfully with a rising anticapitalist, antioppressive, anarchistic political ethic in the Global North that would prove a significant engine of the global justice movement and even inform waves of radicalism since. Despite the important and provocative nature of the movement dynamics explored in the course of my research tracing the transnational resonance of Zapatismo—what I have described elsewhere as the ethnography of a transnationalized political imagination (Khasnabish 2013)—the project itself remained limited to archiving the life of a phenomenon that had already been at work in the world. Beyond providing a space and process for critical reflection and a way to trace and document the intersection of activists, movements, and imaginations on a transnational scale, it seemed to have limited significance as a way to contribute to larger social change struggles. In conversations I was having with activists and engaged academics at the time, we began to wonder what it would mean to try to make social movement research work in a way that went beyond cataloging what is and participate in bringing something into being. In other words, what might social movement research look like if we push past movement archaeologies, sifting through what movements leave in their wake and expounding upon those artifacts in an attempt to produce more grist for the academic mill, and instead experiment with research as a practice of prefiguration, a way of working with movements to make manifest a collectively desired end through the research process itself?

Radical Imagination, Method, and Prefiguration

Social movements have long been objects of social scientific inquiry. Particularly from the 1960s on, social movement scholarship has, at its best, shed important light on how, why, and with what consequences people have organized themselves to try to achieve some kind of social change outside of formal political structures and processes (see Staggenborg 2012). In contradistinction to earlier generations of sociological work that cast social movements as little more than irrational, unwashed mobs that functioned, at best, as "escape valves" maintaining the equilibrium of the status quo, social movement research since the 1960s has taken social movement action seriously and sought to understand these collective actors as genuinely political and not merely pathological—or perhaps worse, functional—social eruptions. In this tradition, important attention has been paid to movements with respect to the structural factors affecting their life spans (Tarrow 1988), as well as their capacity to mobilize resources (Zald and McCarthy 1979); to take advantage of openings in the political system (Meyer 2004); to advance claims and frame issues (Benford and Snow 2000); to deploy consciousness, emotion, biography, and culture as social change tools (Goodwin, Jasper, and Polletta 2001; Jasper 1999; Mansbridge and Morris 2001); and to network their efforts across national borders (Bandy and Smith 2005; Della Porta, Kriesi, and Rucht 2009; Keck and Sikkink 1998; Smith 2008). There has been much important and insightful work carried out from this perspective, but the bulk of it also positions social movements as political actors vying for influence and leverage within the established political system, rendering it insufficient for the study of contemporary radical tendencies whose aspirations are a direct challenge to the very *form* of the sociopolitical itself and are embodied by a variety of unconventional actors outside of political parties and nongovernmental organizations (see Sitrin 2012). Rather than offering diagnostics of movements, mapping them onto a political landscape delimited by dominant sociopolitical and economic institutions, powerful actors, and their attendant ontologies and epistemologies, the approach we have utilized in the Radical Imagination Project tries instead to mobilize the weird autonomy—compromised, privileged, imperfect, unjust, but nonetheless potentially productive—of the academic vocation in order to help collectively craft a space and a process capable of calling something into being that is not yet fully present (Haiven and Khasnabish 2014; Khasnabish and Haiven 2012).

In our efforts to assist in "convoking" the radical imagination with radical social movement activists and organizers in Halifax we drew extensively on ethnographic methods. Particularly in recent years, ethnographers and ethnographically informed researchers have produced rich and insightful accounts of social movement activity (Conway 2004; Juris 2008; Juris and Khasnabish 2013; Khasnabish 2008; Graeber 2009; Sitrin 2012; Wood 2012). Engaging social movements as complex sociopolitical ecologies reproduced both through the interactions of those individuals and groups that constitute them and the actions they undertake in the wider social world demands a research methodology that prioritizes living social realities rather than approaches that map movements onto a political landscape delimited by dominant sociopolitical and economic institutions, powerful actors, and their attendant ontologies and epistemologies. There are important threads within the tremendously broad ethnographic methodological field from which draw in order to achieve these ends. Ethnography here needs to be understood not merely as a set of specific qualitative methods including open-ended interviews, participant observation, long-term fieldwork, and writing characterized by "thick description," but also as a research posture grounded in the lived realities of those with whom the ethnographer is engaged and by a willingness to invest in and be transformed by the research process itself.

Methodologically, the Radical Imagination Project proceeded through three separate research phases in our work with radical activists in Halifax. Our four-person research team began with one-on-one open-ended and in-depth interviews with self-identified "radicals" in Halifax, Nova Scotia. Through word-of-mouth, ads in local activist and independent media (radio, print, online), preexisting connections in the activist milieu, and postering and pamphleting, we interviewed thirty individuals in the first months of the project. Intensely aware of the utility social movement research can have for those with vested interests in suppressing social justice movements, our team explicitly avoided collecting information that could be considered of tactical or strategic value and instead focused on activists' narratives of political radicalization, visions of the future, and assessments of strengths and weaknesses in different cultures and milieus of political organizing. Following and flowing from our interview phase, the research team organized three dialogue sessions, open to the public and to which all project participants were invited. Each session was formulated around a key theme that emerged from our interviews with activists in Halifax: social justice struggle in the age of austerity, anticapitalist struggle and the reproduction of oppressions within social movements, and forms of organization for radical social change. Each session was led by a panel of project participants who were invited to give brief introductory statements (lasting five to ten minutes) on the theme followed by an open discussion involving all attendees facilitated by the research team. The final phase of the project was the initiation of the Radical Imagination Speaker Series, in which, with input from the local social justice community, my project codirector and I have brought a variety of activists, academics, and organizers to Halifax to share their experiences and perspectives on issues relating to radical social justice struggles today.

In a nutshell, our research methodology in the Radical Imagination Project was centered on the primacy of using research as a tool to facilitate a deep, open-ended, and protracted process of dialogue. Many of our research collaborators responded favorably—even enthusiastically—to a process aimed not only at "making space" for critical discussions in the Halifax radical milieu but also at "making time" for them in a way that did not tie them to tactical considerations or pressing defensive battles. At the same time, many radicals in Halifax rejected our emphasis on "dialogue" arguing that the urgency of the current moment calls for a greater focus on the form and organization of struggle. Still others chose to avoid the project altogether, seeing it as little more than an attempt to accumulate academic capital on the back of movement struggles. And yet for us the relevance and value of the project was testified to by the fact that we managed to engage a wide swath of self-identified radicals in Halifax, the vast majority of whom remained—and remain—interested and involved in the project throughout its life. By locating the project in the midst of the ways that movements produce and reproduce themselves on a daily basis, we stepped away from a methodology focused on generating "better data," specific outcomes, or "deliverables," choosing instead to practice research as a collaborative process capable of augmenting forms of knowledge making and social reproduction that movements are already engaged in.

Absent from our research process is any description of what the radical imagination looks like at this moment in Halifax among this set of radical social justice activists. This was no omission and its absence neither surprised nor troubled the research team. Our convocatory intervention amid the radical milieu in Halifax aimed not to document, catalog, and archive the nature of the radical imagination of individuals or collectives but to provide a new space, time, and process capable of offering opportunities to those engaged in radical social justice struggles to consider in an expansive, reflexive, and dialogic way where their struggles have come from, where they are now, and how they might move forward. A key outcome of this approach was the realization—derived in part from a key question we asked each participant in our interview phase about what it would mean to "win" (see Turbulence Collective 2010)—that movements do not spend their lives occupying the lofty heights of victory or mired in the depths of defeat but in the hiatus, the gap, between them (Haiven and Khasnabish 2013). The hiatus is the quotidian space of reproduction, that everyday space where as collectives and individuals we work to restore ourselves and undertake the work of care that makes our other labors possible. As such, it is also a critical space shaping struggles for social change. What happens within the space and time of movement reproduction bears directly upon the form, content, limits, and promises of struggles for social justice and social change.

Marxist-feminist scholars and activists Maria Mies (1986) and Silvia Federici (2003, 2012) have critically explored the deeply fraught condition of the work of social reproduction, that is, that labor that brings labor power into existence and that nurtures and sustains it. The degradation and sequestering of this (feminized, unremunerated, concealed) care work actually marks its centrality to capitalist accumulation and its enclosure, and the social divisions upon which it is based, actually constitute the first moments of the process of primitive accumulation (Federici 2012). More broadly, the work of social reproduction is the very source of the diverse forms of social life upon which humanity collectively relies. Social reproduction is taking place all the time and everywhere as people care for themselves, for each other, and reproduce the social by literally living it into existence one day after another. Social reproduction is occurring even when the world, collectivities, and individuals being reproduced are shaped by oppressive and exploitative systems with commensurate oppressive and exploitative outcomes. In this sense, social movements are not merely politics by other means or specific organizational formations; they are also sites of social reproduction. The ways in which this labor is carried out and the ends to which it is directed (what kinds of social spaces and subjectivities it produces) is perhaps all the more significant when we think about radical movements as sites of pre-figuration, spaces where alternative sociopolitical possibilities are innovated and experimented with. In this context, the reproduction of systems of oppression and exploitation within movements themselves is a deeply troubling and poison-ous dynamic that perpetuates injustice and subverts struggles for social justice (see Bishop 2002; Featherstone 2012; Graeber 2009; Martinez 2000; Mohanty 2003; Osterweil 2010; Polletta 2002; Walia 2013). While the dynamics driving the reproduction of oppression are complex, movements—and specifically the relatively privileged actors within them—have often deferred addressing them by appealing to a supposedly more "urgent" or "immediate" set of concerns, cri-ses, or struggles (Bishop 2002; Mies 1986). This kind of rationalization, one we encountered not infrequently, endlessly postpones the work of coming to terms with these toxic dynamics and perpetuates the very violences and injustices so-cial justice movements purport to oppose.

We certainly cannot claim that our research successfully intervened in the reproduction of systemic oppressions in the radical milieu in Halifax. But our dialogic, convocatory method at least furnished preliminary tools and a con-text so that activists and organizers could make time to confront and collec-tively begin to work through these everyday realities. Given its individualistic and psychoanalytic overtones, our research team was averse to conceptualizing research primarily as a form of "radical therapy." Despite this, we are convinced that research with social movements conducted in a spirit of solidarity and will-ing to make canny use of the weirdly and unjustly quasi-autonomous space of the university can offer important opportunities that movements and those who make them up cannot or do not offer themselves. Rather than operationalizing and cataloging movements' perceived political efficacy or lack thereof—steeped in and so reinforcing conventional notions of success and failure—our research encounter with our collaborators compelled us to problematize notions of what counts as success and failure for solidaristic social movement research and to ask honest questions about what engaged research is good for. The outcome of being compelled to confront this tension was not a glossing over of the gap—the hiatus—between success and failure either for movements or for those who study them. Instead, it emphasized the importance of learning to dwell well in the hiatus, particularly once we understand it as a critical space and time of social reproduction and so vital to the innovation of and experimentation with other (more just, democratic, liberated) ways of being.

Research, Crisis, Imagination

Crisis, today, appears ubiquitous. But as Janet Roitman (2013) so astutely observes, declarations of "crisis" are not empirical realities; they are invocations that seek to make possible certain courses of action while foreclosing others. Claims to crisis are disciplinary tools in the hands of powerful and vested interests and they have had powerful effects on institutions like the university and privileged vocations like academic research. Against calls to demonstrate our relevance to and service in defense of the status quo, here I have sought to offer a glimpse of what engaged social movement research practiced in an ethic of solidarity might look like. The Radical Imagination Project is, of course, far from perfect, and as we have worked through the stages of the project, we as researchers have become only more convinced of that. Nevertheless, as an experiment in ethnographically based research methods capable not only of accurately documenting the lives of social movements but also actually and productively engaging them, it has proved promising.

Through this research process we have preliminarily explored the utility of the weird and always unjust autonomy of the academy as a way to work with social movements that contributes something to them that they are not doing for themselves. On the one hand, the Radical Imagination Project provided material resources and neutral space for activists in Halifax to have discussions they were not having elsewhere—particularly about the state and direction of their own movements. On the other hand, it intervened in the frenzied temporality of activism so often characterized by urgent mobilizations to defend against both the erosion of gains won and fresh attacks to the fabric of social justice. This slower temporality offered by our research facilitated critical and collective moments of deep reflection, opening up opportunities for those in attendance to have expansive discussions they felt they did not have the time or luxury for in the course of their day-to-day activities. While it remains our hope that solidarity research can do more than this, it remains a useful place to start. Globe-spanning systems of oppression and exploitation will not dismantle themselves, and while it is far from the most important ingredient in the alchemy of radical social change, engaged research has the capacity to assist social justice struggles in ways that go beyond simply providing accurate analysis. While crisis and catastrophism threaten to completely occlude other possible futures, our collective imagination of the politically possible faces ruthless assault by those with vested interests in enclosing our ability to envision and live otherwise. In the face of this, engaged social research must do more than archive systems of violence, exploitation, and oppression while enumerating their victims and beneficiaries. It must accept that "objectivity" is not principled neutrality; it is the act of turning the world into objects for one's consumptive contemplation. If engaged research is to be worth anything, it must seek to do more than bear witness to systems of oppression, violence, and exploitation. It—and those who practice it—must accept the challenge of working with a multitude of others (activists and organizers, practitioners and collaborators) who have already embarked on diverse paths seeking to imagine and build more just, democratic, liberated, and peaceful possibilities amid the ruins of the Capitalocene.

References

Bandy, Joe, and Jackie Smith, eds. 2005. *Coalitions across Borders*. Lanham, MD: Rowman & Littlefield.

Benford, Robert, and David Snow. 2000. "Framing Processes and Social Movements: An Overview and Assessment." *Annual Review of Sociology* 26: 611–639.

Bishop, Anne. 2002. *Becoming an Ally: Breaking the Cycle of Oppression in People*. Halifax, NS: Zed Books and Fernwood.

Callahan, Manuel. 2004. "Zapatismo and Global Struggle: A Revolution to Make Revolution Possible." In *Confronting Capitalism: Dispatches from a Global Movement*, edited by Eddie Yuen, Daniel Burton-Rose, and George Katsiaficas, 11–18. Brooklyn, NY: Soft Skull Press.

Conway, Janet. 2004. *Identity, Place, Knowledge: Social Movements Contesting Globalization*. Halifax, NS: Fernwood.

Day, Richard. 2005. *Gramsci Is Dead: Anarchist Currents in the Newest Social Movements*. Toronto: Between the Lines.

Dean, Jodi. 2012. *The Communist Horizon*. London: Verso.

Della Porta, Donatella, Hanspeter Kriesi, and Dieter Rucht. 2009. *Social Movements in a Globalizing World*. Basingstoke, UK: Palgrave Macmillan.

Dixon, Chris. 2014. *Another Politics: Talking across Today's Transformative Movements*. Berkeley: University of California Press.

Featherstone, David. 2012. *Solidarity: Hidden Histories and Geographies of Internationalism*. London: Zed Books.

Federici, Silvia. 2003. *Caliban and the Witch: Women, the Body and Primitive Accumulation*. New York: Autonomedia; London: Pluto.

———. 2012. *Revolution at Point Zero: Housework, Reproduction, and Feminist Struggle*. Oakland, CA: PM Press.

Goodwin, Jeff, James Jasper, and Francesca Polletta. 2001. *Passionate Politics: Emotions and Social Movements*. Chicago: University of Chicago Press.

Graeber, David. 2009. *Direct Action: An Ethnography*. Oakland, CA: AK Press.

Haiven, Max, and Alex Khasnabish. 2010. "What Is Radial Imagination? A Special Issue." *Affinities: A Journal of Radical Theory, Culture, and Action* 4 (2): i–xxxvii.

———. 2013. "Between Success and Failure: Dwelling with Social Movements in the Hiatus." *Interface: A Journal for and about Social Movements* 5 (2): 472–498.

———. 2014. *The Radical Imagination: Social Movement Research in the Age of Austerity*. Halifax, NS: Zed Books and Fernwood.

Holloway, John. 2002a. *Change the World without Taking Power: The Meaning of Revolution Today*. London: Pluto Press.

———. 2002b. "Zapatismo and the Social Sciences." *Capital & Class* 78: 153–160.

Jasper, James. 1999. *The Art of Moral Protest: Culture, Biography, and Creativity in Social Movements*. Chicago: University of Chicago Press.

Juris, Jeffrey. 2008. *Networking Futures: The Movements against Corporate Globalization*. Durham, NC: Duke University Press.

Juris, Jeffrey S., and Alex Khasnabish, eds. 2013. *Insurgent Encounters: Transnational Activism, Ethnography, and the Political.* Durham, NC: Duke University Press.

Katsiaficas, George. 2006. *The Subversion of Politics: European Autonomous Social Movements and the Decolonization of Everyday Life.* Edinburgh, UK: AK Press.

Keck, Margaret, and Kathryn Sikkink. 1998. *Activists beyond Borders: Advocacy Networks in International Politics.* Ithaca, NY: Cornell University Press.

Khasnabish, Alex. 2007. "Insurgent Imaginations." *Ephemera: Theory and Politics in Organization* 7 (4): 505–526.

———. 2008. *Zapatismo beyond Borders: New Imaginations of Political Possibility.* Toronto: University of Toronto Press.

———. 2010. *Zapatistas: Rebellion from the Grassroots to the Global.* London: Zed Books.

———. 2013. "Tracing the Zapatista Rhizome; or, The Ethnography of a Transnationalized Political Imagination." In *Insurgent Encounters: Activism, Ethnography, and the Transnational,* edited by Jeffrey S. Juris and Alex Khasnabish, 66–88. Durham, NC: Duke University Press.

Khasnabish, Alex, and Max Haiven. 2012. "Convoking the Radical Imagination: Social Movement Research, Dialogic Methodologies, and Scholarly Vocations." *Cultural Studies ↔ Critical Methodologies* 12 (5): 408–421.

Kingsnorth, Paul. 2004. *One No, Many Yeses: A Journey to the Heart of the Global Resistance Movement.* London: Free Press.

Klein, Naomi. 2002. "Rebellion in Chiapas." In *Fences and Windows: Dispatches from the Front Lines of the Globalization Debate,* 208–223. Toronto: Vintage Canada.

Lal, Vinay. 2002. *Empire of Knowledge: Culture and Plurality in the Global Economy.* London: Pluto Press.

Linebaugh, Peter. 2014. "How Did We Get Here (University Hall) at This Point of Time (the 'Anthropocene')?" *Counterpunch,* May 16. http://www.counterpunch.org/2014/05/16/how-did-we-get-here-university-hall-at-this-point-of-time-the-anthropocene/.

Linebaugh, Peter, and Marcus Rediker. 2000. *The Many-Headed Hydra Sailors, Slaves, Commoners, and the Hidden History of the Revolutionary Atlantic.* Boston: Beacon Press. http://site.ebrary.com/id/10014732.

Maeckelbergh, Marianne. 2009. *The Will of the Many.* London: Pluto Press.

Mansbridge, Jane, and Aldon Morris, eds. 2001. *Oppositional Consciousness: The Subjective Roots of Social Protest.* Chicago: University of Chicago Press.

Marcos, Subcomandante Insurgente. 2002. "Testimonies of the First Day." In *The Zapatista Reader,* edited by Tom Hayden, 207–217. New York: Thunder's Mouth Press.

Martinez, Elizabeth Betita. 2000. "Where Was the Color in Seattle? Looking for Reasons Why the Great Battle Was So White." *Colorlines,* March 10. http://colorlines.com/archives/2000/03/where_was_the_color_in_seattlelooking_for_reasons_why_the_great_battle_was_so_white.html.

Meyer, David. 2004. "Protest and Political Opportunities." *Annual Review of Sociology* 30: 125–145.

Midnight Notes Collective. 2001. *Auroras of the Zapatistas: Local and Global Struggles of the Fourth World War.* Brooklyn, NY: Autonomedia.

Mies, Maria. 1986. *Patriarchy and Accumulation on a World Scale: Women in the International Division of Labour.* London: Zed Books.

Mohanty, Chandra Talpade. 2003. *Feminism without Borders: Decolonizing Theory, Practicing Solidarity.* Durham, NC: Duke University Press.

Moore, Jason W. 2015. *Capitalism in the Web of Life: Ecology and the Accumulation of Capital.* New York: Verso.

Muñoz Ramírez, Gloria. 2008. *The Fire & the Word: A History of the Zapatista Movement*. San Francisco: City Lights Books.

Network of Concerned Anthropologists. 2009. *The Counter-Counterinsurgency Manual; or, Notes on Demilitarizing American Society*. Chicago: Prickly Paradigm Press.

Notes from Nowhere. 2003. *We Are Everywhere: The Irresistible Rise of Global Anticapitalism*. New York: Verso.

Osterweil, Michal. 2010. "'Becoming-Woman?' In Theory or in Practice." In *What Would It Mean to Win?*, edited by Turbulence Collective, 82–89.

Polletta, Francesca. 2002. *Freedom Is an Endless Meeting: Democracy in American Social Movements*. Chicago: University of Chicago Press.

Price, David H. 2011. *Weaponizing Anthropology : Social Science in Service of the Militarized State*. Edinburgh, UK: AK Press.

Reinsborough, Patrick. 2010. "Giant Whispers: Narrative Power, Radical Imagination and a Future Worth Fighting For." *Affinities: A Journal of Radical Theory, Culture, and Action* 4 (2): 67–78.

Reinsborough, Patrick, and Doyle Canning. 2010. *Re:imagining Change: How to Use Story-Based Strategy to Win Campaigns, Build Movements, and Change the World*. Winnipeg, MB: Fernwood.

Roitman, Janet L. 2013. *Anti-Crisis*. Durham, NC: Duke University Press.

Scranton, Roy. 2013. "Learning How to Die in the Anthropocene." *Opinionator* (blog), November 10. http://opinionator.blogs.nytimes.com/2013/11/10/learning-how-to-die-in-the-anthropocene/.

Selbin, Eric. 2010. *Revolution, Rebellion, Resistance: The Power of Story*. London: Zed Books.

Sitrin, Marina. 2012. *Everyday Revolutions: Horizontalism and Autonomy in Argentina*. London: Zed Books.

Smith, Jackie. 2008. *Social Movements for Global Democracy*. Baltimore: Johns Hopkins University Press.

Smith, Linda. 1999. *Decolonizing Methodologies: Research and Indigenous Peoples*. London: Zed Press.

Staggenborg, Suzanne. 2012. *Social Movements*. Don Mills, ON: Oxford University Press.

Tarrow, Sidney. 1988. "National Politics and Collective Action: Recent Theory and Research in Western Europe and the United States." *Annual Review of Sociology* 14: 421–440.

Turbulence Collective. 2010. *What Would It Mean to Win?* Oakland, CA: PM Press.

Walia, Harsha. 2013. *Undoing Border Imperialism*. Vol. 6 of *Anarchist Interventions*. Oakland, CA: AK Press.

Wallerstein, Immanuel. 1996. *Open the Social Sciences: Report of the Gulbenkian Commission on the Restructuring of the Social Sciences*. Stanford, CA: Stanford University Press.

Wood, Lesley J. 2012. *Direct Action, Deliberation, and Diffusion: Collective Action after the WTO Protests in Seattle*. Cambridge Studies in Contentious Politics. Cambridge: Cambridge University Press.

Zald, Mayer, and John McCarthy, eds. 1979. *The Dynamics of Social Movements: Resource Mobilization, Social Control, and Tactics*. Cambridge, MA: Winthrop.

Conclusion

On an Emergent Politics and Ethics of Resistance

Athena Athanasiou and Othon Alexandrakis

IN THESE FINAL PAGES we would like to revisit the idea of figuring out and, more generally, *thinking with* resistance action. What follows is conversation beginning with a very plain observation about incongruence between what one author, Othon, observed on the ground and what he was expecting, building to a more complex discussion about emerging action and where to locate hope and hopefulness—in terms of both analytics and the unfolding reality in Greece. The chapter revisits affect and agency, collectives and horizons, but also attends to more immediate methodological challenges like where is resistance, and what does it look like?

Figuring out is about awareness and reflection, engagement and creativity, but it is also about conscience—a guiding sense. In working through the following, we invite readers to track the progressive undoing of familiar frames of analysis, the resetting of perspective on the field site, the consideration of various analytical perspectives and tool kits, and finally the air of responsibility and urgency that drove this conversation.

The exchange does not "resolve" anything—that's not the point. What we achieve is an opening up and questioning of what appears political, and other more uncertain doings and being that still flirt with and within some expression of the political. We also echo a number of key conversations that emerged in the volume, conversations we would like to highlight: ethnography as a form of political responsiveness, reimagining the human in the political, poststructuralist collectivization and action, political ecologies, and the mindful participant observer. Each of these broader conversations emerged from responses to the challenge of new resistance actions and related forms, to ethnographic method. The next steps, it seems to us, are to take up and consider these various conversations as new points of departure.

* * *

Othon: In 2013, I sat with a political activist, a journalist, and two university students for a broad conversation on responses to the economic crisis in Athens. The journalist opened the conversation with a story about the early days of protesting and the occupation of Syntagma Square. Everyone in the room spoke with nostalgia. They recalled feeling a strong sense of community and hope. My activist interlocutor—a seasoned veteran of the local political scene—explained that the occupation was different from action he had seen in the past. He recalled that people gathered day after day, cooperated creatively, and built a communal ethic he thought could be the foundation of a new social reality. Others echoed the sense of hope he located in the Syntagma occupation. The participants added their own stories of participating in this action, and of the sense of optimism and positivity they felt coming together with others in this way, and in this place.

The tone, however, changed when I asked if the group thought the frequency and intensity of antiausterity protests had abated in Athens. One of the students explained that, in her view, most Greeks had been brought to the verge of poverty by the austerity measures—she suggested that individuals living on the brink of ruin (or beyond), the precariat, were only just surviving, had become demoralized, and had therefore pulled away from the protest scene. Asked to explain further, she mused that a growing sense of shame and a new state of perpetual competition were making participation in politics increasingly unlikely for the majority of Athenians.

As my interlocutors began to connect the effects of crisis and austerity with the will to resist, I challenged the group to think further about competition, and particularly about the assumption that competition driven by insecurity and shame was necessarily individuating—a theme that developed over the course of a few further comments. They responded by insisting that, among the precariat, the "terms of association" were changing: people were coming to see themselves as competitors first and fellow citizens second—collective action was becoming a nonstarter. Put simply, and to borrow from the journalist, "people are acting primarily for themselves. . . . [I]f not dead, the sense of collective [*démos*] is an afterthought—totally incidental." I thought this was a rather bold statement, and it stayed with me. I've since become very interested in rethinking collective action, solidarity, and precarity.

* * *

Athena: In taking my cue from your introductory presentation of various responses to the crisis in Greece, Othon, I think it is important from the outset to mark the limits of the concept of crisis by asking what forms of questioning the issue of crisis enables and what forms of questioning it eclipses or disables. To be able to tackle this question (which entails also questioning crisis as an apparatus of power and knowledge), we might be impelled to navigate between two concurrent and equally problematic assumptions: one that construes crisis as an exceptional, extraordinary condition that deviates from "normality," and a second that casts crisis as a common, "normal," ontological state of human condition.

I would like to suggest that critical thought on crisis is faced with the challenge to put these presuppositions into crisis, as it were. Resistance includes also resisting such epistemological assumptions that underlie the neoconservative manufacture of consent around the narrative of austerity. Critical thought on crisis asks what knowledges become possible and what knowledges become impossible in and/or by regimes of crisis. Thus, critique is about provoking crisis. It is about interrogating established truth claims, including the truth claims of crisis. It is important, for instance, to "provoke crisis" to the neoliberal and right-wing narrative of austerity and its enactment as a means for effecting and legitimizing policies which increase inequalities and benefit the elites. Clearly, what interests me in this truth production process is not its referential function but rather its performative force. (More on the performativity of categories later.)

* * *

Othon: I agree, examining crisis must be our starting point. I recall Janet Roitman's (2014) warning that the term *crisis* seems self-explanatory but actually does particular work, both in terms of critical inquiry and on everyday life. As I will discuss momentarily, we might even find *crisis thinking* in the exchange I describe above. In light of this, your suggestion to provoke crisis is fascinating. I wonder how attention to the kind of provocation you describe could inform an approach to field research. Athenians provoke crisis everyday, both intentionally and not. I am interested in the challenges we might encounter studying these provocations. I am also interested in the broader implications of these sites in terms of our understanding of the political.

Returning to the case I've mentioned, my interlocutors talked as if they understood "crisis" or "the crisis," even as they seemed puzzled by the political state of affairs and were generally uncertain as to how they might find stable ground in the wake of restructuring and cutbacks. What's more, the term appeared to bring back different memories, to signal different implications, and to spark different reactions from person to person. There was no question that "crisis" evoked thoughts of collective struggle among my interlocutors; but the form, content and direction of that struggle differed tremendously. The idea that there would be a multiplicity of crisis experiences, as it were, is not surprising. However, the way crisis seemed to hold multiple worlds and meanings *was* surprising and made me think about regulation.

* * *

Athena: Now, if we draw our attention to the ways in which the state of crisis is deployed as a mode of neoliberal governmentality, and as a distinct assemblage of power, knowledge, and subjectivity, we will have to raise difficult questions about precariousness, solidarity, dispossession, affectivity, and the political.

It is in this context that the question of resistance that you pose requires exploring how the possibility for plural political responsiveness is activated within and against a configuration of advanced capitalist power that depletes certain livelihoods, forms of life, and modes of political action, by subsuming all political discourse under the "unmarked universal" of economic management. So the question of resistance is formulated in terms of power relations: how do bodies, subjects, and collectivities come into play when protesting modalities of power that make it impossible to contest them? One of the normative impulses of current neoliberal regimes in Greece and around Europe is to depoliticize crisis: in other words, to forestall the element of critical agonism and dissent, and to establish a self-evident, uncritical, and authoritarian truth—namely, that neoliberal austerity is the only possible game in town. This totalizing function of closing the space of dissent lies at the core of a power configuration that works to postulate any thinking, imagining, and acting otherwise, impossible. In this sense, the antagonistic spirit of capitalism takes precedence over democratic agonism. According to this compulsory economization of the political terrain, politics is reduced to managerial governing for the market, as Michel Foucault wrote in *Birth of Biopolitics*. As the normative narrative of austerity mandates the dissolution of public services, the role of the state and state institutions is reduced to safeguarding the pervasive functions of the market.

So how do we engage the critical present in a critical way? In arguing that the effacement of agonism and critique is crucial to the project of neoliberal governmentality, I am reminded of the ways in which thinkers such as Foucault (1997) and, later, Judith Butler have reflected on critique as undoing the normative principles that enact subjects into being within particular matrices of power. This process of desubjugation (*désassujettissement*) is at the core of the account of critique I am formulating here, especially in relation to your question on political responses to the disenfranchisement associated with the neoliberal crisis. Current modes of governing through crisis management bring forth the ways in which subjects are interpellated into crisis normality as economized, but also gendered, sexed, and racialized. As this "crisis normality" hails us today as subjects of competitive economic struggle for survival, neoliberal governmentality denotes an authoritative apparatus of producing dispensable and disposable populations, and, at the same time, producing and regulating the normative codes of the human through the intersecting powers of capital, nation, gendering, and racialization that structure the condition of "becoming precarious." So it is important, I think, to grapple with the ways subjects form themselves in desubjugation and yield critical agency from the normative violences of subjectivation.

Thus, we might think of critical agency not as self-contained and self-assertive sovereign subjectivity (according to the prescriptions of humanism but also advanced capitalism) but rather as a mode of becoming outside of oneself, in conditions of precariousness that are both shared and differential (Butler 2004). I wonder whether we could consider critical resistance through an ethics and politics that resist the antagonistically individualizing function of capitalism without reverting to an uncritical idea of the "common." Critical agency, then, pertains to the question of how subjects, through our plural and differential embodiedness and embeddedness, might contest and politically mobilize with others the very terms to which we "owe" our constitution in a world of inequality.

We need to remember that resistance is, in a way, in many ways, always already dependent on power. One of Marx's most compelling insights is that "men make their own history, but they do not make it as they please; they do not make it under self-selected circumstances, but under circumstances existing already, given and transmitted from the past. The tradition of all dead generations weighs like a nightmare on the brains of the living" (*The Eighteenth Brumaire of Louis Bonaparte*, 1852). In Jacques Derrida's (1994, 138) reading of *The Eighteenth Brumaire*, Marx draws a distinction between the spirit and the specter of the revolution. Derrida claims that revolutions to come must break through the protocol of inheritance. Although a certain degree of "inheriting" the past is inescapable and perhaps desirable in formulations of critical discourse, there is something radically contingent and contextual about all revolutionary politics and all critical discourse.

* * *

Othon: Your reminder that critical agency is a mode of becoming outside of oneself and, more to the point, with others, is very important as we move on to discuss political responsiveness. In light of this, and thinking back to provoking crisis, I'd like to consider responsiveness further. Again, in the meeting I described earlier, I proposed to my interlocutors that traditional forms of resistance were tapering off in Athens. This comment was based on my sense that street actions and other kinds of traditional organized resistance were becoming less frequent in the latter years of the current "crisis period." Perhaps, however, this suggestion was wrong or more to the point tied resistance to an altogether narrow definition of action. Thinking with Foucault, as you suggest, perhaps it would be productive to look at resistant subjectivities, the making of political possibility, and the rooting of other forms of political response.

So whereas my interlocutors spoke variously about the experience and meaning of crisis, they spoke rather uniformly about pushing back. It struck me that each member of the group was positive about the early actions they all took part in: actions that hadn't actually brought about any of the specific social, political or other changes my interlocutors claimed they wanted. It also struck me that their desired changes were often at odds with each other, particularly around policy dealing with tax evasion and public-sector restructuring. Further, my interlocutors did not express nostalgia for "the nation," "the people," nor were they particularly fond of each other. Given this, I wonder how we might explain their general positivity toward the actions of the past, their ardent willingness to participate—with each other—in future antiausterity action, and the sense of inclusivity in the room. Something was bringing the group together, something that exceeded the exclusionary logics of traditional political communities, something that cut across gender, age, and life experience. In this, the collective struggle they evoked broke from old political categories and undid uniformities and unities.

I am very interested in the idea that conditions of precarity can produce coherence among diverse individuals. My interlocutors were all struggling with loss and the fear of *losing more*—in fact they cited this fear as a source of motivation in their lives. "Loss. Loss and losing . . . The absolute relentless, endless, habitual, unfairness of the world," as Foucault (1983, xiv) put it in his preface to Deleuze and Guattari's *Anti-Oedipus*, may correspond to a loss of "belief in the world" according to Rajchman (2000, 25). Perhaps this sense of perpetually imminent loss was setting the stage for desubjugation, and the emergence of new forms of resistance? In any case, we should likely begin with a more careful look at resistance.

* * *

Athena: You are asking why the frequency and intensity of the antiausterity and antigovernmental protest sphere forming in Greece in the previous years in the context of the ongoing debt crisis has eventually abated in Athens. I would like to wonder with you about the built-in assumptions of this empirical observation. The trajectories of political practices are often construed in a conventional way, namely, in a linear and teleological way: *from* protest *to* radical change and the production of a new future. It seems to me, however, that the new configurations of political mobilization that we have been witnessing in Istanbul, Athens, Madrid, and elsewhere enable and enact something different and open ended, without guarantees and without programmed outcome. As present neoliberal regimes increasingly—albeit differentially—expose people to the injuries of poverty, demoralization, and racism, a performative politics of protest emerges, one that mobilizes the potentiality of calling into question and perhaps transforming such injurious interpellations. The recent wave of anti-neoliberal movements, public assemblies, square encampments, uprisings, and solidarity collectivities not only has inscribed a popular discontent with the status quo but also has made us capture and wield the possible in the actual. It gives a sense of what "another world" and a "different life" might consist of. In offering the possibility of figuring a break with the present order(ing) of things, it mobilizes radical social imagination.

The "outcomes" of this mobilized radical social imagination are not always immediately visible at the register of a "grand narrative," but are often inscribed in malleable and nuanced ways, scales, and flows of intensity. The proliferation of local solidarity projects and social movements, the invention of new idioms of thinking and acting politically, various "ordinary" acts of camaraderie and solidarity, and the growing influence of the left, which draws extensively on the collective experience of the social movements—they all indicate tangible transformative modes of political responsiveness.

Taking part in public gatherings involves corporeal and affective qualities such as collective motivation and endurance but also exposure to weariness and violence. I think that this alternative economy of bodies, in their injuries and innovations, has made space for enacting a mode of politics that involves insisting on the possibilities of critical agency in the face of its impossibility. While people are relegated to the status of disposable or redundant bodies, new modes of everyday agonistic embodied citizenship have been emerging through which challenges to market logic have been posed. Despite authorities' efforts to produce a monolithic narrative of austerity as the route to "national salvation," people have been seeking to counteract the individuating sense of debt, hardship, fear, and shame by claiming an alternative public space in light of sweeping cuts to public services. They have done so by persisting together in public, by reclaiming the public from corporate power and its "economies of abandonment," to use Elizabeth Povinelli's (2011) term.

Now, I am not proposing that the fantasy of the individualistic, self-sufficient and market-oriented sovereign subject has been effectively challenged once and for all through these collective acts of resistance. In fact, I remain critical of romanticizing and "apocalyptic" readings of the political act as a foundation of total positivity. Resistance, it should be noted, is unavoidably interwoven in the normative violence inherent in the ways we come to imagine and claim political life. At the same time, though, such social movements of resistance and solidarity, in all their incalculable potentialities and misfires, have begun to formulate an ethics and politics of being that is not constrained by and reduced to the mandates of possessive individualism. They have worked to unsettle, even provisionally, the norms that regulate who is admissible to established spaces of intelligibility, including the (physical and imaginary) space of political subjectivity and public protest. I am interested in the performative power of these intervals and interstices in our present historical moment.

* * *

Othon: I'm reminded here of the growing examples of informal experimentation with social solidarity activities I've recently seen around Athens like neighborhood swap meets, open kitchens, and seed exchanges—all activities that flirt with civic forms. These activities have been remarkable—at least to me—in their creativity and inclusivity. What's more, I have become interested in the way participation in these activities expresses a resentment of austerity and, more to the point, a provocation of crisis. In the case of an open kitchen where I've spent time, the unofficial motto was—"I'm okay. Are you okay? We can get through this"—expressing a very basic sense of care and cooperation despite forces driving individuation and competition. These solidarity activities challenge the state while responding to austerity and abandonment.

I find it fascinating that the public space created by individuals who participate in solidarity activities, who express something *other*, can be read as a revision of the space between people in the everyday, of normal relations. I don't mean that social support activities and resistance actions are performances of some ideal social state of affairs; I simply want to suggest that, among other things, they make some desired social difference legible to both participants and observers—they provide a sense of a different life, as you put it.

The proliferation of pop-ups, experiments, and microscale activities that challenge and provoke the neoliberal crisis in positive, multiple, and different ways do not mark a general popular withdraw from established categories and modes of acting politically. The two are not unrelated or disconnected, as you've noted, nor should we think of them as two sides of the same coin (contrary to the approach taken by some analysts). If we figure resistance in terms of the connection of desire to reality, we can see the span of resistance activity in Athens as a combining and recombining of individuals. As individuals move between these spaces, something is communicated to a yet-unanimated public—some desiring for another state of affairs.

* * *

Athena: Certainly. Allow me a caveat at this juncture. In contrast to idealizing tropes of activism, we need to always pose the question who takes to the streets and for what purpose. When it comes to bodies on the streets, we should be attentive to the daily incidents of beatings, stabbings, and fatal assaults against migrant workers, refugees, as well as gay and trans people throughout Greece carried out by organized neo-Nazis. According to the far right and neo-Nazi ideology, immigrants, LGBTQ people, feminists, HIV-positive people, are all considered social abnormalities and national enemies and hence are designated as dangerous and disposable bodies. The neo-Nazi agenda, uncannily converging in this with the ideology of market economy, hinges upon the biopolitical logi(sti) cs of human disposability. Taking advantage of the erosion of welfare systems, members of Golden Dawn have organized food giveaways and blood donations exclusively for "ethnic Greeks." So such racist practices of claiming and demarcating national, masculinist, and heteronormative belonging in the public space mobilize the foreclosures through which the space of the polis is constituted as a vehicle for immunizing and securitizing the body politic.

A certain idea of solidarity is at the heart of nationalism, in the sense of an exclusionary and totalitarian bond, a brotherhood protecting one's "own" women from enemies. So appeals to concepts such as solidarity are far from transparent. There is a need to clarify the conceptual significance of the term *solidarity* and situate it politically by expanding the analytics of solidarity to the concepts and actualities of resistance and dissent. Rather than assuming a Durkheimian mode of solidarity as social cohesion, current projects of agonistic democratic solidarity move toward a more open-ended and contingent conceptualization of solidarity.

So for me, there is always a line of questioning that could and should trouble the euphoria and naive optimism of "commons" and "community": what does it mean for collectivities and communities to define themselves through forms of being-together and having-in-common? On what presumptions of wholeness is their situated partiality built? How does their self-determination work to set and reproduce the norms according to which belonging is construed? And what if these norms operating to render solidarity possible already preclude the acknowledgment of certain modes of relationality as noticeable or valuable? I think that such questioning can help left-wing politics and social movements remain vigilant and critical of the regimes of epistemic violence operative in the engrained mythologies and orthodoxies of "community."

* * *

Othon: Your mention of the neo-Nazi Golden Dawn brings to my mind the recent involvement of undocumented migrants in civic action of various kinds— brave acts by individuals outside juridical categories of citizenship. As Kalyvas (2010) has noted, their involvement in actions like the December 2008 protests in response to the murder of Alexandros Grigoropoulos, their taking up of a kind of de facto citizenship, challenges the sovereignty of the state on multiple fronts. It also challenges us, picking up on your last point, to reconsider "community" and having-in-common. The involvement of Romani protesters in the same action, and in antiausterity actions since, complicates the question of community and citizenship further.

Now, the challenge, it seems to me, will be in part to rethink the effects and potentials of "pluralized" civic formations, both in terms of the broader political scene and in terms of individuals and small groups. In other words, to think beyond solidarity—as you say, a problematic concept that appears to function better as a descriptive category than an analytic framework—to consider not just the dynamics on the ground and what they represent (or not), but the residues, as it were, and reverberations of participation in collective action in coming political forms and initiatives.

* * *

Athena: Although these very diverse dissenting practices did not emanate from a singular political logic, I think that the main impulse of the protests did not have so much to do with achieving self-identity or univocality but rather with collectively avowing both the traumatic component and the critical potential of relationality. Assembled bodies in the street, as Judith Butler (2015) develops in her latest book, and in various collectivities and alternative networks of solidarity reclaim the unconditionality of public space and demand a democracy with demos. Such enactments of plural performativity have manifested a return of "the people," however that is understood. I think there is a lot of theoretical work to be done regarding the ways in which "the people" come into play through these collective practices of reclaiming democracy. Clearly, posing the question itself signals a potential to rework the norms of admissibility through which the neoliberal and neoconservative nation-in-crisis, but also Europe-in-crisis, constitutes itself. This potential has to do with rethinking "the people," again and again, beyond conventional understandings of solidarity as enclosed community (in the way, for example, of the far right). And it has to do with revisiting and re-envisioning solidarity beyond identity politics and in opposition to exclusionary demarcations through which people are bound together "as one." So instead of definitions of solidarity in terms of social cohesion and unity (in accordance with the Latin etymology of *in solidum*—for the whole), I would like to point to a compelling formulation by Sara Ahmed (2004, 189): "Solidarity does not assume that our struggles are the same struggles, or that our pain is the same pain, or that our hope is for the same future. Solidarity involves commitment, and work, as well as the recognition that even if we do not have the same feelings, or the same lives, or the same bodies, we do live on common ground." I would like to expand this a bit, however, and ask: Do we indeed all live on common ground? What does this formulation of "we" mean? And what does it exclude in order to produce a meaning of "common ground"? Perhaps we need to revise this through the perspective of the current "refugee crisis" in the Mediterranean. And then does taking action mean taking to the streets? How would such conception shift from the perspective of people in the boats in the Mediterranean? How would it shift from the perspective of a Europe marked by the authoritarianism of closed borders?

Following Ahmed's lead, but perhaps a little more skeptically, I am proposing that we need to be able to utter with others, the collective demand for another life against and beyond the logic of tradability and disposability, and at the same time revisit the norms of disposability as well as the prescriptive categories through which particular forms of self-determination become available to the normative cultures of intelligibility. We need to be able to utter "We" and, at the same time, countenance the normative presuppositions of first-person self-sufficiency, and even rethink community, with Jean-Luc Nancy, as an occasion in which people share a certain impossibility of being-in-common. I am indicating a politics of critical solidarity which embraces contingency and is always preoccupied with undoing its own foundational(ist) presuppositions.

For me, the challenge is to expose and counter the hierarchies and foreclosures inherent in normative definitions of demos and rework the performative possibilities of becoming-in-common beyond the totalizing and normalizing premises of communitarianism and moral universalism. In other words, the ongoing wager is to formulate claims of the political in ways that are not subsumed by ontological foundations and always leave space for the exigencies of social agonism. It seems to me that the politics of radical, agonistic democracy today is faced with the challenge to creatively engage with this tension.

* * *

Othon: Your warning, Athena, that we must remain critical of our terms and categories echoes one of the central messages of this volume. We must keep this warning at the forefront of our (collective) engagement with the political. The anthropological mode of inquiry—the idea that abstraction flows from our engagement with human lifeworlds—can provide a false sense that our conceptualization is always *grounded*: a classic empirical conceit. Perhaps a way forward might be to attend to the messy entanglements (borrowing from Helmreich 2003) and limit situations (borrowing from Jackson 2009) that render the relation between the political and *anthropos* (the human) uncertain. Feeling one's way through uncertainty and the indeterminate forces the researcher to reflect critically on the tools we use and experiences we draw upon.

* * *

Athena: Indeed, it is important to pose the question, with Michael Jackson (2009), "where thought belongs," that is, to ask about the social spaces where thought arises as inextricably tied to the political and Hannah Arendt's *vita activa*.

And then your question on forms of solidarity draws my attention to the embodied materiality and affectivity of political responsiveness. One way of grappling with this inquiry would be to problematize the very assumptions built in the claim that antiausterity protests have been simply "dropped off," and instead complicate this rather linear perspective by an idiom of eventness. To be sure, these movements have been changing in form, mainly by transforming and translating into the texture of civic experimentations with small-scale and multiscalar solidarity, which I see as one of the most hopeful and incalculable aspects of current collective engagements with the political, precisely because they work to shift and expand the way in which politics is conventionally construed and enacted. Now, there are undoubtedly segments of the society that are withdrawn from political action and interaction, either because of the exhaustion (economic, physical, psychological) enforced by unemployment, debt, state repression, the dissolution of public welfare services, and the austerity policies that have rendered survival a draining everyday struggle, or because of political melancholia and disenchantment.

I wish to contend that the point of these movements is not to have a plan to implement in order to "solve the problems of society" but rather to make way, again and again, for new social and political potentials, spaces, visions, and desires; in other words, to produce and refigure a repertoire of "reverberations," to use your apt word. And this also involves an ethics of social activism that challenges normative representational frameworks of advocacy. So there is an aspect of critical eventness involved in the trajectories and intensities of these movements—a becoming of the political, as it were. We have witnessed how this quality of eventness, which experiments with new modes of being and being-together, is inscribed in various such movements, and not only in Greece certainly: consider the Gezi Park uprising in Istanbul and the Podemos movement in Spain. The transnational reverberations and (mis)translations of these movements and activisms, as they traverse regional and national boundaries, have assumed critical urgency in our times.

It is important, however, to keep in mind that the present-day repertoire of movements of solidarity in Greece draws on earlier "moments" of social resistance and dissent, such as the movements in defense of public education in 2006, the uprising of the youth after the murder of the fifteen-year-old Alexandros Grigoropoulos by a police officer in December 2008, the movement in solidarity of Kostadinka Kuneva (the immigrant trade unionist in the cleaning sector who was attacked brutally over her union activities), the movement of the squares in 2011 (the part of the movement that articulated a radical democratic discourse against austerity, in contrast to the nationalists who attempted to transform the squares into arenas for fashioning a national narrative of crisis), and the movement of protest against the authoritarian, austerity-related closure of the Greek public broadcaster (ERT) and of solidarity with the "redundant" employers in June 2013. To this dense "repertoire" of reverberations one might add also the victory of the Coalition of the Radical Left (SYRIZA) in the European and national elections, despite the persistent mainstream media representations of the left as nothing less than a national danger; SYRIZA's growing power in Greece has made us also think how social movements connect and reverberate with the realm and scale—or, the *potentia*—of political governance.

Each of these actualities indicates that although the antagonistic spirit of capitalism seeks to contain democratic agonism, these initiatives enact alternative engagements with the political, which do not resort, and actively object, to possessive individualism and the commodity logic of accumulation and consumerism. From local clinics, such as the Metropolitan Clinic at Elliniko, to food-sharing schemes, and from informal barter networks to "ordinary" modalities of commitment and camaraderie, we are witnessing today manifold ways in which shared hardship afflicted by neoliberal policies becomes a resource for enacting new modes of political eventness and for pursuing a new sense of the political.

Indeed, the political diacritics and critical dissonances of solidarity are crucial here. While neoliberal capitalism degrades solidarity or reduces it to the production of "vulnerable groups," and while the far-rightists and the neo-Nazis strive to fashion solidarity on the model of an exclusive, totalitarian, and ethnically pure national brotherhood, democratic experimentations with solidarity movements explore solidarity as a political and ethical alternative to both these authoritarian standpoints. Movements of democratic social solidarity enact a collective politics of relationality and responsiveness beyond and against the normative premises of competitive individualization and self-management—and at the same time against the agenda of totalitarian brotherhood that hinges upon the biopolitics of human disposability. These movements contest the governmentality of crisis in ways that point to alternative, radical democratic, social imaginaries: alternative and opposing to neoliberal authoritarianism and the founding myths of the totalitarian *Volk*. Such vexed discords should be taken very seriously, I would think.

I would like to note here that radical democratic anti-neoliberal solidarity movements do not only resist and contest inequalities and exploitation; they also articulate new collective imaginaries, visions, values, and desires against and beyond inequalities and exploitation. In inventing and inspiring new ways of struggling for another world through organizing political responsiveness, these movements bring to the fore the wider question of what makes political responsiveness possible in this era of cruel possessive and competitive individualism. They illustrate how precarity might occasion alternative social modes of solidarity and responsiveness, but also how current forms of grassroots antiausterity solidarity might enable a rethinking of relationality and community and an enactment of a radically different "free economy." Let me note here that there is nothing "free" about any economy, let alone "free economy" of the market. I recall in this vein Vassos Argyrou's (2013) timely latest book, where he develops this idea about the untenability of the notion of free thinking and living, in making a case for an "economy of thought" and a "political economy" against the Enlightenment mandate to "think for oneself" as a foundational marker of autonomous subject.

So, I maintain that we can learn a lot from these movements and perhaps ask ourselves how they depict a new democracy yet to come, a reflexive actualization of relationality, and a different redistribution not only of goods and services but also of political power. So a creative anthropological engagement would consist in exploring how solidarity is made possible and what it makes possible in terms of hitherto unavailable, displaced, or unnoticed potentials. Furthermore, this analytics would give rise to questions such as: how do differently positioned subjects "show up" and "come into play" in addressing assigned and differentiated conditions of precarity? Are collective affects of solidarity premised upon intermeshed economic, gendered, and racialized power differentials? How does solidarity work on local, translocal, and transnational or cross-border levels of "assembling"?

* * *

Othon: I want to connect your comments on solidarity with our earlier consideration of provoking crisis as a methodological approach to studying resistance in Athens. Once again, the question of scale and form comes to mind when I think of research on political possibility. Specifically, I'm thinking about how large and traditional protest scenes or actions orchestrated by or associated with movements and organizations are often perceived as holding greater transformative potential than small-scale scenes or nonlocalized, emergent (but harmonized) individual actions. Your comments to the contrary resonate with Tania Ahmad's challenge to this scaling of resistance in her examination of the "politics of the ordinary" in Karachi (chapter 7, this volume). Attending to one form of action as the primary location of political agency over another obscures the multiplicity, interconnectedness and simultaneity of resistance. This is to say we might complicate our understanding of solidarity—and collective forms—by looking, as you suggest, at spaces where resistance emerges.

Now it is interesting to note—and to echo my comments on the limits of participant observation in the introduction to this volume—one of the challenges of studying resistance among individuals involved in experimentations of being and being together is that they may not yet understand their actions in political terms. Again, this may be an effect of neoliberal regulation, as you explained earlier, or perhaps a sign that these actions depart in fundamental ways from those of earlier collective forms. I'm thinking especially of interlocutors involved in casual, repetitive, and perhaps evanescent responses, in other words, sites not yet fixed but that intensify the potential of desubjugation and the emergence of critique. Thinking with our interlocutors about political becoming when the terms and meaning of conjunction, or becoming together, is still a question is an interesting problem.

We might also see sites of deindividualization, conjunction, and new forms of relatedness in terms of an ecology of political responsiveness, as it were—in terms of multiple connections. For example, you mentioned that the present-day repertoire of movements of solidarity in Greece draws on earlier "moments" of social resistance and dissent. The early antiausterity protests struck me as having brought to the streets a political body that was remarkably similar, at least in form, to the body that assembled in response to the murder of Alexandros Grigoropoulos in December 2008. That is, during both protests we saw the coming together of actors engaged in individual and communitarian politics forming what James Faubion (inspired by Deleuze and Guattari) has called a political assemblage: a political formation that emerges out of the intersection of heterogeneous interests and commitments but that produces effects and finalities that cannot be reduced to a simple coalescence of these. The "We" communicated by this political form was inextricably related to collective practice, its logic exceeding those of its constituent parts. Same can be said for the various food- or resource-sharing schemes, the establishment of informal barter networks, the setting up of home-based child and elderly care centers, and so on. These small, informal sites of response have proliferated in recent years. They are not new responses, but the effect they are having today might be. How we study this—the span of emergent and established forms and scales of action—appears to require a different approach. Perhaps seeing in terms of provocation and assemblages, or, sites emerging of the intersection of heterogeneous interests and commitments, would be productive? Mapping the connections between assemblages might also be a way forward, asking more directly what are the residues of political assemblages that came into being in public spaces? Are there reverberations?

* * *

Athena: Your reference to James Faubion's notion of political assemblage is particularly apposite. I find very insightful the way in which Faubion (2001, 52) speaks of modernity in terms of assemblage and suggests that it is up to the social anthropologist and her or his cross-sectional work to explore what such a multi-scalar assemblage is or what it might be.

It seems to me that appreciating the political significance of these new idioms of activism requires breaking through both celebration of resistance as invulnerable and deploration of injury as depleted of agency. A theoretical "reverberation" of these modalities of social mobilization can be traced in poststructuralist critical pursuits of nonsovereign accounts of agency, such as those we explored with Judith Butler (2013) in *Dispossession: The Performative in the Political*.

As an experimental trope, assemblage politics can be fruitfully put to work to challenge liberal frameworks of representation and to call attention to a varied range of relational and plural political possibilities—feminist, antiracist, anticapitalist, queer, antimilitarist and alterglobalist—in their nonlinear interconnectedness, polyvalent situatedness, and irreducible particularity. Perhaps this pertains also to the difference between assemblage and intersectionality. Jasbir Puar's (2007) important book *Terrorist Assemblages: Homonationalism in Queer Times* is pertinent to our discussion in its elaborating queerness as assemblage, and in its suggesting that intersectionality must be supplemented by a notion of (queer) assemblage.

I am interested in asking how the epistemic viewpoint of political assemblage would serve as an unsettling of the narrative of a self-sufficient human subject and offer a means for enacting forms of being-in-common, beyond and against the premises of communitarianism and anthropomorphism. How do, for instance, the *sans papier*, the queer, and the unemployed (and I don't mean these terms to denote distinct identities here) come together in transformative modes of survival and more-than-survival? And what happens when "we" come together as *sans papier*, queer, and unemployed? What happens to both the "we" and the "come-together"? For me, these are vexed questions, as we struggle today, jointly and partially, through various assemblages and reassemblages of queerness, antiracism, anticapitalism, and companion-species solidarity.

So despite my reservations regarding certain usages of the term, I do find the Deleuzian assemblage to be a potentially creative conceptual resource. My reservations concern especially treatments of assemblage that are premised upon presumptions of ontology and/or functional synthesis; in other words, treatments that employ assemblages as an occasion for reifying discrete and transparent identities and differences (despite the antiessentialist claims). I also endorse various aspects of the insightful feminist critique of "desiring machines" and "becoming-woman." And finally, further questions arise when an outright revolutionary potential of the desiring production is presumed. That said, I think it might be fruitful to address assemblages as matrices of heterogeneous, indeterminate, and situated social contingencies—such as techniques, temporalities, bodies, affects, and power relations—to be construed in nonessentialist and not-totalizable ways. I would like to ask, then, how we might read assemblages with poststructuralist, posthumanist framings of the political in an age of financialized capitalism and tightened borders. What kinds of political subjectivity would such revisiting of the political require (but not assume!) beyond the self-contained and self-legislating sovereign subject of humanism and advanced capitalism? In this sense, as I am neither able nor keen to define what assemblages *are*, I remain interested in their performative potential as they take place in the very texture of the political at the global level.

* * *

The conversation continues, of course.

References

Ahmed, Sara. 2004. *The Cultural Politics of Emotion*. New York: Routledge.

Argyrou, Vassos. 2013. *The Gift of European Thought and the Cost of Living*. Oxford, UK: Berghahn.

Butler, Judith. 2004. *Precarious Life: The Powers of Mourning and Violence*. New York: Verso.

———. 2015. *Notes Toward a Performative Theory of Assembly*. Cambridge, MA: Harvard University Press.

Butler, Judith, and Athena Athanasiou. 2013. *Dispossession: The Performative in the Political*. Cambridge, UK: Polity.

Derrida, Jacques. 1994. *Specters of Marx: The State of the Debt, the Work of Mourning, and the New International*. New York: Routledge.

Faubion, James. 2001. "Currents of Cultural Fieldwork." In *The Handbook of Ethnography*, edited by Paul Atkinson, Amanda Coffey, Sara Delamont, John Lofland, and Lyn Lofland, 39–59. New York: Sage.

Foucault, Michel. 1983. "Preface." In *Anti-Oedipus: Capitalism and Schizophrenia*, edited by B. Deleuze and F. Guattari, xi–xiv. Minneapolis: University of Minnesota Press.

———. 1997. "What Is Critique?" In *The Politics of Truth*, edited by S. Lotringer and L. Hochroth. New York: Semiotext(e).

———. 2010. *The Birth of Biopolitics: Lectures at the Colláege de France, 1978–1979*. New York, NY: Picador.

Helmreich, Stefan. 2003. "Trees and Seas of Information: Alien Kinship and the Biopolitics of Gene Transfer in Marine Biology and Biotechnology." *American Ethnologist* 30 (3): 340–358.

Jackson, M. D. 2009. "Where Thought Belongs: An Anthropological Critique of the Project of Philosophy." *Anthropological Theory* 9 (3): 235–251.

Kalyvas, Andreas. 2010. "An Anomaly? Some Reflections on the Greek December 2008." *Constellations* 17 (2): 351–365.

Povinelli, Elizabeth. 2011. *Economies of Abandonment: Social Belonging and Endurance in Late Liberalism*. Durham, NC: Duke University Press.

Puar, Jasbir K. 2007. *Terrorist Assemblages: Homoniationalism in Queer Times*. Durham, NC: Duke University Press.

Rajchman, John. 2000. *The Deleuze Connections*. Cambridge, MA: MIT Press.

Roitman, Janet L. 2014. *Anti-Crisis*. Durham, NC: Duke University Press.

Contributors

Tania Ahmad is Sessional Assistant Professor at York University. She has also taught at Franklin & Marshall College and the University of Toronto. She has studied at McGill University, Université de Montréal, and Stanford University. Her research interests include urban middle-class formations and public culture in Karachi, Pakistan, and Muslim migrant experiences in Central Mexico.

Othon Alexandrakis is Assistant Professor of Anthropology at York University. He held the Hannah Seeger Davis Post-Doctoral Research Fellowship in Hellenic Studies at the Seeger Center for Hellenic Studies, Princeton University, between 2010 and 2011. His recently published works explore resistance, precarity, and political possibility in Athens.

Athena Athanasiou is Fellow at the Center for the Study of Social Difference at Columbia University and teaches social anthropology at Panteion University of Social and Political Sciences, Athens. Her publications include the books *Life at the Limit: Essays on Gender, Body and Biopolitics, Crisis as a State of Exception: Critiques and Resistances*, and (with Judith Butler) *Dispossession: The Performative in the Political*. She has also edited (with Elena Tzelepis) *Feminist Theory and Cultural Critique, Rewriting Difference: Luce Irigaray and 'the Greeks.'* She is currently working on a book titled *Agonistic Mourning: Counter-Memory and Feminist Political Subjectivity in Post-Yugoslavia*.

Eirini Avramopoulou is A. G. Leventis Fellow at the British School at Athens, working on a research project entitled "Changing Spaces of Refuge: Histories and Geographies of Displacement amidst Politics of Crisis in Greece." She has taught anthropology of human rights and social movements, as well as postcolonial, gender, and queer critical theory at Panteion University (Greece), the University of Cambridge, and Bosphorus University (Turkey). Currently, she is completing her first monograph on affect, performativity, and gender-queer activism in Istanbul.

James D. Faubion is Radoslav Tsanoff Chair of Public Affairs and Professor of Anthropology at Rice University. Publications representative of his interests include *Modern Greek Lessons: A Primer in Historical Constructivism; Rethinking the Subject: An Anthology of Contemporary European Social Thought; Essential Works of Michel Foucault, Volume 2: Aesthetics, Method and Epistemology* and *Volume 3: Power; The Ethics of Kinship; The Shadows and Lights of Waco: Millenarianism Today; Designs for an Anthropology of the Contemporary* (with George Marcus, Paul Rabinow, and Tobias Rees); *Fieldwork Is Not What It Used to Be* (with George Marcus); *An Anthropology of Ethics; Foucault Now;* and *Theory Can Be More Than It Used to Be* (with Dominic Boyer and George Marcus).

Jessica Greenberg is Associate Professor of Anthropology at the University of Illinois, Urbana-Champaign. Her research focuses on the anthropology of democracy, postsocialism, revolution, and youth politics in the Balkans. Her new research looks at legal cultures and the judicialization of democracy in the European Union.

Cymene Howe is Associate Professor and Director of Graduate Studies in the Department of Anthropology at Rice University. She is the author of *Intimate Activism* and *Ecologics: Wind and Power in the Anthropocene*—a collaborative, multimedia duograph that analyzes the contingent social and material formations of renewable energy. Her current project, *Melt: The Social Life of Ice at the Top of the World*, seeks to understand cryo-human interrelations and the implications of climate-induced geohydrological change. She currently serves as coeditor for the journal *Cultural Anthropology* and the *Johns Hopkins Guide to Social Theory*.

Alex Khasnabish is Associate Professor in the Department of Sociology and Anthropology at Mount Saint Vincent University and codirector of the Radical Imagination Project (http://radicalimagination.org). His work focuses on radical social movements, the radical imagination, globalization, and social change. He is the author of *Zapatistas: Rebellion from the Grassroots to the Global* and *Zapatismo beyond Borders*, editor (with Jeffrey Juris) of *Insurgent Encounters: Transnational Activism, Ethnography, and the Political*, and author (with Max Haiven) of *The Radical Imagination*.

Marianne Maeckelbergh is Associate Professor in Cultural Anthropology at Leiden University, Netherlands. She has been participating in (and later researching) social movements since the mid-1990s. Her research focuses on the relation between emerging forms of self-determination and classic notions of democracy. Her other research interests include anthropological approaches to personhood, agency, urban transformation, and media and digital technology. She is the author of *The Will of the Many: How the Alterglobalisation Movement Is Changing the Face of Democracy*. From 2014 to 2016 she is a Marie Curie International Outgoing Fellow at University of California, Berkeley.

Neni Panourgiá is Visiting Associate Professor of Anthropology at the New School for Social Research and Senior Research Fellow at the Institute for Comparative Literature and Society at Columbia University. She is the author of *Fragments of Death, Fables of Identity: An Athenian Anthropography, Dangerous Citizens: The Greek Left and the Terror of the State*, and editor (with George Marcus) of *Ethnographica Moralia: Experiments in Interpretive Anthropology*. Her articles and book reviews have appeared in *Angelaki, Journal of Modern Greek Studies, Anthropology and Humanism, Politis, American Anthropologist, American Ethnologist, Anthropological Theory*, and *Social Archaeology*, among others. She is immediate past editor for the social sciences of *Journal of Modern Greek Studies* and editor of that journal's "Occasional Papers."

Irene Peano is Postdoctoral Researcher at the Department of Political and Social Sciences, University of Bologna, where she previously held a Marie Curie Fellowship. Her doctoral thesis, for which she conducted extensive fieldwork in Nigeria and in Italy, is titled "Ambiguous Bonds: A Contextual Study of Nigerian Sex Labour in Italy." Her research engages with forms of exploitation of migrant labor, specifically in the Italian context, seeking to connect productive and reproductive domains and focusing especially on the links between sexual labor and seasonal farmwork. Irene is also engaged in forms of collective militant research that, alongside critical reflection on existing dynamics, explore the possibilities of creative figurations of alternative social landscapes.

John Postill is Vice-Chancellor's Senior Research Fellow at RMIT University, Melbourne, and Digital Anthropology Fellow at University College London. His publications include the coauthored *Digital Ethnography*, the single-authored *Localizing the Internet* and *Media and Nation Building*, as well as the coedited *Theorising Media and Practice*. Currently he is conducting anthropological research on new forms of digital activism and civic engagement in Indonesia, Spain, and globally. He is also writing a book provisionally titled *Freedom Technologists: Digital Activism and Political Change in the 21st Century* and the coedited volume *Theorising Media and Change*.

Petra Rethmann is Professor of Anthropology at McMaster University. She is the author of *Tundra Passages*, coeditor of *Globality: Frictions and Connections*, and author of articles that have appeared in numerous edited volumes and journals. In her research she examines questions of political possibility through the lens of creative cultural projects and art. Framed in an interdisciplinary way, much of her research is situated at the intersection of anthropology, politics, and philosophy.

Index

Page numbers in italics refer to illustrations.

CPSIA information can be obtained
at www.ICGtesting.com
Printed in the USA
LVOW12s0305111016

508255LV00001B/53/P